T0138654

INTELLIGENT MACHINES

Myths and Realities

Edited by

Clarence W. de Silva
Department of Mechanical Engineering
University of British Columbia

CRC Press

Boca Raton   London   New York   Washington, D.C.

Cover Art: The Honda Humanoid Robot. (Courtesy of Honda Motor Co., Ltd. With permission.)

Library of Congress Cataloging-in-Publication Data

Intelligent machines: myths and realities / edited by Clarence W. de Silva
    p. cm.
Includes bibliographical references and index.
ISBN 0-8493-0330-3
    1. Intelligent control systems. 2. Robotics. 3. Artificial intelligence. I. De Silva, Clarence W.
TJ217.5 .I5445 2000
006.3--dc21
                                          00-030352
                                              CIP

© 2000 by CRC Press LLC

No claim to original U.S. Government works
International Standard Book Number 0-8493-0330-3
Library of Congress Card Number 00-030352
Printed in the United States of America 1 2 3 4 5 6 7 8 9 0
Printed on acid-free paper

FOREWORD

Intelligent Machines: Myths and Realities arises out of a Thematic Lecture Series presented at Green College, University of British Columbia (UBC) during the 1998-99 academic year. The College sponsors thematic lectures each year that highlight important topics in interdisciplinary scholarship and bridge both academic and public interest.

The topic of intelligent machines is of particular significance. It spans several disciplines in science and applied science, especially computer science and engineering. At the same time it raises many public interest and policy questions for social scientists and humanists. While intelligent machines have enormous practical significance and potential, their effects on organizational structures and processes, and on human relations, must be evaluated.

Under the able editorship of Clarence W. de Silva, Professor of Mechanical Engineering and NSERC Professor of Industrial Automation at UBC, this volume brings together distinguished scholars from several disciplines and countries to advance both technical knowledge and broad reflection on the subject. The topics range from the history of intelligent machines to their technical design and impact on human work processes and quality of life. The contributors not only provide original analyses, they also pose important questions for new inquiry.

This book is a value to both specialists and the general reader. While the entire volume bears careful scrutiny, a few features can be highlighted.

The effort to develop intelligent machines is not simply coincident with the age of computers; rather, it began with the industrial revolution. It has always involved complex interaction between what is taken to be knowledge and intelligence in any given time and place, and how these qualities may or may not become embodied in technologies and embedded in technological systems. As such, humans and their knowledge capacities must be seen as part of the technological system: humans always share agency in what those systems can do.

Intelligent machines typically involve large and complex systems with nonconventional performance goals; therefore, standard techniques of control are restricted and significant control engineering issues arise. One control response is to build artificial intelligence into machines used in production processes, so that modeling, sensing, and learning occur simultaneously. Another response is to use robots to control machines intelligently. Last, but not least, intelligent machines are designed to regulate human behavior along the lines of preferred performance goals.

The lectures upon which these published contributions are based sparked lively debate, and continuing reflection and discussion, at Green College. This volume will lead to further insights and new research. We are grateful to Professor de Silva for his most intelligent coordination of the entire project.

Richard V. Ericson
Principal
Green College

PREFACE

Intelligent machines, or machines with a brain, is a popular area of academic research in both engineering and computer science. Also, research prototypes of intelligent machines are being developed, with possible applications in a variety of situations. For example, intelligent robots can be effectively used in modern factories, homes, offices, and applications related to health, human safety, and security. Apart from robots, there are vehicles, home appliances, consumer equipment, and various types of computer-controlled machinery where some capabilities of intelligence, such as reasoning, learning, sensory perception, self-reorganization, and repair; coping with incomplete, inexact, and qualitative information; and effectively dealing with unfamiliar and unexpected situations, are incorporated. In these devices, intelligence is implemented through hardware and software.

There are many important issues that arise when examining the subject of intelligent machines. For example: What is intelligence? What are the key components of an intelligent machine? How are intelligent machines developed, designed, built, and controlled, and what types of technology and tools are needed? What are important research issues of intelligent machines? Are truly intelligent machines a practical reality? Can intelligent machines significantly improve the quality of life for human beings? Can intelligent machines work in harmony with human workers? The book explores questions of this nature and, in general, will address technological, industrial, economic, social, and research issues related to intelligent machines.

The book is intended for both technical and nontechnical readership. In that context, an extra attempt has been made to present complex technical issues in simple and qualitative terms. Nevertheless, some theoretical aspects, research issues, practical considerations, industrial applications, modeling and design issues, and techniques are presented where appropriate throughout the book. Consequently, the book will be useful to engineers, scientists, researchers, and students as well as a general reference tool and information source.

The book contains nine chapters, which are authored by highly distinguished and respected international authorities in the field, from USA, Canada, UK, Hong Kong, and Singapore. Chapter 1 gives a general introduction to the theme of the book and explores the characteristics that make a machine intelligent. Common techniques of knowledge representation and reasoning for decision making (i.e., knowledge processing) are indicated. Both conventional and "soft" methods of computational intelligence are outlined. A simple architecture of an intelligent machine is presented. The incorporation of intelligent control and sensor fusion into such an architecture is addressed. Typical steps in the development of an intelligent machine are given. The material in this chapter provides a foundation upon which the remaining chapters are built.

Chapters 1 through 5 cover fundamentals, general aspects, research issues, and techniques related to intelligent machines. Chapters 6 through 9 primarily discuss practical issues and applications related to the subject. Chapter 2 investigates the topics of information and knowledge as applied to intelligent machines. Within an innovative and versatile paradigm, information, knowledge, and machines are treated as agents that interact with the physical world and with other agents including humans. These considerations are then related to the concept of a knowledge economy. Chapter 3 presents an interesting view of the evolution of intelligent machines, starting from the industrial revolution. It asks the fundamental question of whether we understand the human intelligence and wisdom, and if not, can we realistically impart what we do not understand to a machine. Chapter 4 discusses research challenges of intelligent machines. The basic concepts pertaining to an intelligent machine are presented. Several practical projects related to intelligent machines are outlined. Fundamentals of soft computing are given in Chapter 5. Common techniques of soft computing as applied to intelligent machines are outlined. Chapter 6 presents control issues of intelligent machines. Since these machines often tend to be large and complex systems and their performance goals can be non-conventional, standard techniques of control may not be appropriate. Soft computing control, which incorporates techniques of fuzzy logic, neural networks, and genetic algorithms, is presented as particularly suitable for intelligent machines. Related practical applications, specifically dealing with image enhancement, are presented. Chapter 7 discusses the application of artificial intelligence in manufacturing. From a practical point of view, this chapter discusses how modeling, sensing, and learning can be synergically incorporated into production machines, providing substantial benefits. Chapter 8 surveys intelligent control of machines with an emphasis on robots. Chapter 9 addresses a problem of human–machine interaction. Particularly, the use of an intelligent machine to modify and adapt human behavior, which has important practical applications, is presented.

ACKNOWLEDGMENTS

This book is an outgrowth of a distinguished lecture series on "Myths and Realities of Intelligent Machines," sponsored by Green College of the University of British Columbia. The support of Principal Dr. Richard Ericson and Acting Principal Dr. Mark Vessey and the assistance of Carolyn Anderson were crucial for the success of the lecture series. Other sponsors of the lecture series were the Centre for Integrated Computer Systems Research (Director, Dr. Rabab Ward), BC Advanced Systems Institute (Executive Director, Mr. Brent Sauder), and the Vancouver Chapter of the IEEE Control Systems Society. I wish to thank my students Ms. Roya Rahbari and Mr. Jooyeol Choi for their assistance and my department head, Dr. Dale Cherchas, for encouragement. I am very grateful to Ms. Dawn Mesa, Editor, Ms. Felicia Shapiro, Production Manager, and the staff of CRC Press for their effort in producing this book.

Clarence de Silva
University of British Columbia, Vancouver

THE EDITOR

Clarence W. de Silva, Fellow ASME and Fellow IEEE, is Professor of Mechanical Engineering at the University of British Columbia, Vancouver, Canada and has occupied the NSERC Research Chair in Industrial Automation since 1988. He has earned Ph.D. degrees from the *Massachusetts Institute of Technology* (1978) and the *University of Cambridge*, England (1998). De Silva has served as a consultant to several companies, including IBM and Westinghouse in USA, and has led the development of many industrial machines.

Dr. de Silva is recipient of the Education Award of the Dynamic Systems and Control Division of the American Society of Mechanical Engineers (ASME); Killam Research Prize; Meritorious Achievement Award of the Association of Professional Engineers of BC; the Outstanding Contribution Award of the Systems, Man, and Cybernetics Society of the Institute of Electrical and Electronics Engineers (IEEE); Outstanding Engineering Educator Award of IEEE Canada; IEEE Third Millennium Medal; Outstanding Chapter Chair Award of the IEEE Vancouver Section; Outstanding Chapter Award of the IEEE Control Systems Society; and the Outstanding Large Chapter Award of the IEEE Industry Applications Society.

Dr. de Silva has authored 14 technical books including *VIBRATION Fundamentals and Practice* (CRC Press, 2000), 10 edited volumes, about 125 journal papers, and a similar number of conference papers and book chapters. He has served on the editorial boards of twelve international journals and is the Editor-in-Chief of the *International Journal of Knowledge-Based Intelligent Engineering Systems*, Senior Technical Editor of *Measurements and Control*, and Regional Editor, North America, of *Engineering Applications of Artificial Intelligence — the International Journal of Intelligent Real-Time Automation*. He is a Lilly Fellow, Senior Fulbright Fellow to Cambridge University, ASI Fellow, and a Killam Fellow.

AUTHOR BIOGRAPHIES

Garg, D. P.

Dr. Devendra P. Garg is Professor of Mechanical Engineering at Duke University and Director of the Robotics and Manufacturing Automation Laboratory. Prior to his present position, he taught at the University of Roorkee in India, New York University, and Massachusetts Institute of Technology. While at MIT, he served as the Chairman of Engineering Projects Laboratory as well. From 1992 to 1998, Dr. Garg directed the Dynamic Systems and Control Program at the National Science Foundation (NSF), Arlington, VA. While at NSF, Dr. Garg was appointed as the first Chairman of the Strategic Planning and Evaluation Committee (SPEC) of the Directorate for Engineering.

Professor Garg is a recipient of the TCM award and New York University's Founder's Day award for outstanding scholastic achievement. He is an active member of the American Society of Mechanical Engineers (ASME) and Past Chairman of the ASME's Dynamic Systems and Control Division (DSCD). Dr. Garg has received the Dedicated Service Award and the DSCD Leadership Award from ASME, and the Outstanding Work Performance Award and the Cooperative Team Effort Award from NSF. Professor Garg was a Fulbright Senior Scholar to the former Soviet Union during 1987-88. During 1996 and 1999 he was honored with a Japan Society for the Promotion of Science (JSPS) Senior Fellowship at the Tokyo Institute of Technology and, in 1997, a Japan Science and Technology Agency (STA) Invited Fellowship.

Jamshidi, M.

Professor Mohammad Mo Jamshidi received his Ph.D. from the University of Illinois at Urbana-Champaign in February 1971 and holds an honorary doctorate from Azerbaijan National University. Currently, he is the Regents Professor of Electrical and Computer Engineering, the AT&T Professor of Manufacturing Engineering, Professor of Mechanical Engineering, founding Director of NASA Center for Autonomous Control Engineering (ACE), and founding Director of Computer-Aided Design Laboratory for Intelligent and Robotic Systems at the University of New Mexico, Albuquerque, NM. He was on the advisory board of the NASA JPL's Pathfinder Project mission, the NASA National Board for Minority Small Businesses Utilization, and the National Academy of Sciences NRC Integrated Manufacturing Review Board. Previously he spent 6 years at US Air Force Phillips (formerly Weapons) Laboratory working on large-scale systems and control of optical systems and adaptive optics.

Professor Jamshidi has close to 450 technical publications including 42 books and edited volumes. Six of his books have been translated into at least one foreign language. He is a Founding Editor or Editor-in-Chief of 5 journals (including Elsevier's *International Journal of Computers and Electrical Engineering*) and one magazine (*IEEE Control Systems Magazine*). In 1986 he helped launch a specialized symposium on robotics which was expanded to International Symposium on Robotics and Manufacturing (ISRAM) in 1988, and in 1994 to the World Automation Congress (WAC). Dr. Jamshidi is Fellow of IEEE, Associate Fellow of Third World Academy of Sciences (Trieste, Italy), Fellow of the AAAS, and Associate Fellow of Hungarian Academy of Engineering. He is recipient of the IEEE Centennial Medal and IEEE Control Systems Society Distinguished Member Award.

Karray, F. O.

Professor Fakhri Karray received the Ingineer Diplome degree from the University of Tunis, Tunisia in 1984, and the Ph.D. in the field of systems and control from the University of Illinois, Urbana-Champaign in 1989. He was on the faculty of the University of British Columbia and Lakehead University before joining the University of Waterloo in late 1996 where he is currently an associate professor in the systems design engineering department. Professor Karray's areas of expertise span the fields of advanced controls and intelligent systems design using recently developed tools of computational intelligence with application to a wide range of industries in the manufacturing, automotive, and telecommunication areas.

Professor Karray has published extensively in these areas and has served on a number of international program committees of major conferences and symposia in an editorial board member of related areas. He is also an editorial board member of several journals and international conference proceedings. Professor Karray is the winner of the Anderson Best Paper Award at the 1998 World Automation Congress held in Anchorage, Alaska. He has been invited on numerous occasions as guest speaker for internationally organized workshops and symposia. He is a Senior Member of the IEEE and the author of two patents. He serves on the board of directors of two University of Waterloo spin-off companies in the Kitchener-Waterloo area.

MacFarlane, A. G. J.

Professor Alistair MacFarlane was born in Edinburgh, Scotland in 1931. After graduating in electrical engineering from the University of Glasgow he joined the Metropolitan-Vickers Electrical Company in Manchester in 1953. Following some years working on a variety of feedback and signal processing problems, he served as group leader of the Moving Target Indication and Receiver Laboratories of that company in 1956-58. In order to pursue research on feedback and control mechanisms, he moved to a series of university appointments, becoming in 1966 Reader in Control Engineering in the newly established Control Systems Center in the University of Manchester Institute of Science and Technology and then Professor of Control Engineering there in 1969. Following this he was elected to a new Chair of Engineering at the University of Cambridge in 1974, and became Head of the Control and Management Systems Department of the Engineering Department at Cambridge. He retired from the position of Principal and Vice-Chancellor of Heriot-Watt University in Edinburgh in 1996.

Professor MacFarlane's main research interests are in the fields of feedback, dynamics, and interactive computing, for which he is a recognized world authority. For work in these areas he was awarded an ASME Centennial Medal in 1980, the Hartley Medal in 1982, the IEE Achievement Medal in 1992, and the Faraday Medal for outstanding contributions to electrical science in 1993. He is an Honorary Fellow of Selwyn College, Cambridge; a Fellow of the Royal Academy of Engineering; and a Fellow of the Royal Societies of London and Edinburgh. For services to engineering he was awarded a Commander of the British Empire (CBE) in 1987. In the Highlands of Scotland, he retains an active interest in research and engineering and is a non-executive director of British Nuclear Fuels, Plc.

Modi, V. J.

Professor Vinod J. Modi received his Ph.D. in aerospace engineering from Purdue University in 1959. He joined the University of British Columbia where he has been a Professor since 1968 and Professor Emeritus since January 1995. Dr. Modi's contributions to the fields of aerospace engineering, aerodynamics, dynamics of ocean-based systems, and biomechanics are recognized worldwide. His versatility is reflected through research in areas as diverse as the human heart, offshore oil platforms, wind energy, the International Space Station, and mobile robotic manipulators. He has served as a consultant to a number of industrial and government agencies including the United Nations.

Professor Modi's contributions are recognized by more than thirty awards including: The Meritorious Achievement Award, the Association of Professional Engineers (1985); Gold Medal, Science Council of BC (1986); The Dirk Brouwer Award, American Astronautical Society (1991); The McCurdy Award, Canadian Aeronautics and Space Institute (1993); Mechanics and Control of Flight Award, American Institute of Aeronautics and Astronautics (1995); The John V. Breakwell Memorial Lecture and Plaque, International Astronautical Federation (1996); and The Pendary Aerospace Literature Award, American Institute of Aeronautics and Astronautics (1999). Professor Modi served as a member of the NASA's Advisory Committee for Application of Tethers in Space and chairman of the Astrodynamics Committee of the International Astronautical Federation. He is a Fellow of the American Institute of Aeronautics and Astronautics (AIAA), American Astronautical Society (AAS), American Society of Mechanical Engineers (ASME), British

Interplanetary Society (BIS), and Royal Society of Canada. He is an Academy Member of the International Academy of Astronautics (IAA).

Poo, A. N.

Professor Aun-Neow Poo received his B.Eng. degree with first class honors from the University of Singapore in 1968 and his M.Sc. and Ph.D. degrees from the University of Wisconsin in 1970 and 1973, respectively. After spending a year with IBM Research at its Watson Research Center, he joined the National University of Singapore (NUS) where he is now professor of mechanical engineering. At NUS, he has held the positions of Head of the Mechanical Engineering Department, Dean of the Faculty of Engineering, Director of the Graduate School of Engineering, and Director of the Bachelor of Technology Program.

Professor Poo's field of research interest is mechatronics, including intelligent automation and control and their applications to robotics and computer numerical control machines. He has published numerous book chapters and over 130 technical papers, in both journals and conference proceedings. Professor Poo has been a president of the Institution of Engineers, Singapore (IES); a consultant to many companies on industrial problems; a Fellow of IES; and a management board member of various organizations and companies.

Repperger, D. W.

Dr. D. W. Repperger received his B.S.E.E. and M.S.E.E. degrees from Rensselaer Polytechnic Institute, Troy, NY and the Ph.D. in Electrical Engineering from Purdue University. He is a member of Eta Kappa Nu, Tau Beta Pi, and Sigma Xi. From 1973-1974, he was a National Research Council Postdoctoral Fellow, then joined the federal government at Wright Patterson Air Force Base in Ohio where he has remained to the present time. He has authored or co-authored over 45 journal publications, 15 technical reports, and over 180 conference papers. The creator of 11 patents and 18 Air Force inventions, he has applied this technology to disabled people in the health care sector in joint programs involving the US Air Force and the Department of Veterans Affairs. In 1985, he ran experiments on two space shuttle missions.

Dr. Repperger serves as an Associate Editor of *IEEE Transactions on Control Systems Technology, Control Engineering Practice, Journal of Intelligent and Fuzzy Systems*, and *Journal of Knowledge-Based Intelligent Engineering Systems*. In addition to these activities, he presently serves on numerous conference committees and has been The Chair of the First International Conference on Control Applications. In 1995 he was elected Distinguished Member and in 1996 elected

Fellow of the IEEE (Institute of Electrical and Electronic Engineers). He is a recipient of the IEEE Third Millennium Medal for his past IEEE activities.

Tang, P. L.

Mr. Poi Loon Tang was born in Penang, Malaysia in 1974. He received his Bachelor of Engineering degree with First Class Honors in Mechanical Engineering from the University of Malaya, Malaysia, in 1998. His final-year thesis was devoted to real-time control of servomechanisms and liquid level systems using fuzzy logic. He is currently working for his Master of Engineering degree at the National University of Singapore, Singapore. His research interests include intelligent control, control theory and application, automation, and robotics.

Venuvinod, P. K.

Professor Patri Venuvinod has carried out research in the broad field of machining science, machining tools, AI applications in manufacturing, computer-integrated manufacturing and assembly; supervised numerous Ph.D., M.Phil., and M.Sc. students; and published over 90 scientific papers. He has established research links with a number of overseas and local organizations and holds honorary professorship at Shandong University, Jinan. He has been a member in a number of government and industrial committees. He has served as Honorary Director of the Institute of Industrial Engineers (IIE) in Hong Kong, Steering Committee Member of the City/Hong Kong Productivity Council Rapid Prototyping Center, and a Judge for the Hong Kong Special Administrative Region Award for Productivity.

Professor Venuvinod has organized a number of regional and international conferences, chaired many technical sessions, and served as reviewer for many international journals and conferences. His current areas of research include compensation of machining errors, fusion of modeling and sensing, intelligent geometric feature recognition, and chip control in machining. He is a Fellow of the Institution of Electrical Engineers (UK) and the Hong Kong Institute of Engineers. He is Senior Member of IIE and Active Member of the International Institute for Production Engineering Research (CIRP).

Addresses of the Authors

(INTELLIGENT MACHINES — Myths and Realities)

Chapter 1:

Professor Clarence W. de Silva
Department of Mechanical Engineering
University of British Columbia
2324 Main Mall
Vancouver, BC
Canada V6T 1Z4

Tel: (604) 822-5291
Fax: (604) 822-2403
e-mail: desilva@mech.ubc.ca

Chapter 2:

Professor Alistair G.J. MacFarlane
Dalnacroich
Strathconon
Muir of Ord
Ross-shire IV6 7QQ
UK

Tel and Fax: 01997 477 281
e-mail: alistair.macfarlane@groupwise.uhi.ac.uk

Chapter 3:

Professor Vinod Modi
Department of Mechanical Engineering
University of British Columbia
2324 Main Mall
Vancouver, BC
Canada V6T 1Z4

Tel: (604) 822-2914
Fax: (604) 822-2403
e-mail: modi@mech.ubc.ca

Chapter 4:

Professor Devendra P. Garg
Department of Mechanical Engineering
Box 90300
Duke University
Durham, NC 27708-0300

Tel: (919) 660-5330
Fax: (919) 660-8963
e-mail: dpgarg@duke.edu

Chapter 5:

Professor Fakhri Karray
Systems Design Engineering
University of Waterloo
200 University Avenue West
Waterloo, Ontario
Canada N2L 3G1

Tel: (519) 885-1211
Fax: (519) 746-4791
e-mail: karray@watfor.uwaterloo.ca

Chapter 6:

Professor Mo Jamshidi
AT&T Professor
NASA Center for Autonomous Control Engineering
Department of Electrical & Computer Engineering
University of New Mexico
Albuquerque, NM 87131

Tel: (505) 277-5538
Fax: (505) 291-0013
e-mail: jamshid@eece.unm.edu

Chapter 7:

Professor Patri K. Venuvinod, Head
Department of Manufacturing Engineering
City University of Hong Kong
83 Tat Che Avenue
Kowloon
HONG KONG

e-mail: mepatri@cityu.edu.hk

Chapter 8:

Professor A.N. Poo and Mr. Poi-Loon Tang
Department of Mechanical & Production Engineering
National University of Singapore
10 Kent Ridge Crescent
Singapore 119260

Tel: (65) 874-6283
Fax: (65) 777-2264
e-mail: mpepooan@nus.edu.sg
       engp9479@nus.edu.sg

Chapter 9:

Dr. D.W. Repperger
Building 33 AFRL/HECP
Air Force Research Laboratory
Wright Patterson Air Force Base
Dayton, OH 45433-7022

Tel: (937) 255-8765
Fax: (937) 255-8752
e-mail: daniel.repperger@he.wpafb.af.mil
       d.repperger@ieee.org

CONTENTS

1 | WHAT MAKES A MACHINE INTELLIGENT?

C.W. de Silva
Industrial Automation Laboratory
Department of Mechanical Engineering
The University of British Columbia
Vancouver, Canada

In its attempt to define an intelligent machine, this chapter indicates characteristics and capabilities of a machine that are considered intelligent. Common techniques and approaches that will be useful in the development of an intelligent machine are introduced and will form a common foundation for the remaining chapters of the book. It is the knowledge system that enables a machine to display intelligent characteristics. Representation and processing of knowledge are central functions of a knowledge system. Associated techniques are outlined. Conventional machine intelligence has relied heavily on symbolic manipulation for processing descriptive information and "knowledge" in realizing some degree of intelligent behavior. Approximation is a "soft" concept, and the capability to approximate for the purposes of comparison, pattern recognition, reasoning, and decision making is a manifestation of intelligence.

This chapter discusses several concepts of approximation. Humans commonly employ approximate reasoning in their intelligent behavior. Soft computing is an important branch of computational intelligence where fuzzy logic, probability theory, neural networks, and genetic algorithms are synergetically used to mimic reasoning and decision making of a human. The chapter introduces the subject of soft computing, with an emphasis on fuzzy logic, probabilistic decision making, and genetic algorithms, and then presents a general structure for an intelligent machine. Intelligent control refers to a group of analytical and synthesis methods that fall outside the scope of traditional control theory and that are useful in autonomous control and supervision of an intelligent machine. Multiple sensing and intelligent sensor fusion are also important in intelligent machines. This is motivated by the observation that humans routinely and effectively employ sensor fusion in executing real-time tasks. The chapter outlines intelligent control and intelligent sensor fusion and ends by indicating the main steps in the development of an intelligent machine for practical use.

1 Introduction

This chapter provides a general introduction to the subject of intelligent machines and forms a common foundation for the remaining chapters of the book. The presentation given here is intended to be neither exhaustive nor highly mathematical. A more rigorous treatment of some of the topics introduced here is found in other chapters.

An intelligent machine is a machine that can exhibit one or more intelligent characteristics of a human. In the context of the present book, an intelligent machine is not necessarily treated as an "intelligent" computer alone, and may consist of a structural system for carrying out the intended functions of the machine. According to this viewpoint, a recent example of an intelligent machine is the Honda Humanoid Robot (see cover photo), which contains an intelligent control system [1]. An intelligent machine embodies machine intelligence. The term *machine intelligence*, however, is synonymous with computer intelligence, as the machine in this context implies a computer. Loosely speaking, artificial intelligence (AI) as well may be considered synonymous with computer intelligence. Computers that can be programmed to perform "intelligent" tasks such as playing chess or understanding a natural language are known to employ AI techniques for those purposes, and may be classified as intelligent machines either by themselves or in conjunction with other structural devices such as robotic hands and visual, sonic, chemical, and tactile interfaces.

The first digital computer may be traced back to the development of universal Turing machines in the mid 1930s, but it is in the 1960s that significant activity in the field of artificial intelligence began with the objective of developing computers that can think like humans. Just like neurons in the brain, the hardware and software of a computer are themselves not intelligent, yet it has been demonstrated that a computer may be programmed to demonstrate some intelligent characteristics of a human. In this context it is the outward characteristics (outputs) of a computer that may be termed "intelligent," rather than any similarity of the computer programs to how a human processes information. The field of study that deals with analyzing and modeling of the information processing capabilities of a human is known as *cognitive science* and is important in AI. Nevertheless, in developing an intelligent machine it is not essential to master cognitive science.

Future generations of industrial machinery may be expected to carry out round-the-clock operation, with minimal human intervention, in manufacturing products or providing services [2]. It will be necessary that these machines maintain consistency and repeatability of operation and cope with disturbances and unexpected variations in the system, its operating environment, and performance objectives. In essence, these machines should have the capability to accommodate rapid recon-figuration and adaptation. For example, a production machine should be able to quickly cope with variations ranging from design changes for an existing product to the introduction of an entirely new product line. This will call for tremendous flexibility and some level of autonomous operation in automated machines, which translate into a need for a higher degree of intelligence in the supporting devices. Smart machines will exhibit an increased presence and significance in a wide vari-ety of applications. Products with a "brain" are found, for example, in household appliances, consumer electronics, transportation systems, industrial processes, manufacturing systems, and services. There is clearly a need to incorporate a greater degree of intelligence and a higher level of autonomy into automated ma-chines. This will require the appropriate integration of such devices as sensors, actuators, and controllers, which themselves may have to be "intelligent" and, furthermore, appropriately distributed throughout the system. Design, develop-ment, production, and operation of intelligent machines have been possible today through ongoing research and development in the field of intelligent systems and control.

In an attempt to define an intelligent machine, the present chapter will indicate characteristics and capabilities of a machine that are considered intelligent. It is the knowledge system that enables a machine to display intelligent characteristics. Representation and processing of knowledge are central functions of a knowledge system. Capability to acquire information, presence of a knowledge base, use of a reasoning procedure, and availability of a human–machine interface are all impor-tant features of a knowledge system and are crucial for the operation of an intelli-gent machine. The chapter will introduce approaches for representation of knowl-edge and reasoning with knowledge in the task of intelligent decision making [3].

Human reasoning is predominantly approximate, qualitative, and "soft." Humans can effectively handle incomplete, imprecise, and fuzzy information in making intelligent decisions [4]. Soft computing is an important branch of computational intelligence where fuzzy logic, probability theory, neural networks, and genetic algorithms are cooperatively used with the objective of mimicking the reasoning and decision-making processes of a human [5]. Accordingly, this is an important branch of study in the area of intelligent machines. This chapter will give an intro-duction to the subject of soft computing, with an emphasis on fuzzy logic and evolutionary computing or genetic algorithms. Neural networks will be covered in more detail in another chapter. A general structure for an intelligent machine will be presented here. Sensory perception and control are important functions of such an architecture. *Intelligent control* refers to a group of analytical and synthesis methods that fall outside the scope of traditional control theory and that are useful in autonomous control and supervision of an intelligent machine. Multiple sensing and intelligent sensor fusion are also important in intelligent machines. The chapter will introduce these topics and will conclude by giving the main steps in the development of an intelligent machine for practical use.

2 Machine Intelligence

In the context of machine intelligence, the term *machine* is normally used to denote a computer or a computational machine. In this sense *machine intelligence* and *computational intelligence* are synonymous. An *intelligent machine*, however, may take a broader meaning than an *intelligent computer*. It may be used to represent any process, plant, system, device, or machinery that possesses machine intelligence. Historically *machine intelligence* and *artificial intelligence* (AI) also have come to mean the same thing. The field of soft computing is important here, developments of which have taken a somewhat different path from traditional AI, yet they have contributed to the general goal of realizing intelligent machines, thereby broadening the meaning of machine intelligence.

According to Marvin Minsky of the Massachusetts Institute of Technology [1], "artificial intelligence is the science of making machines do things that would require intelligence if done by men." In this definition note that it is the outward behavior of a machine rather than the physical makeup that is considered in ascertaining whether the machine is intelligent. Specifically, an analogy may be made here with intelligent behavior of a human whose brain itself is a physical entity that assists in realizing that behavior. A considerable effort has gone into the development of machines that somewhat mimic humans in their actions. Because it is the thought process that leads to intelligent actions, substantial effort in AI has been directed at the development of artificial means to mimic the human thought process. This effort is somewhat related to cognitive science.

Conventional AI has relied heavily on symbolic manipulation for the processing of descriptive information and "knowledge" in realizing a degree of intelligent behavior. The knowledge itself may be represented in a special high-level language. The decisions that are made through processing of such "artificial" knowledge, perhaps in response to data such as sensory signals, should possess characteristics of intelligent decisions of a human. Knowledge-based systems and related expert systems are an outcome of the efforts made by the AI community in their pursuit of intelligent machines.

In the problem of knowledge-based decision making, sensory information and any other available data on the process are evaluated against a knowledge base for the specific application, making use of an inference-making procedure. Typically, this procedure consists of some form of "matching" of the abstracted data, with the knowledge base [3]. In particular, for a knowledge base K and a set of data or information D on the process, the procedure of arriving at a decision or inference I may be expressed as [1]

$$I = M[P(D), K] \qquad (1)$$

in which the "preprocessing operator" $P(.)$ converts the context information on the process into a form that is compatible with K.

2.1 Appearance of Intelligence

At the basic or atomic level of implementation what a computer does is quite procedural and cannot be considered intelligent. Similarly, one may argue that the 20 billion neurons in a human brain perform operations that are hardly intelligent when taken individually. It is these same neurons, however, that govern the intelligent behavior of a human. A definition for *intelligence*, then, has to be closely related to the characteristics or outward "appearance" of an intelligent behavior. There exist many characteristics that can be termed *intelligent*, and partly due to this reason, it has not been possible to give a precise definition for intelligence.

It is commonly accepted that an intelligent system possesses one or more of the following characteristics and capabilities:

- Sensory perception
- Pattern recognition
- Learning and knowledge acquisition
- Inference from incomplete information
- Inference from qualitative or approximate information
- Ability to deal with unfamiliar situations
- Adaptability to new, yet related situations (through expectational knowledge)
- Inductive reasoning
- Common sense
- Display of emotions
- Inventiveness.

Even though significant advances have been made, particularly in the first five capabilities listed above, the current generation of intelligent machines do not claim to have all these capabilities, particularly the last three in the list. Clearly this list of items does not represent a formal definition of an intelligent system. It is known, however, that humans possess these characteristics and capabilities and that humans are intelligent beings. A handwriting recognition system is a practical example of an intelligent system. The underlying problem cannot be solved through simple template matching, which does not require intelligence. Because handwriting can vary temporally for the same person, due to various practical shortcomings such as missing characters, errors, nonrepeatability, sensory restrictions, and noise, a handwriting recognition system has to deal with incomplete information and unfamiliar characters and should possess capabilities of learning, pattern recognition, and approximate reasoning, which will assist in carrying out intelligent functions of the system.

2.2 Dynamics of Intelligence

In attempting to make a machine "intelligent," it is useful to first explore the meaning of the term itself. A complete yet simple definition of *intelligence* is not available. As noted before, it is the outward characteristics of a system that qualify it to be classified as being intelligent; for example, possession of a memory, ability to learn and thereby gain knowledge and expertise, ability to satisfactorily deal with unexpected and unfamiliar situations, and ability to reason, deduce, and infer from incomplete information. In particular, pattern recognition and classification play an important role in intelligent processing of information. For example, an intelligent system may be able to recognize and acquire useful information from an object that is aged or distorted, having been previously familiar with the original, undistorted object. Somewhat related are the concepts of approximation, which may lead one to treat the ability to approximate as also a characteristic of intelligence [3].

A simplified and qualitative model for the dynamics of intelligence [1,3] is shown in Figure 1. This model illustrates the hierarchical nature of the associated processes as well. In the model of Figure 1, intelligent preprocessing is identified as the operation that converts information into knowledge and knowledge into expertise. A degree of intelligence is needed to carry out these preprocessing operations, and simultaneously the intelligence itself will be broadened or enhanced through preprocessing, as indicated by the bi-directional activity lines. Knowledge may be interpreted as "structured information" that is acquired by an intelligent object, and expertise as "specialized knowledge." In this sense, then, preprocessing operations will carry out structuring and acquisition of information in gaining knowledge and will specialize knowledge in gaining expertise. Note that knowledge and expertise can depreciate, and be outdated or lost, in the absence of continuous usage, learning, and updating (i.e., intelligent preprocessing). The blocks of "Knowledge Dynamics" and "Expertise Dynamics" account for such appreciation and depreciation, in the present simplified model. Similarly, the block of "Intelligence Dynamics" allows for variations in the level of intelligence. Another interpretation of information and knowledge is given in Chapter 2.

Knowledge and expertise form the "knowledge base" of an intelligent system. Then, with any new information that may arrive from external sources such as sensors and human interfaces, the knowledge-based system can make perceptions (sensory perception) and new inferences or decisions by interpreting the meaning and implications of the new information within the capabilities of the existing knowledge base. The associated decision-making task is an intelligent processing activity which in turn may lead to enhancement, refinement, and updating of the knowledge base.

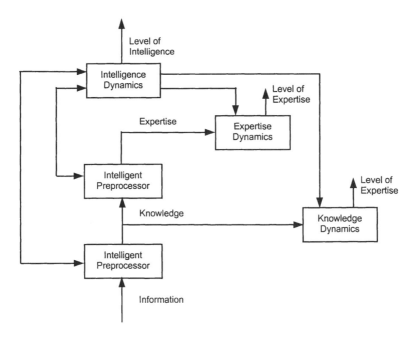

Figure 1: A schematic model for the dynamics of intelligence.

3 Soft Computing

Soft computing has effectively complemented conventional AI in the area of machine intelligence. Computing paradigms of fuzzy logic, neural networks, and genetic algorithms are the main constituents of soft computing, which can be utilized in intelligent machines either separately or synergistically. Fuzzy logic is useful in representing human knowledge in a specific domain of application and in reasoning with that knowledge to make useful inferences or actions. For example, fuzzy logic may be employed to represent, as a set of "fuzzy rules," the knowledge of a human operating a machine. This is the process of knowledge representation. Then, a rule of inference in fuzzy logic may be used according to this "fuzzy" knowledge base to make decisions on operation of the machine for a given set of machine observations. This task concerns "knowledge processing" [3]. In this sense, fuzzy logic serves to represent and process the knowledge of a human in operating a given machine.

Artificial neural networks (NN) are massively connected networks of computational "neurons." By adjusting a set of weighting parameters of an NN, it may be "trained" to approximate an arbitrary nonlinear function to a required degree of accuracy [5]. Biological analogy here is the neuronal architecture of a human brain. Since machine intelligence involves a special class of highly nonlinear decision making, neural networks may be appropriately employed there, either separately or in conjunction with other techniques such as fuzzy logic. Fuzzy-neural techniques are applicable in intelligent decision making, in particular when machine learning is involved and parameter changes and unknown disturbances have to be compensated for.

Genetic algorithms (GA) are derivative-free optimization techniques that can evolve through procedures analogous to biological evolution [5]. Genetic algorithms belong to the area of evolutionary computing. They represent an optimization approach where a search is made to "evolve" a solution algorithm that will retain the "most fit" components in a procedure that is analogous to biological evolution through natural selection, crossover, and mutation. It follows that GAs are applicable in machine intelligence, particularly when optimization is an objective.

In summarizing the biological analogies of fuzzy, neural, and genetic approaches, fuzzy techniques attempt to approximate human knowledge and the associated reasoning process; neural networks are a simplified representation of the neuron structure of a brain; and genetic algorithms follow procedures that are crudely similar to the process of evolution in biological species.

Techniques of soft computing are powerful by themselves in achieving the goals of machine intelligence. Furthermore, they have a particular appeal in view of the biological analogies that exist. This is no accident because in machine intelligence it is the behavior of human intelligence that is sought to be mimicked. Biological analogies and key characteristic of several techniques of machine intelligence are listed in Table 1. Conventional AI, which typically uses symbolic and descriptive representations and procedures for knowledge-based reasoning, is listed as well for completeness.

Table 1: Techniques of computational intelligence.

Technique	Characteristic	Biological Analogy
Fuzzy Logic	Uses fuzzy rules and approximate reasoning	Human knowledge
Neural Networks	Network of massively connected nodes	Neuron structure in brain
Genetic Algorithms	Derivative-free optimization	Biological evolution
Conventional AI	Symbolic processing of information	Symbolic languages

3.1 Approximate Reasoning

In fuzzy logic, the knowledge base is represented by if-then rules of fuzzy descriptors [3]. For example, "If the speed is slow and the target is far, then moderately increase the power" is a fuzzy rule, which contains the fuzzy descriptors *slow, far,* and *moderate.* A fuzzy descriptor may be represented by a membership function, which is a function that gives a membership grade between 0 and 1 for each possible value of the fuzzy descriptor it represents.

Mathematically, a fuzzy set A is represented by a membership function, or a "possibility function" [6,7] of the form

$$Fz[x \varepsilon A] = \mu_A(x): \mathfrak{R} \rightarrow [0,1] \qquad (2)$$

in which each element of A, as denoted by a point x on the real line $\mathfrak{R}$, is mapped to a value μ which may lie anywhere in the real interval of 0 to 1. This value is the "grade of membership" of x in A. If the membership grade is greater than 0 but less than 1, then the membership is not crisp (i.e., it is fuzzy), and the element has some possibility of being within the set and also some complementary possibility of being outside the set. In this case, the element falls on the fuzzy boundary of the set.

The conventional binary (bivalent) logic is crisp and allows for only two states, represented by 0 and 1, of set membership; an element is either completely inside or completely outside a set. This logic cannot handle fuzzy descriptors, examples of which are "fast" which is a *fuzzy quantifier* and "weak" which is a *fuzzy predicate.* They are generally qualitative, descriptive, and subjective and may contain some overlapping degree of a neighboring quantity, for example, some degree of "slowness" in the case of the fuzzy quantity "fast." Through the use of membership grades which lie between 0 and 1, fuzzy sets and associated fuzzy logic allow for a realistic extension of binary, crisp logic to qualitative, subjective, and approximate situations, which often exist in problems of intelligent machines where techniques of artificial intelligence are appropriate.

A fuzzy rule itself may be represented as a grouping of membership functions. An example of two rules:

> If *A1* and *B1* then *C1*
> If *A2* and *B2* then *C2*

is sketched in Figure 2, where triangular membership functions are used. Here *A1* and *A2* may represent two fuzzy states such as "near" and "far" of the variable "destination;" *B1* and *B2* may represent two fuzzy states such as "fast" and "slow" of the variable "speed;" and *C1* and *C2* may represent the fuzzy actions "decrease" and "increase" of the variable "power." If the actual distance to the target is x_o and the actual speed is y_o, then each fuzzy rule will contribute an action as shown by the shaded region of the membership functions for *C1* and *C2* in Figure 2. The net power-change action (decision) corresponding to these readings of distance and speed is given by the overall shaded region, indicated by *C'* in the figure. This is arrived according to a particular decision-making procedure (*sup-min* composition) that is commonly used in fuzzy logic [3]. If a crisp decision is required, one may use the centroid z_o of the decision membership function *C'* as shown.

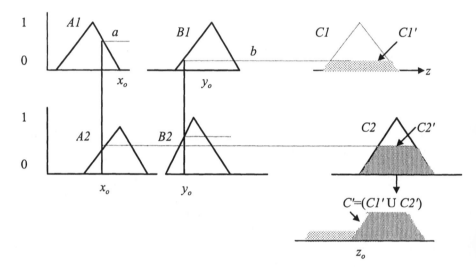

Figure 2: An illustration of fuzzy decision making.

Now consider the general problem of approximate reasoning. In this case the knowledge base *K* is represented in an "approximate" form, for example, by a set of if-then rules with *antecedent* and *consequent* variables that are fuzzy descriptors. First, the data *D* are preprocessed according to

$$F_D = FP(D) \tag{3}$$

which, in a typical situation, corresponds to a data abstraction procedure called "fuzzification" and establishes the membership functions or membership grades that correspond to *D*. Then for a fuzzy knowledge base F_K, the fuzzy inference F_I is obtained through fuzzy-predicate approximate reasoning, as denoted by

$$F_I = F_K \circ F_D \tag{4}$$

Here, the fuzzy matching operator *FM* that corresponds to *M* in Equation (1) is in fact the composition operator ° and may be expressed as

$$\mu_I = \sup_X \min(\mu_K, \mu_D)$$ (5)

where

μ_K = multidimensional membership function of the fuzzy rule base

μ_D = membership function of the fuzzified data

μ_I = membership function of the fuzzy inference

$x \varepsilon X$ = common set of context variables used in knowledge base matching.

Also, the supremum (*sup*) and minimum (*min*) operations are given by the usual definitions [3]. Often, a crisp value $\hat{c}$ is needed for the intelligent action that has to be carried out in the physical process (intelligent machine) and may be determined by the *centroid method*; thus,

$$\hat{c} = \frac{\int_s c\mu_I(c)dc}{\int_s \mu_I(c)dc}$$ (6)

where *c* is the independent variable of the inference *I*, and *S* is the support set (or the region of interest) of the inference membership function.

The simple example of goal pursuit (vehicle driving) shown in Figure 2 was given to illustrate the similarity of fuzzy decision making to approximate reasoning, which is commonly used by humans. One may argue that there is no intelligence in the associated decision-making process because the rules are fixed and no learning and improvement are involved. Even in the example of Figure 2, however, there exists a process of "approximation" and the use of approximate reasoning. These, as commonly performed by humans, may be interpreted as manifestations of intelligence. Much more complex problems of knowledge-based decision making may be required in intelligent machines for practical applications. Fuzzy logic is a valuable and appealing technique in such problems, particularly because of the associated process of approximate reasoning. Learning may be introduced through a process of reinforcement where valid rules in the rulebase are retained and new rules are added (learned), while inappropriate rules are removed. Techniques of neural networks and evolutionary computing may be used in such tasks of learning [5].

3.2 Approximation and Intelligence

Approximation is a "soft" concept that is related to intelligence [1,3]. The capability of approximation for the purpose of comparison, pattern recognition, reasoning and decision making is a manifestation of intelligence (e.g., dealing with incomplete and subjective information, unfamiliar situations, comparison, and judgment). There are many concepts of approximation, examples of which include imprecision, uncertainty, fuzziness, and belief. These concepts are not identical even though the associated methods of information representation and processing may display analytical similarities.

Several concepts of approximation [7] that may be useful in knowledge-based reasoning are summarized in Table 2. In particular, uncertainty deals with crisp sets, while belief and plausibility may be defined with respect to both crisp and fuzzy sets. It is possible to incorporate and employ these various concepts into a knowledge base in a complementary, rather than mutually exclusive, manner. In particular, uncertainty and belief levels may be included as qualifiers in a fuzzy rule; for example [1],

If A then B with probability p

If A then B with belief b

In each case, the antecedent A and the consequent B can be either crisp or fuzzy quantities. In the fuzzy case the level of fuzziness of the knowledge base is determined by the membership functions of the associated fuzzy sets. Apart from that, a level of certainty p, a truth value m, a level of belief b, etc. may be associated with each rule, so as to qualify the exactness of each rule on the basis of additional statistical information, perception, evidence, and so on. In this manner, the concepts of approximation may be used in a complementary way to more realistically and authentically represent a knowledge base and to make valid inferences using it.

It is important to recognize the characteristic features of the concepts of approximation listed in Table 2, so that one can avoid using them incorrectly and inappropriately. In Table 2 the main characteristic that differentiates each concept from the others is indicated, and an example to illustrate that characteristic is also given. In representing and analyzing these concepts, one may treat a condition as membership in a set. The set itself may be either fuzzy or crisp depending on the concept. In particular, it should be noted that both uncertainty and imprecision deal with crisp sets and fuzziness uses fuzzy sets. Belief and plausibility are applicable to both crisp and fuzzy sets.

Suppose that the intersection ($\cap$) of fuzzy sets is represented by a T-norm [3] such as $min(x,y)$ and xy, and the union ($\cup$) of fuzzy sets is represented by an S-norm such as $max(x,y)$ and $x+y-xy$. Then, for two fuzzy sets A and B, the following axiom holds:

Table 2: Several concepts of approximation and their characteristics.

Concept	Property	Example
Ambiguity	The condition has a finite number of different possibilities.	The machine response "may or may not" satisfy the specification.
Vagueness	The condition is not precisely (clearly) defined.	The machine response "may have" met the specification.
Generality	The condition may apply to many (finite or infinite) situations depending on the specific context.	The machine response is "x" times the specification.
Imprecision	Condition can assume a state within a clearly defined (crisp) tolerance interval.	The machine response is "within ±5%" of the specification.
Uncertainty	There is a degree of probability associated with occurrence of the condition.	There is a "90% probability" that the machine response meets the specification.
Fuzziness	The membership of the condition is not crisply defined (set boundary of the condition is not crisp).	The machine response is "close to" the specification.
Belief (Subjective Probability)	The level of belief on the condition (membership of a crisp or fuzzy set) is through knowledge and evidence.	It is believed at a level of 90% that the machine response meets the specification.
Plausibility	The plausibility of nonmembership fully complements the belief of membership (dual condition of belief). $Bl(x \varepsilon A) + Pl(x \notin A) = 1$	It is plausible at a level of 95% that the machine response meets the specification.

$$Fz(A \cup B) = Fz(A) + Fz(B) - Fz(A \cap B) \tag{7}$$

in which $Fz()$ denotes the grade of membership of an element x in the set that is specified within ( ).

The concept of approximation (uncertainty) deals with the "probability of membership" in a crisp set, not a fuzzy set. In this case, a probability function $p(x)$ may be defined for a crisp set A as follows:

$$Pr[x \varepsilon A] = p(x): \Re \rightarrow [0,1] \tag{8}$$

The axiom that describes the probability of combined sets is analogous to Equation (7). Specifically,

$$Pr(A \cup B) = Pr(A) + Pr(B) - Pr(A \cap B) \tag{9}$$

in which, A and B are crisp (non-fuzzy) sets, and $Pr(S)$ is interpreted as the probability that an element x belongs to set S. From Equations (2) and (7) through (9), some form of analytical similarity between fuzziness and uncertainty may be established. But, clearly these two concepts of approximation are not identical. Nevertheless, probabilistic and statistical techniques may be employed in fuzzy logic, and similarly, probabilistic approaches may be augmented with fuzzy-logic techniques. Specifically, a membership function of a fuzzy set may be estimated by using statistical data on membership and nonmembership of the set, as determined by, say, polling a set of experts. For example, a set of trials may be conducted among a group of experts to determine whether a particular state is "fast" or not. Then the grade of membership may be estimated as the ratio of the number of positive polls to the total number of polls. An entire membership function can be estimated by repeating this experiment for different conditions of speed. This practical link between fuzziness and uncertainty may be extended to establish an analytical link as well, while giving due consideration to the dissimilarity between the two concepts [8]. To further establish a link of this form, another interpretation for fuzziness, that is somewhat akin to probability, is also available [6]. Here, a crisp set A is considered. Then, the level of fuzziness of an element x is interpreted as the truth value, the level of belief or the level of certainty that $x \varepsilon A$. Another common way of jointly exploiting the concepts of fuzziness and uncertainty is through the use of *fuzzy modifiers*. An example would be "fast with a certainty level of 90%."

Yet another useful concept of approximation is *belief*, as listed in Table 2. Here, $Bl(A)$ denotes the level of belief that the element x belongs to set A. A belief value may represent the subjective level of confidence (or belief) that a particular object is a member of a given set and may be based on available knowledge, experience, common sense, experimentation, and other evidence. A belief may be defined regardless of whether the set is crisp or fuzzy. The axiom of combination for belief is

$$Bl(A \cup B) \geq Bl(A) + Bl(B) - Bl(A \cap B) \tag{10}$$

with

$$Bl(X) = 1; \quad Bl(\Phi) = 0 \tag{11}$$

in which X denotes the universal set and Φ denotes the null set. When A and B are disjoint sets, one has

$$Bl(A \cup B) \geq Bl(A) + Bl(B) \tag{12}$$

It follows that the level of belief can improve when two sets are considered jointly within a common context over when they are considered separately and independently. Also, it follows from (12) that

$$1 \geq Bl(A) + Bl(A') \tag{13}$$

where, A' is the negation (complement) of A.

Expression (13) states that, the belief of a nonoccurrence of A is less than the complement of belief of A. In other words, the belief of occurrence of A and the belief of nonoccurrence of A are not full, and there exists some level of belief that is indecisive. This deficiency is compensated for by introducing the concept of plausibility, which satisfies

$$Pl(A') = 1 - Bl(A) \tag{14}$$

From Equation (14) it also holds that

$$Pl(A) = 1 - Bl(A') \tag{15}$$

Furthermore, it can be shown that

$$Pl(A) \geq Bl(A) \tag{16}$$

and

$$Pl(A') \geq Bl(A') \tag{17}$$

In view of the inequalities (16) and (17) one could argue that, on the basis of a given body of knowledge (including evidence, experience, and common sense), the level of plausibility that a particular situation occurs is greater than the level of belief of occurrence of the situation. Hence, plausibility is a more liberal, weaker, or more flexible form of belief. As for belief, plausibility may be applicable to both crisp sets and fuzzy sets. The complement relationship for plausibility is given by

$$1 \le Pl(A) + Pl(A') \tag{18}$$

which further supports the weaker or more liberal nature of plausibility over belief (inequality (13)).

Analogous to the manner in which fuzziness and uncertainty are jointly applied to a condition by the use of fuzzy modifiers, fuzziness may be applied jointly with either belief or plausibility as well. In this context *fuzzy beliefs* or *fuzzy plausibilities*, which are akin to fuzzy truth values [3,7], may be employed. This combination of approximators may be achieved, for example, by using expressions of the form "fast with a 90% level of belief."

Some useful properties of four common concepts of approximation are summarized in Table 3. Note that all these concepts can be described in terms of an "inexactness" of set membership. Nature and origin of the inexactness, however, are unique to the particular concept itself. The type of set used is also not the same for all four concepts. Specifically, uncertainty concerns crisp sets and fuzziness deals with fuzzy sets, whereas belief and plausibility are applicable to both crisp and fuzzy sets. All four concepts are useful in knowledge-based decision making of intelligent machines, where representing and processing of knowledge are crucial [1,3]. Even though the mathematical formulations are somewhat similar and the physical characteristics would be lost in the procedures of numerical computations, it is important to understand the differences in meaning of these concepts when employing them in practical applications.

3.3 Probabilistic Approximate Reasoning

In probabilistic approximate reasoning, the concept of approximation that is applicable is *uncertainty*. Here, probability distribution/density functions are employed in place of membership functions. The formula of knowledge-based decision making that corresponds to Equation (1), in this case, depends on the specific type of probabilistic reasoning that is employed. The Bayesian approach [9,10] is commonly used. This may be interpreted as a classification problem. Suppose that an observation d is made, and it may belong to one of several classes c_i.

The Bayes' relation states [3]

$$\max_i P(c_i|d) = \frac{P(d|c_i) \bullet P(c_i)}{P(d)} \tag{19}$$

Table 3: A comparison of several concepts of approximation.

Concept	Qualitative Definition	Combination Axiom	Complement Relation
Uncertainty	Probabilistic/statistical inexactness of occurrence of an event (Crisp set)	$Pr(A \cup B) = Pr(A) + Pr(B) - Pr(A \cap B)$	$Pr(A) + Pr(A') = 1$
Fuzziness	Inexactness in human perception about a situation (Set boundary is non-crisp)	$Fz(A \cup B) = Fz(A) + Fz(B) - Fz(A \cap B)$	$Fz(A) + Fz(A') = 1$
Belief	Inexactness in human belief or confidence about a condition (Crisp or fuzzy set)	$Bl(A \cup B) \geq Bl(A) + Bl(B) - Bl(A \cap B)$	$Bl(A) + Bl(A') \leq 1$
Plausibility	A more liberal form of belief. Level is higher than belief, with the same amount of evidence (Crisp or fuzzy set)	$Pl(A \cup B) \leq Pl(A) + Pl(B) - Pl(A \cap B)$	$Pl(A) + Pl(A') \geq 1$

where

$P(c_i|d)$ = given that the observation is d, the probability that it belongs to class c_i (the *a posteriori conditional probability*)

$P(d|c_i)$ = given that the observation belongs to the class c_i, the probability that the observation is d (the *class conditional probability*)

$P(c_i)$ = the probability that a particular observation belongs to class c_i, without knowing the observation itself (the *a priori probability*)

$P(d)$ = the probability that the observation is d without any knowledge of the class

In the Bayes' decision-making approach, for a given observation (data) d, *a posteriori* probabilities $P(c_i|d)$ are computed for all possible classes ($i = 1,2,...,n$), using Equation (19). The class that corresponds to the largest of these *a posteriori* probability values is chosen as the class of d, thereby solving the classification problem. The remaining $n-1$ *a posteriori* probabilities represent the error in this decision.

Note the analogy between Equations (19) and (1). Specifically, $P(d)$ represents the "preprocessed" probabilistic data that correspond to the observation d. The knowledge base itself constitutes the two sets of probabilities:

1. $P(d|c_i)$ of occurrence of data d if the class (decision) is $c_i, i = 1,2,\cdots,n$
2. $P(c_i)$ of class (decision) $c_i, i = 1,2,\cdots,n$ without any knowledge of the observation (data) itself

The knowledge-base matching is carried out, in this case, by computing the expression on the right side of (19) for all possible i and then picking out the maximum value.

Formulas for knowledge-based decision making that correspond to Equation (1) may be identified for other concepts of approximation (e.g., belief, plausibility, truth value) as well. For example, in the case of belief, the knowledge base may constitute a set of belief values for a set of rules. Then, knowing the belief value of an observation, the decision-making problem will become a matter of picking the segment of the rule base that matches the data and also has the highest belief. More often, however, such concepts of approximation are used as modifiers within a knowledge base of different category (e.g., fuzzy or probabilistic) rather than stand-alone tools of decision making, as alluded to previously.

3.4 Uncertainty and Fuzziness

Uncertainty is statistical inexactness due to random events. Fuzziness arises when the decision of whether a particular object belongs to a given set is a matter of perception, which can be subjective. An analytical (not conceptual) similarity between fuzziness and uncertainty was identified previously. Besides, probabilistic and statistical techniques may be employed in conjunction with fuzzy logic in a complementary manner. Conceptual differences remain despite the analytical similarities of the two methods. The two concepts are compared in Table 4 with respect to their advantages and disadvantages in practical applications.

Application areas of fuzzy logic include smart appliances, supervisory control of complex processes, and expert systems. Application areas of probabilistic methods include forecasting, signal analysis and filtering, and parameter estimation and system identification.

Table 4: An application-oriented comparison of fuzziness and uncertainty.

	Fuzziness	Uncertainty
Advantages	• Incomplete information can be handled • Particularly useful in representing and processing human-oriented knowledge • Approximate reasoning is possible, with qualitative and linguistic knowledge • It is a technique of soft computing	• Useful in situations having random influences with known probability distributions • Governs many practical situations • Mathematical procedures are well established • System parameters can be determined using crisp experiments
Disadvantages	• May introduce a degree of inaccuracy • Needs prior knowledge and experience of the problem in generating the knowledge base • Can be slow	• Not related to fuzzy sets • May fail under incomplete information • Results are directly affected by the type and accuracy of the probability distributions

3.5 Evolutionary Computing [5]

In nature, individuals of a population compete with each other for resources such as food, water, and shelter. Also, members of the same species often compete to attract a mate. Those individuals who are more successful in surviving and attracting mates consequently will produce a larger number of offspring [11]. Weaker individuals will often produce few, or even no, offspring. This means that the genes from the highly adapted or "fit" individuals will spread in an exponential manner in successive generations. The combination of good characteristics from different ancestors can result in "super fit" offspring, whose fitness is greater than that of either parent. In this way, species evolve to become increasingly better suited for their environment [12]. In the present context of intelligent machines, intellectual fitness rather than physical fitness is what is important for the evolutionary process. Evolutionary computing relies on related principles and can play an important role in the development of an optimal and self-improving intelligent machine.

Derivative-free optimizing algorithms that make use of evolutionary searching fall into the category of evolutionary computing. Inspired by biological evolution, evolutionary computing [11,12,13], where optimization is conducted through a search procedure that hardly uses information on the search space, has the following characteristics:

1. It is based on multiple searching points or solution candidates (population based search)
2. It uses evolutionary operations such as crossover and mutation
3. It is based on probabilistic operations

Paradigms that employ evolutionary computing include the genetic algorithm (GA), evolution strategy (ES), evolutionary programming (EP), and genetic programming (GP).

In a GA, the solutions for chromosomes are represented by bit coding (genotype) and better solution candidates in the genotype space are searched using the operations of selection, crossover, and mutation. Crossover is the dominant operation.

In ES the solutions, as expressed by chromosomes, are represented using real number coding (phenotype), and better solutions in the phenotype space are searched using the operations of crossover and mutation. The mutation of a real number is realized by adding Gaussian noise, and ES controls the parameters of a Gaussian distribution allowing it to converge to a global optimum.

EPs are similar to GAs. The primary difference is that the mutation is an EP operation. EPs use real number coding, and mutation may change the structure (length) of the EP code.

GPs use tree structure coding to represent a computer program or create new structures of tasks. The crossover operation is done not on a numerical value but on a branch of the tree structure. The rest of the present section will focus on GAs and will illustrate how a GA searches for a solution.

The basic principles of genetic algorithms were first laid down by Holland [14]. GAs strive to mimic those processes in a biological population that are essential to evolution. Exactly which biological processes are essential for evolution and which processes have little or no role to play is still a matter of research. As a result, open research issues of GAs themselves abound.

GAs use a direct analogy of natural behavior (see Figure 3). They work with a population of individuals, each representing a possible solution to a given problem. Each individual is assigned a fitness score according to how good its solution to the problem is. The highly fit (in the intellectual sense) individuals are given opportunities to reproduce by crossbreeding with other individuals in the population. This produces new individuals as offspring, who share some features taken from each parent. The least fit members of the population are less likely to get selected for reproduction and will eventually die out.

A whole new population of possible solutions is thus produced by selecting the best individuals (i.e., individuals with best solutions) from the current generation and mating them to produce a new set of individuals. This new generation will contain a higher proportion of the characteristics possessed by the "fit" members of the previous generation. In this way, over many generations, desirable characteristics are spread throughout the population, being mixed and exchanged with other desirable characteristics, in the process. By favoring the mating of the individuals who are more fit (i.e., who can provide better solutions), the most promising areas of the search space would be exploited.

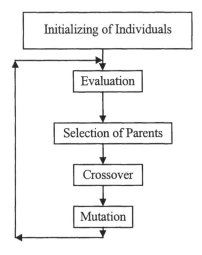

Figure 3: The flow of a GA process.

A GA determines the next set of searching points using the fitness values of the current searching points, which are widely distributed throughout the searching space. It uses the mutation operation to escape from a local minimum. A key disadvantage of GAs is that their convergence speed near the global optimum can be quite slow. Some advantages are:

1. Fast convergence to near-global optimum
2. Superior global searching capability in a space that has a complex searching surface
3. Applicability to problems where the gradient information of the search space cannot be used

Some common definitions of the technical terms used in GAs are given below [11,13]:

Chromosome: a vector of parameters that represents the solution of an application task; for example, the dimensions of the beams in a bridge design (These parameters, known as *genes*, are joined together to form a string of values called *chromosomes*.)
Gene: a solution that will combine to form a chromosome
Selection: the process of choosing parents or offspring chromosomes for the next generation
Individuals: the solution vectors of chromosomes
Population: the collection of individuals
Population size: the number of chromosomes in a population
Fitness Function: the function that evaluates how each solution is suitable for a given task
Phenotype: the expression type of solution values in the task world; for example, "red," "blue," "80kg"
Genotype: the binary (bit) expression type of solution values used in the GA search space; for example, "011," "000111011"

Two important activities of a GA are selection and reproduction.

Selection: Selection is an operation that will choose parent solutions. New solution vectors in the next generation are calculated from them. Since it is expected that better parents generate better offspring, parent solution vectors that have higher fitness values will have a higher probability of selection. There are several methods of selection. In the method of roulette wheel selection [12], the probability of winning is proportional to the area rate of a chosen number on a roulette wheel. According to this analogy, the selection procedure assigns a selection probability to individuals in proportion to their fitness values.

The elitist strategy is an approach that copies the best n parents into the next generation. The fitness value of an offspring does not always become better than those of its parents [13]. The elitist strategy prevents the best fitness value of the offspring generation from becoming worse than that in the present generation, by copying the best parents to the offspring.

Reproduction: During the reproductive phase of a GA, individuals are selected from the population and recombined, producing offspring which in turn will make up the next generation. Parents are selected randomly from the population using a scheme that favors the individuals who are more fit. After two parents are selected, their chromosomes are recombined using the mechanism of crossover and mutation [15,16].

Crossover takes two individuals and cuts their chromosome strings at some randomly chosen position to produce two "head" segments and two "tail" segments. The tail segments are then swapped over to produce two new full-length chromosomes (see Figure 4). Each of the two offspring will inherit some genes from each parent. This is known as a single-point crossover. Crossover is not usually applied to all pairs of individuals that are chosen for mating. A random choice is made, where the likelihood of the crossover being applied is typically between 0.6 and 1.0.

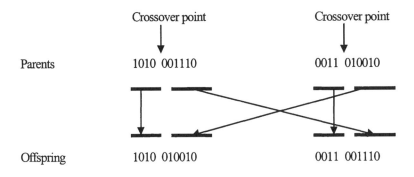

Figure 4: Single-point crossover.

Mutation is applied individually to each child, after crossover. It randomly alters each gene at a small probability (typically 0.001). Figure 5 shows an example where the fifth gene of a chromosome is mutated. The traditional view is that crossover is more important than mutation for rapidly exploring a search space. Mutation provides a small degree of random search and helps ensure that every point in the search space has some probability of being examined.

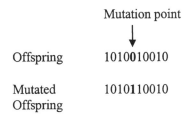

Figure 5: A single mutation.

4 Production Systems

Production systems are rule-based systems that are appropriate for the representation and processing of knowledge (i.e., knowledge-based decision making) in intelligent machines [3,17]. An expert system is one example of a production system. The structure of a typical knowledge-based system is shown in Figure 6.

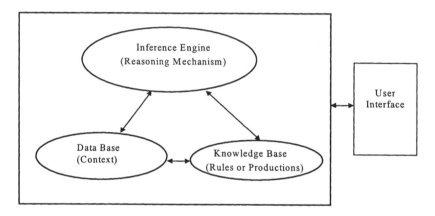

Figure 6: The structure of a production system.

4.1 Blackboard Architecture

A suitable structure for a knowledge-based system would be a blackboard architecture [3], which is a cooperative problem-solving architecture. This architecture has a common (global) data region called *blackboard* which is shared by and visible to the entire system, several intelligent modules called *knowledge sources*, and a *control unit* which manages the operation of the system. Generally the knowledge sources are not arranged in a hierarchical manner and will cooperate as equal partners (specialists) in making a knowledge-based decision. The knowledge sources interact with the shared data region under the supervision of the control unit. When the data in the blackboard change, which corresponds to a change in the context (data condition), the knowledge sources would be triggered in an opportunistic manner and an appropriate decision would be made. That decision could then result in further changes to the blackboard data and subsequent triggering of other knowledge sources. Data may be changed by external means (for example, through the user interface) as well as due to knowledge-source actions. The operation of a general production system is somewhat similar to that of a blackboard system. This topic is addressed next in some detail.

In a production system, knowledge is represented by a set of rules (or productions) stored in the knowledge base. The data base contains the current data (or context) of the process. The inference engine is the reasoning mechanism, which controls rule matching, coordinates and organizes the sequence of steps used in solving a particular problem, and resolves any conflicts. The user interface is the link between the knowledge-based system and its operating environment inclusive of the user. Manual commands and sensory signals from external objects (agents) all will enter the system through this interface.

Knowledge representation using a set of if-then rules is not an unfamiliar concept. For example, a maintenance or trouble-shooting manual of a machine (e.g., automobile) contains such rules, perhaps in tabular form. Also, a production system may be used as a simple model for human reasoning: sensory data fire rules in the short-term memory, which will lead to the firing of more complex rules in the long-term memory.

The operation (processing) of a typical rule-based system proceeds as follows: new data are generated (say, from sensors or external commands) and stored in appropriate locations within the data base of the system. This is the new context. The inference engine tries to match the new data with the condition part (i.e., the *if* part or the *antecedent*) of the rules in the knowledge base. This is called rule searching. If the condition part of a rule matches the data, that rule is "fired," which generates an action dictated by the action part (i.e., the *then* part or the *consequent*) of the rule. In fact, firing of a rule amounts to the generation (inference) of new facts, and this in turn may form a context that will lead to the satisfaction (firing) of other rules.

Example: Consider a knowledge base for selecting a control technique, as given by the following set of rules:

1. *If the plant is linear and uncoupled then use Control Category A.*
2. *If the plant is linear and coupled then use Control Category B.*
3. *If the plant is nonlinear use Control Category C.*
4. *If Category A and a plant model is known then use Subgroup 1.*
5. *If Category B and a plant model is known then use Subgroup 2.*
6. *If Subgroup 2 and high model uncertainty then use H-infinity control.*

Now suppose that the data base receives the following context:

> *Linear*
> *Coupled*
> *Model Available*
> *Model Uncertainty High*

In this case, the first two items in the context will fire Rule 2. The results will form a new item in the context. This new item, along with the third item in the old context, will fire Rule 5. The result, along with the last item of the old context, will fire Rule 6, which will lead to the selection of $H\alpha$ control.

4.2 Reasoning Strategies

Two strategies are available to perform reasoning and make inferences in a production system:

1.   Forward chaining
2.   Backward chaining.

Forward chaining is a data-driven search method. Here, the rule base is searched to match an *if* part of a rule (condition) with known facts or data (context), and if a match is detected, that rule is fired (i.e., the *then* part or "action" part of the rule is activated). Obviously, this is a direct strategy and is a bottom-up approach. Actions could include creation, deletion, and updating of data in the data base. As seen in the previous example, one action can lead to firing of one or more new rules. The inference engine is responsible for sequencing the matching (searching) and action cycles. A production system that uses forward chaining is termed a *forward production system* (FPS). This type of system is particularly useful in knowledge-based control. In the previous example on control-technique selection, forward chaining was tacitly used.

In *backward chaining*, which is a top-down search process, a hypothesized conclusion is matched with rules in the knowledge base in order to determine the context (facts) that supports the particular conclusion. If enough facts support a hypothesis, the hypothesis is accepted. Backward chaining is useful in situations that call for diagnosis and theorem proving, and generally in applications where a logical explanation has to be attached to each action. A production system that uses backward chaining is called a *backward chaining system* (BCS).

In the previous example on control-technique selection, if one had hypothesized the selection of another control technique (say, the LQG method) and proceeded backwards in searching the rule base for the context information that satisfies this hypothesis, one would arrive at a set of requirements (premises). But these premises would not match the entire context of the situation (specifically, "model uncertainty high" will not be matched) and hence the hypothesis would be false. Then, one should try another hypothesis and proceed similarly, until a suitable match is obtained.

4.3 Conflict Resolution Methods

When the context data are matched with the condition parts of the rules in a rule base, it may be possible that more than one rule is satisfied. The set of rules that is satisfied in this manner is termed the *conflict set*. A method of conflict resolution has to be invoked to select from the conflict set the rule that would be fired. Methods of conflict resolution include the following:

1. First match
2. Toughest match
3. Privileged match
4. Most recent match

In the first method, the very first rule that is satisfied during searching will be fired. This is a very simple strategy but may not produce the best performance in general. In the second method, the rule with the most condition elements, within the conflict set, will be fired. For example, suppose that the conflict set has the following two rules:

If the temperature is high then increase the coolant flow rate.

If the temperature is high and the coolant flow rate is maximum, then shut down the plant.

Here, the toughest match is the second rule.

The rules in a rule base may be assigned various weightings and priorities depending on their significance. The privileged match is the rule with the highest priority, within the conflict set. For example, a priority may be assigned in proportion to the toughness of the match. In this case the methods 2 and 3 listed above are identical. Alternatively, a priority may be assigned to a rule on the basis of the significance or consequences of its acts.

The most recent match is the rule in the conflict set, whose condition part satisfies the most recent entries of data. In this method, a higher priority is given to more recently arrived data in the data base.

5 Expert Systems

An *expert system* is a knowledge-based system and contains the traditional constituents of the latter such as a knowledge base, a data base, an inference engine, and a human/machine interface, as indicated in Figure 7. The interface is used for both development, particularly knowledge acquisition, and utilization of the expert system. The knowledge base of an expert system embodies human knowledge and understanding, somewhat imitating a human expert in the particular domain of expertise (e.g., specialist, engineer, scientist, doctor, lawyer, financial consultant). The inference engine is a "driver" program that traverses the knowledge base in response to observations and other inputs from the external world, and possibly previous inferences and results from the expert system itself, and will identify one or more possible outcomes or conclusions [3,5,18]. This task of making inferences for arriving at solutions will involve "processing" of knowledge. It follows that representation and processing of knowledge are central to the functioning of an expert system [3]. The data structure selected for the specific form of knowledge representation determines the nature of the program that serves as an inference engine. Monitors and keyboards, sensors and transducers, and even output from other computer programs including expert systems, usually provide communication links between an expert system and the external world.

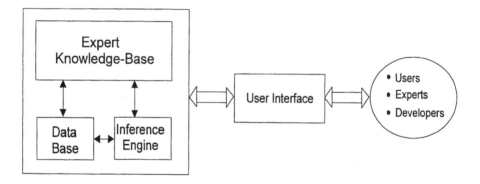

Figure 7: A typical expert system.

An expert system is intended to take the place of a human expert in an advisory capacity. It can be used by a nonexpert to improve problem-solving abilities or by an expert to obtain supporting or corroborating information in her decision making process. An expert system is typically used in a consultation mode. It receives problem descriptions (for example, in a question-answer form) and provides advice through knowledge-based reasoning. An expert system should be able to explain its advice; that is, it should possess an explanation facility.

5.1 Development of an Expert System

The development of an expert system requires the combined effort of domain experts, who are human experts in the field of interest, and knowledge engineers, who acquire and represent/program the knowledge in a suitable form. This process will require a knowledge acquisition facility. Other engineers, programmers, etc. are needed for the development of the system interface, integration, and so on. The experts will be involved in defining the problem domain to be solved and in providing the necessary expertise and knowledge for the knowledge base that will lead to the solution of a class of problems in that domain. The knowledge engineers are involved in acquiring and representing the available knowledge and in the overall process of programming and debugging the system. They organize the acquired knowledge into the form required by the particular expert system tool [19]. Forms of knowledge representation may include logic, production systems (rules), semantic scripts, semantic primitives, frames, and symbolic representations [3]. Experts and knowledge engineers both will be involved in testing and evaluating the system.

Typically, what is commercially available for developing expert systems is an expert system "shell." It will consist of the required software programs, but will not contain a knowledge base. It is the responsibility of the user, then, to organize the creation of the required knowledge base, which should satisfy the requirements of the system with respect to the form of knowledge representation that is used and the structure of the knowledge base [20].

While the quality and performance of an expert system is highly dependent on the knowledge base that is contained within it, this knowledge alone does not constitute a powerful expert system. A poorly chosen formalism may limit the extent and nature of the knowledge; accordingly, the structure of knowledge representation plays an important role. The formalism that is employed should closely resemble how an expert uses knowledge and performs reasoning. The skill of both the domain expert and the knowledge engineer will be crucial here. The techniques of representation and processing will be dependent on the type of knowledge. The reasoning scheme that is employed will directly affect the search speed and how conflicts are resolved. In particular, retrieval and processing of information will not be fast or efficient without a good formalism for representing knowledge and a suitable inference-making scheme to process it. In real-time expert systems, speed of decision making is a very crucial factor, and it depends on hardware/software characteristics, the inference-making scheme, and the particular technique of knowledge representation.

In developing the knowledge base of an expert system, the experts involved may rely on published information, experimental findings, and any other available information in addition to their own knowledge. Testing and evaluation may involve trials where the experts pose problems to the expert system and evaluate the inferences made by the system. Many of these test problems may have solutions that are already known. Others may not be so clear cut and hence the responses of the expert system should be carefully scrutinized by the experts during the testing and evaluation phase. The tests should involve the ultimate users of the system as well.

In this regard, the features of the user interface, including simplicity, use of a common language, graphics, and voice facilities, are important.

5.2 Knowledge Engineering

Tasks of knowledge engineering include the following:

1. Acquisition of knowledge that is pertinent, from different sources (experts, literature, media, etc.)
2. Interpretation and integration of the knowledge (from various sources and in different forms)
3. Representation of the knowledge within the knowledge-based system (Suitable structure, language, etc. have to be chosen. Here, one should consider aspects of incomplete knowledge, presence of analytical models, accessibility of system variables for measurement, and availability of past experience.)
4. Processing of knowledge for making inferences (This operation has to be compatible with the knowledge-base, objectives of the system, etc. Speed of decision making is crucial, particularly in real-time applications. The form of the inferences should be consistent with the system objectives.)
5. System needs and constraints (accuracy, implications of incomplete knowledge, and cost of an incorrect inference)
6. Economic considerations (development cost; cost to the user in comparison to the benefits)

5.3 Applications

An expert system may be equally useful to both an expert and a layperson. For example, it is difficult for one expert to possess complete knowledge in all aspects of a problem and, furthermore, the solutions to a problem can be quite complex. Then, the expert may turn to a good expert system that will provide the necessary solutions, which the expert could evaluate further (perhaps with the assistance of other experts) before adopting. Ideally, an expert system should have an "evolving" knowledge base, which has the capability to learn and continuously update itself.

Expert systems have been developed for a variety of applications such as medical diagnosis and prescription of treatment, mineral exploration, interpretation of satellite imagery, financial advising, legal consultation, tax return preparation, system troubleshooting and maintenance, planning and scheduling, weather forecasting, operation and maintenance of plants and machinery, and system control. An expert system that is used to supervise the control system of a plant is called a *control expert system*. Such expert systems are directly applicable at a high level of operation, for monitoring, supervision, diagnosis, and control of intelligent machines.

Performance goals of the next-generation expert systems are:

- Automatic generation of code and knowledge representation
- Automatic learning and system enhancement from experience
- Voice recognition
- Communication through a natural language
- Automated translation of documents into knowledge bases
- Cooperative problem-solving architectures
- Generic problem-solving shells
- Multilevel reasoning systems

5.4 Use of Fuzzy Logic

Fuzzy logic is particularly useful in the development of expert systems [3]. Expert systems are built by capturing knowledge of humans; however, such knowledge is known to be qualitative and inexact. Experts may be only partially knowledgeable about the problem domain, or data may not be fully available, yet decisions are still expected. In these situations, educated guesses have to be made to provide solutions to problems. This is exactly where fuzzy logic can be employed as a tool to deal with imprecision and qualitative aspects that are associated with problem solving.

Rationale for the use of fuzzy logic in expert systems may be summarized as follows:

- The knowledge base of expert systems encapsulates knowledge of human experts
- Human knowledge is often inexact and qualitative, and fuzzy descriptors (e.g., large, small, fast, poor, fine) are commonly used in its communication
- Problem description of the user may not be exact
- Knowledge base from experts may not be complete, yet satisfactory decisions are still expected
- Educated guesses need to be made in some situations

6 An Intelligent Machine

An *intelligent machine* is a machine that displays what would be considered as "intelligent" behavior if displayed by a human. In view of this rather qualitative and circular definition it is essential to know what is considered as intelligent behavior. Again, a precise and complete definition is not available. Yet it is generally accepted that an intelligent system possesses one or more of the following characteristics and capabilities: sensory perception, pattern recognition, learning and knowledge acquisition, inference from incomplete information; inference from qualitative or approximate information, dealing with unfamiliar situations, adapting to new yet related situations (through expectational knowledge), inductive reasoning, common sense, display of emotions, and inventiveness. The attributes of knowledge acquisition — making logical inferences, learning, and dealing with incomplete or qualitative information and uncertainty — are all associated with human intelligence.

As much as neurons themselves in a brain are not intelligent but certain behaviors that are effected by those neurons are, the physical elements of a machine are not intelligent but the machine can be programmed to behave in an intelligent manner. In the present context a "machine" is not just a computer but rather a computer-integrated process or machinery. Sensors, actuators, and controllers will be integral components of such a process and will work cooperatively in making the behavior of the process intelligent. Sensing with understanding or "feeling" what is sensed is known as *sensory perception*, and this is very important for intelligent behavior. Humans use vision, smell, hearing, and touch (tactile sensing) in the context of their intelligent behavior. Intelligent machines too should possess some degree of sensory perception. The "mind" of an intelligent machine is represented by machine intelligence. For proper functioning of an intelligent machine it should have effective communication links between various components. By taking these various requirements into consideration a general-purpose structure of an intelligent machine is given in Figure 8.

In broad terms, an intelligent machine may be viewed to consist of a *knowledge system* and a *structural system*. The knowledge system effects and manages intelligent behavior of the machine, loosely analogous to the brain, and consists of various knowledge sources and reasoning strategies. The structural system consists of physical hardware and devices that are necessary to perform the machine objectives yet do not necessarily need a knowledge system for their individual functions. Sensors, actuators, controllers (nonintelligent), communication interfaces, mechanical devices, and other physical components fall into this category. The broad division of the structure of an intelligent machine, as mentioned above, is primarily functional rather than physical. In particular the knowledge system may be distributed throughout the machine, and individual components by themselves may be interpreted as being "intelligent" as well (for example, intelligent sensors, intelligent controllers, intelligent multi-agent systems).

It needs to be emphasized that an actual implementation of an intelligent system will be domain specific, and much more detail than what is alluded to in Figure 8 may have to be incorporated into the system structure. Even from the viewpoint of system efficiency, domain-specific and special purpose implementations are preferred over general purpose systems.

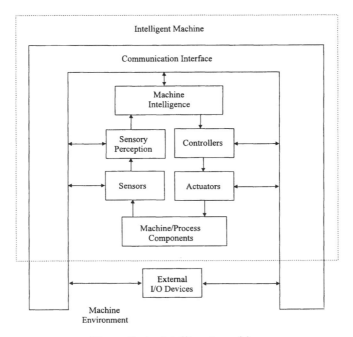

Figure 8: An intelligent machine.

6.1 Intelligent Control

Modern machinery and devices are often called upon to perform complex tasks with high accuracy, under ill-defined conditions. Conventional control techniques may not be quite effective in these systems, whereas intelligent control has a tremendous potential [3,5]. The term *intelligent control* may be loosely used to denote a control technique that can be carried out using the "intelligence" of a human who is knowledgeable in the particular domain of control [3]. In this definition, constraints pertaining to limitations of sensory and actuation capabilities and information processing speeds of humans are not considered. It follows that if a human in the control loop can properly control a machine, then that machine would be a good candidate for intelligent control. Information abstraction and knowledge-based decision making, which incorporates abstracted information, are considered important in intelligent control. Unlike conventional control, intelligent control techniques possess capabilities for effectively dealing with incomplete information concerning the machine and its environment and unexpected or unfamiliar conditions.

Intelligent control refers to a group of analytical and synthesis methods that fall outside the scope of traditional control theory and that are used for autonomous control and supervision of complex machinery and processes. The need for intelligent control is evident from the emergence of engineering systems exhibiting an increasingly greater degree of complexity and sophistication. These systems are found in applications such as process control of industrial plants, traffic control, distributed simulation, military command and control, communication networks, power generation and distribution, aircraft and robot operation, automotive control, household appliances, and generally in intelligent machines. The field of intelligent control has grown in recent years at an impressive rate. This is due primarily to the proven capabilities of the algorithms and techniques, particularly with soft computing, developed in the field to deal with complex systems that operate in ill-defined and dynamically varying environments.

Industrial applications using tools of intelligent control have risen substantially and continue to increase at a rapid rate. Advances in digital electronics, technologies of semiconductor processing, and micro-electromechanical systems (MEMS) have set the stage for the integration of intelligence into sensors, actuators, and controllers [2]. The physical segregation between these devices may well be lost in due time as it becomes possible to perform diversified functionalities such as sensing, conditioning (filtering, amplification, processing, modification, etc.), transmission of signals, and intelligent control all within the same physical device.

6.2 Intelligent Sensor Fusion

When several sensors are available for acquiring the same information regarding a particular process, the combined and synergetic use of that information can increase the reliability, accuracy, and overall effectiveness of the sensor-based operation. A systematic method for the combination of sensory data obtained from different sources is known as *sensor fusion* or *data fusion*. Important contributions of sensor fusion have been made in several areas of application such as robotics [21], flexible manufacturing [22], target detection [23], process monitoring, and sorting [24]. Typically, techniques of combining evidence [25] and particularly statistical approaches such as the Bayesian estimation [26] are used for sensor fusion, in view of the uncertainty associated with information from different sensors [27]. Furthermore, since the knowledge used in sensor fusion may be heuristic, some work has been carried out in applying knowledge-based approaches in that context [28]. Intelligent machines typically make use of multiple sensors for information acquisition, decision making, and control. It follows that the subject of sensor fusion is particularly applicable in intelligent machines.

Intelligent sensor fusion is motivated by the observation that humans routinely and effectively employ sensor fusion in executing real-time tasks. The incorporation of knowledge-based techniques into sensor fusion should yield significant benefits. Such techniques of sensor fusion are useful in intelligent machines. For example, it is possible to combine the robustness of knowledge-based soft computing with the flexibility of distributed systems to provide an adaptive solution for sensor fusion in an intelligent machine. In particular, the fusion of data from sensors may be achieved through knowledge-based decision making using fuzzy logic [3].

The information that goes into the fusion system could be preprocessed through a series of sensor models [29]. The result could be available at any level of information abstraction from raw sensor data to data features to target classifications and sophisticated decisions. The fusion process may be tuned and optimized using a global nonlinear optimization algorithm such as genetic search [30]. A fuzzy representation of the sensors and their interactions may be used to provide a robust sensor fusion engine. Furthermore, using communication protocols and distributed intelligence, it will be possible to create a flexible system that can be easily adapted to existing sensor-based controller of a machine.

A knowledge-based sensor fusion system may utilize soft computing techniques. A general architecture for a knowledge-based sensor fusion system is shown in Figure 9. The system has three main modules:

(1) A fuzzy fusion module, which receives preprocessed sensory information, combines it using knowledge-based inference, and produces the necessary result

(2) A bank of sensor models, which model the individual sensors that are present, to generate standard outputs compatible with the fusion system

(3) An adaptive module used for tuning and optimizing the fusion action

Specific methodology that may be employed are outlined below.

Fuzzy Fusion System: A fusion formula that uses techniques of fuzzy inference may be incorporated. The input to the system will be membership functions of the sensory information. The knowledge base of the system will be a set of fuzzy rules that governs the execution of tasks such as machine monitoring, diagnosis, product quality assessment, machine performance assessment, and low-level control. The knowledge base will also reflect the expertise of human sensor fusion. The inference engine may be based on the compositional rule of inference [3]. The output of this module will be information such as control commands, task planning sequences, and quality/performance decisions related to the machine.

Sensor Models: Sensor models may be implemented using fuzzy-neural units [31] as a separate module. This module will provide preprocessed and interpreted sensor readings to the main fusion center. Consistent with a distributed design for the machine, the sensor modeling system may incorporate local adaptive components for sensors with highly nonlinear or variable behavior.

Optimizing Rule Tuner: Sensor fusion can be regarded as an optimization problem. The initial inference rules may be based on the knowledge of expert operators; however, that knowledge is not necessarily optimal. The rule tuner may use a global nonlinear optimization algorithm to adapt the sensor fusion rules to the current environment. The rule-tuning component should modify the fuzzy rules to minimize the overall error in the fused results. This rule-tuning criterion would be particularly well suited for use with a global nonlinear optimization strategy such as an evolutionary algorithm or simulated annealing.

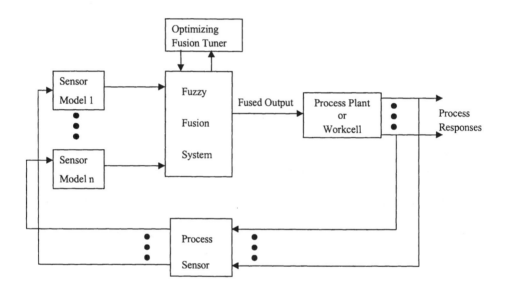

Figure 9: A structure for intelligent sensor fusion.

Communication Protocol: The communication protocol is intended to be a standard interface between the sensors and the fusion engine. The protocol will not only allow highly flexible implementations of sensor fusion systems, but will also allow the system to use distributed intelligence to perform preprocessing and information understanding. The communication protocol should be based on an application-level standard. In essence, it should outline what the different sensors can communicate with each other and with the fusion system, without defining the physical data link and network levels. The communication protocol should allow for different sensor types and different sensory data abstractions to be interchanged within the same framework. It should also allow for information from geographically removed locations to be communicated to the sensor fusion system. A client-server architecture may be adopted here, where the sensors are the clients and the fusion system is the server [32].

6.3 Stages of Development

Development of an intelligent machine will require a parallel development of the knowledge system and the structural system of the machine. It may be the case that the structural system (a nonintelligent machine) is already available. Still, modifications might be necessary in the structural system in order to accommodate the needs of the intelligent system, for example, new sensors, transducers, and communication links for information acquisition. In any event, the development of an intelligent machine is typically a multidisciplinary task often involving the collaboration of a group of professionals such as engineers (electrical, mechanical, etc.), domain experts, computer scientists, programmers, software engineers, and technicians. The success of a project of this nature will depend on proper planning of the necessary activities. The involved tasks will be domain specific and depend on many factors, particularly the objectives and specifications of the machine itself. The main steps would be:

1. Conceptual development
2. System design
3. Prototyping
4. Testing and refinement
5. Technology transfer and commercialization.

It should be noted that generally these are not sequential and independent activities; furthermore, several iterations of multiple steps may be required before satisfactory completion of any single step.

Conceptual development will usually evolve from a specific application need. A general concept needs to be expanded into an implementation model of some detail. A preliminary study of feasibility, costs, and benefits should be made at this stage. The interdisciplinary groups that would form the project team should be actively consulted and their input should be incorporated into the process of concept development. Major obstacles and criticism that may arise from both prospective developers and users of the technology should be seriously addressed in this stage. The prospects of abandoning the project altogether due to valid reasons such as infeasibilty, time constraints, and cost-benefit factors should not be overlooked.

Once a satisfactory conceptual model has been developed, and the system goals are found to be realistic and feasible, the next logical step of development would be the system design. Here the conceptual model is refined and sufficient practical details for implementation of the machine are identified. The structural design may follow traditional practices. Commercially available components and tools should be identified. In the context of an intelligent machine, careful attention needs to be given for design of the knowledge system and the human–machine interface. System architecture, types of knowledge that are required, appropriate techniques of knowledge representation, reasoning strategies, and related tools of knowledge engineering should be identified at this stage. Considerations in the context of user interface would include graphic displays; interactive use; input types including visual, vocal, and other sensory inputs; voice recognition; and natural language processing. These considerations will be application specific to a large degree and will depend on what technologies are available and feasible. A detail design of the overall system should be finalized after obtaining input from the entire project team, and the cost-benefit analysis should be refined. At this stage the financial sponsors and managers of the project as well as the developers and users of the technology should be convinced of the project outcomes.

Prototype development may be carried out in two stages. First a research prototype may be developed in laboratory, for the proof of concept. For this prototype it is not necessary to adhere strictly to industry standards and specifications. Through the experience gained in this manner an industrial prototype should be developed next, in close collaboration with industrial users. Actual operating conditions and performance specifications should be carefully taken into account for this prototype. Standard components and tools should be used as much as possible.

Testing of the industrial prototype should be done under normal operating conditions and preferably at an actual industrial site. Prospective operators and users of the machine should be involved cooperatively with the project team during this exercise. This should be used as a good opportunity to educate, train, and generally prepare the workers for the new technology. Unnecessary fears and prejudices can kill an industrial implementation of advanced technology. Familiarization with the technology is the most effective way to overcome such difficulties. The shortcomings of the machine should be identified through thorough testing and performance evaluation where all interested parties should be involved. The machine should be refined (and possibly redesigned) to overcome any shortcomings.

Once the machine is tested, refined, and confirmed to satisfy the required performance specifications, the processes of technology transfer to industry and commercialization could begin. An approved business plan, necessary infrastructure, and funds should be in place for commercial development and marketing. According to the existing practice, engineers, scientists, and technicians provide minimal input into these activities. This situation is not desirable and needs to be greatly improved. The lawyers, financiers, and business managers should work closely with the technical team during the processes of production planning and commercialization. Typically the industrial sponsors of the project will have the right of first refusal of the developed technology. The process of technology transfer would normally begin during the stage of prototype testing and continue through commercial development and marketing. A suitable plan and infrastructure for product maintenance and upgrading are musts for sustaining any commercial product.

7 Summary

In exploring the question "What makes a machine intelligent?" this introductory chapter outlined several important characteristics and capabilities of a machine that are considered to exhibit intelligent behavior. Common techniques and approaches that are useful in the development of an intelligent machine were introduced. A simplified model for the dynamics of intelligence was given. An intelligent machine relies on computational intelligence in generating its intelligent behavior. This requires a knowledge system in which representation and processing of knowledge are central functions. Associated techniques were outlined. Conventional machine intelligence has relied heavily on symbolic manipulation for processing descriptive information and "knowledge" in realizing a degree of intelligent behavior.

Approximation is a "soft" concept. The capability of approximation for the purpose of comparison, pattern recognition, reasoning, and decision making was emphasized as a manifestation of intelligence. The chapter discussed several concepts of approximation. Humans commonly employ approximate reasoning in their intelligent behavior. Soft computing is an important branch of computational intelligence where fuzzy logic, probability theory, neural networks, and genetic algorithms are synergetically used to mimic reasoning and decision making of a human. The chapter introduced the subject of soft computing, with an emphasis on fuzzy logic, probabilistic decision making, and genetic algorithms. The chapter presented a general structure for an intelligent machine. Intelligent control refers to a group of analytical and synthesis methods that fall outside the scope of traditional control theory and that are useful in autonomous control and supervision of an intelligent machine. Multiple sensing and intelligent sensor fusion are also important in intelligent machines. This is motivated by the observation that humans routinely and effectively employ sensor fusion in executing real-time tasks. The chapter outlined intelligent control and intelligent sensor fusion, and concluded by giving the main steps in the development of an intelligent machine for practical use. The material in this chapter forms a common foundation for the remaining chapters of the book.

References

[1]   De Silva, C.W., "Intelligent Control of Robotic Systems with Application in Industrial Processes," *Robotics and Autonomous Systems*, Vol. 21, pp. 221-237, 1997.

[2]   De Silva, C.W., Lee, T.H., Poo, A.N., Ang, M.H., Wu, J.Q.M., Tan, K.K., and Tan, K.C., *NUS-UBC Centre for Intelligent Machines and Control*, A Proposal, Centre for Integrated Computer Systems Research, University of British Columbia, Vancouver, Canada, 1999.

[3]   De Silva, C.W., *Intelligent Control: Fuzzy Logic Applications*, CRC Press, Boca Raton, FL, 1995.

[4]   Zadeh, L.A., "Making Computers Think Like People," *IEEE Spectrum*, pp. 26-32, August 1984.

[5]   Filippidis, A., Jain, L.C., and de Silva, C.W., "Intelligent Control Techniques," *Intelligent Adaptive Control*, (Editors: Jain, L.C. and de Silva, C.W.), CRC Press, Boca Raton, FL, 1999.

[6]   Dubois, D. and Prade, H., *Fuzzy Sets and Systems: Theory and Applications*, Academic Press, Orlando, FL, 1980.

[7]   Klir, G.J. and Folger, T.A., *Fuzzy Sets, Uncertainty, and Information*, Prentice Hall, Englewood Cliffs, NJ, 1988.

[8]   De Silva, C.W., Gamage, L.B., and Gosine, R.G., "An Intelligent Firmness Sensor for an Automated Herring Roe Grader," *International Journal of Intelligent Automation and Soft Computing*, Vol. 1, pp. 99-114, 1995.

[9]   Anderson, T.W., *An Introduction to Multivariate Statistical Analysis*, John Wiley & Sons, New York, 1984.

[10] Pao, Y.H., *Adaptive Pattern Recognition and Neural Networks*, Addison-Wesley, Reading, MA, 1989.

[11] Takagi, H., "Introduction to Fuzzy Systems, Neural Networks and Genetic Algorithms," Tutorial Notes, *International Conference on Knowledge-Based Intelligent Electronic Systems* (KES'97), Adelaide, Australia, May 1997.

[12] Davis, L., *Handbook on Genetic Algorithms*, Van Nostrand-Rienhold, New York, 1991.

[13] Grefenstette, J.J., "Optimization of Control Parameters for Genetic Algorithms," *IEEE Transactions on Systems, Man, and Cybernetics*, Vol. 16, pp. 122-128, 1986.

[14] Holland, J.H., *Adaptation in Natural and Artificial Systems*, MIT Press, Cambridge, MA, 1975.

[15] Vonk, E., Jain, L.C., and Johnson, R.P., *Automatic Generation of Neural Network Architecture Using Evolutionary Computing*, World Scientific Publishing Co., Singapore, 1997.

[16] Van Rooij, A., Jain, L.C., and Johnson, R.P., *Neural Network Training Using Genetic Algorithms*, World Scientific Publishing Co., Singapore, 1997.

[17] Staugaard, A.C., *Robotics and AI*, Prentice Hall, Inc., Englewood Cliffs, NJ, 1987.

[18] Forsyth, R. (Editor), *Expert Systems,* Chapman & Hall, New York, 1984.

[19] Hart, A., *Knowledge Acquisition for Expert Systems*, McGraw-Hill, New York, 1986.

[20] Bernold, T. (Editor), *Expert Systems and Knowledge Engineering*, North-Holland, Amsterdam, 1986.

[21] Mongi, A.A. and Gonzalez, R.C., *Data Fusion in Robotics and Machine Intelligence,* Academic Press, Orlando, FL, 1992.

[22] Thien, R.J. and Hill, S.D., "Sensor Fusion for Automated Assembly Using an Expert System Shell," *Proceedings of the 5th International Conference on Advanced Robotics*, Pisa, Italy, Vol. 2, pp. 1270-1274, June 1991.

[23] Kreithen, D.E., Halversen, S.D., and Owirka, G.J., "Discriminating Targets from Clutter," *The Lincoln Laboratory Journal,* Vol. 6, No. 1, pp. 25-51, 1993.

[24] Alexander, S.M., Vaidya, C.M., and Kamel, K.A., "An Architecture for Sensor Fusion in Intelligent Process Monitoring," *Computers in Industrial Engineering*, Vol. 16, No. 2, pp. 307-311, 1989.

[25] Shafer, G., *A Mathematical Theory of Evidence*, Princeton University Press, Princeton, NJ, 1976.

[26] Berger, J.O., *Statistical Decision Theory and Bayesian Analysis,* Springer-Verlag, New York, 1985.

[27] Luo, R.C. and Kay, M.C., "Multi-sensor Integration and Fusion in Intelligent Systems," *IEEE Transactions on Systems, Man, and Cybernetics*, Vol. 19, No. 5, pp. 901-931, October 1989.

[28] Filippidis, A., Jain, L.C., and Martin, N., "Fuzzy Rule Based Fusion Technique to Automatically Detect Aircraft in SAR Images," *Proceedings of the International Conference on Knowledge Based Intelligent Electronic Systems* (KES'97), Adelaide, IEEE Press, Piscataway, NJ, pp. 435-441, 1997.

[29] Gupta, M.M. and Rao, H., *Neural Control Theory and Applications,* IEEE Press, Piscataway, NJ, 1994.

[30] Davis, L., *Handbook of Genetic Algorithms,* Van Nostrand Rienhold, New York, 1991.

[31] Lee, T.H., Yue, P.K., and de Silva, C.W., "Neural Networks Improve Control," *Measurements and Control*, Vol. 28, No. 4, pp. 148-153, 1994.

[32] Gu, J.H. and de Silva, C.W., "Client-Server Architecture for Implementing Real-Time Robot Control in Industrial Processes," *Proceedings of the Asian Control Conference*, Seoul, Korea, Vol. 3, pp. 259-262, July 1997.

2 | INFORMATION, KNOWLEDGE, AND MACHINES

A.G.J. MacFarlane
Emeritus Principal
Heriot-Watt University
Edinburgh
Scotland, UK

Adam Smith's vision of an economic future determined by a division of labor can be replaced by one determined by an accumulation and division of knowledge. In order to understand the nature and evolution of such a knowledge economy, and the role of machines within it, a comprehensive survey and discussion is given of the concepts of information and knowledge. Information, knowledge, and machines are considered in the context of agents interacting both with the physical world and with other agents. In a knowledge economy, information is seen as the currency of agency, and objective knowledge as the capital of a society of agents. The future of machines in a knowledge economy, and their relationship to human agents, is considered in terms of the growth of objective knowledge and the consequent development of knowledgeable and intelligent machines.

1 Prologue

In the opening sentence of the first chapter of *The Wealth of Nations*, Adam Smith [1] introduced the key theoretical importance of the division of labor:

> The greatest improvement in the productive powers of labour, and the greater part of the skill, dexterity and judgement with which it is everywhere directed, or applied, seem to have been the effects of the division of labour.

He went on to give his famous example from the trade of the pin-maker, describing how ten persons acting through a co-ordination of basic tasks:

could make among them upwards of forty-eight thousand pins a day
... [while] they could certainly not each of them have made not
twenty, perhaps not one pin in a day.

The increase of productivity, giving rise to the greater volume of goods which
Adam Smith observed, is usually described as resulting from a division of *labor*.
The associated de-skilling of individual tasks opened the way for a widespread use
of technology in manufacturing.

The principle of division can be more widely applied. The design of complex objects, like a modern aircraft, requires a very large body of *knowledge* which is divided among a wide range of specialists — aerodynamicists, structural engineers,
metallurgists, electronic engineers, production planners, and so on. Their very high
degree of specialization derives from years of formal training built upon a sound
basic education. Furthermore, the production of higher quality objects requires a
proliferation of skills because it demands more attention to every part of their detail. A Rolls-Royce costs more not because it is functionally different from a
cheaper car but because it has absorbed more specialised, and so more highly
skilled, effort in creating it to a higher standard in every aspect of its functionality
and construction. Also, when activities are divided, they must be co-ordinated.
This co-ordination of skills, together with the ability to respond effectively to uncertainty and to change, requires yet further capacities in the workforce — these
include the abilities to plan, learn, innovate, adapt, motivate, supervise, and coordinate. They require *intelligence* as well as knowledge.

In the future, both an individual's work and larger-scale industry will develop in
the context of a *knowledge economy*. To understand what this means, to discuss the
evolving role of machines in it, and to see how humans and machines could complement each other within such an economy, we need to define carefully the concepts of *information* and *knowledge*. An approach to information, knowledge, and
machines is developed here which leads to a powerful economic metaphor in
which information is seen as the currency of agency and objective knowledge is
seen as the capital of a society of agents. The quantization of information allows
growth rates of objective knowledge to be estimated, and a view can then be
formed of the likely future role of machines in society.

2 Agents

We take a wide view of agency: agents can be humans, animals, insects, machines,
computers, robots, and even some very large molecules [2].

AGENTS are defined as entities with the capacity to perceive and act in the world.

Agents interact by exchanging and processing information. Something, for our
present purposes, is an agent if and only if it has the abilities to sense, to process
what is sensed, and to act on the result of this processing. You and I are agents,

and so is a thermostat which is capable of sensing the value of a temperature, processing it in such a way as to classify it as too high or too low, and communicating the result to a computer.

Imagine two engines, one fitted with a speed control system and one without, driving fluctuating loads so that the speed of one engine's output shaft always varies much more than the other. With nothing else to go on in the way of a description, we could say that one engine has a *disposition* to run at a constant speed. Looking at the engines in more detail to find out what underpins this disposition, we could identify that extra part which enables one to run with less variation in speed. This control system is the *mechanical agent* which carries out the necessary compensating actions. The agency is achieved by arranging for the control system to be able to accept *data* representing engine speed and execute an appropriate control *process* on a *processor*. It, thus, has three defining abilities:

- an ability for perception — an ability to accept and use data, to sense engine speed and how it changes

- an ability for action — an ability to take hold of the throttle and influence fuel flow

- an ability to execute process — an ability to relate perception and action, to compare a representation of sensed speed with a representation of desired speed, and to signal an appropriate action to reduce the error between them

In a generalized form, these are the defining attributes of any agent. Our model for an agent perceiving and acting in the world requires that it can receive data and execute process on a processor. Its coupling to the wider world will normally be via sensors and actuators. Mechanical agents are *designed*, and in this case the processor will be, for example, a computer, signal processing system, or neural network (see Chapter 5). It does not have to be any specific form of symbol-processing serial or parallel computer to qualify as an agent under our definition. Biological agents have *evolved*, and their processing is affected by their nervous systems. In calling them agents — and in particular when we are talking about human agents — we assume [3,4] that they can be described for our specific purposes in terms of data, process, and processor. We do not assume, however, any specific form of data and process representation, or any specific kind of processor, in our discussion of human agents. When we refer to explicit symbolic representations and manipulations by a human agent, these are taken to be *external* to the agent.

3 Information

We will consider the concept of information first in a qualitative sense, and then in a quantitative sense. When we interact with our environment, there are two fundamentally different aspects to our experience of it. One aspect is of the order which we experience in the world as passively sensed. This is of *patterns* in space and time formed by shapes, colors, smells, tactile sensations, tastes, and sounds. The other aspect is of the order which we experience when we actively engage with the world. This is of *mechanisms*, of relationships in a world described by cause and effect, of the order imposed by what David Hume called the "cement of the universe" [5]. Pattern and mechanism are dual aspects of the order which we experience in the world: mechanism generates pattern and pattern specifies mechanism.

Agents, as summarized in Figure 1, interact with the world and with each other.

Figure 1: Agency.

Since they inhabit the same physical world, they share a commonality of mechanisms which are grounded in the laws which govern the behavior of objects in the world. Interaction between an agent and an object involves an exchange of energy or matter, albeit possibly in only infinitesimal amounts. Hence, it involves *correlated* changes in the state of both the agent and the object in the environment with which it is interacting. When the amount of energy exchanged is very small the change in the state of the object may be insignificant; it is the possibility of a correlated change in some state of the agent which is important. The feedback arrangement which is necessarily involved in any direct interaction, whereby action changes object, which changes perception, which leads to further action, and so on, sets up a tight correlation between some of an agent's states and those of the object with which it is interacting. Such a set of correlated states in some part of an agent can provide what we can call the agent's *representation* of an object. So, when an agent interacts with an object in its environment, a correlated pattern of states, instantiated as changes in matter or energy, can be generated within the agent. This in turn can be transformed into some form external to the agent, and thus communicated to other agents. Agents can communicate if and only if their interactions are coherent within their shared external environment: what one sends the other receives, what one encodes the other decodes. This *coherent* encoding and decoding requires a commonality of mechanisms grounded in the laws which govern the behavior of objects in their shared world. If the communicating agents share appropriate features of their physical make-up and internal mechanisms, there will exist *sharable* representations of aspects of their common world, as illustrated in Figure 2.

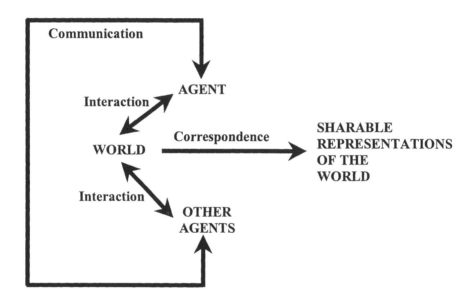

Figure 2: Information as shareable representation.

These sharable representations link internal states of both agents to objects in the external world. The agents interact with the world which they share and with each other. Their interactions with the world produce changes in their internal states, and their interactions with each other allow these internal changes of state to be mutually co-ordinated. These co-ordinated states correspond to representations of a shared perception of their common external environment.

Information, in an abstract sense, consists of sharable representations of the world; it is what we use to characterize the order in the world in terms of pattern and mechanism. Information, in a concrete sense, consists of physical instantiations of these sharable representations; it is a distribution of matter or energy which is meaningful for an agent in terms of description, prescription, or communication. It can thus be used to represent some aspect of that order which is experienced in interacting with the world. When patterns are physically instantiated as spatial or temporal distributions of matter or energy, they can be exchanged between agents for the purposes of communication. Such physically instantiated distributions can also be used to describe and specify physical mechanisms. When information instantiates the representation of pattern without any further qualification, we will call it *data*, and when it specifically instantiates the representation of prescriptions for action we will call it *process* [6]. In summary:

INFORMATION is a physical instantiation of sharable representations of the world. It enables agents to represents the world in terms of data and process. DATA is a physical instantiation in matter or energy which represents a pattern in the world. PROCESS is a physical instantiation in matter or energy which represents a mechanism in the world.

Information represents patterns and mechanisms in terms of individual components called *symbols*. Any characterization of the way in which physically instantiated patterns are used for communication between agents must define:

- the way in which symbols are combined to form data and to specify process
- the way in which this enables agents to represent and interpret patterns and mechanisms in the world and to communicate with each other
- the way in which data and process represent and relate to patterns and mechanisms in the world

This means that the characterization of information must have:

- a syntactic dimension which comprises the rules stipulating how symbols are combined into data and into representations of process
- a semantic dimension which comprises relationships between the patterns of symbols and what they mean for the communicating agents
- a physical dimension which relates information to the characterization of the physical world in terms of matter and energy

Our ability to *measure* amounts of information follows from the fact that *information is quantized*. Agents necessarily work in terms of:

- a quantum of perception — the distinction between something being present or absent
- a quantum of action or choice — the distinction between something being done or not done, between choosing or not choosing something

- a quantum of communication — the distinction between receiving or not receiving something, between sending or not sending something

The instantiation of any representation as information, therefore, must be reducible ultimately to distinctions involving the existence or nonexistence of quanta of perception, action, and communication. Presence or absence of a defined quantum determines *one bit* of information. The *bit* is the unit of measurement of information. (A larger unit, the *byte*, is usually taken to be eight bits.) Hence, adopting Wheeler's dictum [7], we get the:

IT FROM BIT PRINCIPLE: All information derives ultimately from agent-elicited answers to yes-or-no questions, binary choices, bits.

The three dimensions (syntactic, semantic, and physical) of the characterization of information are reflected in theoretical discussions of information in the literature. In engineering texts the term *information* is usually confined to a syntactic or quantitative sense. Two such quantitative theories have evolved: one appropriate to data and developed from an analysis of communication and signals, and the other appropriate to process and arising out of the analysis of models and formal structures.

- The theory appropriate to communication was developed by Shannon [8]. This is based on information as a measure of improbability or *uncertainty*. In this approach a signal is characterized by its entropy. *Entropy* is a measure of the average uncertainty in a random variable; it is the number of bits on average required to describe the random variable [9]

- The theory appropriate to modeling and algorithms was developed by Kolmogorov [10] and Chaitin [11]. This is based on information as a measure of *complexity*. Again, the information is measured in bits.

The Kolmogorov-Chaitin theory (see Section 7 below) is often called *algorithmic information theory* to distinguish it from Shannon's earlier theory. Since quantitative information theory has two aspects, the corresponding measures — entropy and complexity — will appear in complementary roles. There is a large body of technical literature on syntactic information theory and its applications. Excellent general references are Cover and Thomas [9], which deals with both forms of the quantitative theory, and Resnikoff [12], which looks at an interesting range of applications.

The approach which is often used in biological studies such as Kuppers [2] characterizes information in a wide or semantic sense. For other treatments of semantic approaches to information see Dretske [13,14] and Devlin [15].

The physical dimension of information theory has been comprehensively treated by Frieden [16]. The relationship between energy and information has been discussed by Tribus and McIrvine [17].

Figure 3 summarizes some aspects of the above discussion and relates it to the terminology used in the following sections. The duality between an agent's being acted on by the world and acting on the world — that is between patterns and mechanisms — is reflected throughout the whole of our terminology for dealing with information and knowledge:

- When dealing with the physical world we use the terms *pattern* and *mechanism*

- When dealing with information we use the terms *data* and *process*

- When dealing with agency in general we use the terms *descriptions and prescriptions*

- When dealing with a human agent's knowledge we use the terms *concepts* and *schemata* (see section 5.3 below)

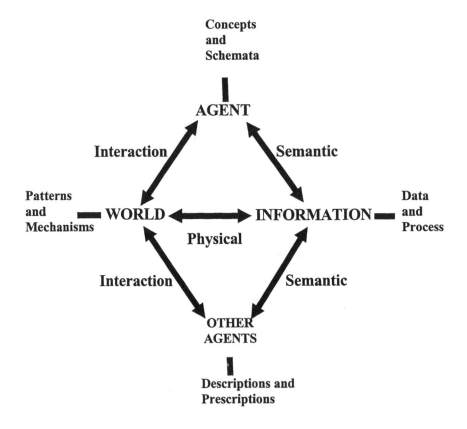

Figure 3: Aspects of information.

3.1 Data and Process

A unifying overview of pattern theory has been given by Mumford [18], which discusses the relationships between data representations and process representations. He deals with two definitive forms of representation: a maximum a priori reconstruction of data and a minimum descriptive length (see Section 8 below) construction of process. His approach reconciles these two forms of representation by showing their equivalence and advocating in practice a combined approach which works bottom up by creating process from data and top down by creating data from process, in an iterative fashion until both forms of representation can be reconciled.

Given data which exhibits regularities, one can *compress* from it a process which will reproduce these regularities. The word *compress* is used because the minimum descriptive length of the resulting process is usually less than that of the original data. Wholly random data is data from which no process can be compressed. It is a data set whose measure in bits is also its minimum descriptive length.

A good illustration of the difference between data and process can be found in a consideration of representations of the phenomena of fractals and chaos [19]. In chaos *data dominates process*; the complexity of chaos is real — a chaotic system is associated with unbounded data. In fractals *process dominates data*; the complexity of a fractal data set is only apparent — the process defining a fractal imposes self-similarity on the generated data and binds it into a tightly self-referential structure of limited complexity. In a way, fractals and chaos provide an instructive parable for theory and experiment. Theory generates process. Like fractals, theory can generate only limited amounts of information (see Section 8.1 below), although it may at times seem overwhelmingly complicated. Experiment generates data. It can, like chaos, generate unbounded amounts of information. All scientific and technical endeavor is an unending struggle to resolve the conflicting demands of process and data, to compress data into process, and to manage the trade-offs between them.

4 Objective Knowledge

Knowledge and information are different things. *Knowledge* is a name we give to a capacity for action, and *information* is a name we give to abstract representations or concrete instantiations of pattern and mechanism. Knowledge arises from the execution of process on a processor. This executable process can be specified in terms of information. Hence knowledge can be shared by sharing information. This is acknowledged in everyday speech where the two words — *information* and *knowledge* — are often used as though they mean the same. We however need to continue to distinguish between them.

KNOWLEDGE is a capacity for action which an agent has by virtue of information instantiated as processes which can be carried out by a processor.

In applying this definition for a human agent (see Section 5 below), we make no specific assumptions about the nature of the processor involved.

An agent's knowledge — its capacity for action — stems from the different sources summarized in Figure 4: knowledge specific to an agent we will call *subjective knowledge*, knowledge shared by a society of agents we will call *societal knowledge*, and knowledge instantiated as information which can be externally accessed by, and shared between, agents we will call *objective knowledge* [70].

OBJECTIVE KNOWLEDGE is sharable, externally accessible information which can endow an agent with a capacity for effective action.

The use of the qualifying adjective *objective* maintains the distinction between knowledge and information. Objective knowledge is information which can specify or enable effective action. Having said this, we can cease to labor the distinction, and informally use the terms *information* and *objective knowledge* as though they were synonymous.

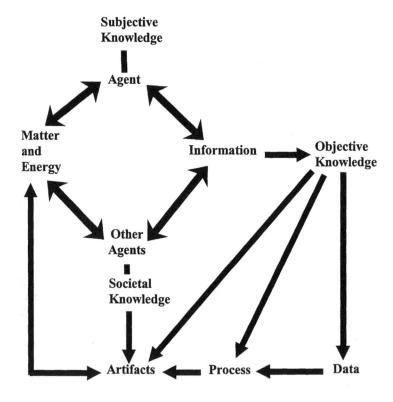

Figure 4: Types of knowledge.

We regard *artifacts* as forms of objective knowledge on the basis that:

1. They are physical instantiations of solutions to problems arrived at by a society of agents. Artifacts are instantiations of societal knowledge.

2. They are, from another point of view, instantiations of pattern and mechanism in matter and energy, and so can be regarded as a form of information which enables action.

Objective knowledge is information which is instantiated externally to an agent in a formal, explicit, stable, persisting, and interactively accessible form which the agent can use as a basis for action. To provide objective knowledge, the information must be suitably encoded. One agent's objective knowledge is another agent's indecipherable information. Examples of symbolically-encoded objective knowledge for a human agent are books, videos, computer programs, diagrams, pictures, railway timetables, and maps.

Information and knowledge allow us to describe ways in which agents can collaborate and interact effectively. Information can be thought of as the *currency of agency*, because it is the medium of exchange for *societies of agency*, that is, for groups of agents working together. Objective knowledge, instantiated in information-processing structures and in artifacts, can be thought of as the *capital of agency* for such societies, because it allows groups of agents to pool and share their capacities for action. The story of the evolution of civilization is a story of the formation of societies of agency, of the successive additions to human agency of material agency in the form of artifacts, and of machine agency in the form of instantiated processes. The result is an ever-increasing pool of objective knowledge. Among the most important artifacts in future knowledge economies will be universal machines [20] on which could be run all the processes comprising objective knowledge, and which will be used to create virtual worlds with which agents can interact and explore.

Objective knowledge grows by feedback processes which are implicit in Figure 4. Objective knowledge, when instantiated in artifacts which agents can use, adds material agency to the stock of agency. And, when instantiated in processes, it adds mechanical agency. These increases in agency augment the capacity of a society of agents to interact effectively with the world. As a result of this interaction further objective knowledge is generated, which in turn leads to a still further augmentation of agency, and so on, increasing the capital of agency stored in objective knowledge. This feedback process creates a pool of objective knowledge which represents the agents' shared perception of, and ability to interact with, their environment with an increasing accuracy and effectiveness. The instantiation of knowledge as externally stored information is essential to this growth.

The agents sharing objective knowledge can be — as in the case of human agent and computer — of different kinds. The fact that it can be stored, transmitted, and shared across species-of-agent boundaries is what makes the generation of objective knowledge one of the most important aspects of modern technology and one of the main drivers of economic development. Objective knowledge can be thought of as giving us a lens through which we view the world, and the feedback mechanism by which agency grows can be thought of as continually generating, refining, correcting and polishing that lens. When we work in collaboration with other agents, including mechanical agents, this can be thought of as increasing the power and versatility of the lens. In the same way as a microscope allows us to look at the arbitrarily small, and a telescope allows us to look at the arbitrarily large, the accumulated objective knowledge of a society of agents allows it to create systems with which it can grapple with the arbitrarily complex. There is a similar metaphor by Joel de Rosnay [21] who called the capability endowed by systems theory and computing a *macroscope*. Modern technology puts within our grasp the possibility of effectively creating and using huge amounts of objective knowledge. Peering through the evolving macroscopes provided by such knowledge systems will open up new vistas of the arbitrarily complex and enable us to create hitherto unimaginably high levels of agency.

5 Human Knowledge

Before discussing how machine and human agents can work together, we have first to characterize human knowledge in appropriate detail.

5.1 Human Belief

Our behavior is determined by a vast, and different, repertoire of beliefs instantiated as pattern-processing structures in our brains. Pause for a moment, and listen. Every sound, near and far, will add a belief to your store, or modify one which you hold. A passing car or a distant airplane, footsteps in a corridor, an announcement in a radio programme — each set of sounds, second by second, changes your set of beliefs. Something is moving, someone is coming or going, something good or bad has happened. Now look around. Your perception of your environment, strange or familiar, will add to or modify your beliefs about your immediate surroundings. You may even — Good Heavens ! When did that happen? — realize on a close inspection that you have been quite mistaken about some part of your everyday habitat. Many of your beliefs are transient; others persist. You probably believe that electrical phenomena are associated with the flow of particles called electrons; that the Moon rotates in orbit round the Earth which in turn rotates in orbit around the Sun, as well as about its own polar axis; that these satellite and planetary motions determine why night follows day, and why the seasons vary throughout the year. The range and depth of your beliefs, and the facility with which you can recall them, sift through them, form associations among them, inspect them, and think about them at will is staggering. Some of your beliefs, you will feel, are more secure than others. You probably feel much more secure in your belief that two plus two is four than that a bus, train, or airplane for which you happen to be waiting will arrive on time, and to the precise fraction of a second. You may even believe that there is a country in which such a paragon of precision would be commonplace, although you have not yet had the good fortune to visit it.

The complexity of the brain [3,4] is such that a precise and all-embracing scientific description of its functioning is not at present available. So we have no alternative, when dealing with human agents, but to characterize their beliefs from an external or dispositional point of view. We will therefore, following Quine (see, in particular, [22] and [23]), take a belief to be a disposition to respond in certain specifiable ways when an appropriate issue arises. Your flexible and coherent responses to the complex and ever-changing environment in which you live and act — crossing street intersections at a green light, going to an airport to catch a plane, writing checks, whatever — are all driven by your beliefs. Each adaptation or modification of your behavior, of your disposition to act, implies an adaptation or modification of the pattern-processing system which instantiates your beliefs. When we compare human and machine capabilities, we are comparing the relative levels and complexity of their agency, of their capacities for action as instantiated in process.

5.2 Human Knowledge

Among our beliefs are some which are somehow strongly secured against transient or trivial modification, which we act on with great confidence, and which we use to integrate abstractions from our experience into a capability for effective action. Such beliefs we call our knowledge. Knowledge is what underpins human agency; it is a complex and elusive concept. There is an entire branch of philosophy — epistemology — which is devoted to its study [24]. Knowledge is also being studied increasingly from a scientific and engineering point of view, in fields such as artificial intelligence and artificial life [25,26]. Although any simple definition risks being misleading, it may be helpful to supply one.

HUMAN KNOWLEDGE is an ability enabled by a coherent system of rational beliefs, which is used as a continuing and reliable basis for action.

Knowledge and belief are both capacities for action. Knowledge is distinguished from belief on the following grounds:

- Rationality and coherence
- Continuity and persistence
- Reliability and effectiveness

These distinguishing characteristics merit individual comment.

- Rationality and coherence imply that the particular kind of belief which we call knowledge is formal and explicit, robust against criticism, proved in the fire of discussion and argument, and free from internal contradictions.

- Continuity implies a significant degree of permanence. Knowledge is hard earned and, once secured, tends to be maintained and safeguarded.

- Reliability and effectiveness are pragmatic criteria. What we call knowledge is what we find to be useful, trustworthy, and of wide and lasting social and practical utility.

5.3 Concepts and Schemata

Concepts and schemata are fundamental building blocks of human knowledge systems (see Section 7 below). From our experience of the world as sensed, we construct one form of belief, whose units may be called concepts. From our experience of the world as acted upon, we construct a dual form of belief whose units may be called *schemata*. The pattern-processing structures which are instantiated in our brains as concepts and schemata underpin our capacity for effective action. Since our actions will be, to the greatest extent which we can manage, based on knowledge, that is, on beliefs which are as securely based and as soundly justified as we can make them, we will refer to concepts and schemata as building blocks of knowledge rather than of belief. Skemp has given a very useful discussion of the psychology of learning mathematics in terms of concepts and schemata [27].

Concepts [28] are *descriptive* components of human knowledge:

CONCEPT: A concept categorizes experience and so provides a descriptive component in a human knowledge system.

Concepts have a *hierarchical structure* and can be associated with the following list.

- To have a concept of X is to be able to distinguish X-ness from non-X-ness, to be able to identify or re-identify Xs or cases of X.

- A concept requires for its formation a number of experiences which have something in common.

- Concepts of a higher order than those which learners already have cannot be communicated to them by definition, but only by arranging for them to encounter a suitable set of examples.

- If any of these examples involves concepts it must be ensured that these have been previously formed in the minds of the learners.

Schemata are dual to concepts. They are *prescriptive* components of human knowledge.

SCHEMATA: A schema (plural schemata) is a coherent, integrated, logically interconnected component in a human knowledge system which stipulates how to deal with a specific situation in a prescriptive way.

Knowledge comes in chunks. Our limited raw pattern-processing capability compels us to interact with only a severely restricted part of our environment at any specific time. Thus when we learn we can only learn about, and acquire a facility in dealing with, a highly limited version of part of the world. We will say that the sort of coherent, restricted, and organized scheme of knowledge which an agent can use in any specific situation, and at any specific time, characterizes a *microworld*. Schemata can be associated with a list in the same way as concepts, by regarding them in terms of a *capacity to perform in a stipulated way for a specific microworld*.

- To have a schema for Y may be, variously, to be able to do or make Y, to be adept in Y-ness, to know when and why, as well as how, to do Y, and so forth.

- Schemata encapsulate an understanding of microworlds.

- Schemata link concept and action, knowing and doing, observation and explanation for specific microworlds.

- Assimilation of schemata is manifested by an ability to give explanations of a microworld and to solve problems posed in terms of it.

- Schemata are acquired by interactions with an appropriately structured environment, by interactions with instantiated knowledge, and by their organization into prescriptions for purposive effective action with reference to a specific microworld.

Concepts and schemata, taken together, can be thought of as providing a "user guide" for a microworld. We use concepts and schemata in a discussion of knowledge systems in which human and machine agents collaborate (Section 7 below).

6 Intelligence

We need one more ingredient before we can adequately characterize agency. To describe the world completely, and so to provide all the explicit knowledge which an agent would need for every possible interaction with its environment, would require an unbounded amount of information. An infinity of bits would be needed to enable an infinity of decisions. Therefore, to function effectively in an uncertain world, an agent (of other than the simplest, most rigidly inflexible form) requires something in addition to knowledge. It requires intelligence.

INTELLIGENCE is the capacity to learn, the capacity to acquire, adapt, modify and extend knowledge in order to solve problems. If knowledge is a capacity to use process, then intelligence is a capacity to create process (see Chapter 1 for a discussion of intelligence).

Intelligence is the growth factor of agency. It gives agency the robustness and flexibility needed to develop in an uncertain world. It enables an agent to deal with situations which have not been previously encountered. An airline-timetable voice-synthesising query-answer system is a *knowledgeable agent* if it can answer a wide, but fixed, range of questions about aircraft flight times and destinations. Its knowledge capacity may need to be augmented by the intelligence necessary to solve problems arising from ambiguities of phrasing, lack of intelligibility in speech, or ambiguity and lack of precision in the questions which are put to it. It would then be an *intelligent agent*. Intelligence involves the creation of *new process*. The instantiation of intelligence in a machine agent thus involves the creation and installation within it of special classes of generic processes which *generate and test processes* until one is found which solves the problem at hand [29,30]. Human intelligence is thought to depend on a similar generative ability, on the interplay of imagination and rationality, on conjecture and refutation, on sophisticated forms of search, and on the generation and testing of trial solutions until a satisfactory one is found. A powerful knowledge capability derives from access to large amounts of prespecified process and to large amounts of appropriately structured and organized data. A powerful intelligence capability derives primarily from access to powerful information processing capability, because the need to generate and test new process is of itself processor-intensive.

7 Knowledge Systems

Imagine that you are standing in any big library, say before the stacks of technology-related journals. You are surrounded by information, but it is not in an immediately useful form. *You are surrounded by data but what you need is process.* The knowledge with which the library is filled is very difficult to access, and even more difficult to turn quickly into either illuminating insight (in the form of concepts) or practical use (in the form of schemata). This — the difficulty of harnessing such forms of objective knowledge to useful effect — poses a very real and a very formidable problem. A major challenge facing modern technology is how to use machine agency to produce knowledgeable machines which will help to:

- Organize and make interactively accessible the large and growing amount of objective formal knowledge which is available.

- Develop a coherent, communicable, synoptic overall view of any specific subject which can be used to illuminate and organize this objective knowledge.

- Make the knowledge useable by practitioners, to provide them with user guides and powerful toolkits.

- Relate the knowledge to reality, that is, to experimental and practical investigations.

To use objective knowledge in this way, we must be able to create appropriate *knowledge systems*. In particular, we must devise arrangements by means of which human agents and knowledgeable machine agents can work together effectively. The emergence of such systems will have a profound effect on education and training, and they will enable lifelong learning to become a reality. Knowledgeable agents will become an embedded aspect of almost all manifestations of machine agency, giving help and advice and answering queries. They will become ubiquitous, encountered in almost every aspect of daily life in both embedded and autonomous manifestations. The limitations on the development of knowledgeable agents lie in the difficulty of extracting knowledge from human agents. Design activity will be carried out almost entirely by interactive knowledge-support systems [31,32], whose refinement and extension will become of determining importance for industrial competitiveness. Such knowledge systems will also become indispensable in the support of teaching, learning, and training at all levels [33].

In such a knowledge system, the overall characterization of our knowledge of some specific object — say, the Arc de Triomphe in Paris — will come from three complementary frameworks.

- A data framework, comprising the raw information necessary to describe the object. We generate this information by seeing it, touching it, photographing it, measuring and drawing it, and so forth, generating as much information as is needed for our purposes.

- A conceptual framework, comprising a set of generic concepts related to this type of object — say, the generalized idea of arches, the many ways in which they may be built and used, and so forth.

- A schemata framework, comprising a set of schemata which give a detailed prescription of how that particular type of arch, of which the concrete Arc de Triomphe is an instantiation, could be constructed, or, more usually, of how its construction could in principle be detailed. For most of us this prescription would be restricted to some general understanding of how such an object could be created, to complete the way in which we could coherently and intelligibly talk about it. Only in the knowledge system of a master builder would there be a complete and fully detailed specification of how to proceed in actually fabricating its components and then constructing it.

For an example of how the parts of a knowledge system would fit together, and work in action, consider the legal problem of determining whether someone is guilty of a crime such as manslaughter or murder. This may be carried out in terms of a knowledge system with the following three frameworks:

- a data framework consisting of the evidence and testimony about the alleged crime, as collected and classified and available in documents and artifacts

- a conceptual framework, consisting of the relevant concepts on which the law is based, as interpreted by a judge and jury, and

- a schemata framework, consisting of the relevant and formally codified law, which details the appropriate procedures to be followed, how the relevant penalties are to be determined, and so on.

To resolve a question of guilt requires that the prescriptive application of the law be related both to the concepts for which the events which took place are specific individuations, and to the descriptions of the actual events and circumstances involved. It is important to note how the *open-ended* nature of the normal legal-judicial system allows all three frameworks to come into play. This is because the formal structure of codified law contains *exit points*, for example, by referring to the concept of "reasonable force" which must be *interpreted* by the judge and jury against the generic framework of relevant concepts rather than the prescriptive framework of codified law. The extreme flexibility with which human agents use their knowledge systems seems to stem from the ease with which such a set of three meshed frameworks are used simultaneously, slipping effortlessly from one to the other as required.

This structure allows us to consider how human and machine capabilities can complement each other best in using knowledge. In this context, the remark above about "open-endedness" is crucially important. Any accurate description of a knowledge system involving both humans and machines must show how explicit and tacit knowledge mesh together. A machine can supply in principle any amount of information, and so it obviously can provide immensely powerful support for the data framework. It can also provide very powerful support for a user's (or learner's) conceptual and schemata frameworks. This can be done with appropriate data and process in the form of structured (e.g. hyperlinked) texts, film, animation, simulation, narrative, interactively accessible databases, automated reasoning processes, and expert systems. A machine could clearly offer powerful help as an assistant to human agents in using knowledge. The degree to which it could function on its own is set by the difficulty of making the tacit knowledge of human agents explicit [34,35]. The success of arrangements in which humans and machines work together will depend critically on a complete and coherent meshing of the human and machine knowledge systems, joined together at the relevant entry and exit points. In an ideal combination of human and machine agency, the machine will underpin all the formal, explicit, and rational activities of the human, imposing coherency and supplying logical, computational, and organizational power; and the human will supply intuition, experience, inventiveness, ingenuity, and flair.

The structure of an ideal knowledge system is shown in Figure 5. It is characterized in terms of:

- an ideal computer (an implementation of a universal Turing machine, or equivalent) on which all formal processes, algorithms, etc. could be run.

- an ideal subject, described in terms of the most up-to-date neurological and psychological knowledge available, and

- an error-correcting feedback mechanism driven by the ideal subject's ability to learn from experience.

A good example of how physiological knowledge can illuminate a practical approach to epistemology is given in Dehaene's treatment of number sense [36]. The relative roles in such a knowledge system of the Ideal Computer and the Ideal Subject are shown in Figure 6.

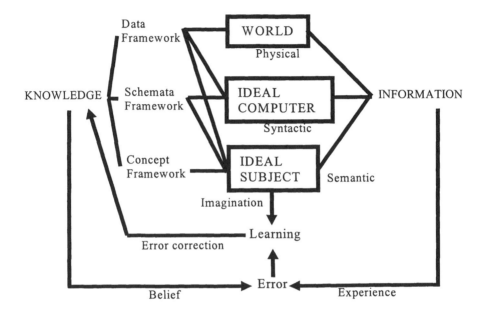

Figure 5: Knowledge system.

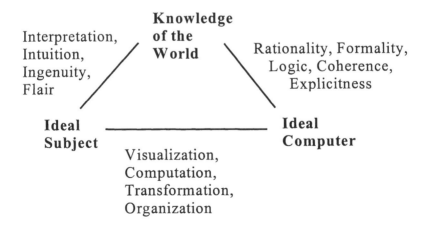

Figure 6: Relation of subject, computer, and knowledge.

8 Complexity

It is useful, and illuminating, to try to estimate roughly the amount of information which we absorb day by day. A standard single screen's worth of reasonably good quality video on a monitor display requires about a million bytes or, say, eight million bits. For the acceptable rendering of motion this needs to be refreshed at least 25 times per second. If we take _all_ the sensory input we receive in every second in all modalities — sight, hearing, taste, touch, smell — to be around 100 times that needed for the generation of acceptable video, then our bit input over a lifetime is of the order of ten-to-the-power-twenty bits (10^{20} bits). Compare this with the following examples of information quantification:

- viral DNA: 10^4 bits
- bacterial DNA: 10^7 bits
- human DNA: 10^{10} bits
- Oxford English Dictionary: 10^{12} bits
- British Library: 10^{16} bits.

These numbers must be interpreted with some care; _we must always remember to distinguish between data and process._ The bit estimates for the dictionary and the library are estimates of data, whereas the bit estimates for DNA are estimates of process. What is encoded in DNA is a program compressed out of data accumulated over billions of years.

So anyone with a lifetime's experience to think about has had an input of around 10,000 times more data bits than the entire contents of the British Library. Our ability to recall past events at will shows that a substantial fraction of this data input is retained. Thus, we are able to quickly, freely, and flexibly roam around in a storage system whose potential contents are comparable in amount with the entire contents of a huge library. The power, richness, and flexibility of the mental processes which enable us to do this are inspiring. The size and sophisticated organization of the pattern-processing systems which are involved currently defy detailed description. To be able to compare the size, organization, and functionality of different forms of agency we need some measure of complexity other than a simple enumeration of the bits in encoded data.

8.1 Kolmogorov Complexity

The quantitative theory of complexity [10,37,38] is a valuable tool when comparing the functionality of different forms of agent. Chaitin [39] has given an illuminating discussion of complexity and makes many and subtle uses of the concept. The interested reader may consult his collected papers [11]. For our present purposes it is useful to give one of the characterizations which he uses in his own words, and then use the term in the spirit of this characterization ([40], p. 5).

The complexity of a binary string is the information needed to define it, that is to say, the number of bits of information which must be given to a computer in order to calculate it, or in other words, the size in bits of the shortest program for calculating it. It is understood that a certain mathematical definition of an ideal computer is being used, but it is not given here, because as a first approximation it is sufficient to think of the length in bits of a program for a typical computer in use today.

Chaitin characterizes a related approach by Solomonoff ([40], p. 5) in the following way:

[In] Solomonoff's model a theory that enables one to understand a series of observations is seen as a small computer program that reproduces the observations and makes predictions about possible future observations. The smaller the program, the more comprehensive the theory and the greater the degree of understanding. Observations that are random cannot be reproduced by a small program and therefore cannot be explained by a theory. In addition the future behavior of a random system cannot be predicted. For random data the most compact way for the scientist to communicate his observations is for him to publish them in their entirety.

Cover and Thomas ([9], p. 144) give an illuminating discussion of Kolmogorov complexity and some of its uses.

KOLMOGOROV COMPLEXITY of an agency is the length in bits of the smallest computer program which will instantiate the process which enables that agency.

MINIMUM DESCRIPTIVE LENGTH: The Kolmogorov complexity of a computer program is also called its minimum descriptive length.

An illuminating characterization in terms of complexity has been given for Godel's Theorem. This famous result in logic theory ([41], p. 17) states that any formal system will necessarily have associated with it propositions which may be formulated validly in terms of the system but which cannot be shown to be true or false by using that formal system. Stewart ([42], p. 115) has succinctly stated this in information-theoretic terms as: the theorems deducible from an axiom system cannot contain more information than do the axioms themselves. This means that all formal systems, and thus the processes built on them and instantiated in machines, are limited in what they can do by the amount of information which they contain. The only way to increase their power is to increase the information base by adding more independent axioms, and this increase can only come from the creation of new processes, that is from the use of intelligence. The ultimate source of all the necessary new information is an experimental interaction with the world.

8.2 Simple Measures of Complexity

While the Kolmogorov definition gives a sound basis for a quantitative theory of complexity, it is necessary to have other measures which allow one to make estimations in a simpler way. This is particularly useful for a rough and ready estimation of the complexity of artifacts. The design or fabrication of any artifact can be considered as resulting from a sequence of decisions, which in turn can be reduced to a series of yes-no decisions. Information in bits and the number of yes-no decisions which an agent makes are logarithmically related. As N bits specify 2^N different yes-no possibilities, information in bits is the logarithm to base 2 of the number of different yes-no decisions which an agent can take. (When using numbers of decisions as measures of complexity, logarithms can in practice be taken to any convenient base, since only a scaling factor is introduced when using a different base.) The complexity of an artifact can thus be estimated by taking the logarithm of the number of decisions involved in its creation. When considering the design or construction of a complicated artifact like an aircraft (see Section 10.1 below) we can, on the reasonable assumption that designers and constructors are working steadily at an average decision rate, take the complexity of the artifact to be roughly measured by the logarithm of the total number of working hours absorbed in its design or construction. Such a measure of complexity for an artifact can be regarded as a quantification of the agency which went into its creation.

Another approach is to consider the *structural complexity* of an artifact, where this is defined in terms of the number of *functionally* distinct interrelated components out of which it is constructed. Each individual functionally distinct part of an artifact can be called a *technounit* [43]. The logarithm of the total number of distinct technounits which make up a complete working artifact is then taken as a simple measure of its complexity. Both of the above measures can be related to the basic Kolmogorov definition by thinking in terms of programs which specify design and construction processes for artifacts and of programs which specify the fabrication of individual technounits. Simpler measures of complexity are also being developed for computer programs themselves [44].

8.3 Logical Depth

Bennett [45,46] has given an illuminating and valuable discussion of the complexity of an object in terms which we can interpret as a quantification of the natural agency associated with its evolution. He calls this its *logical depth*. This is defined as the plausible number of computational steps required to prescribe an object's causal history on a universal computing machine. A logically deep object is one containing internal evidence of having resulted from a long computation, or from a dynamical process which requires a long time for a computer to simulate. An object or process is to be called deep only if there is no shortcut path, physical or non-physical, to reconstruct it from a concise description. In these terms the combined myriad processes which constitute human cognitive engines are logically very deep, and the processes currently storable in a computer are in comparison shallow.

9 AI and You-and-I

When attributing agency to an entity we are taking what Dennett [47] calls a *stance* — we deal with it on the basis of arbitrarily giving it those properties which we have defined to be those of agency, and justify this move by the degree to which its consequences fulfil our purposes. In this way we can characterize both computers and humans as agents. In one case the attributed agency is the result of evolution, in the other of design. How to design agency and how to compare designed and evolved agency are the fundamental problems of Artificial Intelligence (AI). There is a large body of literature on this topic, enlivened by vigorous polemic and battles between opposing camps. A good introduction to the controversies which are involved can be found in Dreyfus [48], and there is a wealth of excellent background surveys and anthologies [25,26,49-55]. From an agency point of view the arguments surrounding AI over, for example, whether computers can or cannot think largely miss the point that a *spectrum of agency* exists ranging from that embodied in the functionality of large molecules through simple cellular organisms, insects, control systems, robots, and so on up to that embodied in the higher animals and in humans [56]. The way in which this enables one to deploy a form of *spectrum argument* has been illustrated by Dretske [14] in a discussion of consciousness:

> [If] I am conscious and my very distant ancestors were not, *when* did my less-distant ancestors start being conscious? At the same time a poor man becomes rich as you keep giving him pennies.

Thus an answer to the question: "When could we say a computer is thinking?" is that, if we keep giving it process, then there will come a time when that is indeed so. Rather than ask badly posed questions, we need to find ways, quantitative if possible, which allow us to compare and contrast machine and human agency.

What sort of comparisons can we make between the brain's complexity and that of current artifacts in terms of data and process? The on-line storage capacity on the global Internet has been estimated [72] as 2 exabytes (exa=10^{18}), and its increase over the next three years is estimated as taking it to about 60 exabytes. One estimate of the number of distinct possible brain neural states has been given as 10 to the power 100,000,000,000,000 [57], whereas the total number of atoms in the visible universe has been estimated as of the relatively modest order of 10 to the power 79 [58]. Thus the potential of the brain for data storage seems staggeringly large. Comparison in terms of process is much more meaningful, but of course is much harder. If we were to take the 10^{10} bits of human DNA as a measure of a fully compressed program for fabricating human agency, this would give an upper bound (since the brain is only one component of our body) on one part of brain function complexity. To this estimate we would have to add that component of complexity which arises from learning by interactions with society and the environment, which we have estimated above as around 10^{20} data bits, which could, in theory, be compressed into a process having a bit size many orders of magnitude lower. A *very* crude upper bound for the complexity of brain process might then be of the order of petabits (peta = 10^{15}). The largest current machine programs are smaller by many orders of magnitude [44].

All that I think we can reasonably conclude from such very crude calculations is that the estimated complexity of the human brain is very much greater than that of any currently achievable artifact. Against this, however, we must note the crucial fact that much of the knowledge on which human agency now depends is objective, formal, and explicit, *and is thus of a form which is wholly compatible with machine function.* The more knowledge evolves, the more important the role of machines in handling it will become. What we really need to determine is how humans and machines can work best together. One way to get a feel for the depth and complexity of human agency, when comparing it with machine agency, is to look at language.

9.1 Languages

A richness of communication between agents is possible only if each agent has a rich internal representation of some relevant part of their shared external environment. It follows that the mutual possession of a richly detailed internal representation of a common environment is a necessary condition for there to be a richly expressive means of communication between agents. It further follows that the means used for communication must then, in some sense, contain and convey the richness of this internal model representation. Natural language thus embodies our shared perception of an external world and instantiates a shared theory of that world. *It is the most powerful means of knowledge representation which we have.* The instantiation of shared knowledge in language is characterized by physical embodiment as information, commonality of access, and accumulation over time.

It is the sharing and use of physically embodied information which enables knowledge to be stored, to grow, and to be continually refined. The role of language in the growth of objective knowledge is of fundamental importance. Essig [59] has given an interesting discussion of the generic features of natural language. He takes a basic feature of natural language to be the representation of *categorization*: the process of ascribing relationships between objects, where these relationships may be in themselves categories. For an idea of how many linguistic function representations could be handled by a natural language we can take Essig's estimates of 4,500 verbs and 26,000 nouns and pronouns to get a feel for how many categories could be involved. If we take only associations between a single verb and a single noun/pronoun, then we immediately have over 100 million potential categories. Associating a verb with two nouns or pronouns increases this by three orders of magnitude, taking us up into the billions of categories. Adding adjectival and adverbial modifiers, more complex syntactical constructions, and specialized lexicons rockets the number of potential categories up into the trillions. The rich expressiveness of natural language and other important aspects of languages are discussed in an illuminating and entertaining way by Pinker [60]. Natural language is the most convincing illustration of the depth of the cognitive engine which runs its underlying processes, and its complexity poses the most severe challenge to devising effective systems in which humans and machines can collaborate effectively.

Natural language is keyed into cognitive processes of vast depth, and for this reason we must accept that most of our knowledge, however we choose to store it or to access it, will continue to be represented in a natural language form or in some stylised sub-language derived from it. This will have a definitive effect in setting the relative roles of human and machine in executing combined tasks involving knowledge. Since the processes required are too deep for a machine to handle natural language at present other than in a relatively trivial sense (store, reproduce, search, display, and give highly structured and stylised responses), the machine is required currently to play a complementary role. This leaves most of the *knowledge-interpretation* tasks to the human agent.

9.2 Hierarchy of Knowledge Representations

The relative roles of natural language and specialized, simple, formal languages used for communication with machines (microlanguages) will play an important part in any discussion of human–machine interaction. It is the nature of a language that it has a formal, explicit, persisting structure (syntax, semantics, pragmatics). Thus, knowledge so instantiated must be formal and explicit. We can call knowledge represented in natural language *linguistic knowledge* . Knowledge represented in a microlanguage we can call *formal knowledge*, because such languages are much more rigidly structured than natural language [61]. Thus we have a *hierarchy* of knowledge representations of progressively increasing depth:

- formal knowledge (explicit)
- linguistic knowledge (explicit), and
- tacit knowledge.

Tacit knowledge [34,35] — memorably described in Polanyi's phrase "We know more than we can tell" — dwarfs linguistic knowledge in complexity, which in turn dwarfs formal knowledge in complexity. Tacit knowledge involves all the senses — sight, sound, taste, smell, and touch — and all the products of our imagination. These nonlinguistic aspects of a supportive environment for learning must not be forgotten as we grapple with ways of representing, storing, and transmitting knowledge.

Human *tacit* knowledge is both vast and inaccessible. All *explicit* knowledge however is grist to a machine's mill. We conclude that, at the present level of technology, human and machine agency are complementary, and that future technology should be developed in such a way as properly to exploit this complementarity in societies of agency. In particular, the deployment and use of large amounts of objective knowledge will require societies of machine and human agents.

10 The Future of Machines

When Robert Reich [62] made a study of possible forms of 21st Century capitalism, he paid homage to Adam Smith by his choice of title, calling his book *The Work of Nations.* In it Reich divided the future forms of work into three categories which he called: routine production services, in-person services, and symbolic-analytic services. We may extend his classification by a further division of production services and a renaming of his last category. Our classification of the future forms of work in knowledge economies then becomes:

- routine production services
- in-person services
- general production services, and
- knowledge-based services.

Routine production services entail all forms of stereotyped repetitive procedures which are associated with all high-volume and mass-producing enterprises. They include the routine handling of information as well as material, and they include all the routine supervisory jobs done by low-level and mid-level managers. Such activities will involve an increasing deployment of mechanical agency.

In-person services are closely supervised and cannot be supplied in bulk; they must be supplied person-to-person. These activities depend on tacit human knowledge and are less likely to be supplanted by machine agency.

General production services sustain volume production but require much broader skills and more knowledge than routine production services. These would include, for example, farmers, miners, many government employees, many workers in public and private utilities, and teachers. General production services will specifically include all production processes whose output is trained and knowledgeable people. There will be an increasing use of machine agency in such services. Knowledgeable agents will become major providers and will be intensively developed. The mechanization of knowledge will be as spectacular in its impact on general production services as was the mechanization of labor on the routine production sector in the Industrial Revolution.

Knowledge-based services (Reich's symbolic-analytic services) include all the problem-solving, problem-identifying, and strategic-brokering services associated with engineers, scientists, research workers of all kinds, investment bankers and brokers, accountants, engineering and management consultants, architects, strategic planners, system analysts, journalists, film editors, writers, musicians, composers, system analysts, aircraft designers, metallurgists, brain surgeons and doctors, and so on and so forth, that is, everyone whose stock in trade is derived from knowledge-based skills. Most knowledge-based service providers will have had a university education, and many of them will have postgraduate degrees. In this area there will be an ever-increasing use of knowledge systems in which knowledgeable machine agents support human agency.

A general question regards what will determine the role of machines in future knowledge economies. To address it we need to consider how machine agency might develop. There are three aspects to such a consideration:

- Complementarity
- Knowledge
- Intelligence

At present, and for the foreseeable future, human and machine agency are complementary. The vast complexity of human cognitive processes cannot at present be matched by any comparable depth of machine process. Complementarity will require that powerful knowledge systems will involve a meshing together of knowledgeable machine agents and highly-skilled human agents. Ultimately the most profound impact on future knowledge economies will arise from the continued development of intelligent agents. Constantly increasing processing power, coupled with a bootstrapping of knowledgeable and intelligent agency in design environments, will mean that intelligent agents will become increasingly powerful and ubiquitous. The limitations on the development of intelligent agents will arise from the need to equip them with processes of great logical depth. The only way of getting any feel for the possibility of mechanical agents emerging with the necessary very high levels of intelligent functionality is by looking at the way in which artifacts are evolving.

10.1 The Evolution of Machines

The emergence and evolution of artifacts can be described in terms of complexity: creation, management, and deployment. The ingredients out of which artifacts are created are labor, knowledge, and intelligence. Each of these ingredients is divisible, and for human agents each has a tacit and an explicit component. When part of an ingredient is divisible the task of creating an artifact can be shared between communicating agents. The ability of human and machine agents to collaborate — to form societies of agency — coupled with an ability to store, share, and so accumulate objective knowledge in such a society, means that the knowledge accumulated in artifacts, and so their complexity, can continually increase. This conjecture is based on an *active* interpretation of knowledge. Knowledge enables agents to ask questions, and the answers to these questions increases knowledge, which in turn enables the agents to ask more questions, and so forth. If one assumes that the amount of knowledge which a society of agents possesses sets the *rate* at which decisions can be made, and so sets the rate at which the society's knowledge increases, then one would expect its knowledge to increase exponentially as a result of this feedback process. Thus the complexity of the society's artifacts, taken as the logarithm of the number of decisions involved in their creation, would then be expected to increase linearly. The simple assumption of linearity implies of course an absence of resource limitations or other forms of likely constraint. Given an appropriate set of conditions which ensure that resources are deployed at a level which ensures a rate of design and development activity which is proportional to the full level of knowledge then available, we can conclude that the complexity of a society's artifacts could, in principle, increase linearly with time.

Some support for this conclusion can be drawn from a consideration of the evolution of aircraft. Figures 7 and 8 show, on a logarithmic scale, the growth in aircraft design effort and aircraft manufacturing effort over five decades [63]. These imply that aircraft complexity is increasing linearly. Similar conclusions can be drawn from well-known data on the development of semiconductor devices. Cotterell and Kamminga [43] have, using the idea of measuring complexity in terms of numbers of technounits (the functionally distinct constituent parts of an artifact), considered the growth of artifact complexity over the last million years. This linear growth of complexity is sketched in Figure 9 adapted from Cotterell and Kamminga [43].

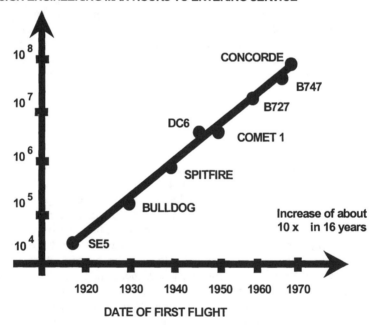

Figure 7: Growth in design effort.

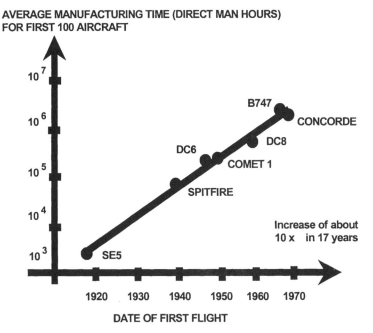

Figure 8: Growth in manufacturing effort.

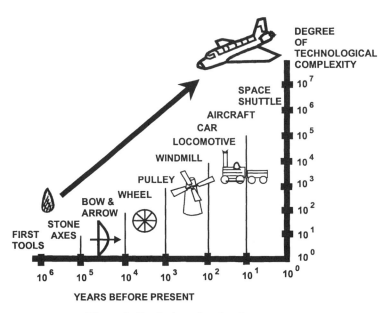

Figure 9: Evolution of technology

11 Epilogue

Adam Smith's vision of an economic future determined by a division of labor can be replaced by one determined by an accumulation and division of knowledge. Objective knowledge, stored and shared in the form of information and used in the form of artifacts, will steadily increase. Machine agency will play an indispensable role in its development and use. The iterative bootstrapping (a form of positive feedback) of design capability by knowledge growth will ensure that machine processor power will continually increase. The development of meta-processes — processes which create process — and hence the development of intelligent agency, is limited only by the amount of processor power which can be made available. This means that, in principle, there is no barrier to a continuing development of machine intelligence.

Information theory and complexity theory offer a powerful perspective from which to consider the evolution of machines. The development of a quantitative theory of knowledge, and knowledge systems, from them would offer the prospect of measuring and predicting the progress of the development of societies of agency. It would replace sterile argument about metaphysical speculations concerning the nature and limitations of computers with testable hypotheses about the evolution of objective knowledge. Tentative initial conclusions imply that humans and machines are now co-evolving [64,65] in a way parallel to the co-evolution of the human brain and language [66]. Thus, the complexity of the artifacts which are the essential components of civilization are increasing linearly, have been increasing linearly for many millennia, and could in principle continue to so evolve for many more millennia. One can also argue that the complexity of the human brain is so vast, and that the plastic component of the human mind is so great, that human agency could continue to keep pace with the development of machine agency in a complementary fashion, thus allowing this co-evolution to continue. Some distant future society of complementary human and machine agency could then have artifacts which are of a complexity relative to the space shuttle, as that of the space shuttle is relative to the stone axe. All new information necessary to continually expand the pool of objective knowledge can come only from experimental interaction with the physical world. There is nothing intrinsically mysterious about intelligence; it is simply the capacity to create new process and test it in action. The likely rate of increase in the complexity of information processors could in time bring into play very high levels of machine intelligence, since the ability to create new process puts an absolute premium on great processing power. Thus the emergence of intelligent machines with processes of great logical depth seems possible, although it may take a very long time. Such machines would form with humans an entirely new form of society. It is an awesome prospect.

Acknowledgement

The study whose results are reported here was carried out while the author was the holder of a Leverhulme Emeritus Fellowship. The support of the Leverhulme Trust is gratefully acknowledged.

References

[1]   Smith, A., *The wealth of nations*, (first published in London in 1776) Penguin Books, London, 1986.

[2]   Kuppers, B-O., *Information and the origin of life*, MIT Press, Cambridge, MA, 1990.

[3]   Churchland, P.M., *Neurophilosophy*, MIT Press, Cambridge, MA, 1989.

[4]   Churchland, P.S. and Sejnowski, T.J., *The computational brain*, MIT Press, Cambridge, MA, 1992.

[5]   Mackie, J.L., *The cement of the universe: a study of causation*, Oxford University Press, Oxford, UK, 1974.

[6]   Simon, H.A., *The sciences of the artificial*, 2nd edition, MIT Press, Cambridge, MA, 1981.

[7]   Wheeler, J.A., "Information, physics, quantum: the search for links" in [37].

[8]   Shannon, C.E. and Weaver, W., *The mathematical theory of communication*, University of Illinois Press, Urbana, 1949.

[9]   Cover, T.M. and Thomas, J.A., *Elements of information theory*, Wiley, New York, 1991.

[10]   Kolmogorov, A.N., "Logical basis for information theory and probability theory," *IEEE Transactions on Information Theory,* Vol. IT-16, pp. 662-664, 1968.

[11]   Chaitin, G.J., *Information, randomness and incompleteness* (second edition), World Scientific, Singapore, 1990.

[12]   Resnikoff, H.L., *The illusion of reality*, Springer-Verlag, New York, 1989.

[13]   Dretske, F.I., *Knowledge and the flow of information*, MIT Press, Cambridge, MA, 1981.

[14]   Dretske, F.I., *Naturalizing the mind*, MIT Press, Cambridge, MA, 1995.

[15]   Devlin, K., *Logic and information*, Cambridge University Press, Cambridge, UK, 1991.

[16]   Frieden, R., *Physics from fisher information*, Cambridge University Press, Cambridge, UK, 1998.

[17]   Tribus, M. and McIrvine, E.C., "Energy and information," *Scientific American*, Vol. 225, pp. 179-188, September 1971.

[18]   Mumford, D., "Pattern theory: a unifying perspective" in [67].

[19]   Peitgen, H-O., Jurgens, H., and Saupe, D., *Chaos and fractals,* Springer-Verlag, New York, 1992.

[20]   Herken, R. (Editor), *The universal Turing machine: a half-century survey*, Oxford University Press, Oxford, UK, 1988.

[21]   Rosnay, J. de, *Le Macroscope - Vers une vision globale*, Editions du Seuil, Paris, 1975.

[22]   Quine, W.V. and Ullian, J.S., *The web of belief*, Random House, New York, 1978.

[23]   Quine, W.V., *From stimulus to science*, Harvard University Press, Cambridge, MA, 1995.

[24]   Moser, P.K., and Vandernat, A., *Human knowledge*, Oxford University Press, New York, 1987.

[25]   Boden, M.A. (Editor), *The philosophy of artificial intelligence*, Oxford University Press, Oxford, UK, 1990.

[26]   Boden, M.A. (Editor), *The philosophy of artificial life*, Oxford University Press, Oxford, UK, 1996.

[27]   Skemp, R.R., *The psychology of learning mathematics*, Penguin Books, New York, 1971.

[28]   Peacocke, C., *A study of concepts*, MIT Press, Cambridge, MA, 1992.

[29]   Newell, A., *Unified theories of cognition*, Harvard University Press, Cambridge, MA, 1990.

[30]   Simon, H.A.: "Machine as mind" in [55].

[31]   MacFarlane, A.G.J., Grubel, G., and Ackermann, J., "Future design environments for control engineering," *Automatica*, Vol. 25 (2), pp. 165-176, 1989.

[32]   MacFarlane, A.G.J., "Interactive computing: a revolutionary medium for teaching and design," *Computing and Control Engineering Journal*, pp. 149-158, July 1990.

[33]   MacFarlane, A.G.J., "Universities in a knowledge economy: the impact of technology" in [71].

[34]   Polanyi, M., *Personal knowledge: towards a post-critical philosophy*, University of Chicago Press, Chicago, IL, 1958.

[35]   Polanyi, M., *The tacit dimension*, Peter Smith, Gloucester, MA, 1966.

[36]   Dehaene, S., *The number sense: how the mind creates mathematics*, Oxford University Press, New York, 1997.

[37]   Zurek, W.H. (Editor), *Complexity, entropy and the physics of information*, Santa Fe Studies in the Sciences of Complexity, Addison-Wesley, Reading, MA, 1991.

[38]   Li, M. and Vitanyi, P., *An introduction to Kolmogorov complexity and its applications*, Springer-Verlag, New York, 1993.

[39]   Chaitin, G.J., *Algorithmic information theory*, Cambridge University Press, Cambridge, UK, 1987.

[40]   Solomonoff, R.J., "A formal theory of inductive inference," *Information and Control*, Vol.7(1), pp. 1-22, 1964.

[41]   Shanker, S.G. (Editor), *Godel's theorem in focus*, Croom Helm, London, 1988.

[42] Stewart, I., "The ultimate in undecidability," *Nature*, Vol. 332(6160), pp. 115-116, 1988.

[43] Cotterell, B. and Kamminga, J., *Mechanics of pre-industrial technology*, Cambridge University Press, Cambridge, UK, 1990.

[44] Jones, C., "Sizing up software," *Scientific American*, Vol. 279(6), pp. 2-7, December 1998.

[45] Bennett, C.H., "Logical depth and physical complexity" in [20].

[46] Bennett, C.H., "Complexity in the universe" in [68].

[47] Dennett, D.C., *The intentional stance*, MIT Press, Cambridge, MA, 1987.

[48] Dreyfus, H.L., *What computers still can't do*, MIT Press, Cambridge, MA, 1992.

[49] Gardner, H., *The mind's new science*, Basic Books, New York, 1987.

[50] Johnson-Laird, P., *The computer and the mind*, Fontana Press, London, 1993.

[51] Posner, M.I. (Editor), *Foundations of cognitive science*, MIT Press, Cambridge, MA, 1991.

[52] Beakley, B. and Ludlow, P. (Editors), *The philosophy of mind: classical problems, contemporary issues*, MIT Press, Cambridge, MA, 1992.

[53] Goldman, A.I. (Editor), *Readings in philosophy and cognitive science,* MIT Press, Cambridge, MA, 1993.

[54] Ford, K.M., Glymour, C., and Hayes, P.J. (Editors), *Android epistemology*, AAAI Press and MIT Press, Cambridge, MA, 1995.

[55] Luger, G.F. (Editor), *Computation and intelligence*, AAAI Press and MIT Press, Cambridge, MA, 1995.

[56] Kenny, A., *The metaphysics of mind*, Oxford University Press, Oxford, UK, 1989.

[57] Flanagan, O., *Consciousness reconsidered*, MIT Press, Cambridge, MA, 1992.

[58] Emiliani, C., *The scientific companion*, Wiley, New York, 1995.

[59] Essig, G., "Naturalware: natural language and human-intelligence capabilities" in [69].

[60] Pinker, S., *The language instinct*, Penguin Books, New York, 1995.

[61] Abelson, H. and Sussman, G.J., *Structure and interpretation of computer programs*, MIT Press, Cambridge, MA, 1985.

[62] Reich, R.B., *The work of nations: a blueprint for the future*, Simon and Schuster, London, 1991.

[63] Brooks, P.W., "Aircraft and their operation" in [73].

[64] Mazlish, B., *The fourth discontinuity: the co-evolution of humans and machines*, Yale University Press, New Haven, CT, 1993.

[65] Donald, M., *Origins of the modern mind: three stages in the evolution of culture and cognition*, Harvard University Press, Cambridge, MA, 1991.

[66] Deacon, T., *The symbolic species: The co-evolution of language and the human brain*, Penguin Press, New York, 1997.

[67] Atiyah, M. and Iagolnitzer, D. (Editors), *Field's medallists' lectures,* World Scientific, Singapore University Press, Singapore, 1997.

[68] Halliwell, J.J., Perez-Mercader, J., and Zurek, W.H. (Editors), *Physical origins of time asymmetry*, Cambridge University Press, Cambridge, MA, 1994.

[69] Leebaert, D. (Editor), *The future of software*, MIT Press, Cambridge, MA, 1995.

[70] Popper, K.R., *Objective knowledge - an evolutionary approach,* Clarendon Press, Oxford, UK, 1972.

[71] Smith, D.C. and Langslow, A.K. (Editors), *The idea of a university,* Jessica Kingsley Publishers, London, 1999.

[72] Taylor, J., "Engineering the information age," *Engineering Management Journal*, Vol. 8(6), pp. 277-287, 1998.

[73] Williams, T.J. (Editor), *A History of Technology, Volume VI*, Clarendon Press, Oxford, UK, 1978.

3 | MACHINES AND THE ELUSIVE WISDOM

V.J. Modi
Department of Mechanical Engineering
The University of British Columbia
Vancouver, BC, Canada V6T 1Z4

Since the dawn of the industrial revolution, we have witnessed remarkable expression of ingenuity in creations ranging from steam engines to sewing machines, airplanes, robots, information highways and many more. The presentation focuses on achievements in space technology from Sputnik to the proposed International Space Station and the on board mobile robotic manipulator system. These creations are often considered to be endowed with "artificial intelligence."

Several fundamental questions surface at this stage: What is intelligence? Wisdom? Do we control our own intelligence? Can we impart to a machine what we do not understand or control?

Faith, intellect, experience, memory, and intuition are cornerstones of our lifestream. Thought cannot stir without faith and to that extent the machine is a creation of our faith. But it will never be able to search the outermost bounds of nature and the innermost depths of man, and can never comprehend the force that unites them. No machine, no computer, no robot will ever be able to enjoy the sunset, nor will it be able to describe its total beauty spontaneously in a haiku, a three-line, seventeen-syllable poem.

Life imposes on us the obligation to be compassionate, considerate, and true. We cannot pass these obligations to the machine. To paraphrase Bernard Shaw (1856-1950): No creation of man manages its affairs as well as a tree does.

1 Evolution

Some of the important stages in the evolutionary history of mankind may be listed as follows [1]:

- 14 billion year ago: creation of the universe

- 2 billion years ago: life began in the form of microscopic bacteria living in the ocean depths

- 70 million years ago: first primate, i.e. the group of mammals that includes man, the apes, and the monkeys

- 0.5 million years ago: transition from ape to human, Peking-Java man

- 250,000 years ago: recognizable human form, Homo Sapiens*

- 75,000-10,000 years ago: the fourth ice age

It was not until 3,000 BC, that the ice reached its present location. By then there were already well developed human settlements in Asia and the Middle East.

On a clear night the sky may appear studded with stars, but actually only around 6000-7000 stars, both the hemispheres put together, are visible to the naked eye. Recognizing that at any instant only half of them are above the horizon, and those near the horizon have poor visibility, it is safe to say that one is lucky to see more than 2000 stars at any one time.

With a good binocular the number increases to 50,000, and a simple telescope can reveal around a million stars. Our sun is one such star, one among the 40 billion belonging to the Milky Way Galaxy, with its two spiral arms extending to 100,000 light years (1 light year $\approx 16 \times 10^{12}$ km). In astronomy, numbers become too large so quickly as to make even imagination helpless. Consider, for example, the US budget in 1998 of over 1.6 trillion dollars ($\$10^{12}$). This amounts to having spent around 2.2 million dollars every day since the birth of Christ!

In the Milky Way galaxy with 40 billion suns, some with their own planetary systems, we are located at the outer edge, far away from the center. Christianity has had a long standing difficulty in reconciling with this fact. There are billions of such galaxies! We are truly insignificant, one among the 6 billion souls on earth, and earth tagging along around the sun, one among the multitude. On the other hand, we are blessed with infinite potential.

2 Stages of Knowledge

Man was born in a world threatened by the forces of life and nature. He began from the beginning. Since then, what has progressed is knowledge, not the custodian of the knowledge. The major forces which guided the progress, particularly in the early stages, were: language, fire, and religion. So fundamental have been these three elements of social evolution, that no other subsequent discovery or invention

---

* The accepted interpretation of the Holy Writ gives: 4004 BC, birth of Adam; 2348 BC, Great Flood; 1571 BC, birth of Moses.

has left comparable results. What is relevant in this presentation is the first element, language, the vehicle of thought. The one gift of the space age that has touched the life of humanity in all parts of the world is the communications satellites. We saw the Olympics in Tokyo, the Pope's visits to far off countries, hunger in Ethiopia, turmoil in the Middle-East, Nicaragua, and Bosnia. The world has become a stage in our living room.

It took five months to convey the message to Queen Isabella that the voyage of Columbus was a success, two weeks for Europe to hear about Lincoln's assassination, and about 1.3 seconds to get the word from Neil Armstrong that man could walk on the moon. With communications satellites the world has become a community of instant neighbors.

Thus communication has been one of the central parameters in the evolution of our civilization. The same is true with robotics. Robot, a synthesis of lifeless mechanical /electrical components, comes virtually alive with controlled behavior when an algorithm-driven code is communicated to it (Figure 1).

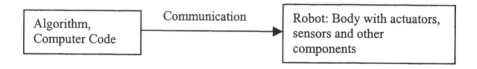

Figure 1:   Communication is a key parameter in robot operation.

3 The March of Industrialization

Advent of the industrial revolution (1750) accelerated the tempo of the technological developments:

- 1850: sewing machine invented by Elias Howe

- 1903: the first powered flight of an airplane by the Wright Brothers

- 1957: Sputnik

- 1969: the first landing on the moon

- 1992: Internet: information highway

- 2004: International Space Station

This technological super express is pushed ahead at such an extravagant speed that even spectacular achievements of science and technology, such as the moon landing, fade away rather quickly. The first one captured our imagination, the second was o.k. By the time the fourth moon landing came, a lady in Texas called the local TV station vigorously protesting a change in the schedule, and demanded that the station should get on with "The Tom Jones Show." What was extraordinary yesterday has become ordinary today. What appeared impossible to one generation seems to become elementary to the next. Jules Verne (1828-1905), well known for his *Around the World in 80 Days, Journey to the Center of Earth, 20,000 Leagues Under the Sea*, and other scientific fictions, conceived the ideas of the submarine for underwater propulsion as well as the rocket for space travel. He said [1]:

"Anything that one can imagine, someone else can make it real."

Spectacular achievements in space are testimony to this observation. It would be instructive to touch upon a few milestones to help appreciate evolution of space science and technology.

4 The Space Age

As a contribution to the International Geophysical Year, the USSR launched Sputnik in 1957 to herald the beginning of the space age. With a diameter of 58 cm and weighing 83.6 kg., it tracked an elliptic trajectory (227 km perigee, 947 km apogee) having a period of 96 minutes. It was a dramatic confirmation of the three orbital laws arrived at by Kepler through correlation of thousands of observations, taken over a lifetime, using simple devices including the telescope his contemporary Galileo (1564-1642) had invented. The first law predicts the shape of the orbits as conic sections. The second law determines speed of the satellite at different locations in the orbit in terms of the area swept by the radius vector. The third law relates period of the orbit (τ) in terms of its semi-major axis (a), $\tau^2 \propto a^3$.

Newton was also interested in planetary motions. Through the gravitational law of mutual attraction, he provided mathematical foundation for Kepler's laws. Newton invented calculus, a new branch of mathematics, to solve the equations (nonlinear) of planetary motion. Also, he discovered the principle of dispersion of light, i.e., light separates into seven colours as it passes through a prism. These three contributions of far-reaching consequence came in the same year, when Newton was 23! He lived to the age of 85. In his remaining 62 years, there were no major contributions from Newton.

Sputnik stayed in orbit for 92 days and gave information about density of the upper atmosphere as well as radio wave propagation in the ionosphere. It was a humble beginning. However, within 20 years of Sputnik we were exploring the space beyond earth and its moon. Taking advantage of the planetary alignment that occurs only once in 176 years, Voyager 2, launched in 1977, completed a twelve-year grand tour of 7 billion km covering four planets: Jupiter (1979), Saturn (1981), Uranus (1986), and Neptune (1989).

Within 12 more years, we were ready for another spectacular mission which is still in progress. The Galileo spacecraft began its 3.8 billion kilometers voyage to Venus and Jupiter in 1989. After a journey of six years, the Galileo spacecraft arrived at Jupiter. On 7 December, 1995, it released a tear-drop shaped probe with six experiments into Jupiter's stormy atmosphere, thus becoming the first man-made object to make a direct contact with an outer planet. Launched from the Shuttle Atlantis, the 4 ton spacecraft studied composition of Jupiter (mostly hydrogen and helium), its complex cloud system, and bursts of lightening.

By any standard, it was one of the most violent maneuvers and an equally sophisticated control strategy in the history of spacecraft. The probe came screaming at a speed of 170,000 km/hour, with an acceleration reaching 230g! It parachuted down around 100 km into the Jovian atmosphere, transmitting data throughout the mission time of 57 minutes. Eventually the probe succumbed to the crushing pressure (approximately equal to that at a depth of 250 m below earth surface) and baking temperature (150° C). The spacecraft itself is now heading for a series of encounters with Jupiter's moons Europa, Callisto, and Io.

The spacecraft honors Galileo, the 16th century professor at the University of Pisa. Galileo was forced to resign his teaching position at the university when he proved Aristotle's assertion, that the heavier the object, the faster it falls, to be in error. A simple experiment with a feather and a stone, conducted on the moon, proved that Galileo was correct. Unfortunately, on yet another point, for asserting that the sun is the center of our planetary system and not earth, he was persecuted by the Vatican. Here is the case where unveiling of knowledge has come with a price, even exacting cruelty, inflicted by ignorance. Galileo was forced to live in misery, in exile, wandering from city to city, to end up in prison. Only recently (1984), after more than 350 years, the council appointed by the present Pope "absolved" him of the "crime" of telling the truth. The council called it a case of "mutual incomprehension."

The upholding of truth often demands the utmost sacrifices.

One cannot overlook the celebrated Hubble Space Telescope launched in 1990. After the initial problem of lens alignment, which was corrected by dramatic efforts of the space shuttle-based astronauts, it has provided remarkable information never before possible to acquire. It successfully extended the frontiers of astronomy and our understanding of it including the ever puzzling blackholes. The 12-ton telescope is named after the American astronomer Edwin P. Hubble (1889-1953), who discovered galaxies beyond our Milky Way. He also found that the universe continues to expand. The age of the oldest galaxy photographed by the Hubble Space Telescope is around 12 billion years. This is remarkable, as the big bang is estimated to have occurred 14 billion years ago.

Who can forget NASA's spectacular success with the Rover crawling on Mars? After exploration of the Red planet from the mid-sixties to late seventies by Mariner and Viking probes, NASA's Mars Pathfinder Sojourner Rover was the demonstration of technology at its best. Launched on December 2, 1996, it took around seven months to cover the 500 million km journey and arrived on July 4, 1997. The Pathfinder sent back excellent photographs of the surrounding terrain (Lander, 16,000; Rover, 550). The six-wheel Rover, 65 × 48 × 30 cm and weighing 16 kg, crawled at a speed of 0.6 m/min and conducted spectrographic analysis of rocks as well as soil. It was designed for a 30-day lifetime. It survived for 83 days (until September 27, 1997).

These are only four examples. One can cite many more. Flawless operation at such great distances in unfriendly environment, according to command, and return of information appears incredible. It is tempting to say that these spacecraft represent intelligent machines. However, let us hold back the judgment for a while.

5 International Space Station

Our current focus is on the International Space Station. Proposed by President Reagan in 1984, it is led by the USA in partnership with Canada, Japan, and the European Space Agency (ESA). In 1994, Russia joined the group. The space station is a gigantic structure, 112m × 75m, larger than a soccer field. In a circular trajectory at a height of 400m with an orbital inclination of around 51° to the equatorial plane, it will carry a crew of 7 astronauts working in a shift of 120 days.

Obviously, such an enormous structure cannot be carried to the operational altitude in its entirety. It will be constructed in modular fashion with components launched by more than 60 flights of the space shuttle and Russia's Proton rocket. ESA's Ariane and Japan's H-II rockets may also play small roles. The cargo left in orbit will be integrated by the extravehicular activity of astronauts as well as the Canada supplied manipulator, Mobile Servicing System (MSS). The MSS involves a robotic arm having two links (each 8.5 m long) with revolute joints. The arm has seven degrees of freedom. The system also carries the Special Purpose Dexterous Manipulator (SPDM), 5 m in length, having 19 degrees of freedom. As with cranes used in construction of high-rise buildings, MSS will act as a crane in space assisting in integration, operation, and maintenance of the space station.

At the outset it must be recognized that we are dealing with an evolving structure whose geometry, inertia, stiffness, and damping characteristics are changing. Figure 2 shows "milestone configurations" established by NASA, for one of the earlier designs of the space station, with details given in Table 1. A striking feature of the space station is its flexibility as illustrated in Figure 3 for the Assembly Complete Configuration (ACC). It is of interest to recognize that the first forty modes are compressed within a frequency range of 0.1 - 1.0 Hz! Note also the closely packed and overlapping character of the frequencies. This makes dynamics and control of the system a challenging task.

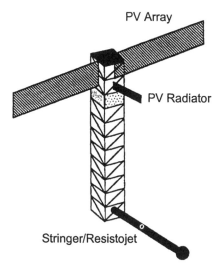

First Milestone Configuration

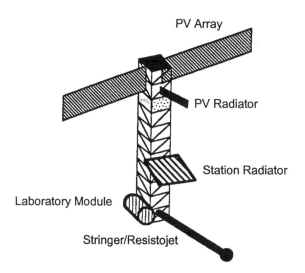

Man-Tended Configuration

Figure 2:   Milestone configurations (first milestone and man-tended) of the space
station *Freedom*. The evolving character leads to variations in geometry, inertia, flexibility, and damping characteristics.

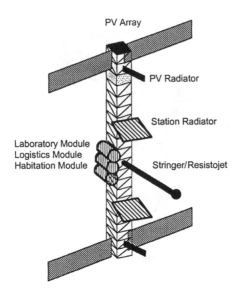

Permanently Manned Configuration

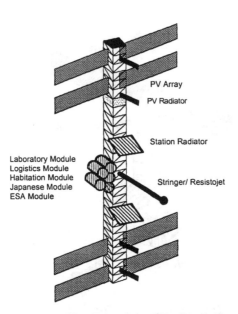

Assembly Complete Configuration

Figure 2 (cont.):   Milestone configurations (permanently manned and assembly complete) of the space station *Freedom*. The evolving character leads to variations in geometry, inertia, flexibility, and damping characteristics.

Table 1: Details of evolving stages of the space station *Freedom*.

MILESTONE FLIGHTS		
First Milestone (FMC)	Main Truss (60m), PV Arrays (2), PV Radiator (1), Stinger Resistojet.	**Mass (Kg)**
		21,580
Man-Tended (MTC)	Main Truss (60m), PV Arrays (2), PV Radiator (1), Stinger Resistojet, Station Radiator (1), US Lab Module, Pressure Docking Adapter	73,779
Permanently Manned (PMC)	Main Truss (115m), PV Arrays (4), PV Radiator (2), Stinger Resistojet, Station Radiator (2), US Lab Module, Logistics and Habitat Modules.	150,490
Assembly Complete (ACC)	Main Truss (115m), PV Arrays (4), PV Radiator (2), Stinger Resistojet, Station Radiator (2), US Lab Module, Logistics and Habitat Modules, Japanese and ESA Modules.	273,647

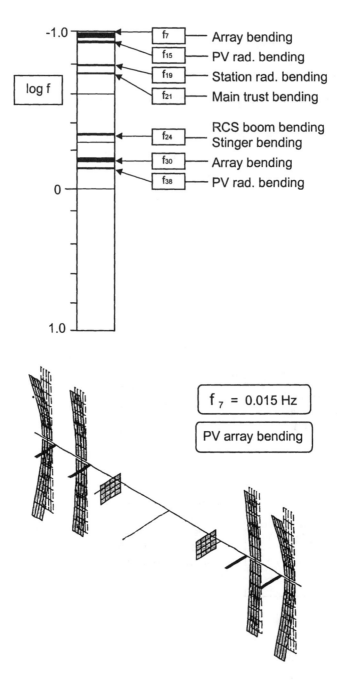

Figure 3:   Frequency spectrum and a representative mode for the Assembly Complete Configuration (ACC) of the Space Station *Freedom*.

The space station will be subjected to the environmental induced disturbances such as solar radiation pressure and thermal deformations and interactions with earth's gravitational and magnetic fields, as well as free molecular reaction forces due to the rarified atmosphere. Docking of the space shuttle will be the most critical excitation, not to forget the effect of manipulator maneuvers. These will be augmented by internal disturbances associated with astronauts' activities. The excitations lead to interactions between the space station's orbital, librational (roll, yaw, pitch), and elastic responses. Figure 4 attempts to summarize basic issues associated with large-scale, space-based systems such as the space station.

Thus space engineers are faced with a formidable task of predicting and controlling the dynamics of a highly elastic orbiting platform, supporting a mobile flexible manipulator, carrying a compliant payload (see Figure 5). This class of problems has never been encountered before. Newton, Euler, Lagrange, and Hamilton, pioneers of the classical mechanics, never envisaged such a situation. Yet their elegant theories are effective in casting such problems into mathematical molds. For the space station, the governing equations of motion turn out to be extremely lengthy, even in the matrix notation. They are highly nonlinear, nonautonomous, and coupled. Control of the space station using the conventional Feedback Linearization Technique (FLT), applied to the rigid degrees of freedom during a docking maneuver, gave remarkably detailed information about the system response. A small amount of data obtained from the response time-histories is summarized in Table 2. Abscissa lists disturbances: docking, intravehicular activity in the longitudinal and transverse directions, walking and jogging on treadmill, extravehicular activity while connected to tether during the space station integration, even clearing the throat. Ordinate lists important locations: position of modules, tips of solar panels, photo-voltaic radiators, stinger, reaction control system boom, and station radiators. The last row states the control moment demands. For example, during the docking maneuver, peak displacement and acceleration at the solar panel tip are 35,000 μm and 2,330 μg, respectively. The control efforts involved with the FLT are 2,194 Nm in pitch (ψ), 42 Nm in roll (ϕ), and 3,035 Nm in yaw (λ). More recently, the focus has been on a novel manipulator with slewing as well as deployable links (Figure 6). It seems to have advantages in terms of reduced coupling leading to simpler equations of motion and inverse kinematics, fewer singularities as well as improved effectiveness in obstacle avoidance (Figure 7).

It was at this stage when "intelligent" control caught my attention. Navigating spacecraft to distant planets, landing robots, gathering information including pictures and sending them to earth or a mobile manipulator on a flexible platform ferrying an elastic payload along a precise trajectory to avoid collision represent only isolated complex situations among many. These missions have been highly successful although they used conventional procedures. Maybe they are intelligent machines. That set me thinking: What is intelligence? Consciousness? Experience? Wisdom? Intuition? Do we understand our intelligence and control it? Can we impart to machines what we do not understand or control?

STRUCTURAL DYNAMICS

- Highly nonlinear, nonautonomous, and coupled system
- Extremely low and clustered frquency spectrum
- Configuration growth; evolving structures
- Not amenable to modeling with ground-based simulation facilities
- Response in the presence of environmental forces

CONTROL

- Control of flexible structures in the presence of environmental forces
- Closely packed resonant frequencies within the bandwidth of control system
- Optimum selection and location of sensors and actuators
- Model reduction
- Necessity of robust controllers due to parametric uncertainties

ENVIRONMENTAL EFFECTS

- Free molecular flow, earth's magnetic field and solar radiation environment
- Prediction of short- and long-term variations of environmental parameters
- Structure–environment interaction mechanisms

Figure 4: Major issues associated with the dynamics and control of large flexible systems such as the International Space Station: structural dynamics, control, and environmental effects.

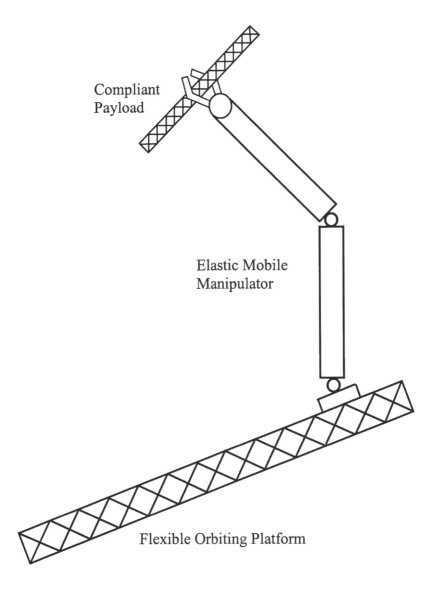

Figure 5: Schematic diagram of an elastic platform in orbit, supporting a compliant mobile manipulator carrying a flexible payload. Dynamics and
control of this class of systems represent problems never before encountered.

Table 2: Peak control efforts, displacements, and accelerations experienced by the space station due to the shuttle-docking and crew-motion disturbances.

Location		Assembly Complete Configuration (ACC)		
		Disturbance (Local Horizontal)		
		Docking	IVA Long.	IVA Trans.
Modules	Disp., μm	260	3.5	2.9
	Acc., μg	18	0.22	0.23
Solar	Disp., μm	35,000	820	580
	Acc., μg	2,330	46	35
Photo Volt. Radiator	Disp., μm	500	210	210
	Acc., μg	18	6	6
Stinger	Disp., μm	300	4	3.6
	Acc., μg	18	0.22	0.23
RCS Boom	Disp., μm	200	2	1
	Acc., μg	10	0.11	0.14
Station Radiator	Disp., μm	240	3	1.7
	Acc., μg	16	0.22	0.2
Control	ψ, Nm	2,194	30	29
	ϕ, Nm	42	0.5	0.5
	λ, Nm	3,055	33	40

Table 2 (cont.):   Peak control efforts, displacements, and accelerations experienced by the space station due to the shuttle-docking and crew-motion disturbances.

Location		Assembly Complete Configuration (ACC)			
		Disturbance (Local Horizontal)			
		Tread. Walk	Tread. Jog.	EVA Tether	Cough
Modules	Disp., μm	2.3	10	13	2.1
	Acc., μg	0.4	2.1	2	0.05
Solar	Disp., μm	570	810	1,942	540
	Acc., μg	59	262	267	13
Photo Volt. Radiator	Disp., μm	210	220	213	210
	Acc., μg	6	6	6	6
Stinger	Disp., μm	2.3	11	13	4
	Acc., μg	0.41	2	2	0.1
RCS Boom	Disp., μm	1.6	5	7	1.5
	Acc., μg	0.14	1.2	1.1	0.05
Station Radiator	Disp., μm	1.1	8	11.4	0.8
	Acc., μg	0.35	2	2	2.2
Control	ψ, Nm	50	252	244	2.4
	ϕ, Nm	1.3	5	4	0.5
	λ, Nm	76	371	333	14

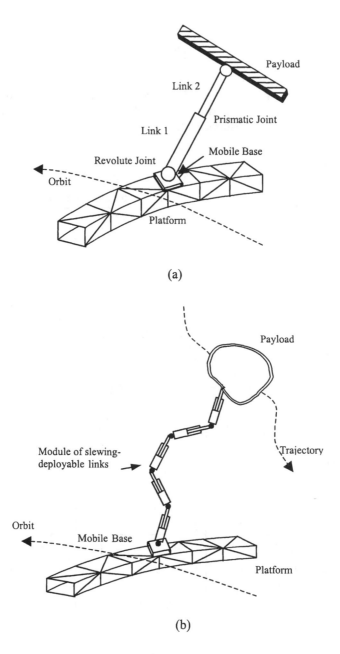

Figure 6:   (a) A single module manipulator with two links: one free to slew (revolute joint) while the other is permitted to deploy; (b) Multi-module manipulator can vary its geometry in the snake-like fashion.

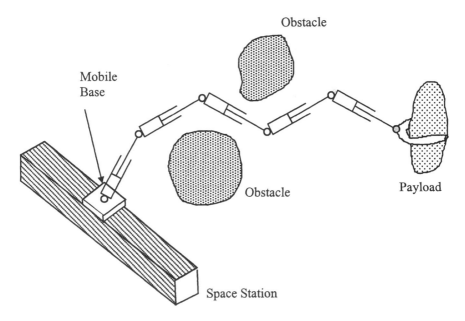

Figure 7:   Variable geometry manipulator is well suited for obstacle avoidance.

6 "Intelligent" Machines

Can a machine think? Probing of a new thought carries with it freshness of the breeze at spring. There are competing colors and fragrances. One hopes for the outcome of an inquiry to be enlightening. In fact, scientists have been discussing the "thinking machine" for around fifty years.

History tells us that Germans, during the first world war, trained pigeons to carry secret messages as well as tiny amount of explosives, thus using them as missiles. Swedes taught seals to carry information. Russians trained dogs to carry bombs. But now we are face to face with the new world of so-called "intelligent" machines (see Chapters 1 and 2).

The term *intelligence* has always been associated with life, something living. One may venture to state, at some risk, that it serves as one of the factors to distinguish the living from the dead. Thus, consciousness, experience, understanding, and intelligence are attributes which seem to be connected by the invisible thread of life. Our ability to think, learn, and make decisions in a wide variety of unplanned situations is attributed to our intelligence. Now there is a suggestion that machines can be constructed with such intelligence and can virtually replace humans.

We encounter reference to intelligent systems, expert systems, knowledge-based systems, fuzzy and neural network procedures, etc. so persistently that, in the future, it may be difficult to find an ordinary, conventionally controlled machine. Fortunately, it is merely a distortion of terminology. Robots may be endowed with enormous sophistication in design and operation and may display technological achievements of a higher order. However, in reality they are all ordinary and far from being "intelligent." Good engineering does not have to result into an "intelligent" machine.

Of course, I recognize that most of us use the terms *intelligent system* and *intelligent control* to distinguish them from conventional procedures. However, this is grossly misleading. "Intelligent" control is not only firmly founded on conventional methodology but is an extension of it (see Chapters 6 and 8). The committee struck by IEEE Control System Society to look into the area of intelligent control essentially came to the same conclusion ([2], p. 4). The Committee prefaced its report by saying: "... the task force has not attempted to address the issue of intelligence in its generality. It focused on only working characterization of intelligent control." Even at that level it suggested that "intelligent" systems have their bases in the conventional methodology. The "general" character of intelligence that the IEEE committee decided not to address is the issue of fundamental importance here.

We seem to have particular fancy, almost approaching obsession, for the word *intelligence* so that its use has become indiscriminate. Let us look at some examples:

(1)   Intelligent Computer

Some of you may remember Hal, the computer of great "intelligence" in the movie *2001: A Space Odyssey*. Its last words began:

"I am a HAL Nine Thousand Computer Production Number 3. I became operational at the Hal Plant in Urbana, Illinois, on January 12, 1977. The quick brown fox jumps over the lazy dog" ([15], p. 156).

HAL's final observation contains all the letters of the English alphabet. Some intelligence!

(2)   Intelligent Football

A Spaniard inventor, Fernado Lopez, claims to have designed an "intelligent" football which enables players to score more goals by following precise trajectories. Instead of containing just one central mass of air, the "intelligent" football has small pockets beneath each panel. This is said to provide firmer grip to the foot on impact and hence the guided path to the goal.

(3)   Smart Self-Opening Envelope

Carlos Castro, president of Lanyard Envelopes, Inc., in Budd Lake, N.J., USA, has patented an envelope (Patent No. 5,752,652) with a built-in opener. A piece of string with a small tab is attached on one edge. Pull the tab and the string slices through the fold from bottom to top.

(4)   Smart Luggage Tags

British Airway is testing a system of "smart tags" designed to reduce the risk of lost baggage. The disposable tags are fitted with pinhead-size computer chips which communicate through a radio system, allowing the airline to keep track of where each suitcase is in an airport's vast baggage-handling system. A two-month test at Heathrow Terminal 1, for flights from Manchester and Munich, ended on January 31, 1999. The results are not conclusive.

(5)   Intelligent Stadium

Bank One Ballpark in Phoenix, Arizona, has an indoor/outdoor stadium. It is the first stadium ever labeled *intelligent*. It uses an extensive network of fiber-optic cables conveying information to and from the command-post concerning the stadium operation, environment, and communications. Thus from this mission control center, stadium lights, temperature, electronic scoreboards, up-to-the-minute player statistics, radio and television broadcasts, etc. can be regulated.

(6)   Cyber-Pet

Of course, one should not forget the cyber-pet Tamagochi, which literally means "baby-egg." The electronic infant demanded owner's attention for feeding, playing, cleaning, putting it to bed, just about everything. It also grew with time.

(7)   Intelligent Cello

The cello-playing robot called Mubot was demonstrated at the Tokyo International Robotic Exhibition in 1997. Designed by Professor Makoto Kajitani, it can play 30 tunes, from popular to classical.

(8)   Intelligent Toilet

Toto, Japan's largest toilet maker, unveiled in April 1999 the "intelligent toilet." It will do everything that its unsophisticated predecessors did plus perform urine and stool analysis as well as record the results. The first model measures the amount of sugar for diabetics. The company plans to follow that up with a range of other medical tests.

One can list many more: smart phones that find the cheapest rates for long distance calls (The Long Distance Manager by United America Corp.); smart homes where every electrical appliance will communicate its health status by e-mail (steam-iron has not been switched off, ice-maker in the refrigerator is not functioning, two milk bottles have passed the expiration date, etc.); smart cars negotiating automated highways; a mannequin with a large number of sensors to monitor injuries during simulated car accidents. We must not forget "smart" bombs, guided by laser, although those used during the Persian Gulf War in 1991 did not always live up to their name. Reports suggest that they could not be used during bad weather or beyond a certain distance, and they often required pilots to guide them to targets.

Under the sponsorship of World Automation Congress, there is an international competition aimed at designing robots that play soccer. Of course, they are called "intelligent" or "smart" robotic soccer players. Many universities around the world participate in this contest. An enormous amount of effort goes into the selection of the latest in sensors and actuators. Banks of computers work with sophisticated algorithms involving demanding control procedures. I had an opportunity to see a video of one of the recent finals. I must confess that it was the most disheartening experience to witness the unbelievable level of crude imitation of soccer players by a group of "intelligent" robots, supported by the cutting edge technology. No robot, irrespective of the level of its imparted "intelligence," will ever be able to duplicate lightening-speed decisions and the footwork of Pele, or the graceful glide of Michael Jordan, almost like a ballerina, to the basket. In the absence of life, clay substitutes are only pathetic jesters.

Some are searching for intelligent life on Mars, some are looking for intelligent machines, and still others are planning to use intelligent machines to search for intelligent life on Mars. We are so carried away with the idea of intelligent products that soon it will be impossible to find an item without it. When every product is intelligent, there is no need to use that label and suddenly things become ordinary, normal, conventional; what they really are.

Just because a robot is able to execute complicated tasks does not make it intelligent. The phrase *intelligent machine* is a misnomer. Robots merely execute instructions. Whatever intelligence involved is in algorithms and programs written by scientists. Intrinsically, the functional aspect of the machine does not change; it still follows instructions.

Mathew Golombek, a project scientist, called the Mars Rover, "... a remarkably dumb machine. It cannot roll and chew gum at the same time." This, of course, is true for any robot, no matter how sophisticated it may be, and not many can approach the engineering marvel of Rover. What is suggested here is the fact that spontaneous, independent expressions are foreign to robots. They are chained to previously established algorithms, computer codes, instructions, plans. Robots do not have minds of their own. They are merely obedient servants. By calling them "intelligent" we degrade the meaning of *intelligence*.

The "mind" of the robot must transform itself into nature's own mind and become the interpreter between nature and science. Isaiah Berlin, the Oxford University philosophy professor who died in 1998 at the age of 88, asserted: "There is no substitute for a sense of reality." Robots miss this fundamental blessing.

The above remarks in no way are meant to belittle great the contributions of robotics. Its achievements are many and magnificent. I have already touched upon a few in the context of space application. Robots have started to assist in surgery. The military is involved in developments of mini-helicopters and airplanes, even robotic birds and insects, for surveillance. Microsoft has experimented with ways to use human nervous system to control a computer. Dr. Ray Bakay of Emory University implanted electrodes in the brains of disabled people so that they could control computers by the power of thought. The implants enabled two paralyzed persons to move the cursor on the screen by simply thinking about it. Thus they were able to convey simple messages such as "I am thirsty" or "Please switch off the light" by moving the cursor to appropriate locations.

Robots have often attempted to mimic human physiology and motions. In fact, almost 500 year ago, Leonardo da Vinci made sketches of a humanoid robot that could wave its arms and move its head through a flexible neck. These drawings were discovered only in the 1950s by da Vinci scholar Carlo Pedretti. He called it "Robot Knight." Recently NASA, as well as Mark Rosheim, a US robotic expert, got interested in Leonardo's design. Rosheim said:[*]

"Leonardo's anatomy drawings are unique because he drew through the eyes of an engineer. They gave me the information I needed to emulate the complex joints and muscles of human body."

Using a stainless steel skeleton and linear motors, Rosheim built the "Automaton" for NASA, at a cost of 3.25 million dollars, and delivered it in September 1997. NASA is presently testing this product of unusual collaboration between the 15th century visionary and a 20th century cybernetics expert. Possible application include maintenance of the International Space Station and construction of habitats on the moon and Mars.

NASA has another project aimed at construction of tiny robots (mechanical platforms) capable of imitating such movements of insects as rowing, burrowing, hopping, hovering, and flying. These "biomorphic explorers" will carry sensors, relay data, reach locations normally not possible, and function on miniscule amount of power. They will be used for planetary exploration. These miniature robots, like worms, could crawl under rocks, move into cracks, dig tunnels in loose soil, and transmit information. Swarms of mosquito-like robots may fly into the Martian atmosphere and provide a detailed profile of the environment. Flight demonstration

---

[*] "Leonard – Inspired Robot Tested by NASA for Mars," *Vancouver Sun*, 12 August 1998.

of such devices under the New Millennium Program (meant for validation of new concepts) is likely to be in 2004.

Micro-machines employing nano-technology promise to bring molecular devices with a new range of applications including repair of minute veins and arteries.

One of the requirement for a robot to mimic "intelligence" is to acquire ability to store more information and process it faster. This requires putting more transistors on a given silicon chip. Intel's cofounder Gordon Moore predicted that the number of microscopic transistors packed on a chip would double every two years [3]. This "Moore's Law" has proved to be remarkably correct.

Chips continue to become smaller, more powerful and, with enormous amount of packed information, quite versatile. Robots with computers using these chips and advanced softwares will scale great heights. Their achievements in diverse areas of ocean, earth, and space will continue to marvel us.

Having said this, one cannot escape the fact that genius innovates what one must, and talent contributes what one can, while our "intelligent robots" merely follow instructions as well as they can.

Robots are often called "smart" and "intelligent" because they try to display attributes of learning, decision making, etc. and their operation depends on acquired knowledge. Knowledge is based on the collection of information, an ever incomplete process. Wisdom, on the other hand, is illusive but absolute. It is like butter floating at the surface of the churned buttermilk. Wisdom goes beyond the realm of knowledge, intellect, even intuition. One can talk about incomplete knowledge but not about incomplete wisdom.

In 1997, Gary Kasparov, the world chess champion, lost to IBM's Deep Blue-II supercomputer in a much publicized man–machine tournament. Does this not prove the superior intelligence of the machine? Far from it. It was not the contest between man and machine but between man (Kasparov) and machine (Deep Blue-II) assisted by a team of experts in the development of complex algorithms. The defeat only emphasized the nature of the game that required rapid computational skill, superior storage and retrieval capability, and enormous memory to select the desirable move from a wide spectrum of options for the long-term advantage. In this realm, machine's superiority is well established. Thus, for each tentative move, all the possible variations in the game, literally thousands of them, were at hand. The computer then followed the move that was most promising. This was repeated at every move. In fact, the IBM team developed the master software that enabled change of softwares in mid-match. It was the collective intelligence of the programmers, with the enormous speed and memory of the computer, that won the match. Kasparov lost to the joint efforts of men and machine. The ability of the Deep Blue to implement instructions cannot be equated with intelligence. Can the Deep Blue feel the living thought process Kasparov went through to arrive at his decisions? Can it experience his excitement, anxiety, enjoyment, and frustrations? Machine is beyond experience. Like a pen, it can write a letter without experiencing the beauty of the message. Intelligence and emotions spring from consciousness, not from a mass of metal and electronics. Kasparov played the game, the Deep Blue executed instructions.

There are machines which read aloud books to blind. Translating machines are gradually improving. In the future we will have machines that will translate the text into a desired language before spoken delivery. Thus a Japanese patient afflicted with blindness will still be able to enjoy the plays of Shakespeare (1564-1611). But the machine involved will never feel the beauty of the language and emotions involved.

The Greek poet Archilochus said: "The fox knows many things but the hedgehog knows one big thing."

Robots do many things, and quite well too, such as super-fast calculations (i.e. execution of instructions), lift tons of weight, fly at great heights and speeds, dive to the bottom of the deepest ocean, and other incredible feats. No human can match that. But we have one unique thing that is life, the basis of consciousness, experience, and intelligence.

Many have depended on the dictionary definitions of *intelligence* and *machine*, and synthesized them to evolve a crude notion of intelligent machines. However, illusive intelligence is more than definition. No matter how detailed the description of a robot based on functional attributes (knowledge-based, logic, decision making, learning, etc.), we all have experienced intelligence and hence recognize that something vital is left out.

The genius of creativity is foreign to robots. Exquisite beauty in the creations of Michelangelo, Beethoven, and Renoir are beyond their reach. Not only do they lack creativity but also they fail to express appreciation. No robot will be moved to write a poem on a gently gliding autumn leaf or carry the expression of wonder and disbelief on seeing the Pietà, as well as shed a few tears of grief.

Can a robot, a mechanical contraption, have awareness of consciousness? Can it think? Feel? Can it have emotions and ethical values? There are so many fundamental questions demanding response that one does not know where to start. In such an uncertain state, an assessment from the scientific point of view is a helpful beginning.

7 The Turing Test

As pointed out earlier, terms such as *thinking* and *smart machines, intelligent systems, expert systems, mechanisms with artificial intelligence* have become relatively common nowadays. We are led to believe that machines with artificial intelligence are here and, in the not too distant future, robots controlled by computers will be able to do what humans are able to achieve through their minds. Perhaps a clearer way of describing the situation would be as follows:

A robot controlled by a computer which, in turn, is governed by an algorithm based computer code written by a human mind can be represented as:

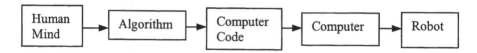

The question now is: Can the confluence of algorithm, code, computer, and robot be equated to the human mind?

Alan Turing (1912-1954), a Cambridge graduate, was a brilliant mathematician. During World War II, he played a leading role in breaking German codes. In 1950, through an article in the philosophical journal *Mind*, Turing proposed a test to identify a machine with human intelligence [4]. Let us say a new computer model has been introduced which the manufacturer claims to think like human. How to assess the validity of that claim? According to the Turing Test, first a competent moderator (Q) is established whose task is to ask questions, receive answers, and pursue further questioning based on the answers received. Next, a human participant (H) in the test is identified. Both the participant (H) and the computer (C) are behind a curtain, thus beyond the view of Q. The interrogator communicates, i.e. questions the two (H and C), in an indirect way through key-boards and monitors (see Figure 8). If over a series of tests, the moderator is consistently unable to identify the human (H), then the computer (i.e. the designer and the programmer) is termed *intelligent*.

Although, on the surface this seemed to be convincing, scientists quickly recognized that the test has several fundamental limitations:

(1)   It does not address the important issues of consciousness, experience, understanding, sense of aesthetics, and ethics.

(2)   The test is not fair and is subject to manipulation. The human volunteer (H) is expected to give honest answers; however, the machine may lie to hide its identity in order to look human.

(3)   The outcome depends on the nature of the questions and answers received and the ability of the moderator to pursue them further.

Penrose [5] has discussed these issues at considerable length. For us, it is sufficient to realize that science does not have a reliable way to judge human intelligence and its presence in machines.

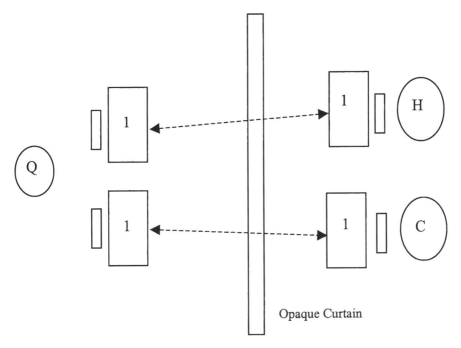

Opaque Curtain

1: Monitor with keyboard

Figure 8: Set-up for the Turing Test.

8 Turing Machine and Gödel Theorem

Turing in England and Hungarian born John von Neumann in the USA are considered pioneers of the modern computer age. Von Neumann developed the theory of games and invented the notion of stored programs for digital computers. He used to say: "A Hungarian enters the revolving door after you and comes out ahead of you."

For code-breaking, Turing developed a mechanical contraption, referred to as "The Turing Machine" [5], which was the forerunner of modern computers. Computer runs according to an algorithm based code, which is nothing but a set of instructions, the methodology for solving a given problem. Perhaps the most ancient as well as famous algorithm, associated with Euclid (around 300 BC), is that for finding the highest common divisor of two numbers. The algorithm is rather simple. For example, consider numbers 3,264 and 1,320:

Remainder

3,264 ÷ 1,320	⟶	624
1,320 ÷ 624	⟶	72
624 ÷ 72	⟶	48
72 ÷ 48	⟶	24
48 ÷ 24	⟶	0

Thus 24 is the highest common divisor.

Performing of the above operations using a modern computer would involve storing numbers obtained during execution of the algorithm in the computer's memory. As there is no limit as to the value of the numbers chosen, the memory needed may be quite large. In theory, for complex algorithms involving large numbers, or peculiar combinations of numbers, infinite memory may be demanded. According to knowledgeable scientists in the field, this suggests limit to the operational capability of computers [6].

Another problem rests with the ability of computers to solve problems according to algorithms. The great German mathematician David Hilbert posed a question in 1928: Is there some general procedure for answering all mathematical problems, belonging to a broad but well-defined class? In 1931, the brilliant Austrian logician Kurt Gödel [5,7,8,9] came to the conclusion: No. The Gödel theorem suggests that, no matter how comprehensive the algorithm is, there always exists a problem which cannot be solved by following its steps. For example, if the algorithm involves "Fermat's last theorem" to determine combinations of integers x, y, z, n for which the following equation is valid,

$$(x+1)^{n+3} + (y+1)^{n+3} = (z+1)^{n+3},$$

the Turing Machine or a modern computer will keep on searching the combination forever. Leaving aside the weighty issues of consciousness, experience, etc., Gödel's theorem points out the fundamental limitation of algorithm-driven computers.

9 Some Thoughts on Core Issues

9.1 Basic Attributes

Is the brain a computer? Can a machine think? The central issue is not the ability of computers to mimic certain human behavior, however inadequate the imitation may be (and it is so as indicated earlier), but to understand the fundamental basis behind the behavior. What really transpires when one sees a beautiful painting or listens to a pleasing music? This involves the life-based consciousness with unique fundamental attributes of experience, understanding, emotions, intuition, memory, and others. One may call them *basic attributes* forming cornerstones of our lifestream. Let us pose a few questions at this stage:

1. Do we understand these basic attributes? What tools have we to try to explore them? Are these tools adequate?

2. Can the basic attributes be transmitted to machines? Is it possible to impart to computers what we do not know?

The mind is more than a computer made of meat. Our sense perceptions transcend transducers. Machine vision may scan a Renoir or witness a sunrise but can it experience the flood of esthetic feelings aroused and the accompanying sense of tranquility, satisfaction, uplifting of the unknown inner being, development of an invisible bond with the rest of the universe? A computer is beyond consciousness. It is unaware of pleasure and pain, appreciation of aesthetics, obligation and duty, meditative detachment, unexplainable inclination, and intuition. These are beyond clever algorithms of an ingeneous programmer. Execution of instructions is not experience. A robot may grasp a baby's hand but will miss my interplay of emotions when I touch the same hand.

Philosopher Ludwig Wittgenstein, perhaps the greatest authority on human thought this century has produced, pointed out [6] that in order to become conscious, a machine will have to have life experiences such as pleasure and pain, grief and joy. Conclusions not confirmed by experience have no legs on which to stand. Biologist J.B.S. Haldane asserted that mind transcends matter, hence regardless of how sophisticated the machine can get, it will never be able to capture and display that mysterious force called intelligence [6]. Computers may attempt to imitate human sense perceptions through vision cameras, tactile sensors, and other transducers, something like artificial flowers vainly attempting to capture nature. However, no plastic flower can fool a bee. Electric wires conducting electrons cannot replace arteries and veins carrying the life-giving blood. Our intrinsic uniqueness is beyond computers. Intelligence is more than organization of instructions. There is no substitute for life. The shadow of life has no life.

Another important aspect concerns transmissibility of the "basic attributes." It is apparent that what we cannot comprehend, cannot be transmitted. However, it must be emphasized that the "basic attributes," even if understood, cannot be transferred to other humans or robots. The life process is unique. Experience cannot be cast into an algorithm. Consciousness cannot be explained. Any attempt to do so only leads to copies.

9.2 The Two Worlds

We try to understand the world around us through sense-based experiences. But experiences can be so diverse, have so many facets, that they have to be observed from several angles, using different branches of sciences. Inquiries into gravitational field, Plank's constant, genes, fusion, black holes, and many more involve physics, chemistry, biology, astronomy, etc.

Around 3000 BC, Vedic scientists grappled with the questions such as: What is this universe? Who am I? What is the meaning of life? What is my destiny? They discovered that the universe of experiences consists of two broad categories: the subjective and the objective. Modern science has mostly focused on the objective aspect. Only recently it has started to recognize the importance of the other world of consciousness, intellect, experience, and similar basic attributes of life.

The world revealed to us by the data collected by five senses is only a small fraction of the total existence. It gives us knowledge of the world outside which is amenable to sense perceptions. Transducers we use to gather data are merely extensions of our senses. But there is a world beyond sense perceptions, the inner world, which science is slowly beginning to recognize. Thus the present science examines only a part of the total reality, a fraction of the complete truth. The truth remains unchanged no matter how we examine it. It needs no endorsement or sanction because it is universal.

As Sir James Jeans put it: "The world revealed by the twentieth-century science is an abstract world far removed from the world of familiar experiences." Sir Arthur Eddingten suggests that science gives us only the knowledge of structural form and not the insight into content ([10], p. 9).

In 1959, to celebrate the centenary of Darwin's publication of *The Origin of Species*, a symposium entitled "Evolution after Darwin" was organized by Chicago University. The general chairman of the symposium, Sir Julian Huxley, remarked in the opening address:

"This nature, starting as mere cosmic dust and passing through various stages of evolution, entered the biological phase by becoming a living cell, and continued to develop, first a nerve fiber, then the nervous system which, in the stage of human assumed a new dimension through awareness of the inner world in addition to the outer world" ([10], p. 17).

Late paleontologist Teilhard de Chardin said: "We do realize today that the universe has not merely a 'without' but also 'within.' In human, nature has disclosed a 'within' view of itself by itself. We are merely a miniature edition of nature. Ego, self-awareness, ethical values, etc. are merely icebergs floating in the deep uncharted ocean" ([10], p.17)

Science has given us some truths, unchanging principles, "basic attributes," in the external world. To reach the inner world, we need to discipline the mind through meditative objective detachment to penetrate the veil of separation. Just as scientific experiments require controlled conditions for success, so is the case with experiments aimed at comprehending the inner world.

Truths of the inner world will have to be discovered and experienced at the individual level. The search of the inner world is entirely democratic, socialistic to the core. The ultimate reality is accessible to all. Truth cannot be exclusive. However, it can be approached only individually, as experience accepts no substitute.

9.3 Pervasive Intellect

Every cell has a role to play, through the information it carries, in sustaining the process of life. The Human Genome Project, launched in 1989, hopes to identify by year 2004 around 100,000 genes and the physical characteristics they control through instructions in the form of "sentences." Each "sentence" is composed of hundreds of "words," and every "word" is constructed of three "letters" (out of four available). In fact, the Genome Project involves identification of around 3 billion "letters."

Note, here we have just the biochemical representation of genes. The mechanism of their operation and the interactions to control human functions have remained beyond our reach, because they are more than chemistry. Algorithms that govern robotic behavior and the human mind are fundamentally different.

In the universe we live in, everything affects everything else. Newton's law of mutual attraction is only a small aspect of universe. Someone called this phenomenon "The Butterfly Effect" by suggesting that the flapping wings of a butterfly in Peru could affect the weather in Vancouver. The same is true with the inner world. We are talking about consciousness, experience, intelligence, etc. which are globally distributed at the cellular level. Moreover, we have no understanding as to what they mean or the basis of their existence. Action of any cell affects the working of a large group of other cells in a mysterious way. Algorithms and codes we develop to govern actuators have no appreciation as to the pervasive character of consciousness. They merely operate discrete joints. On the other hand, when the eye "sees," just about every cell of the optic system is involved in "seeing." Thus in the miracle "machine" that is human, intelligence is suffused at the most fundamental level, in the living cell. For robot the basic unit may be a transistor on the chip. A frog in a well cannot appreciate the infinite expanse of the ocean.

9.4 Limit of Knowledge

Human ingenuity has scaled many peaks and will continue to do so, however, eventually we face a peak that is beyond our reach. Certain secrets of nature cannot be unlocked and will always remain elusive. We have to accept the fact that beyond certain limit, the nature of life as governed by the "basic attributes" is unknowable and will remain unknown. Life is such a profound puzzle that we meet a wall of silence in attempting to decipher it. In the *Gita*, Shri Krishna says, "Maunam cha Asmi Guhyanam — I am the silence in the inscrutable" [11]. We meet this silence when the life is explored at its utmost depth, as in the case of the previously mentioned "basic attributes." All we can do is to try to make objective observations based on limited sense perceptions and speculations prompted by intuition.

The fact that we know virtually nothing about the "basic attributes" is brought to light by a recent announcement. Dr. Kathleen Akins, a philosophy professor at Simon Fraser University, was awarded (January 1999) the James S. McDonnell Fellowship worth one million dollars (over ten years) to study how the human mind works. We may not be able to unlock the mystery of life, yet we will have to make a beginning, however humble it may be. After all, a journey fulfills itself in every step.

10 Social and Ethical Considerations

The world has witnessed spectacular achievements of the machine age which has also brought with it pollution of the air, earth, and water; smoke-filled cities, noise, and urban ghettoes; smog, acid rain, and diseases. Mass production, which robots made possible, also led to unemployment of the masses. Some do not have to work; many cannot work. Often it has failed to add stature to human dignity and helped deaden the spirit. Robots have narrowed the difference between the living and the dead. What the industrial revolution brought was a promise to help an individual but ended up encroaching upon individuality.

In the bygone days, when a bicycle came to an Asian village, it represented a revolution in transportation. With it came the task of maintenance and repair. The village world stretched its boundaries to the nearby settlements and so did the communication, economic transactions, and social interactions. Now a potter could sell his wares in the village fifty, even a hundred kilometers away, and brides began to arrive from the "distant" worlds. All these took time, maybe 5 to 10 years, and the society progressively adjusted to the gross as well as subtle changes, always remaining in equilibrium.

But now needless technological innovations are thrust upon the society unasked, at such a pace that it has no time to adjust and find equilibrium. The society as a whole is unable to adjust to all aspects of their influence before new models arrive. We are in a perpetual state of instability. With a blank stare of wonder we keep on accepting products, for that is considered modern, being with the times, synonymous with progress. In 19th century Africa, natives accepted colored beads and matches with awe. We find ourselves no different today. We have become a culture without a culture.

In 1997, there were 712,000 industrial robots in operation. Of course, 413,000 were in Japan — one for every 36 workers. In Toyota's car assembly plant, one literally has to search to notice workers because their role has changed to checking and maintaining tuned conditions of robots. Such a high level of automation has led to unexpected problems. Although salary has increased with time, there is no job satisfaction. Workers carry a sense of alienation from the society; they feel unwanted. Mental sickness, family quarrels, divorces, and suicide rates increase. The problem is considered so important that the *Journal of Japan Society of Mechanical Engineers* devoted one of its issues [12,13] entirely to this subject. Thus, as in any area, there is an optimum level of development, which when exceeded hurts rather than helps.

To create with the hands is a natural instinct with which man is born. He takes pleasure in his creation. Here lies an uninterrupted flow of life between the hands and their creation. Such a subtle yet vital interplay in the passage of life is beyond any robot. A canoe of the west coast Indian is a genuine expression of its creator and not an impersonal product of machinery. Robots have dead hands which render living hands dead.

Let us not slip into the illusion that we are succeeding in conquering and exploiting nature through machine. It is a goal that is neither worthy nor attainable. Long ago Thoreau decried the mechanical ugliness of progress. In this war that man and machine are waging against nature there are no victors, only victims.

In the dynamic whirlpool of life, in this restless existence, in these layers of culture, science, technology, and religions that envelope us, we often lose sight of our true being. We are so preoccupied with satisfying the demands of our desires that we have neither time nor inclination to seek the truth. Existence becomes suffering thorough ignorance. Most of our pursuits have very little to do with knowing ourselves a little better. We are reluctant to reevaluate our objectives and priorities in life.

Machine is a product of our intellect. Intellect cannot create life anymore than a flower can bloom according to an equation. If machines have failed, to that extent their creators have failed. If machines have created problems, to that extent our inner being is clouded and turbulent. Unless we find peace and tranquility within, we cannot create instruments of peace and tranquility. Evils of industrialization reflect ignorance and evil within us. "Intelligent" machines are products of what we are, not what we think we are.

11 Closing Comments

The 17th century French philosopher René Descartes observed: "I think, therefore I am." For a thinking individual he implied consciousness, intellect, understanding, memory, emotion, and other "basic attributes" associated with life. Even today, we have only fleetingly vague acquaintance of these elements at the fundamental level. We cannot transfer these properties to robots. The automated cello of Prof. Kajitani mentioned earlier can never play an original score on its own, nor can it provide the feelings of players and improvisations. It is like a trained parrot performing a set of tricks taught by the master.

Of course, this does not mean that robotic devices are not playing useful roles. The robotic revolution is pushing ahead with an incredible force and will dominate all aspects of our society. Automation is often considered necessary, even indispensable. However, let us not be prisoners of the illusion that we are creating intelligent machines. The basis of total human intelligence is beyond our grasp and, I think, will always remain so. Our robots perform according to algorithms developed using the incomplete information of the outer world, based on limited sense perceptions. The level of our knowledge is consistent with the extent of our ignorance. Ability to execute instructions does not equate to intelligence or experience. Our machines, devoid of life-giving consciousness which we do not comprehend, will always remain crude efforts at mimicking reality.

Mind is more than a digital computer. Algorithm is active when engaged. Robot has life only when in operation. However, the mind is alive until the life departs. It transcends sense-based comprehension that is science. Scientific theory of mind does not exist. No algorithm can awaken awareness, nor is there a transducer to measure cognition. We must accept and respect the limit of knowledge. Machines, no matter how cleverly they imitate humans, cannot become human. Robot may be the echo of our voice, but it can never be the voice. The shadow can never replace the self.

Human is an intelligent being. But the being does not consist solely of intellect. Beyond intellect lies intuition. It is the extension of perceptions to regions beyond senses. According to Vedic seers, who were also inquirers like scientists, our inner being is revealed only through intuitive apprehension. We recognize the truth but do not reason about it. Existence cannot be argued about; it must be experienced. What is real cannot be affirmed by reason (algorithm).

Sir Arthur Eddington referred to the electron as "something whose mathematical specification can be given. It works but we do not know why." Poincaré called his mathematical discoveries "artistic intuition." The truth shapes itself from within and leaps forth as a spark from fire. The truth is not so much produced as achieved. Archimedes solved the problem in his bathtub, not in his study [13].

Thought cannot stir without faith and to that extent machine is a creation of our faith. But it will never be able to search the outermost bounds of nature and the utmost depths of our inner world, and can never comprehend the force that binds them. No machine, no computer will ever be able to enjoy a sunset, nor will it be able to describe its total beauty. Intuition is communion between knower and the known. Between me and the robot the link is a switch.

From the beginning of time, we have always strived to be masters, conquerors. As we have failed to decipher the miracle associated with the breath of life, the consolation lies in designing machines which try to imitate nature's magic, and we label them "intelligent." No matter how we manipulate definitions, intelligent machine remains and will continue to remain a mirage. It is a myth perpetuated by designers and algorithm experts. However, it is a pleasant myth that carries a touch of magic, pats our confidence, pampers our vanity, and, perhaps, boosts our ego.

Those who view mind as computer [14] would suggest that nature has not programmed us to comprehend consciousness. However, why we do not possess the algorithm to decipher the mystery of life is, perhaps, the greatest mystery. One can imagine Bernard Shaw reacting to the situation with his curt pithy remark: "Artificial intelligence is the wisdom of the fool; or is it the folly of the wise? After all, no creation of man manages its affairs as well as a tree does."

We should not overlook the ethical consideration which expects us to distinguish between what is possible and what is desirable. Life imposes on us the obligation to be compassionate, considerate, and true. Obviously, we cannot pass these obligations to robots. Ability to create must also evaluate the desirability of the creation. There lies the distinction between intellect and wisdom.

The last 500 years have given us an age of exploration. Columbus explored the West, Vasco de Gama the East. Exploration of the oceans and space have followed. Our instruments have mapped the deepest ocean floor and spacecraft have gone beyond the solar system. Our telescopes have touched the outer fringes of the universe.

Now we are ready to enter a new universe which was always with us, yet we have been a stranger to it all along: the inner world of consciousness from where springs the true intelligence. The time has come when we should ask the question which the Vedic seers posed at the beginning of time: What is that knowing which all the rest is known?

References

[1]   Modi, V.J., "Man, the Unknown: Fleeting Impressions of an Uncertain Mind," *Acta Astronautica*, Vol. 41, No. 2, pp. 63-90, 1998.

[2]   Antsaklis, P., "Defining Intelligent Control," *IEEE Control Systems*, pp. 4, 5, 58-66, June 1994.

[3]   *Time*, p. 58, December 2, 1996,.

[4]   Turing, A.M., "Computing Machinery and Intelligence," *Mind*, Vol. 59, No. 236, 1950; also *The Mind's I*, Editors: D.R. Hofstadter and D.C. Dennett, Basic Books Inc., Penguin Books, Ltd., Harmondsworth, Middlesex, UK, 1981.

[5]   Penrose, R., *Emperor's New Mind*, Vintage Books Publisher, London, England, 1990.

[6]   Casti, J.L., *The Cambridge Quintet*, Addison-Wesley Publisher, Reading, Massachusetts, USA, 1998.

[7]   Gödel, K., "Über Formal Unentscheidbare Sätze der Principia Mathematica und Verwandter Systeme I," *Monatschefte für Mathematik und Physik*, Vol. 38, pp. 173-196, 1931.

[8]   Good, I.J., "Gödel's Theorem Is a Red Herring," *British Journal of Philosophical Science*, Vol. 18, pp. 359-373, 1969.

[9]   Singh, S., *Fermat's Enigma*, Penguin Books, London, England, 1998.

[10]   Ranganathananda, S., *Vedanta and Science*, The Ramakrishna Mission Institute of Culture Publisher, Calcutta, India, 2nd Edition, 1996.

[11]   Chidbhavananda, S., *The Bhagavada Gita*, Sri Ramakrishna Tapovan Publisher, Madras, India, Chapter 10, Verse 38, pp. 572-574, 1974.

[12]   *Journal of the Japan Society of Mechanical Engineers*, Vol. 85, No. 758, January 1982.

[13]   Modi, V.J., "Man and Machine," *The BC Professional Engineer*, pp. 7-9, May 1982.

[14]   Pinker, S., *How the Mind Works*, W.W. Norton Publisher, New York, 1998.

[15]   Clarke, A.C., *2001: A Space Odyssey*, New American Library, New York, 1968.

4 | RESEARCH ADVANCES IN INTELLIGENT MACHINES

Devendra P. Garg, Fellow ASME
Professor of Mechanical Engineering
Duke University
Durham, NC

and

Former Director
Dynamic Systems and Control Program
National Science Foundation
Arlington, VA

Intelligent machines [1,2] have been attracting increased attention and interest worldwide. Such machines have the capability to sense both expected and unexpected changes in their work environment and take appropriate actions quickly and efficiently. IBM Corporation's Deep Blue computer [3], which played the game of chess against Kasparov, is an example of an intelligent machine in action against a human. The current accelerated pace of technological progress holds an excellent promise to make significant advances in many emerging application areas: for example, the development of smart automobiles that would avoid collisions, insect-size sensors that would detect sub-surface deadly mines, and intelligent refrigerators that would withhold unhealthy foods from dieters. The basic challenge in the area of intelligent machines is to integrate computers, sensors, controllers, actuators, software, and machines that would lead to devices that are adaptive, flexible, and robust. In this chapter, in addition to presenting the basic concepts related to intelligent machines, several areas of their application are discussed. This is followed by a description of intelligent systems and of the resources invested in research by the US National Science Foundation. Several examples of projects supported under the Learning and Intelligent Systems (LIS) program and the Knowledge and Distributed Intelligence (KDI) initiative are given. The chapter concludes with a discussion of research challenges in the area of intelligent machines.

1 Intelligent Machines

According to Webster's Dictionary [4], the word *intelligence* originated from the Latin word *intelligentia* and means "the ability to learn, or understand, or to deal with new or trying situations." Also, it implies "the ability to apply knowledge to manipulate one's environment or to think abstractly as measured by objective criteria." The word *machine* is derived from the Latin word *machina* or the Greek word *mechane* and means "a constructed thing, whether material or immaterial; an assemblage of parts that transmits forces, motion, and energy one to another in a predetermined manner; a mechanically, electrically, or electronically operated device for performing a task (e.g., calculating)." Combining the two words together, it would appear that *intelligent machines* could be thought of as those machines that integrate sensors, actuators, software, and computers and have a capability of acquiring information efficiently, and responding safely and rapidly to both deterministic changes and/or unexpected events. A detailed discussion of these concepts was given in Chapters 1 and 2. Currently, most of the intelligent machines research activities appear to be in the robotics area [5,6] wherein an integration of vision [7], force-torque, proximity, and other types of sensors [8] is being implemented, and a variety of nonlinear control strategies [9] such as variable structure control [10], adaptive control [11], optimal control [12], neural network control [13-15], and fuzzy logic control [16,17] is being used for single and multiple manipulators cooperating in an intelligent mode (see Chapters 6-9).

2 Application Areas of Intelligent Machines

Intelligent machines can play a potentially dominant role in a variety of areas such as manufacturing, service industry, space explorations, defense, and nonmilitary operations. Such systems, combined with advanced robotics, are critical to the enhancement of national and international security and technological development of the global community. In the manufacturing sector, they can improve product quality and output, as well as assure a safe and efficient work environment. In the food processing industry, effective use of such devices would eliminate back-breaking work resulting from heavy and dangerous cutting and carving operations. Similarly, the automotive, mining, agriculture, and construction industries can benefit from intelligent systems and the use of intelligent machines incorporating sensor-based control. In addition, there are a number of areas in which the intelligent machines will find immediate applications. These include, for example, assistance to the elderly or the physically challenged; materials handling, food preparation, and services; hazardous waste handling systems; surveillance and military applications; games, sports, and entertainment; and medical and surgical assistance.

In the area of assisting the elderly and the physically challenged, the intelligent machines can increase their mobility and independence, thus leading to a happier life and reducing their health-care costs. In the materials handling area such machines could be used for handling and delivering packages of arbitrary shapes, dealing with material flow of varying viscosity and temperature, and moving heavy material palleted in irregular shapes and sizes.   In the area of food preparation and services, such machines could handle cleaning and cutting of chicken and fish, preparing cuts of meat of various specific grades, and preparing and serving a variety of fast foods.   In the area of hazardous waste handling, intelligent machines could handle nuclear, bio-hazardous, and toxic materials for disposal.

In the military and surveillance area, intelligent machines could perform stealth operations; act as unmanned aerial vehicles that may be quieter and even smaller than helicopters, all-weather, all-terrain ground vehicles possibly smaller than the size of a brief case, equipped with vision and other sensors and communication equipment; and autonomous small submersible vehicles deployable and operable with minimum human training and presence.   In the area of agriculture, mining, and construction industry, such machines could deal with blasting, tunneling, and construction of nonstandard buildings, industrial plants, and futuristic structures. Related to the area of games, sports, and entertainment, there are limitless opportunities to develop innovative games, competitions, and educational activities. Finally, in the area of medical and surgical assistance, intelligent machines could assist in the collection and removal of bio-hazardous waste material, protection from infection, diagnosing illnesses, and performing intricate and micro-surgical procedures and prosthetic functions.

3 Typical Applications of Intelligent Robotics

3.1 Introduction

A large body of literature is available that describes intelligent robots that navigate, map, plan, and operate in the real world.   Most of this work attempts to emulate insect-level locomotion and navigation [18].   In Japan, the Honda Motor Corporation has developed a humanoid robot during a secret ten-year project. The first version of this robot was P2 and the second one was P3.   The project was later opened to other corporations to solicit their cooperation and the collaboration of government laboratories. Also, a "remote-brained robot" was developed in Japan to realize the dream of intelligent robotics in the form of humanoid robots [19].   This was accomplished by combining a large-scale brain and a limber body in the humanoid system. Reactive robots are used in production management and industrial process control.   These reactive robots [20] are well suited for applications in modern industries that necessitate a high degree of autonomy and reactivity to unforeseen events.   The Mobile Robot Surrogate (MRS) is a means of developing autonomy in complex systems [21].   A central aspect of this methodology, which is typically used to analyze and interpret data for landmark identification and navigation, is that the operator receives the same sensor information through a tele-robotic interface as the robot does.

Another research project, called MARTHA, dealt with the management and control of a fleet of autonomous mobile robots for trans-shipment tasks in the harbors, marshalling yards, and airports [22]. The most challenging task in this application was multi-robot cooperation. One of the major goals of the project was to study the use of mobile robots with as little decentralized control as possible. The key solution to the decentralization problem is to give more autonomy to the vehicles, thus allowing them to cope with unexpected events and obstacles, inaccurate environment models, and other vehicles. Smithers [23] argues that the loose and varied use of the term *autonomous* in artificial intelligence, robotics, and artificial life has robbed these fields of the important concept of autonomy. He stresses the fact that robots and other intelligent agents will have to be autonomous, i.e., self-law making, not just self-regulating, if they are to be able to effectively deal with the existing environments. Not only do these environments have significant large-scale spatial and temporal invariant structure, but also they have large amounts of local spatial and temporal dynamic variations and unpredictability.

Mataric and her colleagues [24-28] have developed a methodology for selecting and designing a set of basic behaviors that serves as a substrate for a large repertoire of higher level interactions through the application of two general combination operators that allow for overlapping and switching behaviors. Adaptation of reinforced learning can be applied to basis behaviors in order to have a group of mobile robots to learn a complex foraging behavior in a group. A group of robots, initially equipped with a strategy for foraging, are shown to have learned yielding, proceeding, communicating, listening, and a set of social behaviors, that essentially minimize interference and maximize group effectiveness. In the following section a few typical examples of intelligent machines applications (primarily robotic) from a variety of sectors are discussed.

3.2 Intelligent Industrial Applications

Automation of coal harvesting at a major Australian open cut mine located at Morwell, Victoria, is being studied at Monash University. This mine provides a significant quantity of coal for power generation in Victoria [29]. An intelligent unmanned mining system consisting of computer-assisted remote operation of mining machines and services and robotics technology is devised. As an example of application from another field, CyberGlass robot is an intelligent glass blowing robot developed by a French company [30]. Its intelligent functions for various glass-blowing techniques are adapted from those currently used by highly skilled and well-trained workers.

A fully automated unmanned harvester combines the lunar rover and the terrestrial vehicular technologies for development of mobile agricultural equipment — FieldNav, the digital machine, and FieldHand, the digital operator [31]. It utilizes safety and customized electronics; modifications for drive-by-wire, the event driven behavior-based-architecture; sensing for crop line tracking; and detectors.

3.3 Health Care Applications

Collaborative research is in progress between both the Berkeley and San Francisco campuses of the University of California with Endo-robotics Corporation to develop milli-robotic tools for remote, minimally invasive surgery [32]. Novel techniques have been adapted from the micro-electromechanical systems (MEMS) area for the design of the milli-robots, their actuators, tactile sensors, and displays. A test bed tele-surgical work-station has been set up at Berkeley. RoboDoc is an integrated computer-based medical imaging and surgical robotic system. For many surgeons, this system has far exceeded their initial expectations [33,34]. The Integrated Surgical Systems, a California based company, created RoboDoc, which is used for performing total hip replacement surgery. OrthoDoc, a computer work-station, enables orthopedic surgeons to examine a patient's bone more accurately and devise a pre-operative plan for surgery. Over 850 patients in six hospitals worldwide have received surgical procedures performed by RoboDoc.

Tele-presence systems improve surgeons' performance in minimally invasive surgery (MIS) and microsurgery and also enable them to operate on patients remotely over great distances, whether across the room, across the state, or across countries. In microsurgery, the technology can scale down the surgeons' motions, forces, and field of view allowing them to skillfully operate on microscopic anatomy via force-reflecting manipulators integrated with digital servo controllers, stereo viewing systems, and intelligent communication links [35].

The Sensor-Aided Intelligent Wheelchair Navigation System SENARIO project is aimed toward developing a sensor-aided intelligent navigation system that provides high-level navigational aids to the users of powered wheelchairs [37]. The technical challenges in this research include task/path planning, sensing, and positioning for indoor mobile robots as well as user interface issues. The system can accept typical motion commands through a voice-actuated or standard joystick interface. It supports robot motion with obstacle/collision avoidance features. Similarly, an intelligent white cane called GuideCane, that blind people can use to find their way, was developed by researchers at the University of Michigan [38]. The cane is really a robot that gently guides them around any obstacles in their path. The base of this robot is a crescent-shaped array of ultrasonic sensors that scans the area ahead. A built-in computer interprets the data from the sensors, calculates the best route every 50 milliseconds, and steers the device accordingly. The GuideCane weighs about 4 kilograms and require no maintenance other than recharging its batteries. Still another example is the PLAYBOT, a directable intelligent robot, which may enable physically disabled children to access and manipulate toys [36]. Vision is the primary sensor required to search the environment; users and environments must be natural and dynamic; and safety is of paramount importance.

3.4 Service Sector Applications

In a new approach, an intelligent mobile robot was successfully trained to keep clear an arena surrounded by walls by locating, recognizing, and grasping "garbage" objects and taking the collected objects outside the arena [39]. Intelligent control systems assisted in performing a non-trivial sequence of behaviors using the methodology by canalizing the evolutionary process in the right direction. The RoboKent [40] is a robotic floor-cleaning robot to assist the housekeeping industry. It provides a method of scrubbing and sweeping floors without a human being trailing a machine.

FLIMAR is a four-legged, intelligent, mobile, autonomous robot with intelligent sensing and decision-making capabilities. Multiple sensors with embedded knowledge bases and learning capabilities are used in a novel approach to environmental perception and reaction [41]. The robot has the capability of functioning at various degrees of intelligence made possible by an object-oriented architecture with embedded intelligence at various levels. The robot can walk and turn without dragging and skidding and can turn about its center of gravity. In addition, it responds to light, sound, and touch in different ways, based upon prevailing environmental conditions.

3.5 Games and Sports Applications

Multiple autonomous mobile robots exhibiting cooperative behavior are extremely important for developing games and sports applications. Groups of cooperating mobile robots require solutions to issues such as resolution of conflict, group architecture, level of cooperation, learning, and geometric problems. The RoboCup Physical Agent Challenge [42,43] provides a good test bed for how physical bodies play a significant role in realizing intelligent behaviors. In this robot soccer game playing task, a wide range of technologies needs to be integrated. These single-agent skills and cooperative behaviors include shooting, passing or dribbling the ball in the presence of stationary or moving obstacles; catching the ball from an opponent or a teammate; and passing the ball between two players.

In recent years, the domain of complex board games such as Go, Checkers, Othello, and Backgammon have been widely regarded as ideal testing grounds for exploring the use of artificial intelligence and machine learning. These games present challenges of extreme complexity and sophistication to play at an expert level. One game-learning program, devised by Gerald Tesauro [44], is called TD-Gammon. This is a neural network-based algorithm that trains itself to be an evaluation function for the game of backgammon by playing against itself and learning from the outcome. The term TD stands for Temporal-Difference. The basic idea of these learning methods is based on the difference between temporally successive predictions. That is, the goal of learning is to make the learner's current prediction for the current input pattern more closely match the next prediction at the next time step.

3.6 Space Applications

The tele-robotics Program of the National Aeronautics and Space Administration (NASA) Office of Space Science is developing intelligent tele-robotics technologies to enable or support a wide range of space missions over the next decade and beyond. These technologies fall into several core application areas: landers, surface vehicles, and aero-vehicles for solar applications and science; revers for commercially supported lunar activities; free-flying and platform-attached robots for in-orbit servicing and assembly; and robots supporting in-orbit biotechnology and micro-gravity experiments [45]. Such advanced and intelligent machines will enable missions to explore Mars, Venus, and Saturn's moon Titan, as well as probes to sample comets and asteroids. The Micro-rover Flight Experiment (MFEX) is NASA Office of Advanced Concepts and Technology experiment integrated with the Mars Pathfinder lander and spacecraft system [46]. After landing, the MFEX was deployed from the lander and began a mission to conduct a series of technology experiments, placed an alpha proton x-ray spectrometer on rocks and soil, and imaged the lander.

4 Research in Intelligent Systems

Research in intelligent systems is of great interest to the National Science Foundation. As an example, to support this research effort, the National Science Foundation's Dynamic Systems and Control (DSC) Program initiated research plans and funded a very successful 3-day workshop [47] entitled "New Directions in Intelligent Systems." This workshop was held in Gaithersburg, MD, from June 10 to 12, 1996. The main goal of the workshop was to bring together researchers from universities, practicing engineers from industry, and representatives from the government and private research organizations for identifying new research directions needed for the US industry to prepare for the challenges of the next century.

The areas chosen for discussion were intelligent control, dynamic systems, and innovative strategies for measurement, sensing, and actuation. The deliberations were primarily related to computational architecture, learning and adaptation, and human and machine integration. The specific types of industries included in discussions were automotive, power and energy, semiconductor and computer manufacturing, chemical and materials processing, and biotechnology and medical devices. The workshop provided an outstanding opportunity for members of the research community and potential sponsors of a variety of research projects to hold a face-to-face dialogue and to identify areas of research needs and likely collaborations.

The National Science Foundation recently announced a new initiative for research called the Learning and Intelligent Systems (LIS). Six NSF research directorates were involved in supporting and managing this special initiative via the LIS Coordinating Committee. The main objective of this activity was to stimulate interdisciplinary research to promote the use and development of information and communication technologies spanning a wide spectrum of fields. It encouraged researchers in various disciplines, such as social and behavioral sciences, biology, education, computer science and engineering, and physical and mathematical sciences to share their collective resources to contribute and integrate ideas leading to an enhanced understanding of the learning and intelligence of both living and nonliving systems. Typical areas that were addressed included how humans and synthetic mechanisms operate, how intelligent machines could be built to respond to learner's needs, and what unifying principles underlie and connect the diverse phenomena that constitute intelligence and learning. The National Science Foundation invested over $19.5 M from the FY '97 budget and made a firm commitment for the initiative to continue in FY '98 and beyond.

Since the program's inception, NSF has placed a significant emphasis on research in the area of learning and intelligent systems. Two other related areas of potential interest to the dynamic systems and control research community are New Computational Challenges, and Knowledge Networking. All three of these areas taken together fall under the umbrella of Knowledge and Distributed Intelligence (KDI), a new initiative that has been continuously emphasized by NSF since Fiscal Year 1998.

The ultimate goal of Learning and Intelligent Systems (LIS) research was to understand and enhance our ability to learn and create. However, the attainment of this goal required achievable intermediate goals and strategies. Such strategies included combining the theory, concepts, research tools, and methodologies of two or more disciplines, in order to focus on a tractable component of a larger problem. The initiative sought to achieve these goals by encouraging interdisciplinary research that had the potential to unify disciplinary knowledge about learning and intelligent systems, and to foster technology research and prototype development to explore and test designs and models that could lead to supportive interactions between natural and artificial systems.

LIS-supported research was intended to lead to advances in science and engineering that could foster rapid and radical growth in our ability to understand and support learning, creativity, and productivity in the natural and artificial systems which were important to a society characterized by significant changes in the complexity of human and information interactions. Because of the wealth of knowledge already in existence in the areas of dynamic systems and control and the potential research contributions that this community could make in an interdisciplinary mode, this initiative presented an excellent opportunity to partner with researchers in other communities, such as neurobiologists, computer scientists, sociologists, psychologists, and education experts, to name a few. Thus, an integration of the quantitative approaches traditionally used in the dynamic systems and control areas and the qualitative-experimental-statistical approaches used in some of the other areas mentioned above provided efficient and comprehensive solutions to the future learning and intelligent systems related engineering problems.

In its announcements of various new initiatives, the National Science Foundation is continuing to recognize and emphasize the merits and worth of interdisciplinary research. The development of intellectual integration across disciplines was more than just a constraint that the LIS projects satisfied. The projects necessarily went beyond the scope of traditional disciplines. Evidence of this interdisciplinary co-operation took several forms, including the expansion of an established collaboration involving investigators from different disciplines, a credible plan to use NSF support to build such collaborations or links between disciplines, and a proposal from a single investigator who demonstrated the potential for genuine involvement in collaborative multiple disciplinary research. Research under LIS was a part of the KDI initiative. The United States Congress increased the NSF FY '98 budget allocation and authorized expenditure on the KDI initiative. Thus, in a sense it could be interpreted that there was an appropriation for KDI over and above the traditionally available resources at NSF. With the partnership of various director-ates representing different disciplines at NSF, the funds were leveraged to provide even larger support to the researchers on KDI-related topics.

5 Typical LIS Research Projects

Following are examples of a few typical projects recently funded by the National Science Foundation under the LIS initiative.

Professor P. S. Krishnaprasad of the University of Maryland and his associates — Drs. Terry T. Takahashi of the Institute of Neuroscience, Shihab A. Shamma and Steven I. Marcus of the Institute of Systems Research, and Catherine E. Carr of the Department of Zoology — are working on a three-year research project [48] entitled "Learning Binaurally-Directed Movement," which began on October 1, 1997. The goal of this research project is to investigate time coding in the central nervous system, specifically the auditory system of the barn owl, the early development of such codes, the learning of associated maps, and the exploitation of such sound codes and maps in source localization and sound separation. The approach consists of electro-physiological and anatomical study, coupled with mathematical modeling of neural circuitry, the rigorous investigation of the structure and performance of relevant learning algorithms, and the creation of an experimental robotic test bed. This test bed, a binaural head, is intended to be capable of orienting itself to sound sources in complex acoustic environments through pure auditory servoing, by utilizing the development of control architectures capable of learning maps of the auditory space of the robot and drawing upon an evolving understanding of barn owl auditory system. The results of this research are expected to provide insights into the design of novel roles for auditory sensing, interpretation, and discrimination in autonomous robotic systems. This research could lead to applications in hands-free human–machine communications in acoustically cluttered environments and in monitoring complex environments such as highly automated manufacturing plants.

Another example of LIS-related investigation which began in 1997 is "An Integrated Approach to Concept Learning in Humans and Machines." This research was being carried out by an interdisciplinary team, consisting of Drs. Karl S. Rosengren, Leonard Pill, Gerald F. DeJong, and Gregory L. Murphy, under the leadership of Dr. Brian H. Ross, of the University of Illinois at Urbana-Champaign. The goal of the project [49] was to develop an integrated view of concept learning in humans and machines. The primary focus of the research effort was to combine psychological experimentation with artificial intelligence modeling aimed towards examining the interaction of world knowledge and empirical information during concept learning. The representation of concepts consisted of feature regularities observed in the instances and of features inferred from world knowledge. However, current theories focused on only one type of feature and did not consider how learning each might affect the other. Additional work examined how the use of concepts (such as those used for problem solving) might affect learning; how prior knowledge might be restructured to accommodate new information; and how concepts might change with age and experience. Computational learning theory was adapted to provide a mathematical characterization of the learning process.

The view of concept learning that results from this work will be integrated in that it will (a) investigate and account for a wide variety of concept learning results that are often studied separately, and (b) pool the research strengths of psychology, artificial intelligence machine learning, and computational learning theory. The first goal will place greater constraints on theoretical accounts, suggest new possibilities, and help to decide among competing explanations. The second goal will lead to a theory that is psychologically and computationally plausible, yet sufficiently rigorous to be analyzed with the mathematical tools of computational learning theory. Such a theory will contribute to the generation of new knowledge by broadening the understanding of concept learning in each of the fields and by promoting new research issues and approaches in each field through interdisciplinary work.

Yet another LIS project [50] which also began in 1997 is "Developmental Motor Control in Real and Artificial Systems," which is currently in progress at the University of Massachusetts at Amherst under the direction of Dr. Neil E. Berthier. A key aim of this initiative was to understand how highly complex intelligent systems could arise from simple initial knowledge through interactions with the environment. The best real-world example of such a system is the human infant who progresses from relatively simple abilities at birth to quite sophisticated abilities by two years of age. This research focuses on the development of reaching by infants because (a) only rudimentary reaching ability is present at birth; (b) older infants use their arms in a sophisticated way to exploit and explore the world; and (c) the problems facing the infant are similar to those an artificial system would face.

The project brought together two computer scientists who were experts on learning-control algorithms and neural networks and two psychologists who were experts on the behavioral and neural aspects of infant reaching to investigate and test various algorithms by which infants might gain control over their arms. The proposed research focused on the control strategies that infants used in executing reaches, how infants developed appropriate and adaptive modes of reaching, the mechanisms by which infants improved their ability to reach with age, the role of sensory information in controlling the reach, and how such knowledge could be stored in psychologically appropriate and computationally powerful ways. Preliminary results suggested that computational models that were appropriate for modeling the development of human reaching were different in a variety of ways from traditional computational models. Understanding the mechanisms by which intelligence can develop through learning could have a significant impact in many scientific and engineering domains because the ability to build such systems would be simpler and faster than engineering a system with the intelligence specified by the engineer, and because systems based on interactive learning could rapidly adapt to changing environmental conditions.

As a final example of LIS research projects, "Learning Minimal Representations for Visual Navigation and Recognition" was underway at Brown University under the direction of Dr. William H. Warren [51]. The project was concerned with the intelligence exhibited in interactions among sensory-motor activities and cognitive capacities such as reasoning, planning, and learning in both organisms and machines. Such an interaction was regularly shown in the act of navigation, which was engaged in by the humans and other animals from an early age and seemed almost effortless in normal circumstances thereafter. Whatever there was in navigation that was innate and whatever was learned, it was important to try to understand the interaction of the various cognitive, perceptual, and motor systems involved.

The complexity of these interactions became clear in the development of mobile robots, such as the one recently deployed on Mars, not to mention the more autonomous ones planned for the future. It was still a major and imperfectly understood task to create programs that coordinated sensors and allowed the robot to cross a space efficiently and without collisions with obstacles. An interdisciplinary approach was being taken in this research project, exploring human capabilities through experiments, developing models based on the experimental results and what was already known about human navigation, implementing these models in programs for robot control, then testing these programs in robotic navigation experiments for their efficacy and their reasonableness as models of human navigation. The goals were both to understand the phenomena in humans and machines and to develop robust algorithms to be used in mobile robots. This alliance of researchers studying psychophysics, cognition, computation, and robotics was expected to develop gains in knowledge across many disciplines and to enhance our understanding of spatial cognition and visual navigation in agents, both natural and artificial.

It is evident from the few examples given above that there were ample opportunities for researchers in the dynamic systems and control field to expand the scope of their own activities by establishing collaborative partnerships with individual researchers pursuing investigations in the KDI-related areas. The LIS program aimed to accomplish an effective integration of existing research on learning and intelligent systems from such disparate fields as animal behavior, artificial intelligence, cognitive psychology, cultural anthropology, education, language acquisition, mathematical system theory, neuroscience, and sociology. Furthermore, it facilitated fundamental engineering, methodological and scientific breakthroughs from new crossdisciplinary research teams to combine their knowledge and perspectives in new ways to attack the most important puzzles about learning, intelligence, and creativity. Finally, it emphasized the development of effective new learning tools that integrate the best new research findings from relevant disciplines to produce interactive, collaborative and visual technologies for persons with different capabilities and expectations.

6   The Knowledge and Distributed Intelligence (KDI) Initiative

The National Science Foundation (NSF) had included in its FY '98 budget a request to fund a new initiative [52] named Knowledge and Distributed Intelligence (KDI). The need for this initiative had arisen from a recognition that solutions to increasingly complex science and engineering problems required an integration of knowledge from many and diverse disciplines, manipulation of vast amounts of data, and merger of a variety of models in both time and space. These complex problems presented a unique and challenging opportunity to utilize recent advancements made in the arena of emerging technologies and processing of information-laden data. The KDI initiative was designed to achieve, across the scientific community, the next major step in the human capability to induce or gather and represent more complex and crossdisciplinary scientific data information derived from new sources and at enormously large scales; to transform information into knowledge by combining, classifying, and analyzing it in new ways; and to collaborate in groups and organizations, sharing knowledge and working together interactively across space, time, disciplines, and scientific cultures to multiply these results.

The real challenge for the KDI initiative was to increase productivity and impact of science and engineering to cope with real-world problems of greater complexity and to mobilize the distributed knowledge and capabilities of multiple science communities toward identifying common goals, increasing interactions, improving crossdisciplinary understanding, and raising the collective power of analytical tools and methods. The National Science Foundation had decided that an optimal strategy to carry out the KDI initiative was to support research that would generate a greater understanding of phenomena of distributed intelligence and collective behavior in human, automated, and natural systems; would create the next generation of mathematical, computational, data-oriented, and organizational methods and infrastructure, which will exploit multidisciplinary distributed intelligence to advance science and engineering; and would enhance human capabilities to create and use knowledge in groups, organizations, and communities via advances in human and physical infrastructure, technology, and education. As mentioned earlier, there are three complementary components of intellectual focus for collaborative thinking that are grouped under the overall umbrella of KDI. Learning and Intelligent Systems (LIS) was discussed above. The other two are Knowledge Networking (KN) and New Challenges in Computations (NCC).

Modern computers and communication systems share massive amounts of data across time and space. However, by connectivity alone, it is not assured that useful communication will necessarily take place across disciplines, languages, and cultures, or that appropriate processing and integration of knowledge will be accomplished from different sources, or that meaningful activity or arrangements for teams, organizations, classrooms, or communities will be formulated to work together over distance and time, or that a deeper understanding of the legal, moral, ethical, environmental, or social implications of new developments will emerge naturally. KN research aims to move beyond connectivity to achieve new levels of interactivity, thus increasing the bandwidths in semantics, knowledge, activity, and culture among communities, organizations, and the people. National Science Foundation is indeed the most appropriate agency to sponsor this activity since, in the United States, it singularly represents the large science, engineering, and education communities that could significantly contribute to building these knowledge networks.

Technological advances, many spurred under NSF sponsorship, now enable scientific practitioners, who may be widely dispersed geographically, to become a science network, integrating and sharing data, analyzing information, and synthesizing knowledge. The Foundation wants to expand and scale up these activities in the sciences and engineering, enabling society to apply similar strategies throughout its information infrastructure. The NSF's KN initiative creates a program of closely interconnected activities to facilitate advances enabled by simultaneous developments in technology, society, and content. The intellectual advances and insights are to be integrated for the betterment of society and to provide the scientists and engineers useful and easily implementable solutions to complex problems. In order to sharpen the research agenda for KN, three separate workshops were planned and held in the months of May and June of 1997.

The first workshop was entitled Distributed Heterogeneous Knowledge Networks. It was co-convened by the National Center for Atmospheric Research (NCAR) and the San Diego Supercomputing Center, and was held in Boulder, CO from May 8 to 9, 1997. The second workshop was entitled Knowledge Networking Processes. It was held at the Laboratory for Research on Structure of Matter at the University of Pennsylvania on June 9 and 10. The third workshop was entitled Human Dimensions of Knowledge Networking: Access, Usability, and Impact. It was co-organized by George Washington University and the University of California, Santa Barbara, and was held in Santa Barbara, CA from June 19 to 20, 1997. Each of these three workshops emphasized the identification and prioritization of research agenda and research topics, and the three workshops had common themes that were addressed related to various aspects of Knowledge Networking. These themes included an exploration of need for resources to enable an effective use of widely varying data content in a network environment; identification of knowledge networking processes essential to dealing with information having widely varying content, time, and distribution scales; a discussion of human dimensions to knowledge networking communities; and identification of partnerships within the public and nonpublic sectors of society. Participants in each workshop had ample opportunity to discuss the relevant issues in depth and formulate their recommendations for consideration and implementation by NSF.

NCC focuses on research and tools needed to model, simulate, analyze, display, or understand complicated phenomena; to control resources and deal with massive volumes of data in real time; and to predict the behavior of complex systems. Phenomena, data, and systems of interest so exceed in scope, multiplicity of scale, and dimensionality that which can be handled by present techniques that incremental advances do not suffice. New computational schema, such as quantum or biometic computing, are needed. Models, tools, and resources must be shared among many researchers in different places. Moreover, a key need is for immediacy and control of networked resources in real time and tailored to people's needs and capabilities, as well as on-the-fly analysis and design of data to guide experiments or manage situations as they happen. NCC aims to enable a collective understanding and effective management of complex systems. These aims require major advances in hardware and software to handle complexity, representation, and scale to enable distributed collaboration and to facilitate real-time interactions. Managing large data sets has become a critical task in every area of science and engineering.

KDI requires advances in the interpolation, use, and construction of large distributed repositories by participants including people, artificial agents, groups, and organizations. Interactivity research shows how to build and maintain dynamic, content-rich, multimedia relationships among participants, instruments, tools, and data. Representation research explores how knowledge about processes and phenomena can be encoded and how meaningful data for representations are reconstructed in their contexts for use. Cognition research investigates perception, reasoning, memory, learning, and action by participants, including groups and organizations. Studies of agents investigate the active and sometimes physically embodied algorithms, software, communications, and tools that can assist people in collaborating and networking knowledge. Finally, the research on an entire life cycle involves a study of creation, structuring, storage, maintenance, use, and disposal of general and community-specific knowledge. These areas of research are critical enablers of KDI.

People's ability to collaboratively access, retrieve, and comprehend information from complex databases and distributed sources depends on how that information is created, structured, stored, presented, reasoned about, manipulated, utilized, and managed. It must be amply evident from the above description that KDI is an ambitious Foundation-wide effort designed to take information, communications, computing, and networking to a new technological, economic, educational, and societal level. It draws on past advances made in networking, supercomputing, and learning and intelligent systems. In FY '98, NSF invested over 58 million dollars in a focused multidisciplinary program of activities in support of KDI research, infrastructure development, and education. NSF will continue to have a catalytic role under this new initiative to support development of enabling technologies and to bring together scientific communities ranging across many fields and disciplines. By sharing disparate data and diverse perspectives, new partnerships will emerge and strategies will evolve for understanding and solving complex systems.

7 Typical KDI Research Projects

Following are examples of a few typical research projects funded under the KDI initiative.

In 1999, NSF funded a three-year research project to Dr. Miguel A. Nicolelis of the Neurosciences Department and Professor Devendra P. Garg, Professor Patrick Wolf, and Professor Craig S. Henriquez of the School of Engineering at Duke University entitled "Brain-Machine Interfaces for Monitoring and Modeling Sensorimotor Learning in Primates" [53]. This research effort began in September 1999. The major thrust of this project is that despite advances in computer-controlled automation, the technological capabilities of robotic and "smart" instruments are still far exceeded by the human brain. The next generation of intelligent devices will need to combine features such as the perceptual abilities, high learning rates, and capability of generalization shown by the brain. To clarify a fundamental component of intelligent behavior, this project studies how cellular interactions within the cerebral cortex of the brain underlie problem-solving strategies in behaving primates. New technologies will be used for recording brain activity, for designing microchips, and for pattern recognition analysis. The objectives are to characterize the learning methods used to map sensory cues (from sight, sound, and touch) into relevant motor behaviors (directed arm movements), to see how different learning strategies affect the dynamic relations among functional associations of groups of cortical nerve cells during learning, and to design a brain-machine interface that will sample and process neuronal activity in real time in behaving animals. Technological goals include the use of a special virtual reality environment for behavioral testing, the development of a wireless multichannel microchip for transmitting brain activity to a remote receiver, and the development of pattern-recognition algorithms to analyze complex patterns of brain activity among multiple cells. Results of this project from the Knowledge and Distributed Intelligence initiative will have broad impact on fields such as neurobiology, bioengineering, and computer science; will have potential applications in technology for intelligent interactive robotics; and will provide excellent crossdisciplinary training for a range of students and postdoctoral researchers.

In another KDI-related three-year research project [54] entitled "Artificial Implementation of Cerebro-Cerebellar Control of Reaching and Walking," which began in 1998, is being carried out under the leadership of Professor Jean-Jacques E. Slotine at Massachusetts Institute of Technology in collaboration with Drs. Gill A. Pratt, Munther A. Dahleh, and Timothy J. Ebner. The thrust of this investigation is that humans and other animals are capable of a remarkable range of intricate motor behaviors. Although the brain systems involved in motor control are mostly known, the way in which these systems function interactively in motor control is still only partially understood. The investigators on this project have recently developed a model of cerebellar control in which they propose that the cerebellum implements servo (feedback-based) control of limb movements through the processing of "wave variables."

Wave variables are special linear combinations of command and sensory signals that ensure stability of servo systems despite delays in signal transmission. The previously developed simple wave-variable-based cerebellar control model displays single-joint movement control of two-joint horizontal planar arm movement and also produces several realistic internal signals. The model includes the roles of the intermediate and lateral cerebellum and parts of the cerebrum, spinal cord, peripheral nerve, and muscles. The current project is designed to verify and further develop the cerebellar model by attempting to correlate signals observed in active experimental primates with those predicted by the model and to account for motor behavior of healthy human subjects and humans suffering from cerebellar dysfunction. The performance of the model will be analyzed from the perspective of robot balance and leg control during ambulation. The investigating team seeks to develop a model of human (primate) cerebellar system function which is physiologically, neuroanatomically, and quantitatively accurate, as well as fully comprehensible in engineering terms. It is anticipated that this will contribute significantly to the understanding of the mechanisms, capacities, and limitations of human and animal motor control in health and disease. The project should also provide insights into design principles for intelligent executive systems in general, both natural (brain-based) and artificial (robotic). Anticipated applications of this line of investigation include more precise and specific interpretation of functional neuroimaging data, improved rational design of neuroprosthetic devices and neurosurgical interventions, and the design of more behaviorally adaptable, well-coordinated, and agile robots.

Professors Andrew Barto and John Moore of the University of Massachusetts at Amherst have been funded by the National Science Foundation a three-year research project [55] entitled "Temporal Abstraction in Reinforcement Learning" begun in August 1999. The project investigates a new approach to learning, planning, and representing knowledge at multiple levels of temporal abstraction. It develops methods by which an artificial reinforcement learning system can model and reason about persistent courses of action and can perceive its environment in corresponding terms, and it develops and examines the validity of models of animal behavior related to this approach. The project's main objectives are to develop the mathematical theory of the approach; to refine, extend, and conduct validation studies of related models of animal behavior; to examine the formulated theory's relationship to control theory and artificial intelligence; and to demonstrate its effectiveness in a number of simulated learning tasks.

Most current reinforcement learning (RL) research uses a framework in which an agent has to take a sequence of actions paced by a single, fixed time step: actions take one step to complete, and their immediate consequences become available after one step (modeled as a Markov decision process, or MDP). This makes it difficult to learn and plan at different time scales. Some RL research instead uses a generalization of this framework (semi-Markov decision process, or SMDP) in which actions take varying amounts of time to complete, and the existing theory specifies how to model the results of these actions and how to plan with them. However, this approach is limited because temporally extended actions are treated as indivisible and unknown units. For the greatest flexibility and best performance, it is necessary to look inside temporally extended actions to examine or modify how they are composed of lower-level actions, which is not considered in existing approaches.

This project, by contrast, will model extended courses of action as SMDP actions overlaid upon a base MDP. These courses of action, called *options*, can then be treated as if they were primitive actions, and existing RL can be applied almost unchanged. This approach enables options to be analyzed at both the MDP and SMDP levels and introduces new issues at the interface between the levels. This method is appealing because of its simplicity, its similarity to previous approaches using primitive actions, and its solid mathematical foundation in MDP and SMDP theory. This is being developed further into a general approach to hierarchical and multi-time-scale planning and learning.

Professor Stephen Morse of Yale University is leading a group of four other researchers on a KDI project [56] entitled "Coordinated Motion of Natural and Man-Made Groups" which began in September 1999 for a period of three years. The focus of the proposed research is as follows. Be it a school of fish swimming gracefully through the water, a herd of deer running through a meadow, a flock of birds flying across the horizon, or a swarm of bees circling about a hive, one cannot help but wonder how these, and other similar natural groupings, coordinate themselves and move so flawlessly, often without an apparent leader or any form of centralized control. What kinds of signaling must they use? What role if any, do currents, vortices, or other local environmental disturbances play in this process? Are there universal principles of coordinated group motion and if so what might they be? How might they be used to design a school of autonomous submerged vehicles or a group of ground-based or airborne mobile robots to collectively accomplish a useful task in a coordinated manner? In broad terms, these are the kinds of questions which this research project was aimed to address.

More specifically, the researchers proposed to mount a crossdisciplinary assault on the joint problems of understanding how fish schools coordinate their collective motion and how schools of autonomous submerged vehicles might be designed to move in a coordinated manner. These problems were planned to be addressed experimentally, theoretically, and by means of computer simulation. At the theoretical level, the project's aims were to develop models, which were biologically plausible, and, in addition, to develop operating strategies that would enable coordinated group motion of engineered systems. The ultimate goal was not to derive analytical models nor to develop computer simulations, which were visually satisfactory, but rather to discover the underlying concepts upon which the coordination of group motion might depend. Thus, for example, the investigators hoped to develop concepts which, on the one hand, might help to explain how fish maintained their spacing and, on the other, might serve as guidelines for the design of groupings of man-made autonomous vehicles of all types.

The experimental thrust of this research effort was to proceed in two distinct but parallel directions. With the objective of gathering the world's first database documenting the long-term, three-dimensional motions of individual fish within a large school, timed sequences of stereo video images of actual fish schools living in a large (1000 gallon or more) tank were to be taken. The responses of schools to various stimuli and under various conditions were to be imaged. Using advanced image/vision processing techniques, this data was to be transformed into a form suitable for verifying the validity of proposed behavioral and analytical schooling models. This database together with full documentation was to be made available to the science and engineering communities via the World Wide Web.

With the objective of trying out candidate group coordination strategies in a reasonably realistic setting, an experimental test facility consisting of a school of approximately a dozen, identical, miniature underwater vehicles was to be developed. These experiments were expected to be useful for both the biological and the engineering perspectives. In addition, it was proposed to develop capabilities to test robotic versions of hypothesized biology models not possible in a fish tank. Experiments with this man-made school were to be carried out in an Olympic-sized swimming pool, which was available at Princeton University. The first goal of this research investigation was to instrument these vehicles so that they could function autonomously, without remote control. The next goal was to experiment with a variety of maneuvers including forming groups, cruising, bifurcating, avoiding obstacles, and changing group shapes. The implementation of various biologically inspired goal-seeking strategies such as foraging as well as gradient climbing tasks relevant both to biology and to numerous engineering applications was planned. The proposed research was to be carried out by a cross-disciplinary team consisting of experimental and theoretical biologists together with experts in computer vision, control systems, and robotics. By means of this multi-pronged assault consisting of theoretical analysis, computer simulation, and experimentation with both natural and man-made groups, an understanding of the underlying mechanisms governing the coordinated motion of natural and man-made groups could be attained.

Professors John M. Henderson, Sridhar Mahadevan, and Fred C. Dyer of Michigan State University were funded a 3-year research project [57] entitled "Sequential Decision Making in Animals and Machines" in October 1998 under the KDI initiative. The focus of this project is that mobile organisms make accurate behavioral decisions with extraordinary speed and flexibility in real-world environments despite incomplete knowledge about the state of the world and the effects of their actions. This ability must be shared by artificial agents such as mobile robots if they are to operate flexibly in similar environments. The main goal of the research was to undertake a detailed interdisciplinary study of sequential decision making across animals and robots, with a focus on real-time learning and control of information gathering and navigational behaviors.

The project was to take a comparative approach, combining psychophysical and cognitive research techniques from the study of human eye movement control, behavioral research techniques from the study of insect navigation, and computational methods from the study of mobile robots. All of these systems provided experimentally tractable test beds for studying real-time decision making in partially observable environments. The research was guided by a class of sequential decision-making models called the Markov decision process (MDP). These models were attractive because they provided a formal framework for computing optimal behavior in uncertain environments. However, these models did not fully capture the complexity of decision making in organisms. The researchers planned to explore extensions of the MDP framework using insights gained from the study of behavior in organisms and algorithms in artificial agents. This synergy was expected to lead both to a better theoretical understanding of sequential decision making in biological organisms and to the development of efficient algorithms for artificial agents. A major outcome of the project was to show how the design of artificial creatures (robots) could be guided by, and serve as a guide for, the study of sequential behavior in animals. Understanding the challenges that robot designers faced, and the formal framework that they had developed to tackle these challenges, leads to novel questions about organisms behavior. Similarly, insights gained from organisms could help suggest ways for improving algorithms for building intelligent artificial agents.

Another example of a research project [58] funded under KDI initiative, entitled "Learning, Adaptation, and Layered Intelligent Systems," was proposed by Professors Sanjoy K. Mitter, John N. Tsitsiklis, and Robert C. Berwick of Massachusetts Institute of Technology. The duration of the project was 3 years, and the project started on October 1, 1998. The researchers' approach to building intelligent systems was based on the theoretical ideas of Bayesian statistical signal analysis and control-theoretic motion guidance. These theories had achieved major successes in many widely used systems. However, it had remained a challenge to create systems that integrated the analysis of low-level concrete sensor data and motor control with the use of high-level, more abstract representations of perception and action. The investigators proposed to attack this central issue with a variety of approaches.

A very promising tool was the systematic study of hierarchical compositional data structures, in which larger scale, more abstract objects were built up in stages from small-scale concrete objects. This compositional approach applied to making decisions as well as to perception: subtasks could be combined into larger tasks and reasoned with as units. Doing reasoning in such hybrid systems, it was essential that ambiguity and multiple alternatives be maintained as long as possible, for example, not choosing between inconsistent high-level interpretations of a signal until larger scale context was available or replacing a local "greedy algorithm" decision by a dynamic programming-style list of optimal conditional decisions. In addition to the role of learning in such hierarchical layered systems, understanding the interaction between information and control in such layered systems was a critical research issue. The proposed research was to concentrate on the following aspects of layered intelligent systems: (1) the role of the compositional and hierarchical approach in language and speech recognition, (2) hierarchical decision making in layered systems, (3) learning of hierarchical concepts, and (4) interaction information and control in distributed systems. All of these topics were highly interrelated.

Professor Tomaso Poggio, Earl K. Miller, Gregory W. Wornell, Nancy Kanwisher, and Amir H. Assadi of MIT were funded for three years under the 1998 KDI initiative. Their project [59], "Learning of Objects and Object Classes in Visual Cortex," began in September 1998. The focus of this project was that the ability to learn to categorize and recognize objects was a key feature of the visual system of humans and higher animals. Yet, how the representation underlying these powerful visual abilities was organized and acquired was still largely unknown. The principal investigator and his colleagues tackled the problem of how the visual cortex learns to represent and recognize novel objects and object classes through a combination of computational, physiological, and psychophysical approaches. The physiological experiments on alert monkeys relied on multielectrode recordings for which the investigators developed a tool kit of appropriate data mining techniques, based in part on their own work on learning and classification algorithms. In particular, the investigators undertook a multidisciplinary research project consisting of four interacting components: (1) computational modeling of inferotemporal (IT) cortical neurons, extending their previous work on representations of single objects in IT; (2) cortical physiology using multiple electrodes in awake, behaving monkeys trained on between- and within-class classification tasks on novel classes of stimuli; (3) new data mining techniques for processing multiple electrode data, including classification and learning techniques; and (4) visual psychophysics including MRI studies in humans and monkeys, relating the findings from monkey physiology to object learning in the human brain.

Understanding learning in the human brain means understanding the very core of intelligence. Not only was this one of the remaining fundamental challenges in science but it was also one area where even small steps forward would have significant implications for understanding neurological diseases and disorders, and also for the future of computing and machine intelligence. However, despite enormous progress in the last decade or two, science did not yet know what various areas of the cortex did and how. Because understanding the brain, the most complex system known to man, was a huge endeavor, this project focused on understanding a part of cortex, involved in a key and very difficult task in everyone's daily life — even if subjectively very easy: learning to recognize and categorize visual objects such as faces or cars. Understanding how brain cells represent objects was to be a major breakthrough for neuroscience and also for eventually designing machines capable of achieving human-like performance. More importantly, any significant progress in the specific problem of object recognition would have a major impact on the goals of the KDI program, because it would open the door to understanding broader issues of learning and intelligence in brains and machines.

Professor Stuart J. Russell, S. Shankar Sastry, Ronald S. Fearing, Richard Ivry, and Claire T. Farley of the University of California at Berkeley were funded for a 3-year project [60] entitled "Learning Complex Motor Tasks in Natural and Artificial Systems." This project began on October 1, 1998. The emphasis of this research project was to develop a unified theory of how natural and artificial systems could learn to solve complex motor tasks, such as running, diving, throwing, and flying, that entailed significant sensory input and the coordination, sequencing, and fine-tuning of many low-level activities. Such a project was possible because of significant experimental advances in the understanding of motor control systems in humans and other animals and because of increased sophistication in the mathematical models of control learning. These models were to be used not only to analyze and predict natural phenomena in motor control, but also to derive effective adaptive controllers for artificial systems carrying out complex tasks.

To generate complex behaviors, natural and artificial systems must be organized hierarchically with multiple layers of abstraction. The first research task, therefore, was to identify appropriate levels of representation at which the physical system could be modeled and at which control actions could be defined. For example, in describing an insect flying from A to B, possible levels might be (1) nerve signals and mechanical properties controlling the detailed shaping of each wingbeat, (2) basic wingbeat cycle, (3) "steering" the cycle to direct flight, and (4) takeoff, navigation, and landing. Detailed motion, force, and/or airflow measurements were planned to be made under a variety of experimental circumstances and tasks to establish the correspondence between formal models and physical systems. These experiments were to be carried out for a variety of organisms, possibly including flying in insects, running in cockroaches, and running, diving, and throwing in humans. These studies (and, in the case of insects, neurophysiological studies) would also establish the sensory inputs that were available at each level of the control system.

Given the general structure of the control system and the appropriate sensory inputs, the next step was to design learning algorithms capable of learning to perform the given task successfully. The learning method to be used was reinforcement learning, a technique designed to adjust the control algorithm to optimize an objective function — the long-term accumulated value of a specified reward signal. The reward was supplied to the learning algorithm as part of the sensory input. New reinforcement learning algorithms were planned to be developed that operated using both local and global reward signals within a hierarchical control structure; furthermore, these algorithms were to be proved to converge even using nonlinear representations of the overall objective function. This research should shed light on the central question of whether this form of learning in animals and humans could be viewed as driven by optimization or by some other principle, such as the preservation of fixed interface characteristics among the various levels of the system. Discovery of consistent reward functions in animals, especially humans, would have significant consequences for general theories of learning.

A final example of typical 3-year research projects funded under the KDI initiative is entitled "Statistical Learning and Its Constraints." The principal investigators were Drs. Richard N. Aslin, Marc D. Hauser, Robert A. Jacobs, and Elissa L. Newport of the University of Rochester. The project [61] started in December 1998. Following was the focus of this project. Whereas both humans and nonhuman primates showed remarkable learning abilities, these abilities were often limited to certain domains, developmental periods, or behavioral contexts. For example, nearly all humans acquired one or more complex linguistic systems — that is, languages — but not all humans acquired complex musical systems. Similarly, nonhuman primates were exceptionally adept at learning to forage for and categorize different types of food, but were severely limited in acquiring complex communication systems. Also, both humans and nonhuman primates appeared to learn best in several domains during early periods of development. Thus, learning was nearly always characterized by specializations, rather than by general-purpose mechanisms. Understanding the constraints on learning could contribute to basic research, by accounting for domain- and species-specializations, and to applied research, by refining the understanding of which domains, ages, and contexts were optimal for human learners.

The main goal of the proposed research project was to explore the ability of human adults, children, infants, and nonhuman primates (Tamarins) to learn rapid sequential events. A prime example of a rapid sequential event was language, in which sounds were combined to form words, and words were combined to form sentences. Recent findings had demonstrated that human adults and infants could rapidly extract and remember very detailed "statistics" of linguistic input, such as the frequency and probability that one syllable would follow another. The proposed research was aimed to employ miniature artificial "languages" which simulated some of the structural properties of natural languages, but which could be built with equivalent structures across different domains (speech sequences, tone sequences, visual sequences, motor sequences). At issue was the facility that humans and nonhuman primates showed for the extraction of statistical structure from these different learning materials. Were they equally sensitive to the distributions of elements and higher order structure in the materials? Did learning abilities differ across learners of different ages and species, and across different structures and domains? These were some of the questions that this research investigation was planning to address.

In addition to behavioral experiments with humans and nonhuman primates, a series of computational studies were to allow the researchers to investigate the formal properties of learning mechanisms, in order to ask what architectural and neural differences might underlie such variations in learning abilities. What kinds of computational architectures could learn the types of regularities and patterns that human infants learn? Was the inability of adults or nonhuman primates to learn some types of complex sequential events due to the absence of a learning device specialized for that domain, or could small differences in computation and/or memory lead to large differences in learning outcome?

8 Research Challenges Ahead

In order to accomplish the development of truly intelligent machines, significant scientific advances have to be made in several areas and a number of technical barriers have yet to be overcome. For example, there is an urgent need to develop sensors, actuators, and open architecture controllers similar to those used in personal computers where the components are easily interchangeable. Also, a standardized terminology for intelligent machines and components does not yet exist. The reliability, precision, and accuracy of these machines need to be improved. Research is needed in developing real-time, 3-dimensional, self-calibrating vision systems. The currently available vision systems are far too slow and too difficult to calibrate. It would be very useful if the vision systems were developed such that they were programmable directly from CAD drawings, thus being available even before the physical parts were made.

Smart materials, innovative structural damping techniques, and active control strategies are needed to reduce, and preferably to eliminate, the vibrations associate with intelligent machines. As the size of these machines increases, so does their weight. In order to keep them as flexible as possible, lighter intelligent materials, possibly with embedded sensors and actuators, need to be developed and employed. New and more efficient algorithmic procedures have to be designed for kinematic and dynamic analysis, path planning, trajectory generation, obstacle avoidance, cooperative functioning, and real-time on-line decision making to deal with unanticipated situations. Most end-effectors that are currently available have limited dexterity. There is a need to develop safe, simple, highly efficient, low-cost, and reliable systems with enhanced sensing and response to contact forces.

The area of software development too could immensely benefit from an enhanced research activity related to intelligent machines. Innovative graphically oriented techniques for intelligent machine control and new programming paradigms are needed for low-cost updating and implementation. Efficient computational algorithms are needed incorporating redundancy and fault tolerance for improved robustness and reliability. Sensing planning and actuation needs to be implemented in a single hierarchical-level control architecture in real time.

Radically new thinking is required in developing function-based human-machine interfaces for use in intelligent machines. Efficient ways are needed for a human controller to interact with a distributed colony of intelligent machines. Safety of humans operating in the vicinity of such machines is also an area of substantial concern. How the intelligent machines can be of assistance to people should be examined. A variety of disciplines and persons with varying backgrounds and training in areas such as sociology, psychology, law, ethics, computer science and engineering, design specialists, business management, and environmental scientists would be necessary to develop overall systems in an efficient and systematic rather than haphazard and opportunistic manner.

References

[1]   The Future and Intelligent Machines, Charting the Path, *White Paper of the Robotics and Intelligent Machines Cooperative Council (RIMCC)*, RIMCC Secretariat, Ann Arbor, MI, 1996.

[2]   Musto, J. and Saridis, G., Entropy-Based Reliability Analysis for Intelligent Machines, *IEEE Transactions on Systems, Man, and Cybernetics — Part B: Cybernetics*, Vol. 27, No. 2, April 1997, pp. 239-244.

[3]   Schwarz, F., Artificial What?, *Invention and Technology*, Spring 1998, p. 64.

[4]   *Webster's Seventh Collegiate Dictionary*, G. & C. Merriam Company, Springfield, MA, 1972.

[5]   Shoureshi, R., Baheti, K., and Garg, D. et al., Intelligent Control Systems, *Proceedings of the IFAC World Congress*, San Francisco, CA, June 30 – July 5, 1996, pp. 101-106.

[6]   Ananthraman, S. and Garg, D., Training Backpropagation and CMAC Neural Networks for Control of a SCARA Robot, *Engineering Applications of Artificial Intelligence*, Vol. 6, No. 2, 1993, pp. 105-115.

[7]   Nagchaudhuri, A., Thint, M., and Garg, D., Camera-Robot Transform for Vision-Guided Tracking in a Manufacturing Work Cell, *Journal of Intelligent and Robotic Systems*, Vol. 5, 1992, pp. 283-298.

[8]   Garg, D., Ananthraman, S., and Nagchaudhuri, A., Sensor Integration for Payload Weight Estimation in a Robotic Work Cell, in *Advances in Instrumentation — 1991*, ASME Special Publication No. DSC-Vol. 30, December 1991, pp. 25-29.

[9]   Garg, D., Developments in Nonlinear Control System Synthesis Research, *ASME/DSCD Special Publication*, No. DSC-64, November, 1998, pp. 519-530.

[10]   Johnson, C. and Garg, D., Parameter Selection for Smoothed Variable Structure Controllers in Robotic Applications, *Proceedings of the 23rd Annual Pittsburgh Modeling and Simulation Conference*, Vol. 23, Pt. 4, May 1992, pp. 2041-2048.

[11]   Garg, D., Adaptive Control of Nonlinear Dynamic SCARA Type of Manipulators, *Robotica — The International Journal of Information, Education and Research in Robotics and Artificial Intelligence*, Vol. 9, No. 3, July-September 1991, pp. 319-326.

[12]   Garg, D. and Yang, J., The Near Time-Optimal Motion Control of Robotic Manipulators, *Journal of The Franklin Institute,* Vol. 327, No. 5, 1990, pp. 785-804.

[13]   Garg, D., Ananthraman, S., and Prabhu, S., Neural Network Applications, *Wiley Encyclopedia of Electrical and Electronic Engineers,* (John G. Webster, Editor), Vol. 14, John Wiley, New York, 1999, pp. 255-265.

[14]   Ananthraman, S. and Garg, D., Neurocontrol of Cooperative Dual Robot Manipulators, *Intelligent Control Systems*, ASME Special Publication, No. DSC-Vol. 48, November 1993, pp. 57-65.

[15]   Prabhu, S. and Garg, D., A Labeled Object Identification System Using Multi-Level Neural Networks, *Journal on Information Sciences*, Vol. 3, No. 2, 1995, pp. 111-126.

[16]   Prabhu, S. and Garg, D., Design of a Fuzzy Logic Based Robotic Admittance Controller, *International Journal of Intelligent Automation and Soft Computing,* Vol. 4, No. 2, 1998, pp. 175-189.

[17]   Prabhu, S. and Garg, D., Fuzzy Logic Based Reinforcement Learning of Admittance Control for Automated Robotic Manufacturing, *International Journal on Engineering Applications of Artificial Intelligence,* Vol. 11, 1998, pp. 7-23.

[18]   Brooks, R., From Earwigs to Humans, *Robotics and Autonomous Systems*, Vol. 20, No. 2-4, June 1997, pp. 291-304.

[19]   Inaba, M., Remote-Brained Humanoid Project, *Advanced Robotics*, Vol. 11, No. 6, 1998, pp. 605-620.

[20]   Tzafestas, E., Reactive Robots in the Service of Production Management, *Journal of Intelligent and Robotic Systems,* Vol. 21, No. 2, February 1998, pp. 179-191.

[21]   Masliah, M. and Albrecht, R., The Mobile Robot Surrogate Method for Developing Autonomy, *IEEE Transactions on Robotics and Automation*, Vol. 14, No. 2, April 1998, pp. 314-320.

[22]   Alami, R. et al., Multi-Robot Cooperation in the MARTHA Project, *IEEE Robotics and Automation Magazine*, Vol. 5, No. 1, 1998, pp. 36-47.

[23] Smithers, T., Autonomy in Robots and Other Agents, *Brain and Cognition,* Vol. 34, No. 1, June 19997, pp. 88-106.

[24] Mataric, M., Reducing Locality Through Communication in Distributed Multi-Agent Learning, *Journal of Experimental and Theoretical Artificial Intelligence,* Vol. 10, No. 3, July-September 1998, pp. 357-369.

[25] Mataric, M., Behavior-Based Robotics as a Tool for Synthesis of Artificial Behavior and Analysis of Natural Behavior, *Trends in Cognitive Science,* Vol. 2, No. 3, March 1998, pp. 82-87.

[26] Mataric, M., Reinforcement Learning in Multi-Robot Domain, *Autonomous Robots,* Vol. 4, No. 1, January 1997, pp. 73-83.

[27] Mataric, M., Behavior-Based Control: Examples from Navigation, Learning, and Group Behavior, *Journal of Experimental and Theoretical Artificial Intelligence,* Vol. 9, No. 2-3, 1997, pp. 323-336.

[28] Mataric, M., Coordination and Learning in Multirobot Systems, *IEEE Intelligent Systems,* March/April 1998, pp. 6-8.

[29] Ibrahim, M.Y. and Barfoot, C., Robotization of Coal Harvesting in Open-Cut Lignite Mines, *Industrial Robot,* Vol. 24, No. 5, 1997, pp. 376-383.

[30] Kochan, A., CyberGlass – Glass-Blowing Robot, *Industrial Robot,* Vol. 24, No. 4, 1997, pp. 282-286.

[31] Fitzpatrick, K. et al., Robot Windrower Is First Unmanned Harvester, *Industrial Robot,* Vol. 24, No. 5, 1997, pp. 342-350.

[32] Sastry, S. et al., Milli-Robotics for Remote, Minimally Invasive Surgery, *Robotics and Autonomous Systems,* Vol. 21, No. 3, September 1997, pp. 305-316.

[33] Pransky, J., Surgeon's Realizations of RoboDoc, *Industrial Robot,* Vol. 25, No. 2, 1998, pp. 105-110.

[34] Dario, P., Guglielmelli, E., and Genovese, V., Robot Assistants: Applications and Evolution, Robotics and Autonomous Systems, Vol. 8, No. 1-2, July 1996, pp. 225-234.

[35] Hill, J. and Jensen, J., Telepresence Technology in Medicine: Principles and Applications, *Proceedings of the IEEE,* Vol. 86, No. 3, March 1998, pp. 569-580.

[36] Tsotsos, J. et al., PLAYBOT — A Visually-Guided Robot for Physically Disabled Children, *Image and Vision Computing,* Vol. 16, No. 4, April 1998, pp. 275-292.

[37] Berliner, H., Computer Backgammon, *Scientific American,* Vol. 43, No. 1, 1980, pp. 64-72.

[37] Katevas, N. et al., The Autonomous Mobile Robot Senario – A Sensor-Aided Intelligent Navigation System for Powered Wheelchairs, *IEEE Robotics and Automation Magazine,* December 1997, pp. 60-70.

[38] Beard, J., Robots Lead the Blind, *New Scientist,* 30 August 1997, p. 12.

[39] Nolfi, S., Evolving Non-Trivial Behaviors on Real Robots: A Garbage Collecting Robot, *Robotics and Autonomous Systems,* Vol. 22, No. 3/4, 1997, pp. 187-198.

[40] Larson, J., RoboKent — A Case Study in Man-Machine Interfaces, *Industrial Robot,* Vol. 25, No. 2, 1998, pp. 95-102.

[41]   Mahajan, A. and Figueroa, F., Four-Legged Intelligent Mobile Autonomous Robot, *Robotics and Computer-Integrated Manufacturing*, Vol. 13, No. 1, March 1997, pp. 51-61.
[42]   Veloso, M. et al., The CM United-97 Small Robot Team, *RoboCup-97: The First Robot World Cup Soccer Games and Conferences* (H. Kitano, Ed.), Springer-Verlag, Berlin, 1998, pp. 10-14.
[43]   Asada, M. et al., The RoboCup Physical Challenge: Phase I, *Applied Artificial Intelligence*, Vol. 12, No. 2/3, March-May 1998, pp. 251-263.
[44]   Tesauro, G., Temporal Difference Learning and TD-Gammon, *Communications of the ACM*, Vol. 38, No. 3, March 1995, pp. 58-68.
[45]   Weisbin, C. et al., Robots in Space: US Missions and Technology Requirements into the Next Century, *Autonomous Robots*, Vol. 4, No. 2, 1997, pp. 159-173.
[46]   Matijevic, J. and Shirley, D., The Mission and Operation of the Mars Pathfinder Microrover, *Control Engineering Practice*, Vol. 5, No. 6, June 1997, pp. 827-835.
[47]   Intelligent Systems Activities at the National Science Foundation, *ASME Dynamic Systems and Control Division Newsletter*, Spring 1997, p. 3.
[48]   Learning and Intelligent Systems, Learning Binaurally-Directed Movement, NSF Award Number 9720334, NSF, Arlington, VA, 1997.
[49]   Learning and Intelligent Systems: An Integrated Approach to Concept Learning in Humans and Machines, NSF Award Number 9720304, NSF, Arlington, VA, 1997.
[50]   Learning and Intelligent Systems: Developmental Motor Control in Real and Artificial Systems, Award Number 9720345, NSF, Arlington, VA, 1997.
[51]   Learning and Intelligent Systems: Learning Minimal Representations for Visual Navigation and Recognition, NSF Award Number 9720327, NSF, Arlington, VA, 1997.
[52]   Research Focus – NSF's Knowledge and Distributed Intelligence (KDI) Initiative, *ASME Dynamic Systems and Control Division Newsletter*, Spring 1998, pp. 4-5.
[53]   Knowledge and Distributed Intelligence Award: Brain-Machine Interfaces for Monitoring and Modeling Sensorimotor Learning in Primates, NSF Award Number 9980043, NSF, Arlington, VA, 1999.
[54]   Knowledge and Distributed Intelligence Award: Artificial Implementation of Cerebro-Cerebellar Control of Reaching and Walking, NSF Award Number 9873478, NSF, Arlington, VA, 1998.
[55]   Knowledge and Distributed Intelligence Award: Temporal Abstraction in Reinforcement Learning, NSF Award Number 9980062, NSF, Arlington, VA, 1999.
[56]   Knowledge and Distributed Intelligence Award: Coordinated Motion of Natural and Man-Made Groups, NSF Award Number 9980058, NSF, Arlington, VA, 1999.

[57] Knowledge and Distributed Intelligence Award: Sequential Decision-Making in Animals and Machines, NSF Award Number 9873531, NSF, Arlington, VA, 1998.

[58] Knowledge and Distributed Intelligence Award: Learning, Adaptation, and Layered Intelligent Systems, NSF Award Number 9873451, NSF, Arlington, VA, 1998.

[59] Knowledge and Distributed Intelligence Award: Learning of Objects and Object Classes in Visual Cortex, NSF Award Number 9872936, NSF, Arlington, VA, 1998.

[60] Knowledge and Distributed Intelligence Award: Learning Complex Motor Tasks in Natural and Artificial Systems, NSF Award Number 9873474, NSF, Arlington, VA, 1998.

[61] Knowledge and Distributed Intelligence Award: Statistical Learning and Its Constraints, NSF Award Number 9873477, NSF, Arlington, VA, 1998.

5 SOFT COMPUTING TECHNIQUES FOR INTELLIGENT MACHINES

Fakhri Karray
Pattern Analysis and Machine Intelligence Laboratory
Department of Systems Design Engineering
University of Waterloo
Waterloo, Canada
karray@watfor.uwaterloo.ca

Soft computing represents one of the newest fields in the area of computational intelligence. It employs state-of-the-art computational tools to deal effectively with systems characterized by complex structuring and ill-defined dynamics. These tools involve recently developed computational techniques based on fuzzy set theory, connectionist modeling, and evolutionary computation. Depending on the type of application, these tools could be used in either integrated or stand-alone schemes. This chapter represents an overview on the fundamental components needed to design intelligent machines based on the tools of soft computing. Such systems will be able to take advantage of knowledge represented in linguistic terms, learn from past knowledge gained by the system, and have the capabilities of using state-of-the-art evolutionary computation to optimize some of their operations.

1 Introduction

In this chapter are presented a set of techniques that have become recently used for designing intelligent systems (machines), which are characterized by large capabilities of learning and autonomous behavior. I specifically outline the fundamental concepts needed for designing such systems. An application to this subject is given in Chapter 1. Applications are discussed in Chapters 4, 6, and 8. In the context of this chapter, *intelligent machines*, *intelligent systems*, and *intelligent control systems* are assumed to be synonymous.

The well-known model-based control techniques are usually implemented under the assumption of a good understanding of processes dynamics and their operating environments. These techniques, however, might not be able to provide satisfactory results when applied to poorly modeled processes, which may operate in ill-defined environments. Even when a suitable analytical model is available, the model parameters might not always be completely known or the process might be subjected to unpredictable variations. This is often the case when dealing with complex dynamical systems where the physical processes are either highly nonlinear or are not fully understood. This ultimately leads to difficulties in deriving an adequate model for the system. For a system (machine) for which experimental input-output data are available, system identification techniques have been shown to be quite effective in deriving a good dynamic representation for the system. This, however, comes at the expense of heavy computational resources, the lack of which may hinder the capability of the controller in tackling real-time changes of the system dynamics. Recent research carried out in the area of computational intelligence as applied to process control has shown that it is possible to circumvent some of the aforementioned difficulties by designing a new family of controllers with learning and adaptation capabilities. This makes them more robust and reliable in response to significant and unanticipated changes of the process dynamics and the operating environment, particularly when they are implemented in a hierarchical setting [1].

For the past several years, engineers and system designers have strived to develop systems with capabilities of mimicking to some extent the intelligent characteristics of humans in dealing with complex systems without having access to detailed mathematical modeling or precise physical description of the systems. This could be accomplished through the use of tools with features similar to those of humans in terms of describing systems with linguistic representations and inferring knowledge through learning from past situations. Described here is a set of fundamental techniques of computational intelligence that have become better known in recent years as tools of soft computing. *Soft computing* has been defined by Zadeh, the initiator of the fuzzy set theory, as:[*]

> Soft computing differs from conventional (hard) computing in that, unlike hard computing, it is tolerant of imprecision, uncertainty and partial truth. In effect, the role model for soft computing is the human mind. The guiding principle of soft computing is: Exploit the tolerance for imprecision, uncertainty and partial truth to achieve tractability, robustness and low solution cost.

The material presented here is not meant to be an exhaustive treatment of the area, but is intended instead to provide an overview of the field, the understanding of which is required in the development and design of a large class of intelligent systems. This we believe is necessary in setting the platform for designing systems that might be able to mimic to a certain extent the capabilities of humans in dealing with complex processes. For the sake of conciseness, this material is restricted to include the fundamental components of soft computing as they have been extended today to include fuzzy logic, neural networks, and evolutionary computing (genetic algorithms).

---

[*] http://www.cs.berkeley.edu/projects/Bisc/bisc.memo.html

2 Fuzzy Logic

2.1 Introduction

Systems featuring complexities and ambiguities have been understood and unconsciously addressed by humans since the early days of our existence. In fact humans have learned to make good decisions even in the absence of clearly defined processes. This is carried out based on expertise and general knowledge acquired of the system. Some of human actions can be accomplished very effectively using a well-structured set of *if-then* rules which are developed implicitly over many years through knowledge and experience.

Fuzzy set theory was developed in the early sixties by L. Zadeh. The main attribute of this theory is that it provides designers and scientists means of mimicking the powerful capability of humans in expressing knowledge with linguistic type of information. This is very important in designing systems capable of dealing effectively with complex processes. By definition, a *fuzzy set* is a set containing elements that have varying degrees of membership, unlike classical (or crisp) sets where members of a set would not be members unless their membership is full in that set (i.e., their membership is assigned a value of 1). Elements of a fuzzy set are mapped to a universe of membership value using a function-theoretic form. This function maps elements of a fuzzy set into a real value belonging to the interval between 0 and 1. Fuzzy set theory is very useful in modeling complex and vague systems. It has also been used very effectively in the area of control, as a decision-making system [1].

2.2 Background

Zadeh introduced the fuzzy set as an extension to the crisp set, which is known by a boundary, in that an element x—of the universe of discourse X—either belongs to the set (A) or not. The *classical crisp set* is defined by a characteristic function which determines the boundary of the set. For example, a crisp set A is defined as:

$$x_A(x) = \begin{cases} 1 & if \quad x \in A \\ 0 & if \quad x \notin A \end{cases}$$

In contrast, a *fuzzy set* is defined by a characteristic function called a *membership function*, which expresses the degree to which an element belongs to the set. It assigns to each x of X a number $\mu_A(x)$ in the closed interval [0,1]. Thus the membership function of the fuzzy set A can be expressed as:

$$\mu_A : X \to [0,1]$$

2.2.1 Fuzzy Sets Operations

As with traditional crisp sets, logic operations (e.g., union, intersection and complement) can be applied to fuzzy sets [2]. The union operation (as well as the intersection operation) can be defined in many different ways (see Chapter 1). Here, the most popular definitions are mentioned.

Union: If two fuzzy sets A and B are defined in the universe of discourse X, then the union of A and B, with membership functions $\mu_A(x)$ and $\mu_B(x)$, respectively, is a fuzzy set C, denoted by $C = A \cup B$, with membership function defined by:

$$\forall x \in X : \mu_C(x) = \max\left[\mu_A(x), \mu_B(x)\right]$$

Intersection: According to the min-operator, the intersection of two fuzzy sets A and B with membership functions $\mu_A(x)$ and $\mu_B(x)$, respectively, is a fuzzy set C, denoted by $C = A \cap B$, with membership function defined by:

$$\forall x \in X : \mu_C(x) = \min\left[\mu_A(x), \mu_B(x)\right]$$

Complement: The complement of a fuzzy set A, denoted as $\overline{A}$, is a fuzzy set with the membership function defined as:

$$\forall x \in X : \mu_{\overline{A}}(x) = 1 - \mu_A(x)$$

Moreover, a general way to express the intersection and the union of fuzzy sets is given by the *t-norm* and *t-conorm* respectively.

t-norms: two-parameter mappings of the form:

$$\mu_{A \cap B}(x) \cong t\left[\mu_A(x), \mu_B(x)\right]$$

with

$$t : [0,1] \times [0,1] \to [0,1]$$

To be a norm, the mapping $t(\cdot,\cdot)$ should satisfy the following conditions:

Boundary conditions: $t(0,0) = 0$; $t(\mu_A(x),1) = t(1,\mu_A(x)) = \mu_A(x)$
Commutativity: $t(\mu_A(x), \mu_B(x)) = t(\mu_B(x), \mu_A(x))$
Monotonicity:
If $\mu_A(x) \le \mu_C(x)$ and $\mu_B(x) \le \mu_D(x)$ Then $t(\mu_A(x), \mu_B(x)) \le t(\mu_C(x), \mu_D(x))$
Associativity: $t(\mu_A(x), t(\mu_B(x), \mu_C(x))) = t(t(\mu_A(x), \mu_B(x)), \mu_C(x))$

The intersection and the algebraic product mappings are among the two well-known nonparametric t-norms. They are expressed as:

Intersection: $\mu_A \wedge \mu_B = \min(\mu_A, \mu_B)$.

Algebraic product: $\mu_A \cdot \mu_B = \mu_A \mu_B$

t-conorms: (also called *s-norms*), on the other hand, are two-parameter functions of the form

$$\mu_{A \cup B}(x) \cong s\left[\mu_A(x), \mu_B(x)\right]$$

with

$$s: \ [0,1] \times [0,1] \rightarrow [0,1]$$

with the mapping $s(\cdot,\cdot)$ satisfying the following conditions:

Boundary conditions: $s(1,1) = 1$, $s(\mu_A(x),0) = s(0,\mu_A(x)) = \mu_A(x)$

Commutativity: $s(\mu_A(x), \mu_B(x)) = s(\mu_B(x), \mu_A(x))$

Monotonicity:

If $\mu_A(x) \le \mu_C(x)$ and $\mu_B(x) \le \mu_D(x)$ Then $s(\mu_A(x), \mu_B(x)) \le s(\mu_C(x), \mu_D(x))$

Associativity: $s(\mu_A(x), s(\mu_B(x), \mu_C(x))) = s(s(\mu_A(x), \mu_B(x)), \mu_C(x))$

Typical nonparametric *t-conorm* mappings are the union and the algebraic sum given as,

Union: $\mu_A \vee \mu_B = \max(\mu_A, \mu_B)$

Algebraic sum: $\mu_A \hat{+} \mu_B = \mu_A + \mu_B - \mu_A \mu_B$

Among the well-known parametric *t-norms* and *t-conorms* are those provided in 1980 by Yager and by Dubois and Prade:

Reference	*t-norms (Fuzzy Intersections)*	*t-conorms (Fuzzy Unions)*
Yager	$1 - \min\left\{1, \left((1-a)^w + (1-b)^w\right)^{\frac{1}{w}}\right\}$ $w \in (0, \infty)$	$\min\left\{1, \left(a^w + b^w\right)^{\frac{1}{w}}\right\}$
Dubois–Prade	$\dfrac{ab}{\max\{a,b,\alpha\}}, \ \alpha \in (0,1)$	$\dfrac{a + b - ab - \min\{a,b,1-\alpha\}}{\max\{1-a, 1-b, \alpha\}}$

2.2.2 Extension Principle

In fuzzy sets, just as in crisp sets, one needs to find a means to extend the domain of a function. For a given fuzzy set A and a function $f(.)$, one needs to obtain the value of function $f(A)$. This notion is called the *extension principle* and was first proposed by Zadeh. It is a basic concept in fuzzy set theory. The main idea of the extension principle is to generalize single points mapping of a function f to a mapping between fuzzy sets. To explain this principle, suppose that a function $f : X \rightarrow Y$ and a fuzzy set A in X. A fuzzy set $B=f(A)$ is deduced by applying the extension principle as the following:

$$\mu_B(y) = \mu_A[f^{-1}(y)], \quad y \in Y$$

where $f^{-1}(y)$ is the inverse of f. In the case where the mapping is not one to one, and where two or more distinct points in X with two different membership values in A are mapped onto the same point on Y, then the maximum value is assigned to $\mu_B(y)$.

3 Fuzzy Logic Controllers

3.1 Introduction

A main feature of fuzzy logic control (FLC) is the generation of adequate control decisions created through linguistic descriptions. These are represented by fuzzy rules based on heuristics, knowledge, and experience and are used for controlling a given process. This knowledge base is used in conjunction with some knowledge of the state of the process by an inference mechanism capable of determining a control action at an adequately appropriate rate. As such, fuzzy logic based controllers provide viable alternatives for tackling problems usually raised when attempting to model and design controllers for complex systems. This would be convenient for the actual study given the complex dynamics involved.

The first application of the concept of fuzzy control was initiated by the pioneering approach of Mamdani and Assilian in 1975 [3]. The starting point of this application was a qualitative "algorithmic" description of a control behavior. This application realized the automatic control of a steam engine boiler in a laboratory. Since then, a lot of real-life controllers have been designed, and the era of fuzzy logic moved from the experimental phase to the wide arena of industrial real-life applications. According to Reznik [4], 1991 was the year in which fuzzy technology became an industrial tool. Fuzzy logic has also been successfully applied to other areas such as system classification, pattern recognition, database management, modeling of chemical processes, and operations research. Table 1 summarizes the major steps in the evolution of fuzzy control applications [4,5].

Table 1: Fuzzy control evolution.

1972	Zadeh	A rationale for fuzzy control
1973	Zadeh	Linguistic approach
1974	Mamdani and Assilian	Steam engine control
1976	Rutherford et al.	Analysis of control algorithms
1977	Ostergaard	Cement kiln control
1977	Willaeys et al.	Optimal fuzzy control
1980	Tong et al.	Wastewater treatment process
1983	Hirota and Pedrycz	Probabilistic fuzzy sets (control)
1983	Takagi and Sugeno	Derivation of fuzzy control rules
1983	Yasunobu, Miyamoto et al.	Predictive fuzzy control
1985	Kiszka, Gupta et al.	Fuzzy system stability
1985	Togai and Watanabe	Fuzzy chip
1986	Yamakawa	Fuzzy controller hardware
1988	Dubois and Prade	Approximate reasoning
1990	Siemens	Reconfigurable fuzzy chip

3.2 Structure of a Fuzzy Logic Controller

The main task of a fuzzy controller is to describe the action for a given state using a linguistic description. The basic structure of a fuzzy controller is outlined in Figure 1. The facts that measuring devices give crisp measurements and that the actuators require crisp inputs call for two additional considerations when linguistic descriptions are employed for control purposes: *fuzzifying* the input of the controller and *defuzzifying* its output. The fuzzy controller consists of four main elements: a fuzzification interface, a knowledge base, an inference engine, and a defuzzification interface.

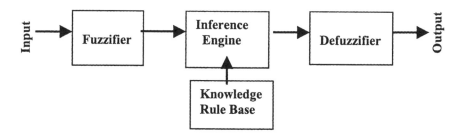

Figure 1: Schematic diagram of fuzzy logic controller.

3.2.1 The Fuzzification Interface

The fuzzification interface can be defined as a mapping from a real-valued point $x \in X \subset R^n$ to a fuzzy set. The role of the fuzzification interface involves measuring the values of the input variables and performing a scale mapping that transfers the input variables into corresponding universe of discourse X. Also, this interface performs the fuzzification of the input that converts input data into suitable linguistic values. The proper choice of the fuzzifier should help simplify the computations involved in the fuzzy inference engine. Among the well-known fuzzifiers are the singleton fuzzifier, the Gaussian fuzzifier, and the triangular fuzzifier. A detailed description of these fuzzifiers is outside the scope of this overview and can be found, for example, in [6]:

3.2.2 The Knowledge Base

The knowledge base is composed of the knowledge about the domain and the control goals of the system. It consists of a database and a linguistic (fuzzy) control rule base. The database is used to define linguistic control rules and fuzzy data manipulation in FLC. In the rule base the control goals and control policy of the application domain are characterized using a set of linguistic control rules.

3.2.3 Inference Engine (Decision Making)

The decision-making logic is the core of FLC. The inference engine works by mimicking the process of human decision making, based on fuzzy concepts and inferring fuzzy control actions. Fuzzy inference systems can be viewed as a computational framework that relies on the principles of fuzzy set theory and fuzzy approximate reasoning. There are three basic types of inference systems: the *Mamdani* system model, the *Sugeno* system model, and the *Tsukomoto* system model.

The Mamdani Model

The Mamdani fuzzy inference system is the first attempt to apply the principles of fuzzy set theory to a real-world controller. The fuzzy rules in Mamdani fuzzy inference systems have the following general form:

$$r_k : \text{If } x_1 \text{ is } A_1^k \text{ and } ......\text{and if } x_n \text{ is } A_n^k \text{ Then } y_1 \text{ is } B_1^k, ..., y_n \text{ is } B_n^k,$$

where $\{A_1, ..., A_n\}$ and $\{B_1, ..., B_n\}$ are the membership functions associated with inputs and outputs, respectively. In this type of inferencing, the qualified output of each fuzzy rule is obtained by choosing the minimum firing strength and the output membership function. Subsequently, the overall fuzzy output is extracted by applying any *t-norm* and *t-conorm* operators to the qualified fuzzy outputs (the common operators are max-min and max-product). To extract a crisp value from the overall fuzzy output, a defuzzification technique is applied to the fuzzy output, and the final crisp value is derived accordingly.

The Sugeno System Model

The Sugeno fuzzy model (Takagi, Sugeno, Kang or TKS fuzzy model) has rules of the following format:

$$r_k : \text{If } x_1 \text{ is } A_1^k \text{ and } ......\text{and } x_n \text{ is } A_n^k \text{ Then } z_1 = f_{1,k}(x_1,...,x_n),...,z_n = f_{n,k}(x_1,...,x_n)$$

where $(A_1^k,....A_n^k)$ are fuzzy sets in the antecedent of rule k, while $z_i = f_{i,k}(x_1,...,x_n)$ is a crisp function in the consequent. The output of each rule is a combination of the input variables plus a constant term. When $z_i = f_{i,k}(x_1,...,x_n)$ is a first order polynomial, the resulting system is called a *first-order Sugeno fuzzy model*. If $z_i = f_{i,k}(x_1,...,x_n)$ is a constant, then the system is called a *zero-order Sugeno fuzzy model*. When using the Sugeno fuzzy inference system, the resulting controller output is a weighted sum of the functions of the controller inputs. This is due to the defuzzification method used in the model. In the Sugeno model, the defuzzification method is efficient (in terms of computation time) and relatively simple to implement. Since each rule has a crisp output, a weighted sum or weighted average is used to extract the overall output.

The Tsukamoto Fuzzy Model

In this model [7], the consequent of each fuzzy *if-then* rule is represented by a fuzzy set with a monotonically increasing or decreasing membership function. The overall output is the weighted average of all outputs.

3.2.4 The Defuzzification Interface

The defuzzification interface performs: a scale mapping that converts the range of output variables into corresponding universes of discourse, and converts the inferred fuzzy control action into a crisp control action.

Several defuzzification techniques have been suggested in the literature. The appropriate choice of a defuzzification method can lead to a significant improvement in terms of speed and accuracy of a given fuzzy controller. The most frequently used methods are the *centroid* or *center of area* (COA) method, the *center of sums* (COS) method, and the *mean of maxima* (MOM) method. Details on these techniques and others suggested in the literature can be found in [8].

4 Connectionist Modeling: Artificial Neural Networks

4.1 Introduction

The immense capabilities of the human brain in processing information and making instantaneous decisions, even under very complex circumstances and uncertain environments, have inspired researchers to study and possibly mimic the computational abilities of this wonder. What a human can achieve in a very short time, for instance, in terms of pattern recognition and obstacle avoidance within an unknown environment, would take a computer very expensive resources (programmers, training experts, expensive hardware) and much more time to produce comparable results. This is mainly due to the way humans process information. Researchers indeed have shown for many years that a brain makes computations in a radically different manner from what is done by a digital computer. Unlike a computer, which is programmed to solve problems using sequential algorithms, the brain makes use of a massive network of parallel and distributed computational elements called *neurons*. The large number of connections linking these elements provides humans with the very powerful capability of learning. Motivated by this very efficient computational biological model, scientists have during the past few decades attempted to build computational systems that can process information in a similar way as the brain does. Such systems are called *neural networks* or *connectionist models*. They are composed of a large number of highly interconnected processing elements analogous in functionality to biological neurons and are tied together with weighted connections corresponding to the brain synapses.

4.2 Features of Artificial Neural Networks

An artificial neural network (ANN) is typically composed of a set of parallel and distributed processing units, called *nodes* or *neurons*. These are usually ordered into layers, appropriately interconnected by means of unidirectional (or bi-directional in some cases) weighted signal channels called *connections* or *synaptic weights*, as shown in Figure 2.

The internal architecture of ANN provides powerful computational capabilities, allowing for the simultaneous exploration of different competing hypotheses. Massive parallelism and computationally intensive learning through examples in ANN make them suitable for application in nonlinear functional mapping, speech and pattern recognition, categorization, data compression, and many other applications characterized by complex dynamics and possibly uncertain behavior. Neural networks gather their knowledge through detection of patterns and relationships found in the data provided to them. Three important features generally characterize an artificial neural network: the network topology, the network activation functions, and the network learning algorithm.

4.2.1 Neural Network Topologies

This feature corresponds to the ordering and organization of the nodes from the input layer to the output layer of the network. In fact, the way the nodes and the interconnections are arranged within the layers of a given ANN determines its topology. The choice for using a given topology is dictated mainly by the type of problem being considered. Some neural networks designers classify ANN according to how the nodes are organized and, hence, how data is processed through the network. The two well-known ANN topologies are the *feedforward* and the *recurrent* architectures.

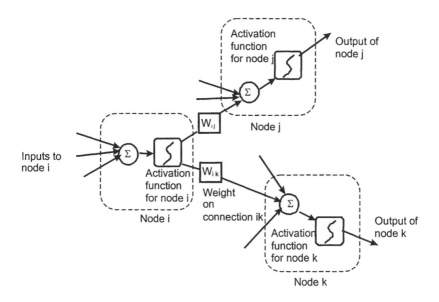

Figure 2: Schematic representation of a series of nodes
connected by synaptic weights.

The Feedforward Topology

A network with a feedforward (FF) architecture has its nodes hierarchically arranged in layers starting with the input layer and ending with the output layer. In
between, a number of internal layers, also called *hidden layers*, provide most of the
computational power of the network. The nodes in each layer are connected to the
next layer through unidirectional paths starting from one layer (source) and ending
at the subsequent layer (sink). This means that the outputs of a given layer feed the
nodes of the following layer in a forward path as shown in Figure 3. Because of
their structure, such networks are known as *feedforward networks*. They are also
occasionally called *open loop networks*, given the absence of feedback flow of
information in their structure.

The feedforward topology has been very popular due to its association with a quite
powerful and relatively robust learning algorithm called backpropoagation learning
algorithm (BPL). The multilayer perceptron network and the radial basis function
network are among the well-known networks using the feedforwrd topology.

The Recurrent Topology

Unlike feedforward networks, recurrent networks (RNs) allow for feedback connections among their nodes as illustrated in Figure 4.

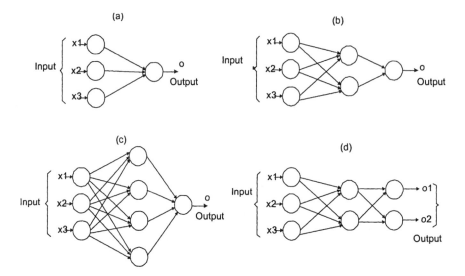

Figure 3: Neural networks with feedforward topology.

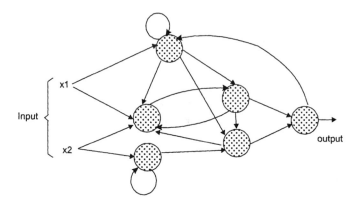

Figure 4: Neural networks with recurrent topology.

They are structured in such a way as to permit storage of information in their output nodes through dynamic states, hence providing the network with some sort of "memory." While FF networks map input into output and are static in the sense that the output of a given pattern of inputs is independent of the previous state of the network, RNs map states into states and as such are very useful for modeling and identification of dynamic systems. This means that the feedback available for a given input node allows it to pass to another state as soon as an output has been delivered at the other end of the network. Several well-known neural networks have been designed based on the recurrent topology. Such networks include, but are not restricted to, the Kohonen Self-Organizing Map, the Hopfield network, and the competitive networks.

4.2.2 Neural Network Activation Functions

The basic elements of the computational engine of a neural network are the neurons. These are, in fact, simple processors which take the weighted sum of their inputs from other nodes and apply to them a nonlinear mapping (not necessarily linear), called *activation function* before delivering the output to the next neuron (Figure 3). The output O_k of a typical neuron (k) having (l) inputs is given as:

$$O_k = f(\sum_l w_{ik} x_i + \theta_k)$$

where f is the activation function of the node, $x_1, x_2, \ldots, x_l$ are the inputs of the node, $w_{1k}, w_{2k}, \ldots, w_{lk}$ are the connection weights, and θ_k is the threshold of k-th node. The processing activity within a given layer is done in a simultaneous way hence providing the neural network with the powerful capability of parallel computing. The bias effect (threshold value) is intended to occasionally inhibit the activity of some nodes. Because neural networks may vary in terms of their structure as described previously, they also may vary in terms of their activation function. Depending on the problem at hand and on the location of the node within a given layer, the activation functions can take different forms: sigmoid mapping, signum function, or a linear correspondence.

4.2.3 Network Learning Algorithms

Learning algorithms are used to update the weighting parameters at the interconnection level of the neurons during the training process of the network. While some designers have classified neural networks according to topologies or architectures, others have classified them according to the learning algorithm used by the network. The three well-known and most often used learning mechanisms are the supervised, the unsupervised (or self-organized), and the reinforced. A brief overview of each one of these weight-updating mechanisms is provided next. For in-depth study of learning algorithms, the reader may also wish to consult [9].

Supervised Learning

The main feature of the supervised (or active) learning mechanism is the training by examples. This means that an external teacher provides the network with a set of input stimulus for which the output is a priori known. During the training process, the output results are continuously compared with the desired data. An appropriate learning rule (such as the gradient descent rule) uses the error between the actual output and the target data to adjust the connection weights so as to obtain, after a number of iteration, the closest match between the target output and the actual output. Supervised learning is particularly useful for feedforward networks. A number of supervised learning algorithms have been suggested in the literature. The backpropagation algorithm first developed by Werbos in 1974 [10], which is also based on the gradient descent optimization technique and the least mean squares algorithm [11], are among the most commonly used supervised learning rules. More on these algorithms and optimization rules is included in subsequent chapters.

Unsupervised Learning

Unlike supervised learning, unsupervised or self-organized learning does not in-volve an external teacher but relies instead upon local information and internal control. The training data and input patterns are presented to the system and, through predefined guidelines, the system discovers emergent collective properties and organizes the data into clusters or categories. Because of the way the network adjusts its connection weights in response to the presented input data, unsupervised learning systems are also known as open-loop adaptation learning schemes. In a simplified manner, an unsupervised learning scheme operates as follows: A set of training data is presented to the system at the input layer level. The network con-nection weights are then adjusted through some sort of competition among the nodes of the output layer in which the successful candidate will be the node with the highest value. In the process, the algorithm strengthens the connection between the incoming pattern at the input layer and the node output corresponding to the winning candidate. In addition to the strengthening of the connections between the input layer and the winning output node, the unsupervised learning scheme may be used as well for adjusting the weights of the connections leading to the neighboring nodes at the output layer. This is controlled by what is called the neighborliness parameter, and it has the major property of making groups of output nodes behave as single entities with particular features. More on the self-organizing mechanisms is provided in [9], in which a class of neural networks using unsupervised learning tools is described.

Reinforced Learning

Reinforced learning (RL), also known as graded learning, has been receiving an increased interest given its many attractive learning features which are considered to model in a satisfactory manner the adaptive behavior of humans when interact-ing with a given physical environment. This is another type of learning mechanism by means of which the network connections are modified according to feedback information provided to the network by its environment. This information simply instructs the system on whether a correct response has been obtained. On receiving a correct response, the corresponding connections leading to that output are strengthened in comparison to others. This type of learning strategy, based on the reward/penalty process, has several similarities with the biological learning system. Unlike supervised learning, RL does not get any information on what the output should be when the network is presented with a given input pattern. RL also differs from unsupervised learning (UL) in that UL does not provide the network with information on whether the output is correct or not, but rather operates on the premise of finding pattern regularity among the examplars presented to the system. Given the nature of this learning scheme, random search strategies have to be used to attain the correct output every time the system is presented with an excitation from its environment. This explorational aspect of learning ultimately leads to an improved capability of the system to deliver the expected output every time the system is presented with an input pattern. Among the strategies used to implement a reinforced learning algorithm are the reinforcement comparison, the adaptive heuristic critic, the Q learning, and the policy only scheme [8].

4.3 Classes of Artificial Neural Networks

A large number of ANN-related topologies and learning algorithms have been proposed which have tackled with success an ever-increasing number of complex problems never thought possible to be solved in the early days of neural networks development. In the following the main features of a number of popular neural networks are outlined, and an overview on their topologies and their learning capabilities is provided.

4.3.1 The Multilayer Perceptron

Topology

The multilayer perceptron (MLP) belongs to the class of feedforward networks, meaning that the information flows among the network nodes exclusively in the forward direction. Figure 5 illustrates a typical representation of a multilayer perceptron with three hidden layers. This structure was first proposed in the sixties to circumvent the nonlinear separability problem of earlier models of the perceptron and the adaline. However, the lack of efficient learning algorithms, at that time, to tackle such a topology hampered the development of the multilayer model. The number of hidden layers required within a multilayer perceptron depends in major part on the type of problem being addressed. In fact there doesn't exist yet a formal explicit theory stating how many hidden layers are needed in a given network to solve a specified task. However, the larger the number, the more classes the system can handle. However this increase in the number of layers could come at the expense of convergence of the learning algorithm. For instance, a system with a single hidden layer is able to solve the problem of the XOR function or other related problems in which the separation boundaries are relatively simple. It was also shown in the work of Cybenko [12] that an MLP network with one single hidden layer composed of an appropriate number of nodes with sigmoidal activation functions can approximate any type of continuous mapping in a compact set.

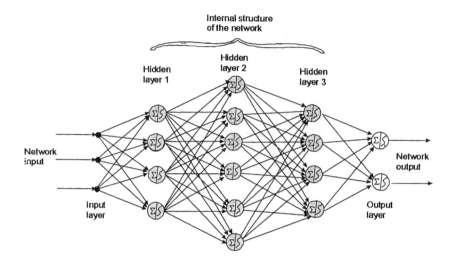

Figure 5: Schematic representation of the MLP network.

Backpropagation Learning Algorithm

It was only in the mid-eighties that the multilayer architecture, first proposed in the late sixties, re-emerged as a solid connectionist model to solve a wide range of complex problems. This occurred following the reformulation of a powerful learning algorithm commonly called the *back propagation learning* (BPL), which was originally developed by Werbos in 1974 [10]. It was later implemented in the multilayer perceptron topology with a great deal of success [13]. The algorithm is based on the gradient descent technique for solving an optimization problem, which involves the minimization of the network cumulative error E_c. Note that E_c represents the sum of n squared errors (Euclidian norm) $E(k)$s which is the Euclidian norm with $E(k)=\sum_{i=1}^{q}[t_i(k)-o_i(k)]^2$ giving the square of the Euclidian norm of the vectorial difference between the k-th target output vector $t(k)$ and the k-th actual output vector $o(k)$ of the network. Also, n is the number of training patterns presented to the network for learning purposes. The algorithm is designed in such a way as to update the weights in the direction of the gradient descent of the cumulative error (with respect to the weight vector). This is done in an iterative way. At the start, patterns are presented to the network. A feedback signal (error between the target signals and the actual outputs) is then propagated backward with the main task of updating the weights of the connections of the layers according to a learning mechanism known as the backpropagation learning algorithm, which is represented in Figure 6 and developed in detail as follows.

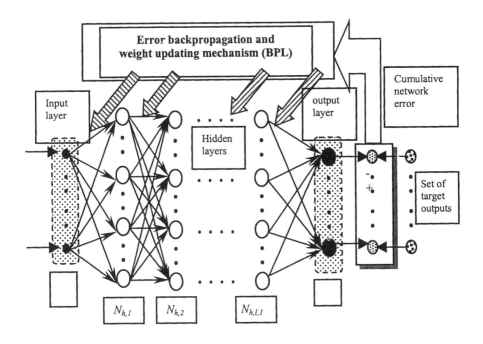

Figure 6: Schematic representation of the MLP network
illustrating the notion of error backpropagation.

Using similar notation as before, and using the sigmoid function as the activation function for all the neurons of the network, we define E_c as

$$E_c = \sum_{k=1}^{n} E(k) = \sum_{k=1}^{n} \sum_{i=1}^{q} [t_i(k) - o_i(k)]^2$$

where the index i represents the i-th neuron of the output layer composed of a total number of q neurons. The formulation of the optimization problem can now be stated as finding the set of the network weights that minimizes E_c or $E(k)$. This depends on whether the learning is made off line (all the training patterns are presented to the system at once) or on line (training is made pattern by pattern). For the first case the optimization problem is stated as:

$$\min_{\mathbf{w}} E_c = \min_{\mathbf{w}} \sum_{k=1}^{n} \sum_{i=1}^{q} [t_i(k) - o_i(k)]^2$$

while, for the second case, the optimization problem is formulated as:

$$\min_{\mathbf{w}} E(k) = \min_{\mathbf{w}} \sum_{t=1}^{q} [t_i(k) - o_i(k)]^2$$

In both formulations, the vector $\mathbf{w}$ denotes the network weight vector with its components corresponding to the interconnection weights among all the neurons of the network. Several authors have discussed and derived the BPL algorithm with ample detail. The reader may wish to consult reference [9] for details. I only derive here the updating rules allowing for the minimization of the cost functions as defined earlier. For the case of on-line training, the generalized delta rule may be expressed as

$$\Delta \mathbf{w}^{(l)} = -\eta \frac{\partial E(k)}{\partial \mathbf{w}^{(l)}}$$

where $\dfrac{\partial E(k)}{\partial \mathbf{w}^{(l)}}$ is the gradient of the error $E(k)$ with respect to the vector $\mathbf{w}^{(l)}$ corresponding to all interconnection weights between a layer (l) and the preceding layer (l-1). Also η denotes the learning rate parameter, which is a small positive number reflecting the convergence and stability behaviors of the learning algorithm and $\Delta \mathbf{w}^{(l)}$ denotes the difference between the vectors $\mathbf{w}^{(l)}(k+1)$ and $\mathbf{w}^{(l)}(k)$ representing the interconnection weights leading to neurons at the layer (l) after and before the presentation of the training pattern k, respectively. Using the chain rule of differentiation in the same way as that carried out in [9], we end up with the expression of the weight update at a given layer (l):

$$\Delta w_{ij}^{(l)} = -\eta \delta_i^{(l)} o_j^{(l-1)}$$

where $\Delta w_{ij}^{(l)}$ is the weight update for the connection linking the node j of layer (l-1) to node i located at layer l, and $o_j^{(l-1)}$ represents the output of the j-th neuron at layer (l-1) (the one located just before layer l). In the case of the layer (l) being the output layer, i.e., $l=L$, $\delta_i^{(l)}$ is expressed as :

$$\delta_i^{(L)} = [(t_i - o_i^L) o_i^L (1 - o_i^L)]$$

The index i represents here the variables pertaining to the i-th unit in the output layer ($l=L$). In the case where (l) represents a hidden layer ($l \neq L$), the expression for $\delta_i^{(l)}$ becomes:

$$\delta_i^{(l)} = o_i^{(l)}(1 - o_i^{(l)}) \sum_{p=1}^{n_l} \delta_p^{(l+1)} w_{pi}^{(l+1)}$$

The index n_l denotes the total number of neurons in the hidden layer (l), the index i represents neurons of the layer (l) and the index p represents the neurons of the layer (l+1). The fact that $\delta_i^{(l)}$ gets its value from the knowledge of $\delta_p^{(l+1)}$ of the next layers lends the algorithm its name: the backpropagation learning algorithm (BPL).

For the case of off-line training, the weight update rule may be expressed as:

$$\Delta \mathbf{w}^{(l)} = -\eta \frac{\partial E_c}{\partial \mathbf{w}^{(l)}}$$

All previous steps outlined for developing the on-line update rules are reproduced here with the exception that $E(k)$ is replaced by E_c. In both cases however, once the network weights have reached steady state values, the training algorithm is said to converge. At every training cycle, the values of the weights are propagated backward starting from the output layer all the way to the first layer of the network structure. While a larger value of η may speed up the convergence of the algorithm, it has been observed that this may lead to oscillations. Several techniques have been proposed in the literature to speed up the BPL while overcoming the convergence stability problem. Some of the techniques proposed involve the addition of the so-called momentum term involving the weight vector at iteration k-1 [8], while others involve normalization procedures for the update formulas outlined earlier. Other speed enhancement approaches have also been proposed in [14].

Applications and Limitations of MLP

Multilayer perceptrons are currently among the most used connectionist models. This stems from the relative ease of training and implementing these networks in either hardware or software. MLPs have been used in a wide variety of applications including signal processing, weather forecasting, financial market prediction, pattern recognition, and signal compression. However, it is well known that MLPs are not a panacea to solve all types of problems involving processes with nonlinear behavior or noisy data. Among the well-known problems that may hinder the generalization or approximation capabilities of MLP is the one related to the convergence behavior of the connection weights during the learning stage. In fact, the gradient descent-based algorithm used to update the network weights may never converge to the global minimum. This is particularly true in the presence of highly nonlinear behavior in the system that is being approximated by the network. Many remedies have been proposed to tackle this issue, either by retraining the network a number of times or by using optimization techniques such as those based on genetic algorithms or simulated annealing.

4.3.2 The Radial Basis Function Network

Topology

Radial basis function networks (RBFN) represent a special category of the feed-forward neural networks architecture. Inspired by the powerful functions of the biological receptive fields of the cerebral cortex, early researchers [15] have developed this connectionist model for mapping nonlinear behavior of static processes and for function approximation purposes. In recent years, the usage of RBFN has been extended to a much wider range of applications involving dynamic systems, pattern classification, prediction, and control. The RBFN structure consists of an input layer, a single hidden layer, and an output layer as shown in Figure 7.

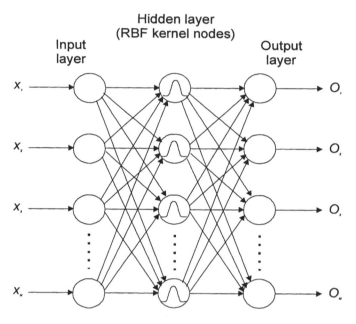

Figure 7: Schematic representation of an RBFN.

The network structure has nonlinear transformations in its hidden layer (typical transfer functions for hidden functions are Gaussian curves), but linear transformations are used between the hidden and output layers. The rationale behind this choice is that input spaces, cast nonlinearly into high-dimensional domains, are more likely to be linearly separable than those cast into low-dimensional ones. Unlike most FF neural networks, the connection weights between the input layer and the neuron units of the hidden layer for an RBFN are all equal to unity. The nonlinear transformations at the hidden layer level have the characteristics of being symmetrical, attaining their maximum at the function center, and generating positive values that rapidly decrease with the distance from the center. As such they produce radial activation signals that are bounded and localized. The two parameters that characterize each activation function are known as the center and the width (normalization parameter). As with other FF networks, an RBFN has to learn its parameters during the training process. For an optimal performance of the network, the hidden layer nodes should span the training data input space. Too sparse or too overlapping functions may cause degradation of the network performance.

In general the form taken by an RBF function is given as

$$g_i(\mathbf{x}) = r_i \left(\frac{\|\mathbf{x} - \mathbf{v}_i\|}{\sigma_i} \right)$$

where $\mathbf{x}$ is the input vector and $\mathbf{v}_i$ is the vector denoting the center of the receptive field unit g_i with σ_i as its unit width parameter. The most widely used form of RBF is the Gaussian kernel function given by

$$g_i(\mathbf{x}) = \exp\left(\frac{-\|\mathbf{x} - \mathbf{v}_i\|^2}{2\sigma_i^2} \right)$$

The logistic function has also been used as a possible RBF candidate:

$$g_i(\mathbf{x}) = \frac{1}{1 + \exp\left(\|\mathbf{x} - \mathbf{v}_i\|^2 / \sigma_i^2 \right)}$$

As such, a typical output of an RBF network having n units in the hidden layer and r output units is given by:

$$o_j(\mathbf{x}) = \sum_{i=1}^{n} w_{ij} g_i(\mathbf{x}) \qquad j = 1, \cdots, r$$

where w_{ij} is the connection weight between the i-th receptive field unit and the j-th output, and g_i is the i-th receptive field unit.

<u>Learning Algorithm for RBF</u>

The standard technique used to train an RBF network is the hybrid approach, which is a two-stage learning strategy. At first, an unsupervised clustering algorithm is used to extract the parameters of the radial basis functions, namely the widths and the centers. This is followed by the computation of the weights of the connections between the output nodes and the kernel functions using a supervised least mean squares algorithm. To tune the parameters of the networks even further, a supervised gradient-based algorithm is applied which makes use of some of the training patterns presented to the network. The reader may wish to consult [9] for detailed description of the algorithm.

<u>Applications</u>

Known to possess universal approximation capabilities, RBFNs have often been used for nonlinear mapping of complex processes and for solving a wide range of classification problems. They have been used in applications such as control, audio and video signal processing, and pattern recognition. They have been used as well for time series prediction [16]. Generally, RBF networks have an undesirably high number of hidden layers, but the dimension of the space can be reduced by careful planning of the network.

4.3.3 Kohonen's Self-Organizing Network

<u>Topology</u>

The Kohonen Self-Organizing Network (KSON) belongs to the class of unsupervised learning networks. This means that the network, unlike other forms of supervised learning based networks, updates its weighting parameters without the need for a performance feedback from a *teacher* or a network trainer. One major feature of this network is that the nodes distribute themselves across the input space to recognize groups of similar input vectors, while the output nodes compete among themselves to be fired one at a time in response to a particular input vector. This process is known as *competitive learning*. When suitably trained, the network will produce a low-dimension representation of the input space that preserves the ordering of the original structure of the network. This implies that two input vectors with similar pattern characteristics excite two physically close layer nodes. In other words, the nodes of the KSON can recognize groups of similar input vectors. This generates a topographic mapping of the input vectors to the output layer, which depends primarily on the pattern of the input vectors, and results in dimensionality reduction of the input space. This is done through an appropriate conversion of the feature space. A schematic representation of a typical KSOM with a 2-D output configuration is shown in Figure 8.

<u>Learning Algorithm</u>

In this case, learning permits the clustering of input data into a smaller set of elements having similar characteristics (features). It is based on the competitive learning technique also known as *winner take all strategy*. Let us presume that the input pattern is given by the vector $\mathbf{x}$, and denote by $\mathbf{w}_{ij}$ the weight vector connecting the pattern input elements to an output node with coordinates provided by indices i and j. In most implementations of the algorithms, the weight vectors are normalized to a unit length. Denote N_c as the neighborhood around the winning output candidate, which has its size decreasing at every iteration of the algorithm until convergence occurs. The steps of the learning algorithm are summarized as follows:

Step1: Initialize all weights to small random values. Set values for the initial learning rate α and the neighborhood N_c.

Step 2: Choose an input pattern $\mathbf{x}$ from the input data set.

Step 3: Select the winning unit c (the index of the best matching output unit) such that

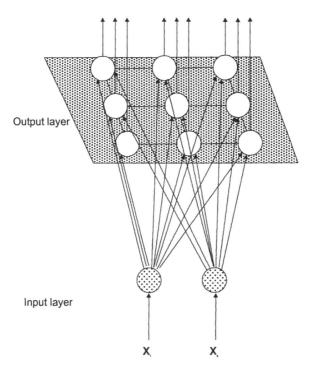

Figure 8: A Kohonen SOM with a 2-D output layer.

$$\|\mathbf{x} - \mathbf{w}_c\| = \min_{ij} \|\mathbf{x} - \mathbf{w}_{ij}\|$$

Step 4: Update the weights according to the global network updating phase from iteration k to iteration $k+1$ as:

$$\mathbf{w}_{ij}(k+1) = \begin{cases} \mathbf{w}_{ij}(k) + \alpha(k)[\mathbf{x} - \mathbf{w}_{ij}(k)], & \text{if } (i,j) \in N_c(k) \\ \mathbf{w}_{ij}(k) & \text{if } (i,j) \notin N_c(k) \end{cases}$$

where $\alpha(k)$ is the adaptive learning rate (strictly positive value smaller than unity) and $N_c(k)$ is the neighborhood of the unit c at iteration k.

Step 5: The learning rate and the neighborhood are decreased at every iteration according to an appropriate scheme. For instance, Kohonen suggested a shrinking function in the form of $\alpha(k) = \alpha(0)(1 - k/T)$, with T as the total number of training cycles and $\alpha(0)$ the starting learning rate bounded by one. As for the neighborhood, several researchers have suggested an initial region whose size is half the output grid and shrinks according to an exponentially decaying behavior.

Step 6: The learning scheme continues until a sufficient number of iterations has been carried out or until each output reaches a threshold of sensitivity to a portion of the input space.

Applications

Given their self-organizing capabilities based on the competitive learning rule, KSONs have been used extensively for clustering applications such as in speech recognition, vector coding, and texture segmentation. They have been used as well in robotics applications and for designing nonlinear controllers. KSONs could be applied in different applications using different parameters of the network, which are the neighborhood size and shape (circular, square, diamond), the learning rate decaying behavior, and the dimensionality of the neuron array (1-D, 2-D, or n-D).

4.3.4 Hopfield Network

Topology

A very special and interesting case of the recurrent (feedback) topology is the Hopfield network. It is the pioneering work of Hopfield in the early 1980s that led the way for designing neural networks with feedback paths and dynamics. The work of Hopfield is seen by many as the starting point for the implementation of associative (content addressable) memory by using a special structure of recurrent neural networks. The associative memory concept means simply that the network is able to recognize newly presented (noisy or incomplete) patterns using an already stored "complete" version of that pattern. We say that the new pattern is "attracted" to the stable pattern already stored in the network memories. This stems from what Hopfield defines as a physical system [17]: *Any physical system whose dynamics in phase space is dominated by a substantial number of locally stable states to which it is attracted can therefore be regarded as a general content-addressable memory.* In other words, this could be stated as having the network represented by an energy function that keeps decreasing until the system has reached stable status.

The general structure of a Hopfield network, shown in Figure 9, is made up of a number of processing units configured in one single layer (in addition to the input and output layers) with symmetrical synaptic connections, i.e., $w_{ij} = w_{ji}$. In the original work of Hopfield, the output of each unit can take a binary value (either 0 or 1) or a bipolar one (either -1 or 1). This value is fed back to all the input units of the network except the one corresponding to that output. Suppose here that the state of the network takes bipolar values. The activation rule for each neuron is then provided by the following:

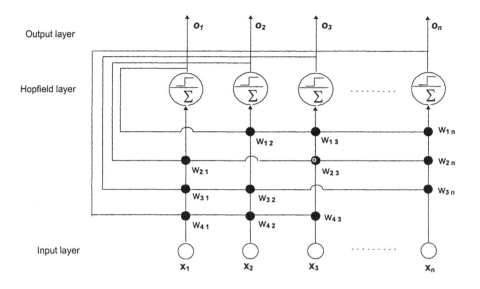

Figure 9: Typical representation of a Hopfield network.

$$o_i = \begin{cases} +1 & \text{if } \sum_{i \neq j} w_{ij} o_j > \theta_i \\ -1 & \text{if } \sum_{i \neq j} w_{ij} o_j < \theta_i \end{cases}$$

with o_i denoting the output of the current processing unit (Hopfield neuron) and θ_i as its threshold value. This also corresponds to the output of the *signum* function. To accomplish the autoassociative behavior of the network according to his physical view of a dynamical system, Hopfield used an energy function for the network given by:

$$E = -1/2 \sum \sum_{i \neq j} w_{ij} o_i o_j + \sum o_i \theta_i$$

To ensure stability of the network, E is so defined that it decreases monotonically with variation of the output states until a minimum is attained. This could be readily noticed from the expression relating the variation of E with respect to the output state variation. In fact it could be easily shown that

$$\Delta E = -\Delta o_i (\sum_{j \neq i} w_{ij} o_j - \theta_i)$$

This expression of the energy error shows indeed that the energy function E of the network continues to decrease until it settles by reaching a local minimum. This also translates into a monotonically decreasing behavior of the energy. Because of this interesting characteristic of the network, it can be shown that any new pattern input presented to the network will get attracted to the locally stable regions of the network. These regions correspond well to what the system has memorized during the learning stage, and hence the connotation of autoassociative memory used to represent the behavior of the Hopfield network.

Few years after his original contribution, Hopfield extended the capabilities of this network to involve possible continuous states. This work is summarized with detail in a seminal paper he presented in 1984 to the National Academy of Science [17].

Learning Algorithm

The learning algorithm for the Hopfield network is based on the so-called Hebbian learning rule, one of the earliest procedures designed for carrying out supervised learning. It is based on the idea that when two units are simultaneously activated, their interconnection weight increases in proportion to the product of their two activities. The Hebbian learning rule, also known as the outer product rule of storage, is applied to a set of q presented patterns $\mathbf{p}_q$, each having a dimension n (n denotes the number of units in the Hopfield network). It is expressed as:

$$w_{ij} = \begin{cases} \dfrac{1}{n}\sum_{k=1}^{q} p_{qj}p_{qi} & \text{if } i \neq j \\ 0 & \text{if } i \neq j \end{cases}$$

The learning stages of a Hopfield network are summarized as:

Step 1: Store the patterns through establishing the connection weights. Each of the q patterns presented is a vector of bipolar elements (+1 or -1). These patterns are also called fundamental memories, given that the connection weights have now become a fixed entity within the network. This reflects the stable status of the network to which newly presented patterns should get "attracted."

Step 2: Present to the network an unknown pattern $\mathbf{u}$ with same dimension as the fundamental patterns. Every component of the network outputs at the initial iteration cycle is set as

$$\mathbf{o}(0) = \mathbf{u}$$

Step 3: Update each component o_i of the output vector $\mathbf{o}$ from time l to time $l+1$ according to the iteration formula:

$$o_i(l+1) = \text{sgn}(\sum_{j=1}^{n} w_{ij}o_j(l))$$

The process is continue until convergence occurs, when the iteration is stopped. The obtained output vector matches best the fundamental pattern closest to it.

Step 4:   Continue the process for other presented unknown patterns by starting again from Step 2.

Applications

Given their autoassociative memory capabilities, Hopfield networks have been used extensively for information retrieval and for recognition of patterns and speech. They have been used as well to solve optimization problems. In fact by making the energy function of a Hopfield network equivalent to a certain performance index or an objective function of a given process to be minimized, the configuration at which the network finally settles will represent the solution to the original optimization problem [18]. The Hopfield network has also been used for solving combinatorial optimization problems such as the traveling salesman problem [19]. As with other types of networks, the Hopfield network, despite many of its useful features and retrieval capabilities, has its own limitations. These limitations are mostly related to the limited stable-state storage capacity of the network and its possible convergence to an incorrect stable state when nonfundamental patterns are presented. Hopfield roughly estimated that a network with N processing units should allow for $0.15N$ stable states. Many studies have been carried out recently to increase the capacity of the network without greatly increasing the number of the processing units.

5 Genetic Algorithms

5.1 Introduction

Life on our planet has persisted through many millions of years and through a variety of environments ranging from extreme cold to intense heat, from arid desert to drenched rainforest, and from the ocean floor to mountain pinnacles. Each different environment presents problems for which solutions must be found in order to survive. Organisms in each environment must live long enough to grow, reproduce, and compete, not only against the elements, but against the other organisms around them.

Evolution is the process by which life adapts to changing environments. The offspring of an organism must inherit enough characteristics of its parents, to be viable but still introduce some differences which will help it cope with new problems presented by its surroundings. Naturally, some succeed and others fail, those surviving winning the opportunity to pass their characteristics on to the next generation. A creature's survival depends, to a large extent, on its fitness within its environment, which is in turn determined by its genetic makeup. Chance, however, is always a factor, and even the fittest can die in unexpected circumstances. Evolution relies on having entire populations of slightly different organisms so that if some fail, others may yet succeed. Researchers have sought to formalize the mechanisms of evolution in order to apply it artificially to very different problems. The pursuit of artificial evolution using computers has led to an area which is known among scientists and researchers in the field as *evolutionary computation,* which basically comprises a collection of techniques among which are genetic algorithms (GAs), evolutionary programming and genetic programming. In this section, we restrict the discussion to the fundamentals of genetic algorithms, indicating their direct pertinence to the design of intelligent systems using soft computing tools as described in this book.

5.2 GAs in the Context of Artificial Evolution

Genetic algorithms borrow the essentials of their operation from natural evolution. The processes involved in cellular genetics, such as DNA replication and recombination, are very complex and are still under intensive study by researchers in different areas of biology, chemistry, and physics. Attempting to simulate even what is known today of these processes poses a serious computational problem in its own right. Thus, in mapping the natural to the artificial, we must simplify and attempt to capture the essence of genetic processes in the hope that these have the problem-solving power that we wish to use. Loosely stated, the problem addressed by natural evolution is, "what combinations of genetic traits result in an organism that can survive in its environment long enough to reproduce?" When considering artificial evolution, we must substitute our own problem in its place. Suppose we were trying to find a set of parameters for a complex equation in order to optimize the result. In this case, we can state our artificial evolutionary goal as, "what combination of parameter values minimizes the result of the equation?" In a particular case, there may be one or more minimal solutions to the equation and we may wish to generate many solutions. This type of problem is one to which genetic algorithms can be applied. The most important task facing a user of genetic algorithms is translating their problem into an evolutionary framework. A major component of this problem has been solved by researchers in the field who have developed several widely accepted tools operating within the context of an artificial evolutionary framework.

The origin of GAs dates back to the early '50s when a group of computer scientists and biologists teamed up to simulate a class of biological processes. But it was only later that Holland and his collaborators introduced the methodology in a more formal and tractable way. Holland was even able to show using the schema theory [20,21] that genetic algorithms have sound theoretical merits and are able to accurately solve a wide range of optimization problems. This is done through a procedure inspired by the biological process of evolution and the concept of survival of the fittest. In recent years GAs have found a wide range of interest, for example, from researchers in the fields of mathematics, connectionist modeling, and approximate reasoning. The search procedure of a GA is stochastic in nature and does not usually provide for the exact location of the optimum as some other gradient-based optimization techniques do. GA-based techniques possess two attractive features placing them at an advantage with respect to their derivative-based counterparts. In fact, given their discrete search nature, they could be easily applied to both continuous and discontinuous functions. Moreover, while GAs may not provide a mathematically exact solution for a given optimization problem, they usually can outperform gradient-based techniques in reaching the global optimum and hence avoid being entrapped in local ones. In the next few sections, the main fundamentals of GA are outlined along with a step-by-step illustration on how to solve a given optimization problem.

5.3 Genetic Algorithms and Optimization

A large number of techniques have been proposed in the literature to solve optimization problems of both smooth functions and piecewise smooth functions. Many of these techniques use the gradient of the function to find the best direction in searching for the optimum. Well known among them are the path-following-based methods and the integral-based procedures. But since the gradient of a function is always zero whether it falls at a local one or at global one, the algorithm always terminates without giving an indication as to whether it reached the global optimum. As such, all gradient-based optimization methods cannot guarantee achieving the global optimum. Several methods have been suggested to overcome this problem, including the path-following methods and the integration-based methods. While alleviating some of the problems, however, most of these techniques still rely on the gradient of the optimization function.

Genetic algorithms were formulated first by Holland [20]. Based on biologic evolution and on the survival-of-the-fittest principle, these techniques have been proposed primarily as effective tools for dealing with global optimization problems. They are derivative-free techniques and, as such, could be easily applied to any function ranging from continuous functions to discontinuous ones. They are based on the evaluation of the function at a set of points in the variable space of the function, usually chosen randomly within the search range. This feature makes them less vulnerable to local optima and, hence, good candidates for solving global optimization problems. The solution is obtained on the basis of an iterative search procedure, which mimics to a certain extent the evolution process of biological entities. The end result of this process, which starts with a randomly selected population of individuals, is a population with a strong survivability index, a phenomena better known as the "survival of the fittest" principle. This translates into finding the location of the point(s) at which the function is maximal. In a more formal way, suppose that the goal is to maximize a function f of m variables given by:

$$f(x_1, x_2, ...x_m) : \Re^m \to \Re$$

at the end of the optimization process one obtains:

$$f(x_1^*, x_2^*, ...x_m^*) \geq f(x_1, x_2, ...x_m)$$

where $(x_1^*, x_2^*, ...x_m^*)$ represents the vector solution belonging to the search space (s) (taken here as $\Re^m = (\Re \times \Re \cdots \times \Re)$). It is presumed that the function f takes positive values. If it is not the case, then one may wish to add a bias term into the function to make it positive throughout the search space. In the case of minimization, one might pose the problem of optimization as that of maximization of a function h, which is the negation of f over the entire search space. In other words, maximize the function h such that:

$$\min f(x_1, x_2, ...x_m) = \max h(x_1, x_2, ...x_m) = \max(-f(x_1, x_2, ...x_m))$$

The basic idea of a GA is to first choose a random population in the range of optimization, with a fixed size n (n usually depends on the search range, the accuracy required, and the nature of the function itself). Using the so-called binary encoding procedure, each variable is represented as a string of q binary digits. This leads to a population of elements represented by a matrix of n rows and qm columns. A set of "genetic" operators is then applied to this matrix to create a new population at which the function f should attain increasingly larger values. The most common operators that have been used to achieve this task are *selection, crossover,* and *mutation*. These operators are described in detail following the definitions of two terms frequently used in the jargon of genetic algorithms: the genotype of a population and its fitness value.

5.3.1 Genotype

When attempting to map natural evolution into the framework of artificial evolution, we must first consider the "data" for the system. In nature, this data consists of living creatures. Each individual represents a potential solution to the problem of survival. Similarly, in genetic algorithms, we consider a set of potential solutions which are collectively referred to as a *population*; each single solution is called an *individual*. Each individual in nature has a form determined by its DNA. Its collection of genetic traits is commonly known as a *genotype*. In genetic algorithms, the term *genotype* is used to describe the encoding of a problem solution represented by an individual. Thus, each individual has a genotype which encodes a solution. Many individuals in a population may have the same or similar genotypes. In the GA literature, an individual's genotype is often referred to as its *chromosome*. However, that term has a more specific meaning in biological genetics and *genotype* will be used in the rest of this overview.

Genotypes in genetic algorithms are typically represented by strings consisting of bits or characters. Each element of the string represents a *gene*, which is a single unit of genetic information. Genes in nature, directly or indirectly, control various traits of the individual. For example, in humans there are genes to determine eye and hair color and for many other characteristics. It is important to note that in nature, several genes often collectively determine a physical trait, and they are not necessarily independent. This is true in genetic algorithms as well, where a solution encoding may employ several interacting genes. Each gene has one or more possible values known as *alleles*. One can imagine that humans have a hair color gene with an allele for each color: brown, blond, black, red, etc. The reality in humans is far more complicated than that, but it serves as an illustration of the idea. The number of alleles for a specific gene is essentially fixed in nature, and in artificial evolution, it is determined by the encoding of solutions. The simplest genes are binary, having only two alleles. This means they can be represented by a single bit. However, some genes may have several alleles and are represented using characters. In genetic algorithms, the number of genes in the genotypes for a particular problem is usually fixed. There have been some applications that employ variable length genotypes but these will not be addressed here. Since the genotype is intended to express a solution to a specific problem, the genes and alleles must be designed for that problem and express the various components of a potential solution. The design of the genotype structure for a particular application is one of the two most difficult and important aspects of using genetic algorithms. Unfortunately, there are no straightforward, general-purpose approaches. The task is highly dependent on the problem and, in many cases, on the particular kind of genetic algorithm one wishes to employ.

5.3.2   Fitness Function

To use genetic algorithms, it is necessary to provide a means for evaluating the "value" or "goodness" of a particular solution. In nature, this is frequently thought to be the "fitness" of a creature (as in the popular concept of "survival of the fittest"), referring to its relative ability to survive in its environment. A "fit" creature must be able to find food and shelter, endure the local temperature and weather, detect and evade predators, and so on. If one creature is able to do this better than another, we say that it is "fitter." This leads us to the concept of a *fitness function*, which measures the *fitness* of a particular solution. In genetic algorithms, fitness functions are also called *objective functions*. An objective function takes a genotype as its parameter and typically gives a real-valued result that represents the "fitness" or "goodness" of the solution. Generally speaking, this fitness is comparative rather than absolute and serves to differentiate between many solutions rather than to discover the ideal solution. The ability to compare solutions is, in most cases, essential to the operation of a genetic algorithm.

In a number of cases, the objective function is quite obvious. In the problem of function minimization described above, the genotype is a set of parameters for the function, and the objective function is simply the value of the equation being minimized, given the genotype. In this case, a lower result from the objective function represents a better solution to the problem. In many cases, however, a good objective function is more difficult to construct and heuristic approaches must be taken at times. If one considers the manufacturing process above, a genotype could consist of a set of values for various control parameters of the process, but the objective function is more difficult. One possibility is to measure the yield from the process (the greater yield the better). Another example might be to measure the quality of the product. Still another might be the cost of the inputs to the process. These quantities might be difficult or slow to measure, and we would probably wish to judge a solution by several of these criteria rather than just one. The objective function is not only problem-specific, but is also inherently specific to the genotype used to represent the solutions. Changing the structure of the genotype generally requires changing the evaluation of the objective function and vice versa. For many problems, the objective function may be expensive to compute, or may offer only an unreliable comparison of two solutions. In some cases, the value of an optimal solution may not be known, even though the objective function is known. The objective function may not be a mathematical function at all, but a measurement taken of the performance of the solution in a simulation or real-world experiment. This makes the design of the objective function among the difficult and important steps in working with genetic algorithms.

5.4 Genetic Algorithm Operators

The foregoing discussion shows how the creatures and environment, which in some sense judge those creatures, in natural evolution must be mapped into a problem-specific genotype and objective function. The other essential components of a genetic algorithm are more generic. These are the processes by which evolution changes the composition of a population. In nature, we commonly look at three major forces: *natural selection, mating,* and *mutation*. The equivalents to these in artificial evolution are *selection, crossover,* and *mutation*. Collectively, these form a large group of processes which act on individuals, sets of individuals, populations, and genes and are known as *genetic operators*.

5.4.1 Selection

This selection procedure is applied to choose the individuals that participate in the reproduction process to give birth to the next generation. Selection operators usually work on a population and may serve to remove weaklings or to select strong individuals for reproduction. In general, selection operators are stochastic, probabilistically selecting good solutions and removing bad ones based on the evaluation given to them by the objective function. There are several heuristics in this process, including the elitist model, where the top 10 to 20 individuals of the population are chosen for further processing; the ranking model, where each member of the population is ranked based on its fitness value; and the roulette wheel procedure where each individual i is assigned a probability p_i to be chosen for reproduction, after which the cumulative probability $c_i = \sum_{j=1}^{i} p_j$ is calculated for each i. In the last model, an individual is selected if c_i becomes greater than a random number r selected a priori. Figure 10 illustrates the process of selection in a GA for an initial population of chromosome.

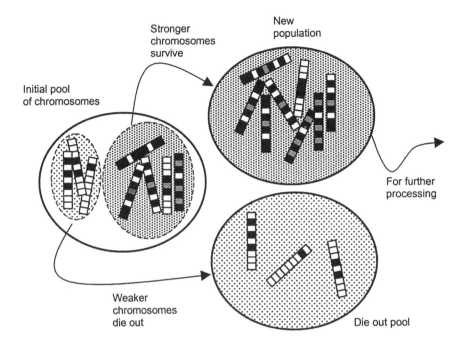

Figure 10:   Illustration of the selection operation in a GA.

5.4.2 Crossover

Crossover (Figure 11) is derived from the natural phenomenon of mating, but refers most specifically to *genetic recombination*, in which the genes of two parents
are combined in a somewhat random fashion to form the genotype of a child. Note
again that this process involves randomness, and thus, most *crossover operators*
randomly select a set of genes from each parent to form a child's genotype. There
exists in the literature a number of crossing operators, but the most common one
consists of choosing a number of points (one for simple crossing) in the binary
strings of the two parents to create the offspring by exchanging the parents' gene
sequences around these points.

5.4.3 Mutation

While crossover might generate new combinations of genes and, therefore, new
combinations of traits, mutation can introduce completely new alleles into a population. It has been widely recognized that mutation is the operator that creates
completely new solutions while crossover and selection serve to explore variants of

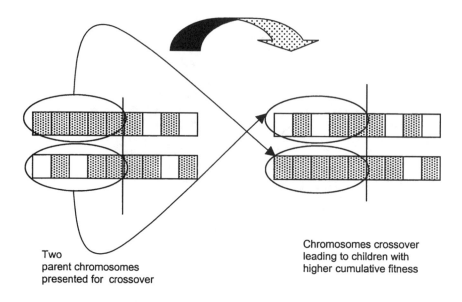

Two
parent chromosomes
presented for crossover

Chromosomes crossover
leading to children with
higher cumulative fitness

Figure 11: Crossover operation for two chromosomes.

existing solutions and eliminate bad ones. In nature, mutations are random altera-
tions in genetic material resulting from chemical or radioactive influences, or from
"mistakes" made during replication or recombination. In genetic algorithms, we
typically design *mutation operators* that select genes in an individual at random
and change the allele. In some cases, the change in allele is random as well, simply
selecting a different allele from those available for that gene. In other cases, especially if the problem structure suggests such a mechanism, alleles are mutated in a
deterministic fashion, and only the selection of genes is considered random. In
terms of implementation, mutation consists of randomly changing one or more
parts of a string. This is done by flipping the digits starting from a randomly chosen order and is illustrated in Figure 12.

5.5 Mode of Operation of a GA

For each population, the GA operators are applied to get the new generation of
individuals, ameliorating in the process the best fitness among the individuals of
the generation. The process is terminated after a fixed number of generations has
been reached, or when the best fitness value is no longer ameliorated from one
generation to the next. Other less standard techniques have been proposed for inducing the new generations, for example, the duplication and inversion technique,
which was proposed by Wienholt [22].

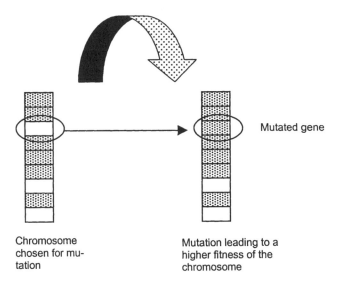

Chromosome
chosen for mu-
tation

Mutation leading to a
higher fitness of the
chromosome

Mutated gene

Figure 12: Mutation operation over a single gene.

Unlike other search-based optimization procedures such as the hill climbing or the random search, GAs have consistently achieved good performance in terms of balancing between the two conflicting objectives of any search procedure. These objectives are the exploitation of the best solution and the exploration of the search space. GAs have a number of other interesting features as well that differentiate them from other search techniques.

- GAs work with a coded version of the parameters.
- They start the search procedure from a population of points (solutions) not from a single point, which makes them suitable candidates for parallel processing.
- They use stochastic reproduction schemes instead of deterministic ones.

The search mechanism of a GA follows a step-by-step algorithm characterized by an iterative procedure having as its main goal the improvement of the fitness measure of the individuals. For a simple optimization problem and at a given iteration, these steps are initialization of the population, encoding of the variables, evaluation of the fitness measure at each generation, and application of the genetic operators that lead to the new generation.

The encoding mechanism permits the representation of the variables belonging to the search space in such a way as it carries all the required information (chromosomes) characterizing the fitness measure of a particular population. The two most used formats for encoding the variables are the binary format and the floating-point format. Traditionally, floating-point format has been used to represent the individuals of a population when dealing with optimization problems involving multidimensional and high precision numerical solutions. Binary format representation is simply not appropriate for these types of problems given the huge search space that may result. For problems that do not require a high level of accuracy and where the range space is small, binary format representation has consistently provided acceptable solutions. Binary representation of individuals requires encoding (into binary) and decoding (into decimal). This is a clear disadvantage in terms of computational time requirement, however, a binary encoded chromosome has considerably more elements (every bit is considered to be an element) than an individual represented by a floating-point. Indeed in genetic algorithms, individuals with more elements carry more information than their counterparts with fewer elements. In using the floating-point representation, each chromosome is created by putting all the floating-point numbers one after another. This means the encoding and decoding steps do not have to take place. For the sake of illustration, only binary representation is considered in what follows. For further details on different format representations, one may wish to consult [23].

With binary encoding, a binary vector composed of n bits is used as a chromosome to represent a real value of each parameter x_i. Here, n can be different for any of the parameters and the length of the chromosome depends mainly on the precision requirements. Suppose that the objective function f has m parameters:

$$f(x_1, x_2, \ldots x_m) : D_1 \times D_2 \times \cdots D_m \rightarrow \Re$$

If each variable (parameter) has its domain of variation within $D_i = [a_i, b_i]$, and if r represents the required precision of the solution, then the domain D_i should be divided into $(b_i - a_i) \cdot 10^r$ little intervals of equal size. If n_i is taken as the smallest integer such that $(b_i - a_i) \cdot 10^r \leq 2^{n_i} - 1$, then each parameter x_i could be presented as a binary string of length n_i. The following formula can be used to determine the value of each parameter:

$$x_i = a_i + dec(string_2) \cdot \frac{b_i - a_i}{2^{n_i} - 1}$$

where $string_2$ is the binary representation of the parameter x_i, and $dec(string_2)$ represents the decimal value of the binary string. Hence, the chromosome is created by putting all encoded parameters one after another. The original values of the parameters may be obtained by decoding the chromosome again.

5.5.1 Steps for GA Design

To illustrate the idea, and without loss of generality, next is outlined the procedure for carrying out the operations achieving a genetic algorithm for a given function of one variable $f(x)$ taken here as $fit(x)$.

Step 1:   Encode the variables of the algorithm as binary chromosomes v_i, where $(i = 1, 2, ..., p)$ and p is the population size of the possible solutions.

Step 2:   Initialize population of chromosomes.

Step 3:   Perform the following steps until the predefined condition is achieved:

- Evaluate (calculate) the fitness function values $fit(v_i)$ for each chromosome $v_i (i = 1, 2, ..., p)$.

- Select a new generation (using the roulette wheel for example).

- Calculate the total fitness of the population:

$$F = \sum_{i=1}^{p} fit(v_i)$$

- Calculate the probability of selection P_i for each chromosome $v_i (i = 1, 2 .. p)$:

$$P_i = \frac{fit(v_i)}{F}$$

- Calculate a cumulative probability q_i for each chromosome $v_i (i = 1, 2 .. p)$:

$$q_i = \sum_{j=1}^{i} p_j$$

- Generate a random float number $r \in [0..1]$.

- If $r < q_1$ then select v_1; otherwise select $v_i (2 \le i \le p)$ such that $q_{i-1} < r \le q_i$.

- Apply genetic operators (crossover, mutation).
    - Generate a random number r from [0 1]. If $r < p_c$ select the given chromosome for crossover (p_c is the crossover probability)
    - Generate a random number r from [0 1]. If $r < p_m$ select the given chromosome for mutation (p_m is the mutation probability)

- Replace the entire population by the children chromosome as the current population.

Step 4:   Go back to step 3 if optimization requirement is not attained.

These steps are shown in the schematic block diagram of Figure 13.

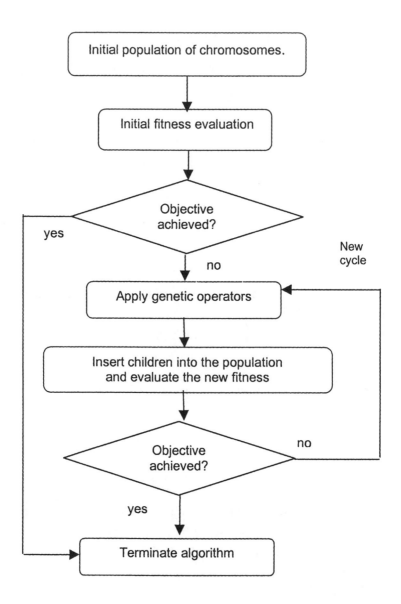

Figure 13: Schematic representation of a genetic algorithm.

5.5.2 Search Process in GAs

The classic genetic algorithm, as stated above, starts with a completely random population of solutions. Iteratively, it selects mating couples with a bias towards the stronger individuals in the population. These couples "mate," producing offspring that are either identical to the parents or that inherit part of their traits from each parent. These children are then subjected to mutation, which may or may not randomly alter their genetic makeup. The entire process is then repeated on the next children, forming a series of generations.

As the algorithm proceeds, the weaker solutions tend to be discarded, are, hence, not selected for breeding, and are unable to pass on their genes. Stronger solutions may breed many times, producing many children that share their traits. The probabilistic crossover means that some of the children will be exact copies, thus increasing the presence of strong solutions in the population. Many will be the result of crossover, inheriting traits from both parents. This recombination may produce a better individual than either parent, but can also produce worse solutions. The hope is that the best traits of the two parents may be combined to create a better individual. However, the probability of this happening is dependent on both the problem and its representation (genotype structure).

In the GA process, mutation serves to introduce alleles and combinations of alleles that may have been selected out or never existed in the population. Since selection and crossover can only recombine existing material, mutation serves an essential role by introducing and reintroducing genetic material, which can lead to still better solutions. Mutation can result in a worse solution, as is observed in nature, but its absence generally leads to stagnation. This leads to a key feature of genetic algorithms, which is related to balancing between *exploration* (the examination of new areas of the problem space) and *exploitation* (the examination of well-known areas of the problem space). In a number of cases, there are several regions containing good solutions. A purely exploratory algorithm (e.g., random search) might search widely through the problem space, but having found a decent solution, it might not search "near" that solution to see if better solutions exist close by. By contrast, a purely exploitive algorithm (e.g., a hill-climber), having found a decent solution, might search only in that area, and not discover a much better solution far away in the problem space. GAs feature exploration (through mutation and, to some extent, crossover) and exploitation (through selection and again through crossover). The degree to which the GA explores or exploits is determined by its parameters and its structure. These are related to the population size, the crossover rate, and the mutation rate. They also depend on the termination conditions, the genotype structure, and the choice of the fitness function. This makes GAs very sensitive to the choice of their parameters, and, hence, a lot of planning and experimentation is required to produce the desired results. Several main issues encountered in GA problem solving are outlined next.

5.6 Integration of Genetic Algorithms with Neural Networks

Using GAs for the purpose of enhancing the learning capabilities of neural networks has been suggested since the early days of the backpropagation learning algorithm in the mid-eighties. But it was only recently that powerful and sound algorithms have been developed for integrating the optimization tools of GAs with learning schemes of a large class of neural networks. This integration has led to more powerful structures of ANN and helped enhance the conventional learning techniques. A number of researchers have since used genetic algorithms for a multitude of applications, particularly for selecting appropriate inputs for neural networks and for improving the learning process of ANN, for instance, those based on gradient-descent procedures. These applications are briefly previewed next.

5.6.1 Use of GAs for the selection of ANN Inputs

Tsoukalas and Uhrig [24] used genetic algorithms to improve the application of neural networks for fault diagnosis in a nuclear power plant. In their work, they used the genetic algorithms to get the best combination of neural network inputs from a large set of the plant variables. The aim of using genetic algorithms for the selection of neural network input was to achieve faster training and improved accuracy with the minimum number of inputs.

5.6.2 Using GAs for NN Learning

This is among the most common applications of GAs in artificial neural networks. Encoding schemes have been proposed in this regard for representing the network parameters such as the connection weights and the bias terms. Whitely and Bogart [25] were among the first to use genetic algorithms for searching for the optimized weights parameters without relying on gradient information. This process is carried out according to the following steps [26]:

1. Encode a complete set of weights in a given string with a well-defined fitness value.
2. Start with a randomly selected population (for which the individuals are strings of weights and biases of the network, ordered in a particular manner) and proceed with the conventional GA operators to construct the children population from those of the parents.

The crossover operation in this process is found to have an important role in assembling good subblocks of strings to build a fitter population of children. One way for encoding the parameters of the networks is to order the weights and the biases in a list structure, as shown in [26] and illustrated in Figure 14. The chromosome can then be expressed as:

$$(0.8, 0.5, -0.1, -0.1, \mathbf{2.3}, \mathbf{1.1}, 0.1, -1, 0.2, -1., 1.2, -0.8, \mathbf{-0.7}, \mathbf{1.3})$$

where the bold face numbers represent the bias terms while all the other numbers represent the weight values. Once encoded in chromosomes, training patterns are presented to the system and errors are computed. In this procedure the fitness function is often taken as the inverse of the network error scaled by the sum total error of the population.

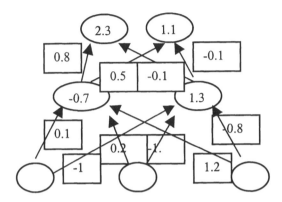

Figure 14: Encoding of a neural network.

A combined scheme of genetic algorithms with neural networks (GANN) has the ability to locate the neighborhood of an optimal solution quicker than what is found using conventional learning methods (such as backpropagation). This is due to the global search strategy of a GA. The only issue here is that once the chromosomes are in the optimal neighborhood, the GANN algorithm tends to converge more slowly to the optimal solution than is the case of the backpropagation learning rule. For this reason, several researchers have added another GA operator known as the gradient operator. This operator takes effect once the solution has reached the neighborhood of the global optimum.

5.7 Integration of Genetic Algorithms with Fuzzy Logic

In a similar manner to what is done with neurofuzzy modeling, fuzzy systems can be improved by providing means for optimizing their parameters, and GAs could be used to improve this aspect. Fuzzy systems can model general nonlinear mappings in a manner similar to feedforward neural networks as they are well-defined function mappings of real-valued inputs to real-valued outputs. All that is needed for practical application is a means of adjusting the system parameters so that the system output matches the training data. Genetic algorithms can provide such a means. Table 2 illustrates the features of the two techniques: fuzzy systems and genetic algorithms.

Table 2: Features of fuzzy logic and GAs.

	Fuzzy systems	*Genetic algorithms*
Stores knowledge	Explicit	None
Learns	Typically No	Yes
Optimizes	Explicitly No	Powerful
Fast	Yes	Yes
Handles nonlinearity	Yes	Yes

Integration of genetic algorithms with fuzzy systems has two main goals:

1. Improving the design process of fuzzy systems
2. Improving the performance of fuzzy systems

This performance can be interpreted as the accuracy of the control action and the efficiency (in terms of the speed of computation). Genetic algorithms could be used to find optimized values for the membership function parameters, particularly when manual selection of their values becomes difficult or takes too much time to attain. The main issue here is to define an appropriate fitness function that serves as an adequate representative of the optimization process. Once the fuzzy rules have been set and the parameterized membership functions have been initialized, the GA module will tune the values of the parameters subject to attaining the optimum of the fitness function. The overall procedure for using genetic algorithms to tune fuzzy systems is illustrated in Figure 15.

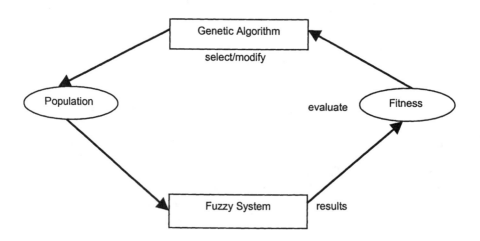

Figure 15: Integrated scheme of GA with fuzzy logic system.

For example, a chromosome can be defined to be a concatenation of the values of all the membership functions. For instance, when triangular functions are used to represent the membership functions, the parameters are the centers and widths of each category. From an initial pool of possible parameter values, the fuzzy system is run to determine how well it will perform. This information is used to determine the fitness of each chromosome and to establish the new population. The cycle is repeated until the best set of values for the membership function parameters is found.

5.8 Issues in GAs

Despite several of their attractive features with respect to parallel search capabilities and abilities in dealing with discrete optimization, GAs, as in the case for other optimization techniques, have a number of drawbacks. These are mentioned next.

5.8.1 Local Minima and Premature Convergence

GAs are typically used on complex problem spaces that are difficult to understand or predict, because they are effective at exploring such spaces. However, *local minima* (or maxima) are often found in complex spaces. These are regions of the space that hold good solutions relative to the regions around them, but which do not necessarily contain the best solutions in the problem space. The region(s) that contain the best solution(s) are called *global minima*. Purely exploitive algorithms, such as hill-climbers, may be entrapped by local minima and may not leave the region.

GAs are less prone to being entrapped because of the effects of mutation and crossover. However, if a GA explores such a region extensively, it may be almost completely dominated by the solutions within that region. A GA that is dominated by a set of identical or very similar solutions is often said to have *converged* (note, however, that there are many different definitions of *convergence*). Converged GAs are often very slow to escape a region of the problem space, because novel solutions are overwhelmed by the dominant solutions. If a GA converges to a set of solutions within a local minimum which is not a global minimum, then the GA is said to have *converged prematurely*, in the sense that it has converged before finding a global minimum. It is important to note that convergence itself is not a bad thing. Convergence to solutions at the global minimum is the ultimate objective, yet a convergence of any kind is a useful means of observing the progress of a GA. Among the most significant factors contributing to convergence is the mutation rate. If it is too low, the population may converge rapidly to a local minimum it encounters and may never escape.

5.8.2 Mutation Interference

Mutation interference occurs when mutation rates in a GA are so high that solutions are so frequently or drastically mutated and, consequently, the algorithm never manages to explore any region of the space thoroughly. Even if it finds good solutions, they tend to be rapidly destroyed. This is the opposite problem to premature convergence. A GA experiencing mutation interference will probably never converge since its population is too unstable. Finding a mutation rate that allows the GA to converge but also allows it to explore adequately is essential, and this often requires experimentation.

5.8.3 Deception

In some cases, a problem space may lead a GA to converge naturally to a suboptimal solution that appears good. This is often the case when there are many decent solutions of similar form but a much better solution that has a radically different form. It may also be that the region of attraction around the global minimum is very small, and there exist other local minima with much larger regions of attraction. Thus, these minima mislead the GA as to the form of the best solution in a manner known as *deception*. This problem is very difficult to deal with because it may simply be inherent in the problem space. One technique for dealing with deception is to emphasise the difference between solutions by altering the objective function or the selection operator such that the best solutions are rated much higher than the deceiving solutions.

5.8.4 Epistasis

Epistasis refers to a condition in the genotype structure where genes are highly interdependent. A set of genes may only produce a good solution when its alleles occur in a particular pattern. It may prove difficult for a GA to discover good solutions because fragments of the patterns will have only a low value and thus do not provide information to guide the construction of better patterns. Again, this is likely to be inherent in the structure of the problem and may be difficult to avoid. It may however be a feature of a particular genotype structure used to represent the problem. If the problem can be restated using another genotype structure and objective function, the epistasis may be avoided.

6 Conclusion

As this overview of the area of soft computing indicated, this area has considerable potential in tackling problems involving complex dynamics and ill-defined processes. I have provided here the fundamentals of the tools used for designing systems capable of providing processes with necessary intelligence to deal with unforeseen events that can hinder the progress of a complex process. This, I believe, is one alternative for the design of intelligent machines of the future. It is obvious that for this area to continue growing, several issues in terms of hardware and software design must be addressed during the implementation stage. Several researchers from around the world are tackling this important aspect. The results have been encouraging.

References

[1]   de Silva, C. W., *Intelligent Control: Fuzzy Logic Applications*, CRC Press, Boca Raton, FL, 1995.

[2]   Zadeh, L., "Fuzzy Sets," *Information and Control*, Vol. 8, pp. 338-356, 1965.

[3]   Mamdani, M. and Assilian, S., "An Experiment in Linguistic Synthesis with Fuzzy Controller," *International Journal of Man and Machine Studies*, Vol. 7, pp. 1-13, 1975.

[4]   Reznik, L. *Fuzzy Controllers*, Newnes, Australia, 1997.

[5]   Lee, C. C., "Fuzzy Logic in Control Systems: Fuzzy Logic Controller — Part I," *IEEE Transactions on Systems, Man, and Cybernetics*, Vol. 2, pp. 404-435, March/April, 1991.

[6]   Wang, L. X., *A Course in Fuzzy Systems and Control*, Prentice Hall, Upper Saddle River, NJ, 1997.

[7]   Tsukamoto, Y., "An Approach to Fuzzy Reasoning Method," *Advances in Fuzzy Set Theory and Applications*, M. M. Gupta, R. K. Ragade, and R. R. Yager (editors), pp. 137-149, Amsterdam, Holland, 1979.

[8]   Jang, J., Sun, S., and Mizutani, E., *NeuroFuzzy and Soft Computing*, Prentice Hall, Upper Saddle River, NJ, 1997.

[9]   Haykin, S., *Neural Networks, a Comprehensive Foundation,* MacMillan Publishing, Englewood Cliffs, NJ, 1994.

[10] Werbos, P., "Beyond Regresssion: New Tools for Prediction and Analysis in the Behavioral Sciences," Ph.D. dissertation, Harvard University, Cambridge, MA, 1974.

[11] Widrow, B. and Hoff, M. E., "Adaptive Switching Circuit," *Proc. 1960 IRE Western Electric Show and Convention*, New York, pp. 96-104, 1960.

[12] Cybenco, G., "Approximation by Superposition of a Sigmoidal Function," *Mathematics of Controls, Signals and Systems*, Vol. 2, pp. 303-314, 1989.

[13] Rumelhart, D., Hinton, G., and Williams, R., "Learning Representations by Backpropagation Errors," *Nature*, Vol. 323, pp. 533-536, 1986.

[14] Shar, S. and Palmieri, F., "MEKA, a Fast Local Algorithm for Training Feedforward Neural Networks," *Proceedings of the International Joint Conference on Neural Networks*, Vol. 3, pp. 41-46, 1990.

[15] Powell, M., "Radial Basis Function for Multivariable Interpolation: A Review," In *Algorithms for Approximations*, J. Mason and M. Cox (Editors), Oxford University Press, Oxford, England, pp. 143-167, 1987.

[16] Katayama, R., Kuwata, K., Kajitani, Y., and Watanabe, M., "Embedding Dimension Estimation of Chaotic Time Series Using Self-Generating Radial Basis Function Network," *Fuzzy Sets and Systems*, Vol. 72(3), pp. 311-327, 1995.

[17] Hopfield, J., "Neurons with Graded Response Have Collective Computational Properties Like Those of Two State Neurons," *Proceedings of the National Academy of Science*, Washington, DC, pp. 3088-3092, 1984.

[18] Hopfield, J. and Tank, D., "Neural Computation of Decisions in Optimization Problems," *Biological Cybernetics*, Vol. 52, pp. 141-152, 1985.

[19] Huetter, G., "Solution of the Traveling Salesman Problem with an Adaptive Ring," *Proceedings of the International Conference on Neural Networks*, pp. 85-92, 1988.

[20] Holland, J., *Adaptation in Natural and Artificial Systems*, University of Michigan Press, Ann Arbor, 1975.

[21] Holland, J. and Reitman, J., "Cognitive Systems Based on Adaptive Algorithms," *Pattern Directed Inference Systems*, D. Waterman and F. Hayes (editors), Academic Press, New York, 1978.

[22] Wienholt, W., "A Refined Genetic Algorithm for Parameter Optimization Problems," *Proceedings of the Fifth International Conference on Genetic Algorithms*, pp. 589-596, Morgan Kaufman, San Mateo, CA, 1993.

[23] Michalewicz, Z., *Genetic Algorithms+Data Structures=Evolution Programs*, Springer-Verlag, Berlin, 1994.

[24] Tsoukalas, L. and Uhrig, R., *Fuzzy and Neural Approaches in Engineering*, J. Wiley Interscience, NY, 1997.

[25] Whitely, D. and Bogart, C., "Optimizing Neural Networks Using Faster More Accurate Genetic Search," *Proceedings of the Third International Conference on Genetic Algorithms*, Morgan Kauffman, San Mateo, CA, 1991.

[26] Lin, C. T. and Lee, C. S., *Neural Fuzzy Systems*, Prentice Hall, Upper Saddle River, NJ, 1996.

6 SOFT COMPUTING CONTROL OF COMPLEX SYSTEMS

Mohammad Jamshidi
Department of Electrical and Computer Engineering
and Autonomous Control Engineering Center
The University of New Mexico
jamshidi@unm.edu
http://ace.unm.edu

One of the biggest challenges of any control paradigm is being able to handle large complex systems under unforeseen situations. A system may be called complex here if its dimension (order) is too high; its model (if available) is nonlinear, time-delayed, and interconnected; and information on the system is uncertain such that classical techniques cannot easily handle the problem. *Soft computing*, a collection of fuzzy logic, neurocomputing, genetic algorithms, and genetic programming has proven to be a powerful tool for adding *autonomy* to many complex systems. For such systems the rule base size of soft computing control architecture will be nearly infinite. Examples of complex systems are power networks, national air traffic control system, and an integrated manufacturing plant. In this chapter a rule base reduction approach is suggested to manage large inference engines. Notions of rule hierarchy and sensor data fusion are introduced and combined to achieve desirable goals. New paradigms using soft computing approaches are utilized to design autonomous controllers for a number of applications which are presented briefly.

1 Introduction

Since the launching of Sputnik in the former Soviet Union, extensive progress has been achieved in our understanding of how to model, identify, represent, measure, control, and implement digital controllers for complex large-scale systems. However, to design systems having high MIQ® (Machine Intelligence Quotient, registered trademark of Lotfi A. Zadeh), a profound change in the orientation of control theory may be required.

Currently, one of the more active areas of soft computing is *fuzzy logic*, and one of the more popular applications of fuzzy logic is *fuzzy control*. *Fuzzy controllers* are

0-8493-0330-3/00/$0.00+$.50

expert control systems that smoothly interpolate between hard-boundary crisp rules. Rules fire simultaneously to continuous degrees or strengths and the multiple resultant actions are combined into an interpolated result. Processing of uncertain information and saving of energy using commonsense rules and natural language statements are the bases for fuzzy control. The use of sensor data in practical control systems involves several tasks that are usually done by a human in the decision loop; e.g., an astronaut adjusting the position of a satellite or putting it in the proper orbit or a driver adjusting a vehicle's air-conditioning unit. All such tasks must be performed based on the evaluation of data according to a set of rules in which the human expert has learned from experience or training. Often, if not all the time, these rules are not crisp, i.e., some decisions are based on common sense or personal judgment. Such problems can be addressed by a set of fuzzy variables and rules which, if properly constructed, can make decisions that are comparable to those of a human expert.

This chapter presents a set of applications of soft computing approaches to complex systems such as mobile robots, flexible arm, and image enhancement. The structure of the chapter is as follows: Section 2 gives a brief introduction to autonomy through soft computing. Section 3 introduces two notions of sensory fusion and rule hierarchy. Section 4 constitutes a few applications of autonomous control for complex systems through soft computing approaches. Section 5 presents a fuzzy expert system for image enhancement. A summary is given in Section 6.

2 Autonomy through Soft Computing

Soft computing is an umbrella terminology used to refer to a collection of intelligent approaches such as neural networks (NN), fuzzy logic (FL), genetic algorithms (GA), genetic programming (GP), and neurocomputing. Soft computing techniques allow one to design an autonomous controller through learning (NN), optimization (GA), or reasoning (FL). Some background material on these subjects is given in Chapters 1 and 5.

Neural networks, genetic algorithms, and genetic programming are augmented with fuzzy logic-based schemes to enhance artificial intelligence of automated systems. Such hybrid combinations exhibit added reasoning, adaptation, and learning ability. In this chapter, three dominant hybrid approaches to intelligent control are experimentally applied to address various robotic control and image processing issues. The hybrid controllers consist of a hierarchical NN-fuzzy controller applied to a direct-drive motor, a GA-fuzzy hierarchical controller applied to position control of a flexible robot link, and a GP-fuzzy behavior based controller applied to a mobile robot navigation task. Various characteristics of each of these hybrid combinations are discussed and utilized in these control architectures. The NN-fuzzy architecture takes advantage of NN for handling complex data patterns; the GA-fuzzy architecture utilizes the ability of GA to optimize parameters of membership functions for improved system response; and the GP-fuzzy architecture utilizes the symbolic manipulation capability of GP to evolve fuzzy rule-sets.

3 Sensory Fusion and Rule Hierarchy

In many real-life problems the number of sensory data is far too many for any reasonable sized rule base. For example for a 4-variable system with 5 linguistic labels per variable, 625 rules are nominally needed. For a 10-variable process, the size of the rule base would be over 9.7 million. In other words, the size of the rule base would quickly approach infinity as the number of variables increases. In an effort to reduce the size of the rule base, many approaches are possible. Two of these approaches are sensory fusion and rule hierarchy which have been detailed in [1]. Sensory fusion employs a linear combination of the two variables x and y to form a fused variable $z = ax + by$, where a and b are arbitrary parameters. In such a technique the number of sensory inputs to the inference engine could be reduced in half. Another approach is to classify the rules of the rule base in groups according to the roles they play in the performance of the system, e.g., rules for stability, rules for tracking, and rules for optimization. In this paradigm, the two most critical variables, say for stability, could first be input to the first subset of rules. Then the output of the first subgroup would be joining the second most important set of sensory variables to be input to the second hierarchy of rules, etc. In practice, it can be assessed that neither method by itself can reduce the rule set substantially when the number of variables is large, say 6 or higher. A third possibility is to combine the rule hierarchy and sensory fusion jointly. Figure 1 shows this structure for rule base reduction. Jamshidi [1,2] has applied this approach for the balancing of an inverted pendulum with a glass of wine on top of it.

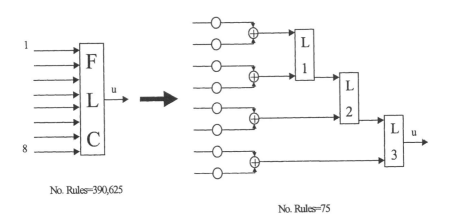

Figure 1: The sensory fusion – rule hierarchy structure for fuzzy control systems.

4 Autonomous Control in Robotics

In this section several applications of soft computing toward rendering various degrees of autonomy in control systems will be presented. There is much detail in each of these case studies than what can be covered in this short chapter. Relevant references will help the readers in all case studies. Since 1993, the University of New Mexico's CAD Laboratory and later the ACE Center have been active in designing the autonomous behavior of many configurations of robots.

4.1 Fuzzy-GP Control

In this application a real-time fuzzy controller was designed to guide a mobile robot through unstructured environments. The paradigm proposed by Tunstel and Jamshidi [3] is based on a hierarchical fuzzy control architecture with respect to primitive and advance behaviors of the robot. The fuzzy rule bases for various behaviors are optimized using genetic programming. Figure 2 presents the architecture of GP-Fuzzy autonomous controller architecture.

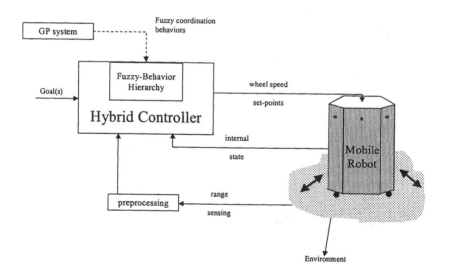

Figure 2: GP-fuzzy mobile robot control architecture.

It is well known [2] that as the number of sensory variables increases, the number of fuzzy rules will reach explosive levels. Therefore, for most complex applications of fuzzy control, such as mobile robot control, a rule reduction approach is a very necessary step of the design process. In an attempt to reduce the rules, the functional operation of the robot is divided into primitive and advanced (composite) behaviors, thereby leading to specialized sets of fuzzy rules to be used on a needed basis at different levels. Figure 3 shows one possible hierarchical decomposition of a mobile robot behavior. As shown, goal-directed navigation of a mobile robot can be decomposed as a behavioral function of goal-seek (collision-free navigation) and route-follow (a path-planning type direction). These behaviors can be further decomposed into primitive behaviors such as avoiding collision and wall-following with associated linguistic rule-base representations. Valid behaviors should conform to the syntactic rules of construction.

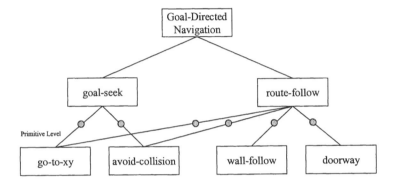

Figure 3: Hierarchical decomposition of mobile robot behavior.

The above theory has been put into both simulation as well as real-time studies. Figure 4 shows the path of the mobile robot under an evolved steady-state genetic programming (SSGP) for coordination and behavior modulation. As compared with a hand-derived coordination and behavior, this approach resulted in a more direct path to the goal due to higher motivation applied to go-to-xy. The resulting path here is executed about 20% faster than the path taken via hand-derived coordination. It is also noted that the behavior modulation under evolved behavior is more complex. Near uniform bouts of competition and cooperation throughout the task are evident in the decision making, thus leading to similar amounts of behavioral influence for each primary behavior. In this section one of many applications of fuzzy logic and its hybridization with genetic programming is represented. The author's research colleagues at the ACE Center have many theoretical and experimental results which cannot possibly be covered here. Interested readers may consult some recent references [1,3].

4.2 Neuro-Fuzzy Control

Another autonomous control approach stemmed from soft computing is the hybridization of fuzzy logic and neural networks for real-time learning (system

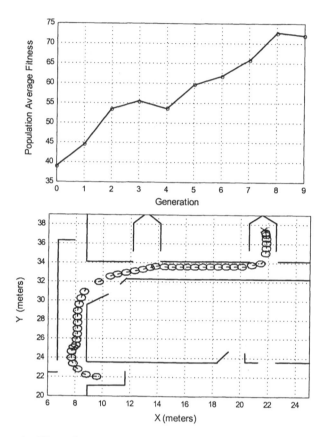

Figure 4: GP performance and resulting goal-seeking task trajectory.

identification) and control. The proposed architecture for autonomous control is based on combining the learning capabilities of NNs and reasoning properties of fuzzy logic paradigms. A neural network learns about the behavior of the plant and uses that knowledge to modify the parameters of an adaptive fuzzy logic controller. The adaptability of the fuzzy controller is derived from a *rule generation mechanism* and modification of the scaling factor or the shape of the membership functions. The rule generation mechanism monitors the system response over a period of time to evaluate new fuzzy rules. Nonredundant rules are appended to the existing rule base during tuning cycles. The membership functions of the input variables are adjusted by a *scaling mechanism*. A multi-layer perceptron neural network classifies the temporal response of the system into various patterns according to oscillatory behaviors, response overshoot, steady state error, etc. This information is used by the decision mechanism which determines the scaling factor of the input membership functions. Another neural network identifies the dynamic system, hence acting as a reference model. This model can be used to determine the stability of the new rules generated before applying to the real system.

In order to implement this hybrid controller in real time, it is necessary to have substantial computing power. The TMS320C30 digital signal processor from Texas Instruments, with its powerful instruction set, high-speed number crunching capability, and innovative architecture is ideally suited for such an application [4]. There are commercially available boards based on TMS320C30 chips, which can be installed on a personal computer. A board from DSP research has been used for this purpose. The software for the control algorithm is developed in C-language and is compiled and downloaded to the DSP board. Collectively, these computing resources are used to implement the neuro-fuzzy controller architecture in real time to control a direct drive motor used as a robot actuator.

Figure 5 presents the neuro-fuzzy autonomous control system which was applied to a direct-drive robot. Figure 6 shows the stabilized response of a typical direct-drive motor of a scalar robot. The fuzzy logic controller has completely learned to control the direct-drive motor after 300 sampling instances.

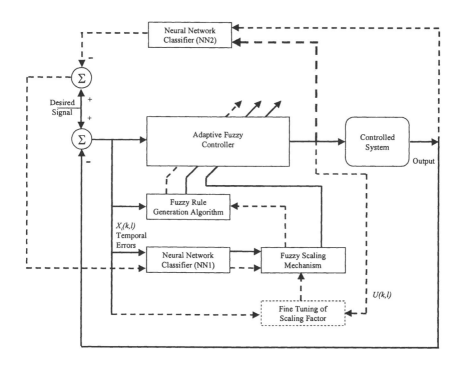

Figure 5: Autonomous control through a neuro-fuzzy architecture.

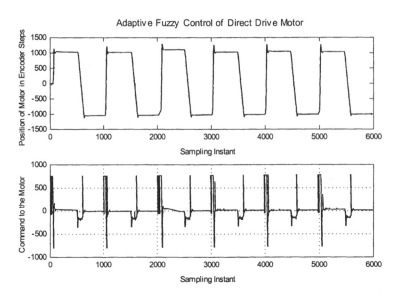

Figure 6: Neuro-fuzzy control stabilizing responses of a direct-drive motor.

4.3 Fuzzy-GA Control

Genetic algorithms are robust optimization routines modeled after the mechanics of Darwinian theory of natural evolution [5]. GAs do not require gradient evaluation. Hence they are capable of solving a great range of optimization problems including determination of optimal parameters of a fuzzy logic rule-set. Genetic algorithms have demonstrated the coding ability to represent parameters of fuzzy knowledge domains such as fuzzy rule sets and membership functions [6] in a genetic structure and, hence, are applicable to optimization of fuzzy rule-sets. Here, several issues pertaining to such integration of the two paradigms are discussed and illustrated through an application on real-time hierarchical fuzzy-GA control of a single-link flexible robotic arm.

To understand the actual mechanism of GAs, one may begin with its three most commonly used operators, namely, reproduction, crossover, and mutation. A member of a given population which has a higher fitness is given a higher chance to reproduce identical replicas of itself in an intermediate population. In this fashion, the optimization routine facilitates reproduction of filter individuals and hampers the reproduction of less fit individuals. After reproduction, crossover randomly "mates" two individuals from an intermediate population and creates offspring which are made up of a random combination of their parents' genetic code. For each generation, the process of crossover is repeated for all individuals in the population. The population size is often a constant and equal to the number of individuals in the initial population. The operations of reproduction and crossover create an environment where every generation benefits from the best genetic codes of the previous generations. However, if the building blocks for the optimal genetic structure are not present in the initial population, these two genetic operators will be unable to find it. The last genetic operator, mutation, randomly mutates one or more of the values in the individual's genetic code in order to create diversity. The mutation operator allows for exploring *new* structures (directions of search) hence allowing the genetic optimization routine to invent new solutions and finally locate the optimal solution even though the individuals in the initial population may not have contained the building blocks for the optimal solution. See Chapters 1 and 2 for further details.

When applying GA to the optimization of fuzzy rule-sets, several concerns arise. First is the design of the transformation function (the interpretation function) between the fuzzy knowledge domain (phenotype) and the GA coded domain (genotype). This is perhaps the most crucial stage of GA design and can significantly degrade the algorithm's performance if a poor or redundant set of parameters is chosen for a given optimization problem. Two important general categories of fuzzy expert knowledge are domain knowledge and meta-knowledge. *Meta-knowledge* is the knowledge used in evaluating rules such as fuzzification (scaling or λ cut), rule evaluation (such as min/max) and defuzzification (such as max membership, centroid, or weighted average) methods. Relatively little research has been performed to study the effect of optimizing the meta-knowledge [7]. Most of the current research, as indicated in this chapter, concentrates on optimizing parameters of the domain knowledge. The domain knowledge consists of the following two categories:

- Membership function: General shape (triangular, trapezoidal, sigmoidal, Gaussian, etc.) and defining points (center, max right, min left, etc.)

- Rule-base: Fuzzy associative memory, disjunctive (OR) and conjunctive (AND) operations among antecedents in the rule base

Even though various methods exist to encode both rule-base and membership functions in one GA representation, such coding can have several potential difficulties. In such situations, in addition to the level of complexity and large number of optimization parameters, the problem of competing conventions may arise and the landscape may unnecessarily become multimodal. This is an important problem since there are often several (or many) fuzzy rule-sets that can represent a given nonlinear function. This means that there is more than one optimal solution to a given optimization problem, which raises the issue of multimodality for fuzzy logic systems or, more specifically, competing conventions where different chromosomes in the representation space have the same interpretation in the evaluation space.

When designing the interpretation function, therefore, the coding needs to contain the fewest possible parameters to avoid the problem of dual representation, and yet the coding needs to have enough complexity to contain all possible optimal or near optimal solutions. Evolutionary approaches such as Niched GA [7] are designed to search in complex multimodal landscapes. As a result, in the present approach, this problem is attended to by limiting the optimization parameter space to membership function parameters only. This was a design decision which was made considering the following:

- The problem of multimodality is introduced when the GA string contains both parameters of membership functions and rules.

- In the control of most physical systems, rules can often be derived either intuitively or through operator experience. The ambiguous and *fuzzy* portion of a knowledge base is often the membership function.

For simplicity in coding of simulation and real-time algorithms, only triangular membership functions are coded for optimization here. Figure 7 illustrates a triangular membership function whose three determining parameters (a,b,c) are shown. Assuming a normalized membership function, the three parameters are real numbers between -1 and 1. The coding in GA is performed as follows: The real parameter a is first mapped to an n-bit signed binary string where the highest bit represents the sign (see Figure 8). This way, the parameter a can take on 2^n different values. Then the binary number is aggregated with other n-bit binary numbers to construct the phenotype representation.

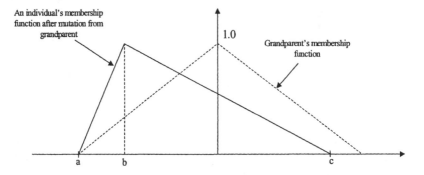

Figure 7: A triangular membership function with its three parameters.

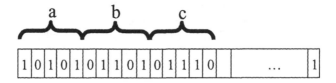

Figure 8: Coding of a GA chromosome.

The second issue which arises is how to utilize initial expert knowledge for a better and faster convergence. In other search routines such as hill-climbing, it is clear that starting from a "good" point can significantly improve computation time needed for convergence to an optimal solution.

However, the conventional GA applications generate a random initial population without using any a priori expert knowledge. This, in general, will provide a more diverse population while sacrificing convergence time. This convention can indeed be adequate if there is no a priori knowledge as to where a "good" solution may exist. However, in fuzzy logic applications, there is usually access to some expert knowledge which, even though it may not be the optimal solution, is often a reasonably good solution. Schultz and Grefenstette [8] addressed the problem of incorporating a priori knowledge by introducing two types of populations, homogeneous and heterogeneous. The homogeneous population consists of individuals created randomly while their string is augmented with the same prior rules. In this sense, they are all identical and hence homogeneous. He concluded that a trade-off exists between manual knowledge and machine learning. The heterogeneous population consists of members that are not identical. This is also referred to as the "seeding" technique. In reference [9] the process of seeding the initial population with one or more experts' knowledge is proposed. The few seeded chromosomes have the chance of reproducing through mutation and crossover with other randomly generated chromosomes in the population. This method improves the performance of a GA by providing the genetic population with a set of highly fit building blocks, as compared with GAs starting with random initial populations. However, such population still requires a large number of iterations before convergence since the "useful" schemata exist in only one or a few seeded members and can only be reproduced as fast as the rate of reproduction. Akbarzadeh [4] proposed the grandparenting scheme where the initial population is composed of mutations of the "knowledgeable" grandparent. This scheme takes advantage of expert knowledge while maintaining the diversity necessary for an effective search. Through grandparenting, an expert's a priori knowledge can be used to improve fitness of the GA's initial population, thereby increasing the speed and performance of the search routine. In the present approach, the method of grandparenting is used to improve the convergence rate of the GA optimization process.

The third issue concerns defining a fitness function. A fitness function is a very important aspect of GA design, because it determines the direction of the search. Fitness functions come in as many different forms as the systems which they are optimizing. In general, for a lumped parameter system (for example, a flexible robot arm), parameters such as control effort $u(t)$, rise-time t_r, overshoot γ, and steady-state error e_{ss} are usually incorporated in a quadratic fitness function. Often, constant multipliers define the relative degree of importance which is given to a specific parameter compared with others.

The above concepts were applied to controller optimization of a flexible link robotic system as shown in Figure 9. The flexible link can be represented by a distributed-parameter system with *spatial* as well as *temporal* parameters. In other words, the states of a flexible robotic system are functions of both space and time. This complicates the modeling of the system and, consequently, the process of designing the controller. Due to the complexity of a mathematical representation for such systems, fuzzy logic is considered an attractive alternative to their control. One of the issues in development of fuzzy controllers is determining faithful expert knowledge. Expert knowledge, however, is difficult to generate since there is often no human expert to consult, and training a human expert may not be a feasible alternative due to cost and other practical considerations. Furthermore, human psychological issues may prohibit a faithful reproduction of a rule-base from an expert. In addition, the unstructured operating environments associated with space and waste handling projects require the robot controller to also adapt to changing conditions. In the process of designing fuzzy rule sets, membership functions are often chosen through an ad hoc process of random selection and evaluation. As a viable alternative, good results have been achieved by employing genetic algorithms to tune membership parameters within a fuzzy controller's knowledge base [10]. Genetic algorithms equip the fuzzy controller with some evolutionary means by which it can improve its rule-base when faced with inadequate a priori expert knowledge or varying circumstances in its operating environment.

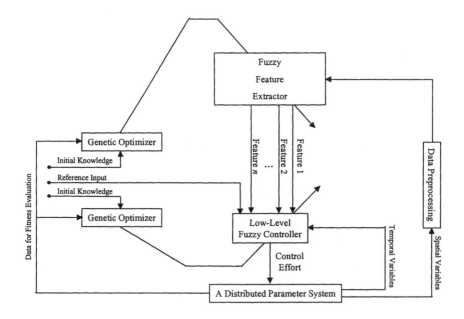

Figure 9: Autonomous control architecture through a fuzzy-GA approach.

Within the hierarchical control architecture, the higher level module serves as a fuzzy classifier by determining spatial features of the arm such as straight, oscillator, and curved. This information is supplied to the lower level of hierarchy where it is processed among other sensory information such as errors in position and velocity for the purpose of determining a desirable control input (torque). In [4] this control system is simulated using only a priori expert knowledge.

To demonstrate the usage of genetic algorithms, GA is applied to optimize parameters related to input membership functions of the upper level of hierarchy. Other parameters in the knowledge base are not allowed to vary. The fitness criterion used to evaluate various individuals within a population of potential solutions was based on the error $e(t)$, effort $u(t)$, and γ as an inverse square function. Consequently, a fitter individual is an individual with a lower overshoot and a lower overall error (shorter rise time) in its time response. Here, results from previous simulations of the architecture are applied experimentally. The method of *grandparenting* [4] was used to create the initial population. Members of the initial population are created through mutation of the knowledgeable *grandparent(s)*. As a result, a fitter initial population results in a faster rate of convergence as is exhibited in Figure 10. Figure 10(a) shows the time response of the GA-optimized controller when compared with previously obtained results through the non-GA fuzzy controller. The rise time is improved by 0.34 seconds (an 11% improvement), and the overshoot is reduced by 0.07 radians (a 54% improvement). The average fitness of each generation is shown in Figure 10(b). A total of 10 generations were simulated. The mutation rate for creating the initial population was set at 0.1. This value was chosen to increase diversity among members of the initial population. A GA depends on this diversity to exploit a large number of differing paths of solutions in parallel. The mutation rate throughout the rest of the simulation, however, was set to 0.6. Initial experimental results demonstrate that the GA-learned controller is able to control the actual experimental system as in Figure 10(c).

5 Expert Systems for Image Enhancement

5.1 Introduction

This research presents a systematic approach to enhancing the quality of images obtained from many different sources, e.g., video, television, scanner, and Internet, using fuzzy expert systems. The input is digitized, passed through a subject of interest (SOI) detector (which could be chosen based on the application), and attributes of the image are calculated and entered into the expert system. The outputs of the expert system are the new optimal settings that result in an enhanced quality image (see Figure 11). In the case of a live input, the image is frozen first before digitization.

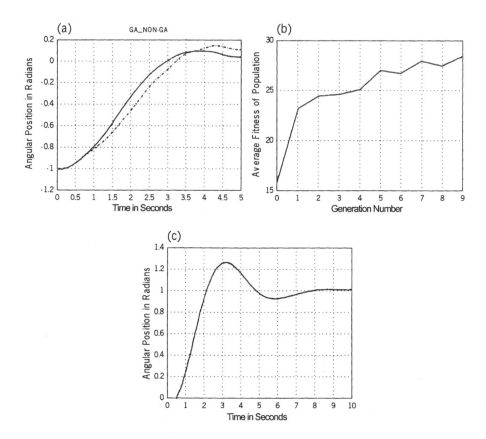

Figure 10:   Computer simulation and experimental results of GA-fuzzy autonomous control system. (a) Simulation, (b) fitness function behavior, and
(c) experimental results.

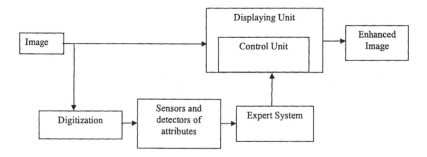

Figure 11: Block diagram for image quality enhancement using an expert system.

In this project the effectiveness of expert systems in enhancing images using fuzzy logic methodologies is demonstrated using two different image sources. The first is digital images that are downloaded from the Internet, and the second is color photos obtained from color negatives. For both sources, the subject of interest is chosen to be skin tone. To implement the expert systems, a software package, SmartPhotoLab©, was developed using Visual C++. The expert systems embedded within SmartPhotoLab© detect unwanted features in an image and enhance the quality of the image in terms of brightness, contrast, color, and tint. Smart-PhotoLab© calculates a set of parameters based on the image under investigation. These parameters are then passed to expert systems. The outputs of the expert systems are the new set of parameters needed to enhance the image. The expert system for enhancing analog images is implemented on a microcontroller board which is also called SmartPhotoLab©.

5.2 Enhancement of Digital Images

SmartPhotoLab© is a software designed to enhance the quality of digital images. An expert system embedded within SmartPhotoLab© detects undesired quantities and enhances the quality of the image. Unlike most of the commercial products on the market this software tool does not require the user to have any image processing knowledge. An image can be enhanced by a click of a button. SmartPhotoLab© is a user friendly, multidocument, and menu-driven software tool. The user has the capability to enhance the image in one shot or to go through the intermediate steps to visually see the process of enhancement. The inputs of the expert system are color, tint, brightness, and contrast. The outputs of the expert system are the new color, tint, brightness, and contrast that will result in an enhanced image. A flow chart of the software is presented in Figure 12. A typical enhancement for Internet-based images using SmartPhotoLab© is shown in Figure 13.

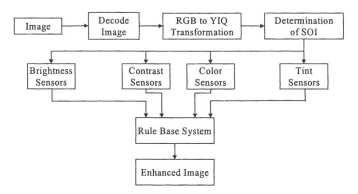

Figure 12: SmartPhotoLab© flow chart.

(a)   (b)

Figure 13: Typical digital images for skin tone and image enhancement:
(a) image before enhancement, (b) image after enhancement.

5.3 Enhancement of Analog Images

The same concept is applied to analog images. An expert system was developed to obtain a good quality photo automatically without the need for a human expert. This application is briefly described in the following subsections. The experimental system is outlined and the steps of the application are given.

5.3.1 Color Photography

Photographic films and paper (color) are manufactured with three separate light sensitive layers of emulsion, one is sensitive to red light, one to green light, and one to blue light. Each of the layers, when exposed and processed, forms a specific color dye. The dyes are the complementary color of corresponding light sensitive layer. The overall density of the recreated color, that is, how dark or light it appears, is dependent upon the densities of the dye layers in the film. The density of a dye layer is directly proportional to the exposure it receives. Consequently, by controlling the light using transparent filters as well as the exposure time, the quality of the image could be controlled.

The current systems require an expert to print the image and then, based on the output, determine the required filtration of light and the exposure time to obtain a good quality photo. Figure 14 demonstrates the process of developing a color photo with a human expert. Generally, the operator selects a filter pack and expo-sure time, and then prints the photo. If the result is not satisfying, a different set-ting will be chosen. Consequently, the process of printing is time consuming and, for nonexperienced users, is difficult and expensive.

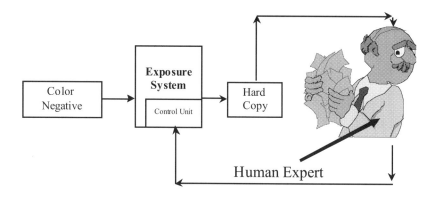

Figure 14: Exposure system controlled by a human expert.

5.3.2 Experimental Setup

The hardware setup is shown in Figure 15. The image from the color negative is digitized and entered into the computer (see Figure 16). The negative image is then transformed into a positive image (see Figure 17). The positive image is then entered into SmartPhotoLab©. The attributes of the image are determined and used as an input to the expert system. The output of the expert system is the new cyan, magenta, and yellow filters and the exposure time necessary to obtain the final good quality image. A typical analog image (35mm color photos) enhance-ment using the SmartPhotoCard© process is shown in Figure 18. For further de-tails on this patented [11] project, interested readers may refer to the works of El-Osery, Jamshidi and others [12-15].

6 Summary

The basic theme of this chapter was autonomous control and autonomy through several architectures of soft computing. A number of robotic applications were used to illustrate these architectures. These autonomous controllers are simple to implement in a laboratory environment on either a PC or on a chip-level board. Soon, autonomous control through intelligent paradigms technology will be a matter of economy and not controversy. It features applications in a wide variety of fields such as control, pattern recognition, medicine, finance, and marketing.

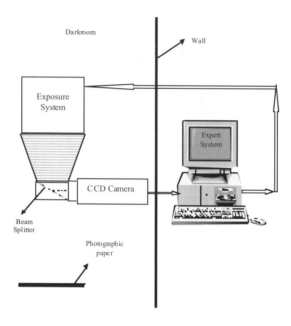

Figure 15: Hardware setup.

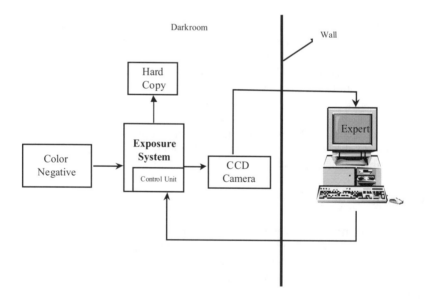

Figure 16: Automated process of enhancing an analog image.

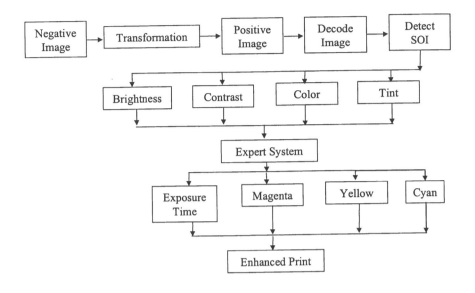

Figure 17: Software flow chart.

(a)   (b)

Figure 18: Typical enhancement of analog images:
(a) image before enhancement, (b) image after enhancement.

These techniques should be given serious consideration as additional tools for the solution of problems that are suitable for this technology, notably, problems where a mathematical model is neither available nor feasible. Applications to complex systems require careful consideration of the system's model, its structure, the behavior and means of sensory data, and rule specialization and hierarchy. Finally, new avenues should be opened for new software design and analysis of control systems using the power and efficiency of tools such as fuzzy logic, neural networks, and genetic algorithms. The expert systems (discussed in Section 5) designed for both analog and digital images have demonstrated very promising results. The results contribute to a software and a hardware product that will automate the process of image enhancement in both analog and digital domains.

Acknowledgements

This work was supported, in part, by NASA Grant Number NCCW-0087. The author wishes to thank many peers and associates. He wishes to thank Professor C.W. de Silva for the invitation to contribute this chapter. Deligent work of his former and current doctoral students Dr. Edward Tunstel, Jr., Dr. Kishan Kumbla, Dr. Mohammad Akbarzadeh, Dr. Ali Asgharzadeh, and Mr. Aly El-Osery is very much appreciated. Last, but not least, he thanks Ms. Sandi Avrit of ACE Center for helping prepare this chapter for the book.

References

[1]   Jamshidi, M., *Large-Scale Systems — Modeling, Control, and Fuzzy Logic,* Prentice Hall Series on Environmental and Intelligent Manufacturing Systems (M. Jamshidi, Ed.),Vol. 8, Saddle River, NJ, 1996.

[2]   Jamshidi, M., "Fuzzy Control of Complex Systems," *Soft Computing*, Vol. 1, No. 1, pp. 42-56, 1997.

[3]   Tunstel, E.W. and Jamshidi, M., "Intelligent Control and Evolution of Mobile Robot Behavior," *Applications of Fuzzy Logic — Towards High MIQ® Systems* (M. Jamshidi, A. Titli, L. A. Zadeh, and S. Boverei, Eds.), Prentice Hall Series on Environmental and Intelligent Manufacturing (M. Jamshidi, Ed.), Vol. 9, Saddle River, NJ, 1997.

[4]   Akbarzadeh, M.R., *Fuzzy Control and Evolutionary Optimization of Complex Systems,* PhD Dissertation, EECE Department and ACE Center, University of New Mexico, Albuquerque, NM, 1998.

[5]   Goldberg, D.E., *Genetic Algorithms in Search, Optimization and Machine Learning*, Addison-Wesley, Bedford, MA, 1989.

[6]   Homaifar, A. and McCormick, E., "Simultaneous Design of Membership Functions and Rule Sets for Fuzzy Controllers Using Genetic Algorithms," *IEEE Transactions on Fuzzy Systems*, Vol. 3, No. 2, p. 129, 1995.

[7]   Akbarzadeh, M., Kumbla, K., Tunstel, Jr., E., and Jamshidi, M., "Soft
        Computing for Autonomous Robotic Systems," *International Journal on
        Computers in Electrical Engineering,* Vol. 26, No. 1, pp. 5-32, 2000.
[8]   Schultz, A.C. and Grefenstette, J.J., "Improving Tactical Plans with Ge-
        netic Algorithms," *Proceedings of the 2nd International Conference on
        Tools for AI,* Herndon, VA, June 1990.
[9]   Lee, M.A. and Takagi, H., "Embedding Apriori Knowledge into an Inte-
        grated Fuzzy System Design Method Based on Genetic Algorithms," *Pro-
        ceedings of the 5th IFSA World Congress,* San Palo, Brazil, July 1995.
[10]   Lee, M.A. and Takagi, H., "Integrating Design Stages of Fuzzy Systems
        Using Genetic Algorithms," *Proceedings of the 1993 IEEE International
        Conference on Fuzzy Systems,* San Francisco, CA, pp. 612-617, June 1993.
[11]   Asgharzadeh, A. and Jamshidi, M., *Fuzzy Logic Control Video Printer,* US
        Patent No. 5, 590, 246, December 1996.
[12]   Asgharzadeh, A. and Gaewsky, J., "Application of Fuzzy Logic in a Video
        Printer," *Proc. World Automation Congress,* Maui, HI, Vol. 4, TSI Press,
        Albuquerque, NM, pp. 445-448, August 1994.
[13]   Asgharzadeh, A., El-Osery, A., and Pages, O., "Enhancement of Images
        Obtained by Digital Cameras Using Fuzzy Logic," *Proc. World Automation
        Congress,* Anchorage, AK, Vol. 8, TSI Press, Albuquerque, NM, pp. 829-
        834, 1998.
[14]   El-Osery, A., *Design and Implementation of Expert Systems for Digital and
        Analog Image Enhancement,* MS Thesis, EECE Department and ACE
        Center, University of New Mexico, Albuquerque, NM, 1998.
[15]   El-Osery, A. and Jamshidi, M., "Image Enhancement: Probability Versus
        Fuzzy Expert Systems," Chapter 7 in *Applications of Fuzzy Logic and
        Probability Theory,* (Booker et al., Eds.), SIAM and American Statistical
        Association, Alexandria, VA, 2000 (to appear).

7 INTELLIGENT PRODUCTION MACHINES: BENEFITING FROM SYNERGY AMONG MODELING, SENSING, AND LEARNING

Patri K. Venuvinod
Professor and Head
Department of Manufacturing Engineering and Engineering Management
City University of Hong Kong
Tat Chee Avenue, Kowloon, Hong Kong

A historical review of manufacturing indicates that the need for the application of reflexive as well reflective intelligence is on the rise. Therefore, there is considerable scope for the application of artificial intelligence (AI) in manufacturing. The interest in AI is mainly utilitarian for manufacturing engineers. This chapter will introduce some AI-related issues at the shop floor level. Attention will be drawn to the concept of holonic manufacturing system and a case study on geometric feature recognition that utilizes a heuristic derived from a theory of human cognition of objects. At the work center level, the desirability of obtaining synergistic interactions among process modeling, sensing, and learning will be highlighted. Finally, a case study on the development of intelligent production machines that are capable of learning to compensate for workpiece errors will be presented.

1 Introduction

Artificial intelligence (AI) is a recently emerging discipline inspired by a desire to emulate human intelligence in a computer. An introduction to this topic is given in Chapter 1. The present chapter discusses some aspects of the relationship between the fields of AI and manufacturing engineering as currently viewed by manufacturing researchers. Manufacturing engineering is a field with a much longer history than AI. It aims to rationalize the societal activity called manufacturing. It is an interdisciplinary field that has adopted concepts drawn from diverse disciplines such as mechanical/electronic/computer engineering, material science, operations research, systems engineering, and management. It is a professional field and its interest in any other discipline is largely utilitarian. Thus, the typical reaction of a manufacturing engineer to AI is "How can AI serve my needs?" In other words, a manufacturing engineer looks at AI as a bag of new tools.

Given the vast scope of both AI and manufacturing engineering, the present discussion can be only sketchy. This chapter will present a historical view of manufacturing, identify the factors driving the contemporary manufacturing scene, refer to a selection of AI-related activities currently in progress, and speculate on how AI could help in resolving some thorny manufacturing issues. In the interest of brevity, references to AI-related manufacturing research activities will be largely drawn from the Center for Intelligent Design, Automation and Manufacture (CIDAM) of City University of Hong Kong. Further, the discussion will mainly focus on machining; i.e., on shaping products through material removal.

2 Development of Manufacturing

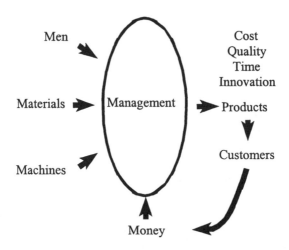

Figure 1: The nature of manufacturing.

Modern manufacturing involves the coordinated integration (management) of human workers, materials, and machines to produce products that satisfy customers (see Figure 1). The role of human workers in manufacturing is threefold. First, wherever mechanization is not feasible, workers have to provide the muscular energy needed to perform the manufacturing tasks. Second, human workers need to possess the dexterity to (a) manually perform the manufacturing processes whenever a machine is not available, and (b) control the machines whenever the machines do not have the necessary dexterity to perform the task. Human dexterity involves the application of human sensorimotor skills that, in turn, require the application of human intelligence. Here the term *intelligence* is used as being synonymous with r*easoning*. However, in the context of dexterity, this reasoning is subconscious, nondeliberate, and reflexive. Hence, we will call such intelligence *reflexive intelligence*.

Finally, the design, planning, and control of manufacturing systems—which, in the modern context, are highly complex—require the application of higher levels of reasoning in a conscious, deliberate, and reflective manner. Such intelligence may be called *reflective intelligence*.

Figure 2 presents a qualitative graph (one that is informative with regard to qualitative trends but not necessarily accurate from a quantitative point of view) of how the patterns of demand for human muscular power, reflexive intelligence (dexterity), and reflective intelligence have been changing.

Prior to the industrial revolution that started in 1760, products were made totally by craftsmen through the application of human muscular power, dexterity (human sensorimotor control), and intelligence. Often, the same person undertook the tasks of designing, manufacturing, selling, etc. There was little separation between the various levels of manufacturing (see Figure 3). Thus, this was the age of unarticulated integration.

The first phase of industrial revolution (1760-1880) saw the development of a variety of powered production machines, viz. lathes, milling machines, etc. [1]. Thus, workers were progressively relieved of the burden of expending muscular power at the machine and work center levels. However, workers continued to expend muscular energy in carrying out material handling at the shop floor level. This decreasing trend in the demand for human muscular power gained momentum during the second phase of industrial revolution (1880-1950) through progressive mechanization of shop floor level activities. It was in this period that Henry Ford, the famed automobile manufacturer, pioneered the assembly line.

The development of powered machines however did not decrease the need for human dexterity. In fact, workers had to continually *learn* new sensorimotor skills. For instance, they had to learn to *control* the carriage of a lathe to move at a constant feed rate so as to ensure good finish on the machined part. This scenario however changed with the development of computer numerical control (CNC) during the third phase (1950-to date) of the industrial revolution. CNC allows a machine's axes to be controlled through computer programs. It makes it possible to economically create different programs for different tasks. Thus, CNC allows flexible automation of manufacturing processes. Likewise, it allows flexible automation of material handling through the use of automated guided vehicles (AGV), robots, etc. As a result, unlike in the past when work center level automation was possible only with large production batches, CNC has made it feasible to automate production in small batches. As a consequence, the need for the application of human reflexive intelligence (dexterity) at the work center level has continued to diminish. For instance, it has been shown recently that a standard robot can be programmed to perform even polishing operations, which hitherto could be performed only by skilled workers [2].

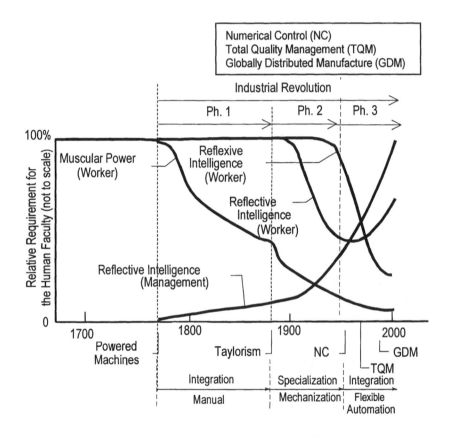

Figure 2: Changing patterns of relative demand for different human faculties in manufacturing.

The advent of powered machines during the first phase of industrial revolution dramatically increased the pace of production activity. This led to the introduction of the factory system that, in turn, led to increased production, improved standards of living at least in the industrialized regions and, hence, to larger markets.

With growth in industrial technology, manufacturing became increasingly complex. Workers needed to apply more than reflexive intelligence. For instance, they had to continually acquire new knowledge concerning the myriad ways in which the workpiece material, size, and shape influence the manufacturing process and the quality (accuracy, finish, etc.) of the parts produced. Further, they had to acquire new decision-making skills such as those needed while determining the cutting conditions (cutting speed, feed rate, depth of cut, etc.) that lead to efficient production. All this required the continued application of reflective intelligence from workers possessing little formal education. Presumably, the workers subconsciously developed qualitative models (cause-effect models, explanation-based reasoning, case-based reasoning, etc.). In time, textbooks (often, under the title of "Workshop Technology") started appearing that captured this kind of qualitative knowledge and reasoning.

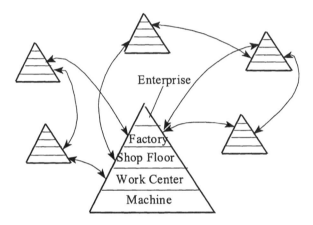

Figure 3: Organization of modern manufacturing.

The second phase of industrial revolution (1880-1950) dramatically changed the higher levels of factory organization. Whereas most production was carried out with small batch sizes during the first phase, many factories engaging in mass production started appearing during the second phase. Workmen became increasingly specialized, i.e., monotonously repeating a set of tasks. Efforts were made to measure (for example, through "Time Study" developed by F.W. Taylor) and work became even more routine and tedious.

Meanwhile manufacturing enterprises were becoming more complex so that several new factory level issues (for example, related to production planning and control) needed to be addressed. The resolution of these issues required more refined and abstract human reasoning. F.W. Taylor, the acknowledged "Father of Scientific Management," realized this need and suggested that "the management take over all work for which they are better fitted than the workmen, while in the past all of the work and the greater part of the responsibility were thrown upon the men" [3]. Thus, the need for the application of reflective intelligence at the level of manufacturing workers decreased while that at the managerial level increased rapidly.

The incorporation of a computer within the machine during the third (current) phase of industrial revolution triggered further dramatic changes at higher levels of manufacturing. Today, machines can communicate with each other through their respective computers. This realization has led to rapid development of shop floor networking and supervisory control in recent years.

By the 1980s, the dream of "unmanned manufacturing" in the form of flexible manufacturing systems (FMS) appeared closer to realization. A few large-scale FMS were actually built. In keeping with the state of technology at that time, these FMS were mainly controlled in a hierarchical manner. However, it was soon recognized that flexible manufacturing was too complex to be controlled in such a fashion. As a result, the role of human reflective intelligence was reasserted and attention shifted to computer-aided technologies such as computer-aided design (CAD) and computer-aided manufacture (CAM), and to their integration through computer-*integrated* manufacturing (CIM). It must be noted that CIM is an ever-receding goal whereas CAD, CAM, and other technologies such as computer-aided process planning (CAPP) and design for manufacture (DFM) are just enablers in our progression towards CIM.

In recent years, several dramatic changes have taken place in the global environment within which a manufacturing enterprise has to operate. The consumer has become the "bull's eye" and the hub of the "manufacturing wheel" [4] and is demanding ever-increasing product variety, quality, and innovation coupled with ever-decreasing product life cycle times. Further, a strong movement has started in favor of sustainable manufacture and ISO14000 so as to protect world ecology from the ravages of manufacturing activities.

The contemporary response to the need for improved product and process quality has been the adoption of ISO9000 and total quality management (TQM) complemented by worker level movements such as quality control circles (QCC) and factory level movements such as just-in-time (JIT). All these are people-oriented movements. As a result, the need for reflective intelligence has rapidly increased at both worker and management levels (see Figure 2). Equally important is the fact that the gap between management and workers is decreasing. Worker specialization is progressively yielding to worker integration. In the 21st century, a manufacturing engineer is expected to be not just a technical specialist but also an operations integrator and a manufacturing strategist [5,6]. Further, individual focus will yield to teamwork, and there will be more human and less technical orientation [5].

The drive towards integration has extended even to the level of communities of enterprises (see Figure 3). Given technological advances such as the Internet, geographic distance between enterprises is no more an issue. This development, coupled with the relaxation of trade barriers in many parts of the world, has resulted in a trend towards globally distributed manufacture (GDM) and virtual enterprises (VE).

To survive in the new global marketing and manufacturing environment, it is no longer adequate that an enterprise just knows how to make products. Rather, it needs to know how to make them *competitively*.

It appears that enterprises usually progress through three successive strategies in the continuing bid to secure competitive advantage—productivity (P), quality (Q), and innovation (I). The game of competing through (P) and (Q) is reasonably well understood at least in the industrialized part of the world. However, the game of competing through (I) is more recent. Enterprises will have to acquire new technologies more rapidly and integrate them into their products, processes, and systems in an agile manner. One such "technology" is AI.

3 Contemporary Manufacturing and AI

The previous section concluded that contemporary manufacturing enterprises need to rapidly assimilate technologies such as AI to remain globally competitive. AI purists may object to the use of the term *technology* here, but that is exactly the way manufacturing view AI.

There is little agreement even within the AI community regarding the intent and role of AI or exactly when a machine can be considered to be intelligent. As early as 1963, Turing [7] had anticipated that an intelligent computer must be "kind, resourceful, beautiful, friendly, have initiative, have a sense of humor, tell right from wrong, make mistakes, fall in love, enjoy strawberries and cream, make someone fall in love with it, learn from experience, use words properly, be the subject of its own thought, have as much diversity of behavior as man, [and] do something really new." Clearly, this is a distant dream (or nightmare?). However, it would certainly be much easier to cope with the complexities of manufacturing in the 21st century if manufacturing enterprises were to have access to computers that are "resourceful," "have initiative," "learn from practice," and "use words properly." See Chapter 3 for another view of this aspect.

Turing's description of an intelligent computer is almost the same as that of a *good* human being. It is not surprising therefore that a large part of the AI community has used AI as a means of understanding and emulating human cognitive processes (see Chapter 1). However, even in this context, there is considerable diversity of opinion. McCarthy et al. suggest that *mind* is logic [8]. Rumelhart and McClelland think that *mind* is a connectionistic network [9]. To Schank, *mind* is a conceptualization [10]. Newell et al. consider *mind* to be rule-chunking [11]. Minsky prefers connectionism and conceptual dependency theory [12].

The manufacturing community however has largely been unconcerned about the anthropomorphic motivations of the AI community. For manufacturing engineers, AI is simply "the study of ways in which computers can be made to perform tasks which require intelligence if performed by humans" (I am paraphrasing Flach [13] who actually belongs to the AI community). In particular, manufacturing engineers would like to either automatically perform or significantly assist human workmen and engineers in performing the myriad manufacturing tasks (such as process/production planning, vendor selection) that typically require human intelligence. Just as Flach, they prefer to assume that the subject matter of AI is the computer rather than the human mind.

Manufacturing engineers prefer to identify AI on the basis of the functionality it provides rather than on the basis of the processes used to achieve the functionality. An AI view that is likely to appeal to manufacturing engineers is the following (from Schank and Jona [10]):

- *AI is learning.* "Intelligence means adapting to the environment and improving performance over time. Thus, if the goal of AI is to build intelligent systems, one of the things that AI has to be about is the study of learning."
- *AI is memory organization and access.* "How a system gains access to its knowledge, and how it organizes memory to facilitate access, provide fundamental functional constraints on the nature of cognitive architectures."
- *AI is functional constraints plus knowledge analysis.* "The discovery and application of functional constraints imposed on cognitive processing and the analysis of the knowledge used in that processing form the bread-and-butter of AI research."
- *AI is scale-up.* "An intelligent system that can only behave intelligently in two or three carefully selected situations is not really intelligent. AI is about building systems that can handle hundreds or even thousands of examples, not just two or three."

There has been considerable interest in AI since the 1980s within the manufacturing community. As early as 1983, Hatvany noted the nondeterministic nature of manufacturing systems and stated that AI had the potential to transform such a system into an intelligent system that is "capable of solving, within certain limits, unprecedented, unforeseen problems on the basis even of incomplete and imprecise information" [14]. CIRP (International Institute for Production Engineering Research) sponsored seminars on intelligent manufacturing systems held at Dubrovnik in 1985, 1987, and 1989. In 1992, Yoshikawa observed that intelligent techniques had become one of the most important fields of manufacturing automation [15]. In 1993, Merchant identified expert systems, neural networks, and smart sensors as the most promising [6]. In 1996, Monostori cited 251 papers on the subject in his CIRP keynote paper on machine learning approaches [16].

A cursory review of AI related literature that is currently available within the manufacturing field leads to the following observations:

- Very few AI tools have seen full-scale application in industrial manufacture. Most papers written on the subject merely establish the feasibility of applying AI tool X in manufacturing application domain Y. Very few seem to have stood up to the "scale up" criterion of Schank [10].
- There has been considerable interest in learning through the use of artificial neural nets (ANN) and fuzzy logic for applications in control and robotics, AGV navigation, etc. that require mainly reflexive intelligence when performed by human operators (for example, [17-21]) and tasks, such as machine diagnostics (for example, [22-24]), requiring specific combinations of reflexive intelligence and low level reflective intelligence. See Chapters 1 and 5.
- Expert systems have been used extensively in the context of higher level manufacturing tasks (for example, [25,26]) that require reflective intelligence. However, in most cases, the production rules have been derived from the intuition (albeit only occasionally informed) of the system writer rather than on the basis of a rigorous application of knowledge engineering approaches developed by the AI community. See Chapter 1.
- There is a significant gap with regard to the use of AI in the context of planning tasks at higher levels of manufacturing.

It is worthwhile dwelling a little more on the last observation. Typically, a professional engineer engaged in planning and design tasks makes extensive use of documented knowledge obtained from textbooks, handbooks, industrial standards, etc. The planner then extracts the relevant knowledge from the documented sources, structures it into a network of qualitative and quantitative models, and applies her/his reflective intelligence to detect and manipulate patterns of information. The reasoning involved in such situations is usually "deep" in the sense that the planner is not just interested in a solution but also needs to know *why* it is a solution so that (s)he could judge the feasibility and value of the decision.

Note that, in the sense used in the previous paragraph, solving a problem using subsymbolic approaches (such as by using a neural net) cannot be called "reasoning." A neural net helps make a decision but it does not explain why; i.e., it does not give the reason. See Chapter 5.

In contrast, a well-developed expert system can provide a reason at least in the sense that it can list the particular set of production rules that have contributed to the recommended decision (see Chapter i). However, note that, in practice, these production rules have often not been explicitly derived from documented knowledge. In fact, many AI scientists themselves question whether expert systems actually emulate human reasoning. For instance, Winograd and Flores say that it "is so patently obvious when you work with *experts*, namely that they have so much difficulty laying out consistent networks and describing relations among concepts in a principled way ..." [27]. Likewise, Clancey thinks that rule-based expert systems can only "replicate mechanical, highly regular actions" whereas "[t]he theory of situated action claims that human behavior is, at its core, inherently improvisatory and nondeliberated" [28].

It can be concluded from the above discussion that the penetration of AI into deep tasks such as planning at higher levels of manufacture has only been "skin deep" so far. Manufacturing engineers therefore need to explore more vigorously the application of symbolic approaches such as explanation-based reasoning (EBR) and case-based reasoning (CBR) [29].

4 The Societies of Mind and Manufacture

A concept called *holonic* manufacturing systems (HMS) has received much attention within the manufacturing community in recent years [30]. The concept has been triggered by the observations Koestler [31] made in 1989 while explaining the structure that is visible in biological systems and real-life complex systems. Koestler argued that complex systems in a demanding environment need to be built from subsystems that are *autonomous* and *co-operative*. In an HMS, these subsystems are called *holons*. Here, *autonomy* means the capability of an entity to create and control the execution of its own plans and/or strategies whereas *cooperation* refers to the ability of the entities to develop mutually acceptable plans and execute these plans. Holons can be physical entities or software entities. All holons have information processing capabilities. Physical holons have, in addition, a physical processing part. A holon by itself need not be complex or intelligent. Complexity and intelligence *emerge* at higher levels through interactions among holons at lower levels.

It is apparent that manufacturing takes place through a *society* of holons in the HMS paradigm. This metaphor of *society* is very similar to that used by Minsky in his book *The Society of Mind* [12]. Minsky says the following: "[M]ind is made up of many smaller processes. These we'll call *agents*. Each mental agent by itself can only do simple things that need no mind or thought at all. Yet when we join these agents in societies — in certain special ways — this leads to true intelligence."

Note that agent theory has already become an established part of AI and agents have many similarities with holons. Russel and Norvig [32] define an *agent* as "a system situated within and a part of an environment that senses the environment and acts on it, over time, in pursuit of its own agenda and so as to effect what it senses in the future." Wooldridge and Jennings [33] define *agent* as "a self-contained problem solver entity (implemented in hardware, software, or a mixture of the two) which exhibits a collection of possible properties ranging from autonomy, social ability, responsiveness, proactiveness, adaptability, mobility, veracity, and rationality."

Likewise, emergent behavior is not new to the AI community. A great deal of literature has been accumulated on emergent computation (for example, see [34]). Hofstadter, an AI scientist, observed long ago that "information which is absent at lower levels can exist at the level of collective activities" [35].

Much work has started within the manufacturing community towards implementing the holonic paradigm. Valckenaers et al. have implemented holonic concepts for steel rolling, NC controllers, machining, assembly, and AGV planning and control [30]. Their work has shown that holonic systems are superior to hierarchical and heterarchical systems in terms of system robustness and the ability to handle disturbances. Kruth et al. have shown that NC holons can be made to exhibit self-assertive (self-repair, and self-configuration) and self-integrative behavior [36]. Although they had not explicitly utilized holonic precepts, Zhao has recently developed an agent-based cooperative framework for process planning [37].

5 Case Study 1: Geometric Feature Recognition

An AI approach applicable to planning activities at all levels of manufacturing (see Figure 3) has been outlined in the previous section. This section will present a brief description of a case study on geometric feature recognition (GFR)—an activity that is common to a large number of planning activities such as process planning, assembly planning, inspection planning, tool and fixture design, and group technology (GT) implementation that are regularly carried out at the shop floor level.

A *geometric feature* is any subset of the geometric model of the object, which is of interest in a particular context. The geometry of an object feature is implicit in its very existence and, hence, context independent. However, from an application viewpoint, the meaning and relevance of the geometry is certainly context dependent. The variety of geometric features encountered in practice is unlimited (the object in Figure 4 includes a representative selection of polyhedral and cylindrical features); yet, this infinite variety of features needs to be recognized using a finite GFR system.

GFR involves arriving at meaningful higher level interpretations of the object model which usually requires sifting through substantial amounts of low level data concerning the part specification (specifications of vertices, edges, faces, etc.). Next, one needs to partition this large volume of low level data into segments of interest (*feature extraction*), pattern-match each segment against a list of descriptions of known features (*feature identification*), and, finally, interpret each of the identified patterns (features) in the context of the application at hand (*feature interpretation*).

All the GFR tasks described above hinge on pattern recognition—an area in which AI can be expected to excel. Hence, not surprisingly, many AI approaches have been applied to the problem of GFR. For instance, Henderson [38] has applied a rule-based expert system approach to extract polyhedral geometric features from CAD model data presented in boundary representation (BRep) format. However, as is usual with many expert systems, the task of writing the rules itself turns out to

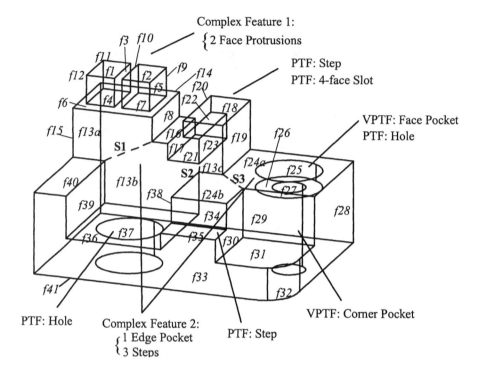

Figure 4: A hypothetical object with a variety of geometric features [42].

be an expert task. A new rule has to be written whenever a new feature is encountered and the robustness of the system depends very much on whether the rule writer is able to capture all the essential attributes of the feature.

I entered the field of GFR around the time experts systems were still dominant. However, I noted that the set of expert rules of the type used by Henderson [38] for each feature could be systematically derived from the face adjacency graph of the feature [39]. This discovery significantly diminished the requirement for human expertise while defining feature identification rules. However, there still remained the need to write a new set of production rules whenever a new geometric feature was encountered.

My team then explored the feasibility of utilizing neural nets for GFR. By that time, there were references in literature about the use of neural nets for object identification from pixel data of computer vision output of the object. We however sought to perform GFR on the basis of CAD model data. We therefore trained a back-propagation network (BPN) by using face adjacency data for each feature as inputs and the feature name (code) as the output (see Chapter 5). The network was found to be reasonably able to identify the test features provided they were essentially similar to training features. The success rate was however significantly below 100%, which was considered unacceptable while solving geometric type of problems. Further, the system often failed whenever it encountered a new complex feature formed through interactions among two or more training features. We were not satisfied with this level of performance and we did not like the fact that the ANN was not able to explain the rationale underlying each feature identification exercise.

We then wondered how human operators had all along been able to recognize geometric features with great facility and browsed through literature on cognitive science. We discovered that Biederman [40] had demonstrated that human recognition of object shape is effected through a decomposition of the object into generalized cylinders called *geons* and that the decomposition is perceived at object locations where two geons exhibit concave adjacency. Thus, for instance, a coffee cup is decomposed into the containing part (a semi-concave cylinder) and the handle (a small "bended" cylinder).

We then discovered that algorithms could indeed be developed that emulate the human object decomposition process described above [41]. In particular we developed a concave triggering algorithm that could extract every depression type of feature and a complementary convex triggering algorithm that could extract every protrusion type of feature. However, this approach, by itself, did not solve the problem of coping with the infinite variety of features that arises in practice.

Next, after extensive work, we realized that one could actually define a finite set of atomic features called *primitive template features* (PTFs) and that all other features could be considered either as *variations of PTFs* (VPTFs) or *complex features* formed through interactions among a specific set of PTFs and VPTFs. We then developed heuristics that were capable of decomposing complex features [42]. Some examples of PTFs, VPTFs, and complex features are included in Figure 4.

Could the above approach to GFR be labeled as an AI-based approach? Some may object to it on the basis that it has not explicitly utilized any specific tools of AI. However, note that the approach has enabled the performance of a task that clearly requires "intelligence if performed by humans" — the criterion for labeling an approach as AI based according to Flach [13]. Further, the approach clearly utilizes heuristics that, according to cognitive scientists, at least partially emulate human cognition of objects. Clearly, such a debate is academic and, as pointed out earlier, manufacturing engineers usually are unconcerned about such debates.

Having developed a systematic approach that could cope with the problem posed by the infinite variety and complexity of geometric features, we turned our attention to the configuration of our feature recognition software. We were sensitive to the fact that the software should be capable of meeting the needs of a variety of customers — process planners, tool designers, etc. drawn from an even larger variety of product sectors. This particular issue had not been addressed before. After debating this issue, we realized that we could largely meet the goal of satisfying multiple customers by adopting the two principles described below.

First, we sought to meet the *Turing test* (at least, our own restricted version of it) within the domain of geometric feature recognition. Turing had envisioned a test in which you have typewriter communication between two rooms [7]. One room has a person and the other a computer. You then pose a set of questions to both and each will provide answers. If the computer is indeed intelligent, you should not be able to distinguish between the computer and the person. We then prepared a framework which could generate a large variety of questions that we believed would be typically asked by a variety of customers interested in GFR. (Naturally, we focused on questions that demanded high levels of reasoning and ignored computationally trivial questions such as "What is the diameter of hole number X?" that merely required data extraction.)

Second, the goal of satisfying the partial Turing test meant that our software should be able to answer any question (albeit falling within the GFR domain) posed on the fly with regard to any given object model. Clearly, we needed a robust software solution. Hence, we sought to develop a holonic GFR system. We created an autonomous software holon for each computational task involved in GFR. Each holon exhibited the property of cooperation by opportunistically taking part in the answering of the question. The following are some of the lessons we have learned from this exercise.

- Much of the programming flexibility required in developing holonic software systems can be achieved by adopting the object-oriented modeling technique (OMT) developed by computer scientists over the last two decades.
- Greater thought needs to be given to what exactly is cooperation (by a holon) and how it should be implemented. Much of this cooperation can be effected through the message-passing feature of object-oriented systems.
- The issues of cooperation and inter-holon communication are closely related. In particular, it is necessary to recognize the differences among cooperation with superiors, peers, and subordinates.
- Holonic systems should be structured so that they are open and expandable. This requires a well-structured approach toward interfacing a new holon to an existing holonic system. Much further research and standardization work is needed in this direction.
- An expandable holonic system enables natural selection from among holons that are seemingly capable of performing the same task. For instance, there are several competing approaches (expert systems based, semantic network based, ANN based, algorithmic, etc.) and several specific GFR methodologies within each approach. Suppose that a selection of these is embedded within a holonic GFR system, each trying to come up with its own answer as each question is posed. Suppose that a separate holon is performing comparative evaluation of these diverse answers and progressively directing more questions to holons

that have shown promise. Clearly, in time, the fitter holons will survive, whereas weaker holons will cease to participate.

6 Some Problems Associated with Machining in Small Batches

Having examined some AI related issues at higher levels of manufacturing, consider now some issues at the work center level.

In the holonic manufacturing paradigm, a work center is viewed as a holon that autonomously executes its tasks while cooperating with other work center holons so as to broadly satisfy the goals set by higher level holons. Each work center holon has its own identity and independent experience defined by the tasks it has been called upon to perform. Quite often this experience is unique to the work center even though there may be other similar work centers on the same shop floor. Ideally, the work center should be aware of its own capabilities and limitations and how these affect its performance and be smart (i.e., intelligent) enough to learn from its own experience so as to perform its future tasks evermore effectively.

Every work center has a manufacturing process at its core. Effective performance of every work center level task requires the utilization of knowledge regarding the manufacturing process.

When manufacturing is carried out in the mass production mode, one often uses a mechanized machine whose operating conditions are determined by a qualified process planner engaging in elaborate reasoning over data collected through operation specific experimentation. The setting of the operating conditions is usually a complex task that requires one to minimize cutting forces, cutting temperatures, dimensional errors, surface roughness on the machined parts, and the number of tool and workpiece settings required while maximizing tool life. However, once the operating conditions have been determined, the job of the machine operator is reduced to one of repeatedly applying the dexterity necessary for implementing an identical and limited operation sequence.

Small batch manufacturing however demands a different approach. Such manufacturing is usually carried out using CNC machine tools each of which is capable of carrying out a variety of machining operations over a range of cutting conditions. Since product variety is very large, it is impractical to carry out process specific experimentation to determine the optimum tooling strategy and cutting conditions (cutting speed, feed rate, depth of cut, etc.) for each machining operation. Hence, it is necessary to develop a practical and reliable way of determining the cutting conditions each time the CNC machine encounters a new part to be machined.

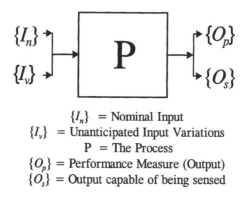

$\{I_n\}$ = Nominal Input
$\{I_v\}$ = Unanticipated Input Variations
P = The Process
$\{O_p\}$ = Performance Measure (Output)
$\{O_s\}$ = Output capable of being sensed

Figure 5: Inputs and outputs of a machining operation [43,44].

Figure 5 illustrates the problem at hand. P is the process that responds to a given set of inputs by producing a set of outputs. Process inputs can be classified into two types: the nominal inputs, $\{I_n\}$, and the unexpected input variations, $\{I_v\}$. The nominal input array, $\{I_n\}$, consists of nominal values of the inputs deliberately set by the process designer or operator. The typical contents of $\{I_n\}$ are nominal tool and work material properties, tool geometry variables (rake angle, clearance angle, cutting edge obliquity; etc.), and cutting conditions (cutting speed, feed, depth of cut, cutting fluid, etc.).

Among the many outputs from a machining process, we are particularly interested in the subset, $\{O_p\}$, containing the performance measures (e.g., cutting forces, cutting temperatures, tool life) which we try to optimize during process design, tool design, process control, etc. Thus, the problem at hand can be expressed as one of predicting $\{O_p\}$ from given $\{I_n\}$ on the basis of prior knowledge derived from similar processes encountered in the past. This would be trivial if the prior knowledge available includes paired combinations of $\{I_n\}$ and $\{O_p\}$ for exactly the same process. But, this is rarely the case for three reasons. First, the new part to be machined is often not exactly the same as a previously encountered part. Second, the performance measures are rarely taken directly on the shop floor. Finally, in practice, many unexpected variations occur in the input conditions. For instance, the process planner might be expecting a tempered structure in the steel being machined. However, it is quite possible that a particular batch of workpieces unexpectedly exhibits a martensitic structure. Such variations cannot often be anticipated and, hence, could lead to unexpected variations in the outputs. $\{I_v\}$ represents this array of unexpected input variations.

The contemporary solution to the problem of selecting cutting conditions is to select a nominal process plan on the basis of a machining database created elsewhere through extensive off-line experimentation and rely on the ability of the machine operator to tweak the plan toward the optimum on the basis of her/his work experience.

Two problems associated with the above CNC machining scenario need to be highlighted. First, the development of a machining database is a tedious and expensive task. Thus, most such databases are relatively sparse in content so that the performance predictions resulting from them are likely to be unreliable. Second, the process at hand will rarely be exactly the same as the one used while collecting data for the nearest neighbor in the machining database. The difference could be significant in terms of unexpected input variations $\{I_v\}$. It is only occasionally that skilled operators can be trusted to detect and respond to all the significant input variations.

The classical response from the machining research community to the above problem has been one of developing competing quantitative models for each of the predicting performance measures.

7 Modeling of Machining Operations

Over the last 50 years, machining scientists have developed a wide variety of process models (M_p, see Figure 6) for each performance measure of engineering importance (for example, cutting force, cutting power, cutting temperature, and tool life) with regard to each practical machining operation (for example, turning, milling, and drilling). Starting from 1945 when Merchant [45] developed a shear plane model for single edge orthogonal cutting (an idealized machining operation), many analytical models (for example, [46-49]) have been developed to enable cutting force prediction from given process inputs (tool/work material properties, tool geometry parameters, and cutting conditions such cutting speed, feed, and depth of cut). More recently some computational models utilizing finite element and finite difference methods have also been developed.

However, notwithstanding the substantial progress made with regard to the development of predictive models for cutting, few such models have found widespread industrial acceptance [50]. One reason for this is that each process model, M_p, that is invoked to predict the output variables, $\{O_p\}$, from given nominal inputs, $\{I_n\}$, requires a priori knowledge of a set of model coefficients, $\{C\}$, that depend on the tool/work material properties and the current state of the process (see Figure 6).

The problem of calibrating model coefficients, $\{C\}$, has traditionally been solved through model databases (MdDb) derived from a limited set of off-line process tests performed under a range of process conditions. However, usually, the coefficients thus determined are only broadly representative of the tool/material combination and, therefore, might or might not reflect the specific material properties prevailing in the actual process. Further, a process may assume different states

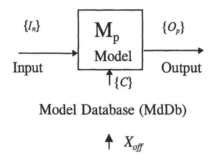

Model Database (MdDb)

$$\uparrow X_{off}$$

Figure 6: Process models require support from databases [43,44].

under different conditions. For instance, which the majority of current machining models assume that chip formation is of the continuous type without built-up edge, the actual process might be quite different—there could be a built-up edge present, the chip could be serrated or even discontinuous, etc.

Thus, all modeling approaches have to face the reality that chip formation in machining is, in general, not uniquely defined. The following summarizes the current limitations of the strategy of relying on process models alone.

- Only very few practical operations have been modeled to the required generality.

- Process models invariably require massive model databases, MdDb (consisting of data on the work material flow stress magnitudes, shear angles, chip flow angles, mechanical and thermal properties of the tool material, etc.), to guide the selection of the magnitudes of an array of model coefficients, $\{C\}$. The creation of an MdDb requires extensive off-line experimentation (note X_{off} in Figure 6) and is therefore expensive.

- Many performance measures still cannot be quantitatively predicted. Process models are reliable only when continuous chips without built-up edge are produced. If a built-up edge exists, chips are discontinuous or serrated, and so on, success is questionable. And, such chip forms occur often and cannot be anticipated. Small perturbations in the input conditions (i.e., the presence of $\{I_v\}$) can lead to substantial changes in the state of the process. Consequently, model coefficients derived from one set of off-line experiments cannot be transported confidently to other instances of the same process. It, therefore, appears that we need to explore other ways of determining the magnitudes of the model coefficients, $\{C\}$.

8 Sensors for Machining

Interest in equipping machine tools with sensors has increased dramatically since the 1980s. However, much of this interest has been stimulated by the need for monitoring and diagnosis of CNC machining operations. CNC machine tools are expensive devices. Hence, they need to be utilized as fully as possible. This means that any unexpected deviations in the operation must be detected early and diagnosed and the appropriate trouble shootings actions must be taken. Often, these deviations can be detected through real-time monitoring of one or more of the sensible outputs, $\{O_s\}$, from the process, e.g., noise, vibrations, motor current, acoustic emission, workpiece dimension detection using on-machine inspection. For instance, it has been shown that there is a perceptible jump in the total mean square (TMS) value of acoustic emission when a cutting tip breaks. Likewise, on-machine inspection using a novel Fine Touch contact probe [51,52] has enabled the detection of the total positioning error (the summation of geometric and thermal errors) of the tool tip in CNC turning [53] (we will return to this technology later in this chapter).

Note that sensing is not necessarily the same as measurement. Measurement aims to monitor the output, $\{O_p\}$, that is sought to be predicted. In contrast, sensing is used to monitor outputs, $\{O_s\}$, that may not include $\{O_p\}$.

It has long been recognized that the greatest challenge with regard to process sensing lies in signal conditioning that enables the detection of signal features, $\{S\}$, implicit in the sensible process output signal, $\{O_s\}$ (see Figure 7). Thus, especially during the 1990s, several advanced techniques such as those using fractal and/or wavelet theories have been developed to identify $\{S\}$. An example of such an approach is the use of wavelet packet transforms of acoustic emission signals for tool wear monitoring [54]. Another major trend has been to rely on artificial neural nets (ANN) to detect $\{S\}$ and use the results to predict $\{O_p\}$. However, success in this regard has generally been limited to predicting a single performance output at a time. An example of such approach is the hybrid learning methodology developed in [55] for tool wear monitoring. However, a major flaw of this approach lies in the fact that extensive training sets of experimental data covering $\{I_n\}$, $\{O_p\}$, as well as $\{O_s\}$ are needed to satisfactorily predict even a single performance measure of a single machining operation over a wide range of cutting conditions. Thus, the search for robust methods of solving this problem has continued to this day. One popular approach towards solving this problem has been to adopt sensor fusion; i.e., to derive the output features, $\{S\}$, of significance in a particular context by fusing the information derivable from diverse sensor outputs, $\{O_s\}$. Several published reports exist demonstrating the power of sensor fusion using an ANN. These demonstrations seem to have prompted Merchant [6] to name sensor fusion as one of the dominant future techniques. Notwithstanding this enthusiasm, it appears doubtful if sensor fusion alone would be adequate and cost effective in solving the problem described in the previous section with regard to process planning in uncertain CNC environments.

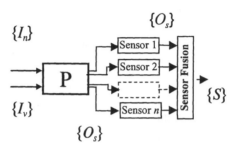

Figure 7: Sensing and sensor fusion.

In theory at least, there seems to be one way of solving the problem posed in the previous paragraph. Returning to Figure 5, note that a process model aims to predict the desired subset of $\{O_p\}$. This subset might or might not overlap with the sensed output array, $\{O_s\}$. In fact, more often than not, it will not overlap. This is because, often, it is impractical to directly measure members of $\{O_p\}$, and the outputs that could be sensed are dictated by the current sensor technologies. However, since both $\{O_p\}$ and $\{O_s\}$ are consequences of the very same process, it is intuitively apparent that there should exist some sort of correlation between the two.

With a view to illustrating the above concept, suppose that we are interested in predicting the power component of the cutting force (i.e., the component of the cutting force in the direction of cutting velocity) on the basis of sensed acoustic emission (AE) signals. For such prediction to be feasible, there must exist a physical association between cutting force and acoustic emission and we must be able to quantitatively model that association.

Fortunately, in the case of acoustic emission (AE), there is evidence that it is physically linked to cutting force magnitudes. AE occurs in machining because of the phenomena of micro-fracture and micro-slip that invariably appear during material shearing and the friction process at the tool/chip and tool/work contact zones. Thus, AE sensing enables the capture of information concerning these phenomena during real time cutting. However, these very same micro-phenomena are known to have profound influence on cutting force and power levels. In particular, both AE energy and cutting energy are likely to increase with increasing cutting volume. Thus, one can expect a fairly strong positive correlation between cutting force magnitudes and the energy content of the AE signal.

Experimental evidence in support of the expectation described above was first reported in [56] through data collected on peripheral milling. Subsequently, these results were verified with respect to end milling by the author's team [57].

However, realizing the existence of a physical relationship is quite different from being able to exploit it. One must be able to quantitatively model the relationship. Unfortunately, few efforts have so far been put into quantitatively modeling the physical origins of AE in machining. A similar situation exists with regard to almost all the other sensing techniques applied so far for machining. Thus, it appears that it will be a long while before one is able to predict machining performance measures directly on the basis of real time sensor signals. Clearly, there is an urgent need for exploring alternative strategies. One such alternative is proposed in the next section.

9 Machine Learning as a Means of Integrating Modeling and Sensing

The previous section has clarified the role of sensing in machining. Much research effort has gone into sensing and sensor fusion in recent years. However, so far, the worlds of process modeling and process sensing have remained largely apart. One reason is that methodologies for processing the dynamic signals output by the sensor into informative features, $\{S\}$, are still in a developing stage. New sensing and signal processing techniques and AI based methods of feature extraction are constantly emerging. Another reason is that robust approaches toward integrating the information derived from sensing with process models are not yet generally available.

Modeling aims to predict $\{O_p\}$ on the basis of given nominal process inputs, $\{I_n\}$. Thus, a machining process model, M_p, can be viewed as a transformation that is capable of mapping from $\{I_n\}$ to $\{O_p\}$. However, this transformation will involve the use of some unknown model coefficients, $\{C\}$. Classically, the magnitudes of $\{C\}$ have been obtained from a model database, MdDb. However, it is impossible to create a comprehensive MdDb that is capable of covering every possible cutting situation. Hence any magnitudes of $\{C\}$ derived from the MdDb can only be taken as initial values, $\{C_i\}$. These values will have to be adjusted on the basis of appropriate on-line process information. Obtaining such information is the task of sensing.

The value of sensing lies in the fact that both $\{O_s\}$ and $\{O_p\}$ are the results of the very same process, P, and, hence, monitoring the former should be able to provide some information that could facilitate the prediction of the latter. Two conditions need to be satisfied for this to be possible (see Figure 8). First, we should select an $\{O_s\}$ that is very closely related (in terms of physical origin) to $\{O_p\}$ (it has already been pointed out that research on this subject has so far been sparse). Second, we need a method by which the model coefficients, $\{C\}$, can either be directly selected or determined through appropriately correcting the initial coefficient array, $\{C_i\}$, derived from a suitable MdDb. Machine learning seems to provide one way of implementing this strategy.

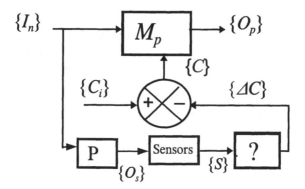

Figure 8: Sensing can help in the determination of model coefficients [43,44].

Figure 9 shows a strategy worth exploring. A learning system (a forte of AI), Ln, is used to integrate model predictions based on model coefficients derived from a MdDb and the features, $\{S\}$, extracted from appropriate sensor signals, $\{O_s\}$. The learning system will have to be trained until the system produces satisfactory results.

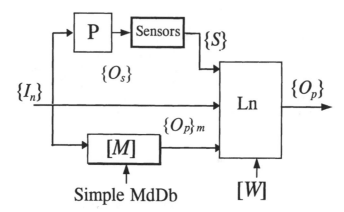

Figure 9: Bringing the worlds of modeling and sensing together through learning.

One possible method of implementing the strategy illustrated in Figure 9 is to use a supervised neural network. Among the various types of supervised ANN, the back propagation network (BPN) has become particularly popular. A supervised ANN operates in two modes: the training mode and the testing or utilization mode. In the training mode, the connection weights of the network are continually adjusted to a randomized initial set (see Figure 9). Off-line or on-line experiments are conducted with the given process using training sets of nominal process inputs, $\{I_n\}$. The measured or estimated process outputs, $\{O_p\}$, are used as training data to yield a set of corrections for the weight matrix. The training cycles are repeated until the outputs agree with the experimental outputs within an acceptable error margin. The matrix of connection weights is then frozen so that the network becomes a trained network that can be used to predict the outputs, $\{O_p\}$, for new instances of $\{I_n\}$.

Early applications of ANN by the manufacturing community were mainly directed toward directly mapping from $\{I_n\}$ to $\{O_p\}$ on the basis of extensive training data. And, for a short while, it appeared that the ANN had succeeded. This generated much euphoria. Here was a method that could learn to predict irrespective of whether we had a deep or shallow understanding of the behavior of the process. However, very soon the euphoria subsided when it was realized that the approach could not be scaled up to real life applications without scaling up the network size itself and/or engaging in impractically long training sessions. Clearly, pure neural net based learning needed to be augmented with information derived from sources other than just the array of process input variables. Two such information sources are sensing and modeling.

Consider, for example, sensing of a machining process through acoustic emission (AE). The upper part of Figure 9 shows one method of augmenting a learning network with a sensor. The author's team recently happened to implement a part of this approach for the purpose of predicting cutting forces in end milling [57]. We used a backpropagation network and augmented it with the true mean square value of the AE signal detected by a piezoelectric AE sensor placed in close proximity to the cutting zone. We found that the prediction error for a given cutter could be reduced from around 9% to 2% through such augmentation.

Figure 9 goes beyond the combination of sensing and learning. It suggests that learning can be further augmented through the inclusion of modeling. It is well known that process models are good at predicting output trends although not necessarily good at quantitative prediction (recall the problems related to the calibration of model coefficients). This is because the models—at least the better ones among them—have much knowledge (laws of physics, material science, etc.) embedded in them. Thus, a model is a knowledge base in itself. The output trends are captured by the outputs, $\{O_p\}_m$, predicted by the model for the given input array. However, every model is based on certain generalized assumptions. Usually the actual process does not behave fully in accordance with one or more of the model assumptions. Capturing the effect of these real time deviations is the role of sensing.

In view of the arguments presented above, I believe that learning augmented with modeling and sensing provides a generalized and powerful method of quantitatively predicting manufacturing process outputs. However, usually, there are several candidate combinations of learning, sensing, and modeling for a given problem. These need to be researched and evaluated before one can develop an effective solution for each problem class. The next section will describe a case study related to the prediction and compensation of workpiece dimensional errors in CNC machining.

10 Case Study 2: Toward CNC Machines that Continually Learn to Perform Error Compensation

It is common knowledge that dimensional errors on parts produced by machine tools are usually several times larger than the axis positioning repeatability error of the machines. For instance, when we tested a CNC turning center of a well-known brand in our laboratory at City University of Hong Kong, it was found that the maximum error was in the range 50 to 100μm although the positioning repeatability was only about 4μm. Thus, it appears that most CNC machines in use in the industry today are working well below their accuracy potential.

Experience shows that the error budget in machining is usually dominated by several quasi-static systematic errors. These errors arise when the positions of the workpiece and the tool are displaced away from the nominal point of contact between the tool tip and the machined surface in a direction normal to the machine surface. We call the algebraic sum of these two displacements the total quasi-static error, δ_{tot}.

It is well known that δ_{tot} is the algebraic sum of error components arising from a variety of assignable causes: (1) geometric error, δ_g, inherent in the machine; (2) thermal error, δ_{th}, arising due to drifts induced by temperature variations in the machine-fixture-workpiece-tool (MFWT) system; (3) δ_f, the deflection error induced by the cutting force; and (4) δ_{other}, induced by other causes such as cutting tool wear and workpiece clamping.

Software-based error compensation is a method of anticipating the combined effect of the above factors on workpiece accuracy and then suitably modifying the conventionally designed (uncompensated) tool path so as to improve machining accuracy. It is widely accepted that such compensation will provide many benefits in terms of productivity and quality at low cost to machining shops.

However, even today, few industrial machine tools are equipped with software error compensation. The main reason for this industrial apathy is that the currently available compensation methods require, *inter alia*, the use of sophisticated instruments such as laser interferometers, load cells, arrays of thermocouples embedded into the machine tools, and sophisticated computational tools (finite element packages). Each machine tool needs to be extensively tested to determine its error profile. Industrial shops could not be bothered to adopt such complex solutions.

I recently attempted a radically different approach. I argued that an error source is recognized as such only by virtue of the fact that it leaves an imprint on every machined dimension of every part. Hence, all one needs to do is to collect and analyze past inspection data in a manner that enables one to anticipate the error on the next part provided, of course, that the inspection database contains enough exemplars of the next part. Following this premise, I initially sought to pursue the software compensation strategy illustrated in Figure 10.

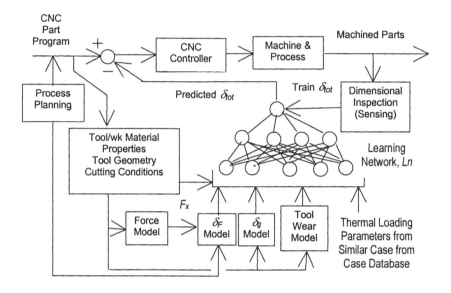

Figure 10: A learning based strategy for intgerating modeling and sensing for workpiece error compensation in CNC machining.

Since the nature of the manufacturing process associated with each operation class (turning, end milling, etc.) is quite distinct, a separate error prediction module needs to be designed for each operation class. Likewise, each machining set up on each machine is unique with regard to its error and stiffness profile. Hence, some of the data needed for the error compensation module are unique to each machine set up. Such information needs to be collected from shop floor experimentation.

My initial strategy assumed that a force prediction model is available for each operation class. Likewise, it assumed that stiffness models for the tool and machine tool corresponding to each machining set up are available. The stiffness distribution of the workpiece is easily determined through a straightforward application of the theory of elasticity. A combination of the force and stiffness models yields the distribution of the deflection error (δ_f). In a similar manner, the strategy assumed that models are available to predict the thermal error (δ_{th}) and other errors such as tool wear (if they are significant). However, since the geometric error (δ_g) must remain invariant in the short term, it is left to the learning network to figure it out. Note that the prediction from each of these models need only be coarse, since the model outputs are not directly used to estimate the total error (δ_{tot}) but only act as inputs to the neural network which acts as a learning system. The model outputs merely convey the knowledge embedded within the models to the neural network.

My approach further assumed that a supervised neural network is used and is trained as follows: Whenever a production batch with a new combination of tool/work material pair, machining set up, and operation class is encountered during routine shop floor work, an appropriate subset of the parts machined with such a combination is first selected. Each part is inspected at a few selected locations to determine the total dimensional error at each location. Each of these values is communicated to the single output node of the neural net during training. The cutting conditions, including tool/work material labels, and tool geometry parameters are extracted from the uncompensated part program and the process plans. These are transmitted to the array of models described earlier so as to estimate the error components coarsely at each selected location on the machined part. The process inputs as well as the model outputs act as inputs to the neural net. Once the network is fully trained, the weight matrix is stored away so that it can be retrieved and used in the prediction of total error whenever a new part of any shape and size but with the same input conditions is encountered.

Next, we proceeded to utilize the above insights toward error compensation in the case of external turning on a CNC turning machine. First, we had to establish a part inspection procedure. Initially we tried post-process measurement using a coordinate measuring machine (CMM). We then thought that this was too elaborate and switched to on-machine inspection. By that time, we had independently tested a new workpiece contact sensing called Fine Touch which enabled contact detection with a repeatability of around 1μm while allowing the turning tool itself to be used as the contact probe [58]. We then combined this technique with the Q-setter available on the turning machine so as to facilitate reliable and automated on-machine measurement [52].

Next, we critically compared the inspection data obtained from the CMM with those from on-machine inspection. We also reviewed the relevant literature. This led to a pleasant realization. We found that the total error, δ_{tot}, determined by post-process measurement could actually be decomposed into δ_g, δ_{th}, and δ_f simply by conducting two further on-machine measurements—one while the machine was still warm and the other after the machine has cooled down (see Appendix 1 for a summary of the theory). The magnitudes of δ_g thus estimated correlated very well with the corresponding magnitudes obtained through independent tests using a laser interferometer.

The discovery mentioned above implied that it was no longer necessary to rely on a neural net, working at the complex level of the total error. We needed only to work at the level of individual error components. In short, we had discovered a sensing protocol that permitted the decomposition of what was a complex problem into a set of more manageable subproblems. Since the subproblems were simpler than the total problem, we could hope to quantitatively model each of them separately. This brought us closer to the dream of achieving synergy among modeling (subproblem models), sensing (fine-touch contact sensing), and learning. We could indeed "divide and conquer." These observations prompted us to reformulate the strategy outlined in Figure 10.

Next, we developed an analytical model for the prediction of deflection error, δ_f. We resurrected the long lost theory of "center of rotation" [58] and arrived at a model for δ_f that consisted of only four coefficients (see Appendix 2 for a summary of the model). Three of these were related to the stiffness of the MFWT system and the fourth was the quasi-static cutting force component, F_x, normal to the machined surface at the particular location along the cutter path. We realized that these four coefficients could be uniquely determined by performing measurements at four different locations on the machined part. The repeated application of this approach yielded statistically significant values (r-values larger than 90%) of the four coefficients.

A by-product of the above approach is the unexpected realization that the radial cutting force (F_x) in turning operations can be estimated simply from past on-machine measurement data. Figure 11 shows the correlation between the OMM-based prediction of F_x with the corresponding force measurements obtained using a piezoelectric cutting force dynamometer. With the regression coefficient equal to 1.004 and the correlation coefficient (r-value) equal to 0.956, it is seen that the correlation is quite acceptable for shop-floor purposes (although the y-intercept is a bit too large at about -6N). Thus, we had inadvertently hit upon a method by which *the machine tool itself could be made to act as its own dynamometer.*

Finally, we tested the new error compensation methodology on a variety of workpiece profiles (cylindrical as well as complex curved profiles) machined with the same tool/work material combination and machining set up. In each case we found that the error on diameter was smaller than $\pm$ 5μm, which was close to the minimum possible given the fact that the repeatability of the machine was of the same order.

The above approach represents one method of obtaining synergistic interactions among quantitative modeling, sensing, and learning. The models supply embedded knowledge, sensing provides the information necessary to train the learning system, and the learning system learns from real life practice and smooths out any wrinkles present within the models. Each is augmented by the other two. Work is in progress to extend the above error compensation methodology to other operation classes (for example, end milling on a machining center).

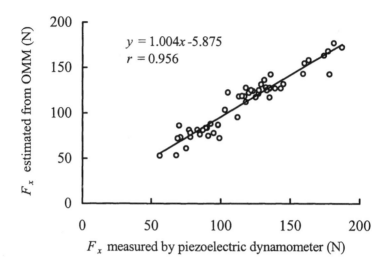

Figure 11: Correlation between F_x estimated from on-machine measurement (OMM) and measurement using a piezoelectric dynamometer.

Clearly the above methodology takes us a long way towards realizing the highly desirable goal of equipping each CNC machine tool on the shop floor with a software that enables the machine to continually learn to perform its own error compensation solely on the basis of historical part inspection data. One method that seems to be attractive in this context is the AI approach called *case based reasoning* (CBR) [29] that has only recently started to catch the imagination of the manufacturing community.

Schank and Jona [10] clarify the nature of CBR as follows: "Most people prefer not to have to think hard if they can help it. They will try to get by with whatever worked before, even if it is less than optimal. We believe that, roughly speaking, people's everyday cognition consists of about 90% retrieving of past solutions and only about 10% or less of actual novel problem solving. Because of our belief about the relative importance of retrieval, it follows that if one wants to understand what it takes to model human intelligence one should focus on the type of processing that contributes the most to people's everyday behavior, namely retrieval and adaptations of old solutions."

It appears feasible to anticipate the error components δ_g, δ_{th}, and δ_f on the next part to be machined by retrieving the most "similar" error compensation episode for each error component from past experience and adapting each of them to take into account whatever differences that exist between the retrieved episode and the current episode. These anticipated error components could then be algebraically summed to obtain the total anticipated total error, δ_{tot}.

Clearly, much further work is needed before the problem can be solved through an application of CBR as described above. However, given the progress in error compensation described above and the success of CBR in other domains, it appears quite feasible to realize the following scenario: *Imagine that you are walking through a production facility. Your guide points to one work center and says "He is a baby. He still has a lot to learn." He then walks to another and says "Ah! This guy is the smartest. He knows what he is doing. He is correct 80% of the time."* We may claim that we have entered the age of intelligent production machines only when we are able to achieve similar levels of intelligent behavior with respect to the more significant of the performance measures associated with a wide range of production operations.

11 Summary

This chapter has introduced the relationship between modern manufacturing and the rapidly growing field of Artificial Intelligence (AI). A review of AI applications in manufacturing over the last fifteen years has indicated that a manufacturing engineer typically views AI as a bag of tools.

At higher levels of manufacturing, a manufacturing engineer seeks to apply AI tools to carry out planning activities such as process planning and production scheduling. In doing so, (s)he needs to balance several concerns related to manufacturing resources (men, materials, machines, and money) while meeting the ever tightening constraints on cost, quality, time, and innovation imposed by the rapid globalization of manufacturing as well as its markets. As a response, the manufacturing engineering community has recently proposed the concept of Holonic Manufacturing Systems (HMS). An HMS is made up of entities called holons where each holon exhibits two essential properties: autonomy and cooperation. A holon can be a hardware, software, or "humanware" entity. A case study on geometric feature recognition (GFR) software based on holonic principles has shown that such a system can exhibit emergent intelligence; i.e., the apparent intelligence of the system emerges through autonomous and cooperative interactions among the holons even though none of the holons has adopted any conventional AI tools. Equally interestingly, the feature recognition algorithms used by the system have been inspired by a heuristic derived from a well-known theory of human cognition of physical objects.

At lower levels of manufacturing, a manufacturing engineer often seeks to apply AI tools to carry out monitoring, diagnostic, and control tasks—mainly related to computer numerical control (CNC) machines. Early applications of AI in this context sought to predict one or more performance measures of the manufacturing process directly from process inputs by means of an artificial neural network (ANN). However, this approach has been found to be inadequate in terms of its ability to be scaled up to the level of complex shop floor situations. Meanwhile two parallel movements have been in progress in the manufacturing field: process modeling and process sensing. Arguments have been presented in this chapter in favor of seeking synergy between the worlds of process modeling and process sensing (which have so far remained apart) through the well-known "learning" capability provided by AI tools such as ANN and case-based reasoning (CBR).

Process models are good at predicting output trends although not necessarily good at quantitative estimation. This is because the models — at least the better ones among them—have much knowledge (laws of physics, material science, etc.) embedded in them. Thus, a model is a knowledge base in itself. However, usually, the actual process does not behave fully in accordance with one or more of the model assumptions. Capturing the effect of these real-time deviations is the role of sensing. The role of learning is to integrate the knowledge embedded in the models with the real-time information gained through on-line sensing. A case study on error compensation in CNC turning has confirmed the feasibility of this approach. The compensation system has enabled nearly 90% of the machining error to be compensated just on the basis of a specifically designed machined part inspection protocol. More importantly, when combined with case-based reasoning, the system enables the machine to learn to compensate (i.e., become smarter) through its routine shop floor experiences — just like a human operator does. Equally importantly, the methodology enables a CNC turning machine itself to act as its own radial force dynamometer. This feature enables the machine itself to autonomously compile a model-based machining database as it proceeds with its normal job assignments.

Acknowledgments

This article would not have been possible without the inspired efforts of many research students of the author. S.Y. Wong has developed the graph-based expert system approach toward geometric feature recognition. C.F. Yuen has investigated how a holonic feature recognition system could be structured. In the process, he has invented feature extraction methodologies that emulate Biederman's observations on human cognition of objects. Liu Zhan-Qiang has investigated how one can perform error compensation in CNC machining solely on the basis of machined part inspection data. The author would also like to acknowledge the financial support received from the Research Grants Council for the funding received in support of CERG project 9040308.

References

[1]   Stearns, P.N., *The Industrial Revolution in World History*, Westview Press, Boulder, CO, 1993.

[2]   Lui, C.H. and Tam, H.Y., "Robotic Mold Polishing Frees up Human Polishers," *Proc. 3rd Int. Conf. Manufacturing Technology*, Hong Kong, pp. 497-501, December 1995.

[3] Taylor, F.W., *The Principles of Scientific Management*, Harper and Brothers, New York, NY, 1911.

[4] *The New Manufacturing Enterprise Wheel*, SME, Dearborn, MI, 1993.

[5] Koska, D.K. and Romano, J.D., *Countdown to the Future: The Manufacturing Engineer in the 21st Century*, A research study conducted by A.T. Kearney, Inc., SME, Dearborn, MI, 1988.

[6] Merchant, M.E., "CIM — Its Evolution, Precepts, Concepts, Status and Trends," *ME Research Bulletin*, Department of Manufacturing Engineering, City University of Hong Kong, Vol. 1, No. 1, pp. 3-18, March 1993.

[7] Turing, A.M., "Computing Machinery and Intelligence," *Computers and Thought*, E.A. Figenbaum and J. Feldman (Editors), McGraw-Hill, New York, NY, pp. 11-35, 1963.

[8] Genesereth, M.R. and Nilsson, N.J. (Editors), *Logical Foundation of Artificial Intelligence*, Morgan Kaufmann, Los Altos, California, 1987.

[9] Rumelhart, D.E., Hinton, G.E., and William, R.J., "Learning and Internal Representations by Error Propagation," *Parallel Distributed Processing: Explorations in the Microstructure of Cognition*, Vol. 1: Foundations, D.E. Rumelhart and J.L. McClelland (Editors), MIT Press, Bradford Books, Cambridge, MA, pp. 318-362, 1986.

[10] Schank, R.C. and Jona, M.Y., "Issues of Psychology, AI, and Education: A Review of Newell's Unified Theories of Cognition," *Contemplating Minds — A Forum for Artificial Intelligence*, W.J. Clancey, S.W. Smoliar, and M.J. Stefik (Editors), MIT Press, Cambridge, MA, pp. 127-140, 1994.

[11] Newell, A. and Simon, H.A., *Human Problem Solving*, Prentice Hall, Englewood Cliffs, NJ, 1972.

[12] Minsky, M.L., *The Society of Mind*, Simon and Schuster, New York, 1985.

[13] Flach, P.A., "The Dialectics of Artificial Intelligence," *Future Directions in Artificial Intelligence*, P.A. Flach and R.A. Meersman (Editors), North-Holland, Amsterdam, pp. 152-159, 1991.

[14] Hatvany, J., "The Efficient Use of Deficient Information," *Annals of the CIRP*, Vol. 32, No. 1, pp. 423-425, 1983.

[15] Yoshikawa, H., *Intelligent Manufacturing Systems Program (IMS): Technical Cooperation that Transcends Cultural Differences*, University of Tokyo, Tokyo, Japan, 1992.

[16] Monostori, L., Markus, A., Van Brussel, H., and Westkamper, E. et al., "Machine Learning Approaches to Manufacturing," *Annals of the CIRP*, Vol. 45, No. 2, pp. 675-712, 1996.

[17] Tong, W.B., Lang, S.Y.T., and Tso, S.K., "Motion Planning Based on Reactive Fuzzy Behavioral Blending in an Unknown Environment," *Proc. 5th Int. Conf. Mechatronics and Machine Vision in Practice*, Nanjing, China, pp. 247-252, 10-12 September 1998.

[18] Xu, W.L. and Tso, S.K., "Intelligent Reactive Navigation of a Mobile Robot," *Intelligent Robotics — From the Structured to Unstructured Environments*, S.K. Tso (Editor), Center for Intelligent Design, Automation and Manufacture (CIDAM), City University of Hong Kong, Hong Kong, pp. 29-34, July 1997.

[19] Tso, S.K., Tong, W.B., and Lang, S., "Fusion of Ultrasonic-Sensor and La-ser-Range-Finder Information for Robot Self-Navigation," *Intelligent Robotics — From the Structured to Unstructured Environments*, S.K. Tso (Editor), Center for Intelligent Design, Automation and Manufacture (CIDAM), City University of Hong Kong, Hong Kong, pp. 19-24, July 1997.

[20] Tso, S.K., Gu, X.P., Zeng, Q.Y., and Lo, K.L., "A Semi-supervised Learning Algorithm Based on BP Framework for NN-based Classification in System Security," *Proc. 3rd Biannual World Automation Congress*, Anchorage, AK, pp. ISSCI 100.1-ISSCI 100.6, May 1998.

[21] Tso, S.K. (Editor), *Intelligent Robotics — From the Structured to Unstructured Environments,* Center for Intelligent Design, Automation and Manufacture (CIDAM), City University of Hong Kong, Hong Kong, 1997.

[22] Tse, P. and Atherton, D., "Prediction of Machine Deterioration Using Vibration based Fault Trends and Recurrent Neural Networks," *Transactions of ASME:J. Vibration and Acoustics*, Vol. 121, No. 3, pp. 355-362, July 1999.

[23] Tse, P. and Atherton, D., "Can Neural Networks Be Robust in Fault Diagnosis and Forecasting?," *Proc. 1st Int. Conf. Eng. Design and Automation*, Bangkok, Thailand, Vol. 1, pp. 299-302, 1997.

[24] Tse, P. and Atherton, D., "Intelligent Fault Diagnostics and Machine Life Prediction Systems for Manufacturing Machinery," *Proc. CIRP Int. Symposium: Adv. Design and Manufacture in the Global Manufacturing Era*, P.K. Venuvinod and A. Djordjevich (Editors), Hong Kong, pp. 166-172, August 1997.

[25] Chin, K.S. and Du, T.C., "Quick Customer Response by Expert Systems: A Case Study," *Proc. 8th Int. Conf. AI and Expert System Applications*, Paris, pp. 229-234, October 1996.

[26] Chin, K.S., "Expert System Based Product Concepts Evaluation for Concurrent Engineering," *Proc. 9th Int. Conf. on AI and Expert System Applications*, Sunderland, UK, pp. 169-174, October 1997.

[27] Winograd, T. and Flores, F., "On Understanding Computers and Cognition: A New Foundation for Design," *Contemplating Minds — A Forum for Artificial Intelligence*, W.J. Clancey, S.W. Smoliar, and M.J. Stefik (Editors), MIT Press, Cambridge, MA. 1994.

[28] Clancey, W.J., Smoliar, S.W., and Stefik, M.J. (Editors), *Contemplating Minds — A Forum for Artificial Intelligence*, MIT Press, Cambridge, MA, p. 169, 1994.

[29] Jona, M.Y. and Kolodner, J.L., "Reasoning, Case-Based," *Encyclopedia of Artificial Intelligence*, S. C. Shapiro (Editor), Wiley, New York, pp. 1265-1279, 1992.

[30] Valckenaers, P., Van Brussel, H., Bongaerts, L., and Wyns, I., "Holonic Manufacturing Systems," *Integrated Computer Aided Eng.*, Vol. 4, No.3, pp. 191-201, 1997.

[31] Koestler, A., *The Ghost in the Machine*, Arkana Books, London, 1989.

[32] Russel, S. and Norvig, P., *Artificial Intelligence: A Modern Approach*, Prentice Hall, Englewood Cliffs, NJ, 1995.

[33] Wooldridge, A. and Jennings, N., "Intelligent Agents: Theory and Practice," *The Knowledge Engineering Review*, Vol. 10, No.2, pp. 115-152, 1995.

[34] Forrest, S. (Editor), *Emergent Computation: Self-Organizing, Collective, and Cooperative Phenomena in Natural and Artificial Computing Networks*, MIT Press, Cambridge, MA, 1991.

[35] Hofstadter, D.R., *Artificial Intelligence: Subcognition as Computation*, Tech. Rep. 132, Indiana University, Bloomington, 1982.

[36] Kruth, J.P. et al., "An NC Holon Architecture," *Proc. CNMU '96 Machine Tool Conf.*, Politechnica University of Bucharest, Bucharest, Romania, pp. 1-10, 1996.

[37] Zhao, F-L., *A Framework for Cooperative Computer-Aided Process Planning*, Ph. D. Thesis, City University of Hong Kong, Hong Kong, July 1999.

[38] Henderson, M.R., *Extraction of Feature Information from the Three-Dimensional CAD Data*, Ph.D. thesis, Purdue University, West Lafayette, IN, 1984.

[39] Venuvinod, P.K. and Wong, S.Y., "A Graph-Based Expert System Approach to Geometric Feature Recognition," *J. Intelligent Manufacturing*, Vol. 6, pp. 155-162, 1995.

[40] Biederman, I., "Human Image Understanding: Recent Research and a Theory," *Human and Machine Vision II*, A. Rosenfeld (Editor), Academic Press Inc., Boston, pp. 13-57, 1986.

[41] Venuvinod, P.K. and Yuen, C.F., "Efficient Automated Geometric Feature Recognition Through Feature Coding," *Annals of the CIRP*, Vol. 43, No. 1, pp. 413-416, 1994.

[42] Yuen, C.F. and Venuvinod, Patri K., "Geometric Feature Recognition: Coping with the Complexity and Infinite Variety of Features," *Int. J. Computer Integrated Manufacture*, Vol. 12, No. 5, pp. 439-452, 1999.

[43] Venuvinod, P.K., "Prediction Augmentation Through Reinforcing Interactions Amongst Modeling, Sensing and Learning," *Session on "Modeling of Machining Operations,"* Working Paper, STC Cutting, CIRP General Assembly, Part II, Tianjin, China, August 1997.

[44] Venuvinod, P.K., "Sensor-Based Modeling of Machining Operations," *Proc. CIRP Int. Workshop on Modeling of Machining Operations*, Atlanta, GA, pp. 397-406, May 1998.

[45] Merchant, M.E., "Mechanics of the Metal Cutting Process I: Orthogonal Cutting and a Type II Chip," *J. Applied Physics*, Vol. 16, No. 5, pp. 267-276, 1945.

[46] Armarego, E.J.A. and Whitfield, R.C., "Computer Based Modeling of Popular Machining Operations," *Annals of the CIRP*, Vol. 34, No. 1, pp. 65-69, 1985.

[47] Whitfield, R.C., *A Mechanics of Cutting Approach for the Prediction of Forces and Power in Some Commercial Machining Operations*, Ph.D. Thesis, University of Melbourne, Melbourne, 1986.

[48] Endres, W.J., Devor, R.E., and Kapoor, S.G., "A Dual-Mechanism Approach to the Prediction of Machining Forces, Part 2: Calibration and Validation," *Trans. ASME., J. of Eng. Ind.*, Vol. 117, pp. 534-541, 1995.

[49] Venuvinod, P.K. and Jin, W.L., "Three Dimensional Cutting Force Analysis Based on the Lower Boundary of Shear Zone, Part I: Single Edge Oblique cutting," *Int. J. Machine Tools & Manufacture*, Vol. 36, No. 3, pp. 307-323, 1996.

[50] van Luttervelt, C.A., Childs, T., Jawahir, I.S., Klocke, F., and Venuvinod, P.K., "The-State-of-the-Art of Modelling of Machining Processes," *Annals of the CIRP*, Vol. 48, No. 2, pp. 587-626, 1998.

[51] Ostafiev, V.A. and Venuvinod, P.K., "A New Electromagnetic Contact Sensing Technique for Enhancing Machining Accuracy," *MED-Vol. 6-1, Manufacturing Science and Technology*, Vol. 1, ASME, New York, pp. 113-119, 1997.

[52] Liu, Z-Q, Venuvinod, P.K., and Ostafiev, V.A., "On-machine Measurements of Workpieces with Cutting Tool," *Int. J. Manufacturing Technology Management*, Vol. 9, No. 3, pp. 168-172, 1998.

[53] Liu, Z-Q and Venuvinod, P.K., "Error Compensation in CNC Turning Solely from Dimensional Measurements of Previously Machined Parts," *Annals of the CIRP*, Vol. 48, No. 1, pp. 429-432, 1999.

[54] Li, X. and Venuvinod, P.K., "Wavelet Packet Transforms of Acoustic Emission Signals for Tool Wear Monitoring," *Int. J. Manufacturing Science and Technology*, 2000 accepted.

[55] Li, X., Dong, S., and Venuvinod, P.K., "Hybrid Learning for Tool Wear Monitoring," *Int. J. Advanced Manufacturing Technology*, 2000 accepted.

[56] Liu, M. and Liang, S.Y., "Monitoring of Peripheral Milling Using Acoustic Emission," *Trans. NAMRI/SME*, pp. 120-127, 1990.

[57] Chiu, Y.H., *Force Prediction End Milling Using Artificial Nets Augmented by Acoustic Emission*, M. Eng. Dissertation, Dept. of Manufacturing Engineering and Engineering Management, City University of Hong Kong, Hong Kong, November 1997.

[58] Murthy, R.L. and Venuvinod, P.K., "Centers of Rotation as an Aid to the Analysis of the Rigidity of Machine Tools," *Proc. 3rd All India Mach. Tool Des. Res. Conf.*, Bombay, pp. 1-7, 1969.

[59] Mou, J. and Liu, C. R, *Transactions of NAMRI/SME*, Vol. XXII, pp. 275-282, 1994.

Appendix 1
An Inspection Protocol Capable of Decomposing the Total Machining Error, δ_{tot}

The total error, δ_{tot}, on a dimension, D (a diameter in turning), of the machined part can be determined from a high precision post-process measurement such as by using a co-ordinate measuring machine (CMM). Let D_{pp} be the magnitude so measured. Then,

$$\delta_{tot} = D_{pp} - D_{des} \tag{A1}$$

where D_{des} is the desired magnitude of D.

The total error can be expressed in terms of component errors as

$$\delta_{tot} = \delta_g + \delta_{th} + \delta_f + \delta_{other} \tag{A2}$$

Recently, Mou and Liu demonstrated that the "difference between CMM measurement (D_{pp}) and on-machine measurement (D_{om}) is positioning error" of the machine [59]. The difference is equal to δ_g when on-machine measurement is performed while the machine is cool. Otherwise, it is equal to ($\delta_g + \delta_{th}$) where δ_{th} is the thermal error associated with the particular thermal state of the machine during on-machine measurement.

Mou and Liu demonstrated the above relationships while describing a method of error measurement using standard artifacts. The author believes that these observations are equally applicable when one uses the machined part itself as the artifact during on-machine measurement.

Let D_{omw} be the part dimension determined by on-machine measurement conducted immediately after the part has been machined so that the thermal state of the machine during measurement is almost the same as that during cutting. Let D_{omc} be the value determined by on-machine measurement after the machine has been allowed to cool down. Then, following Mou and Liu's observations,

$$\delta_g = D_{pp} - D_{omc} \tag{A4}$$

$$\begin{aligned}\delta_{th} &= (\delta_g + \delta_{th}) - \delta_g = (D_{pp} - D_{omw}) - (D_{pp} - D_{omc}) \\ &= (D_{omc} - D_{omw})\end{aligned} \tag{A5}$$

Now, it can be shown by combining Equations (A1) to (A5) that

$$\delta_f = D_{omw} - D_{des} - \delta_{ither} \rightarrow D_{omw} - D_{des} \text{ (when } \delta_{other} \rightarrow 0) \tag{A6}$$

Appendix 2
A Simple Model for Force-Induced Deflection Applicable to Turning Machines

δ_f can be expressed as follows in turning a workpiece held by chucking at one end only:

$$\delta_f = 2F_x \left(1/k_t + 1/k_{wp} + 1/k_{sp}\right) \tag{A8}$$

where F_x is the radial component of the instantaneous quasi-static cutting force, k_t is the overall stiffness of the tool and the structure supporting it in the direction X, k_{wp} is the stiffness of the workpiece on its own, and k_{sp} is the overall stiffness of the chuck/spindle assembly including the headstock side structure. Note that each of these stiffness values should be interpreted as the magnitude of F_x required to act at P so as to cause unit deflection in direction X at point P.

k_t and k_{sp} depend essentially upon the machine, fixture, and tool system. These features are relatively constant for a given turning center. Note however that k_{sp} continuously changes as P traverses the tool path. k_{sp} can be estimated from a finite element analysis (FEA). However, FEA is too complex an approach for routine shop floor use. Further, in FEA, it is difficult to account for the contact deflections occurring at the various mating faces in a given machine tool assembly.

In early literature from the former USSR, there were references to the fact that, at least in the case of some subassemblies within a machine tool structure, the subassembly so behaves under elastic loading as to appear to rotate rigidly about a remotely located but fixed center. Murthy and Venuvinod later demonstrated that this observation is particularly true with respect to the spindle/headstock subassembly of turning machines [58]. This observation is used while modeling k_{sp} for different work holding configurations. In particular, for a workpiece chucked at one end with the other end free (see Figure 12),

$$k_{sp} = K_{csh}/(R - L + z)^2 \qquad\qquad (A9)$$

where z and L are the instantaneous axial distances of the cutting point P from the free end of the workpiece and the chuck face respectively, R is the axial distance between the chuck face and the plane normal to spindle axis and containing the rotation center, and K_{csh} is the rotational stiffness (N.mm/radian) of the chuck-spindle/head-stock assembly about the rotation center. Finally, k_{wp} can be determined by applying well-known principles of theory of elasticity since the instantaneous workpiece shape and the modulus of elasticity of the work material are easily obtained. The author's team has written a simple finite difference program for estimating k_{wp} with less than 1% error even while turning complex workpiece profiles.

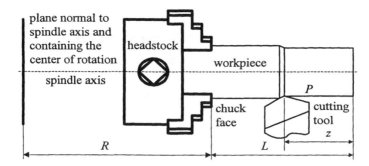

Figure 12: Workpiece set-up and rotation center of chuck/headstock assembly.

A very useful observation follows from Equations (A8) and (A9). Note that, for a workpiece held just by chucking at one end, δ_f can be expressed as an explicit function of seven parameters: F_x, k_t, k_{wp}, K_{csh}, R, L, and z. Of these, L and z are known a priori from the CNC part program; k_{wp} can be directly estimated by using the finite difference program referred to earlier; k_t, K_{csh}, and R should be constants for a given machine tool with given work holding set up; and F_x should be constant for a given combination of tool/work material pair, tool geometry, and cutting conditions.

It follows from the above discussion that the three machine constants (k_t, K_{csh}, and R) and the radial cutting force (F_x) can be estimated just by performing on-machine and post-process measurements of *four* diameters (D) distributed along the machining length during a *single* cylindrical turning operation and then simultaneously solving the corresponding equations for δ_{tot}.

8 INTELLIGENT CONTROL OF MACHINES

A.N. Poo and **P.L. Tang**
Department of Mechanical Engineering
The National University of Singapore
Singapore

An intelligent robot, or an intelligent machine in general, is a mechanical device which has sensors to sense information on itself and the environment it is in, a "brain" or controller to process this information, and actuators to effect its activities and to interact with its environment to perform some useful tasks. Actuators for producing mechanical motion and sensors for sensing such motions and associated forces, together with control theory and techniques for the proper control of such motions, have long been developed. The past has thus seen the development of machines, such as industrial robots, numerically controlled machines, and other automated machines, which have been put to good use for the benefit of man. Recent developments in computer and information technology, in sensing technology, and in artificial intelligence techniques have spawned the rapid development of intelligent techniques to achieve more precise and intelligent control of these machines and robots. Smart sensors such as visual, force, and tactile sensors allow these machines to "see" and "feel" the environment they are in. Power computers, acting as the brain and controller for these machines, allow the incorporation of more powerful control algorithms and artificial intelligence techniques. This has enabled the development of autonomous machines which not only interact intelligently with their environment, but also adapt to changes in the environment around them. This chapter introduces some approaches in the application of artificial intelligence techniques for the control of robots and machines. Some background material is given in Chapters 1, 5, and 6.

1 Introduction

In the present era where we are striving to achieve automation in the physical exertion and mental activities of human being, the idea of building machines automatically comes into mind. Since the emergence of Artificial Intelligence (AI) in designing intelligent computer systems that exhibit some characteristics of human behavior, machine control researchers have helped evolve AI and incorporate it into machines

For the past decade, the idea of creating "intelligent" machines has encouraged many researchers to devote their time and effort to making it a practical reality. Their interest in designing intelligent-controlled machines is diverse, from such applications as robotic devices working in unstructured environments, high-performance aircraft with self-repairing capabilities, to complex industrial plants subject to catastrophic actuator or sensor failures [1]. The development of an effective methodology for designing such intelligent machines or systems undoubtedly requires the synthesis of many concepts and technologies besides artificial intelligence and mechatronics. It includes computing technology (system architecture, object-orientated languages and programming, software engineering, human-machine interaction, etc), operations research, philosophy, physiology, psychology, linguistics, anthropology, and sociology, to name but some. Here we give only a limited overview on the application of artificial intelligence techniques for the control of machines and how machines are made more "intelligent."

The term *intelligent control* means different things to different people. Unfortunately as with any relatively new topic of study it suffers from a considerable amount of hype and terminology abuse. In this case, the term *intelligent* is used very loosely. In order to make a machine appear more modern, thus helping to secure more research funding, people in some areas claim their machines to be intelligent, although sometimes it is just a controller of one type or another. According to *Webster's New World Dictionary*, the term *intelligence* is defined as the ability to learn or understand from experience; to acquire and retain knowledge; and use of the faculty of reason in solving problems. Åström and McAvoy [2] gave the following definition which is favored by the control community: "An intelligent control system has the ability to comprehend, reason and learn about processes, disturbances and operating conditions in order to optimize the performance of the process under consideration." Before going deeper into the definition of intelligent machines, we will discuss some background leading to the necessity for intelligent control of machines.

1.1 Background

For the past thirty-five years, several sophisticated schemes to control automated machines have been developed. These were the so-called conventional control techniques. Although these schemes have been extensively proven and tested in the field, to achieve good control performance most of them require the knowledge of a suitable and often precise dynamic model of the system to be controlled. Many researchers turn to methods of system identification, indicating many complications. Furthermore, the parameters and often structure of the dynamic model may vary with time and the operating point of the system. To overcome this, the fields of robust and adaptive control were developed. Evidently, these approaches require an excessive amount of computation.

Conventional control schemes have shown their inability in controlling systems that exhibit high complexity, uncertainty, inexact information, or an ill-defined structure. They are also unable to process information gathered fast enough to deduce the next appropriate action in real time.

For example, in inverse dynamic control, a popular control approach in robotics, the system model is used to generate the torque input resulting in the desired trajectory and compensation of the highly coupled and nonlinear dynamics of the robot arm. This approach requires on-line identification of the inverse dynamics model, which is highly computation-intensive. Hence, it cannot be used for most practical cases [3].

In designing controllers for complex dynamical systems there are needs that are not sufficiently addressed by conventional control theory as stated above. These relate mainly to the problem of environmental uncertainty and often call for human-like decision making requiring the use of heuristic reasoning and learning from past experience. Learning is required when the complexity of a problem or the uncertainty thereof prevents a priori specification of a satisfactory solution. Such solutions are then only possible through accumulating information about the problem and using this information to dynamically generate an acceptable solution. Such a system will require an intelligent control system [4-7].

1.2 Definition

The focus of building intelligently controlled machines is absolutely not on creating cyborgs or other automatons of science fiction movies. The basic feature of intelligent machines is the ability to adapt to the dynamic environments, with fundamental human-like functions such as sensing, perception, knowledge acquisition, learning, inference and decisionmaking, and acting. Information on changes in the external environment and the state of the machine itself is achieved through sensors. The information acquired from these sensors, together with principles and algorithms gained from "experts" or past experience, forms the knowledge. This knowledge is represented and stored in a unique structured form called the knowledge base. This knowledge base enables the machine to make inferences for decision making, and thus learning from past experience and expertise is achieved. A machine with inference ability will be able to predict the effects and improve from its previous actions. By using knowledge and perceived information obtained from sensors, decision making such as planning, self-improvement, anticipation, goal seeking, and action generation is executed [8-10]. Figure 1 shows the essential concepts of an intelligent machine.

Besides the stated fundamental capabilities, an intelligent machine should preferably also possess the ability of self-maintenance, inter-machine communication, autonomy, creativity, and reproduction. Having self-maintenance ability allows the machine to maintain its own state of readiness through self-diagnosis, preventive self-maintenance and reconfiguration, and self-repair. Communication with other machines is important to accomplish control of, to report to, to receive information from, to engage in competition with, or to collaborate with other machines. Creative machines have the inclination of generating new useful concepts, principles, and methods. The capability of replicating its own soft-computing algorithms in similar or identical forms is also a sought-after intelligent characteristic of a machine [11-13].

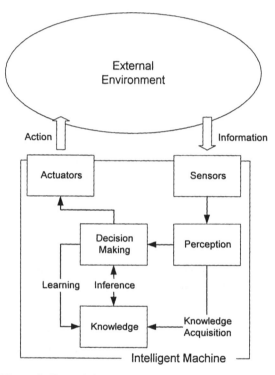

Figure 1: Essential concepts of an intelligent machine.

The participants of the 1997 "Workshop on Research Needs in Robotics and Intelligent Machines for Emerging Industrial and Service Applications" [14] proposed their definitions of what an intelligent machine should have and what they would like to see in intelligent machines. One requires the intelligent machine to be able to work with product designers to ensure manufacturability and then to autonomously reprogram itself to accommodate new product designs. Another proposed smarter automation for the safe dismantling of stockpiles of nuclear, chemical, and conventional explosive weapons. An intelligent machine should also be endowed with human-like dexterity for assembly and material handling. It can also be used for automatic butchery processes in the food industry. The agriculture, construction, and mining industries have the need for autonomous machines that are mobile and driverless with sensor-based control in the field. Intelligent control also has its potential in Just-In-Time (JIT) manufacturing, which demands quick response to customers and a near-zero inventory (See Chapters 4, 7, and 9).

From a different perspective, intelligent machines can be either autonomous or semi-autonomous entities working together with human beings and taking over some of the normal decision-making functions of human experts. These include:

- In industry where heavy objects are routinely and repetitively moved, machines to assist humans, coordinating and working safely with humans and other machines and packages, thus, reducing stress and strain of repetitive motion tasks

- "Smart" houses and robotic assistants which can enable the aging and frail to live independently with a good quality of life

- Service robots which automate the collection of hazardous waste and other routine functions in hospitals

- Surgical assistant robots and dexterity enhancing devices which assist surgeons

- In entertainment parks, robotic characters which are smart and safe enough to directly and intelligently interact with park visitors

- Planetary rovers collaborating with earthbound humans for the exploration of outer space

- Autonomous machines which collaborate with humans to clean up hazardous waste sites, automating repetitive tasks while taking higher level directions from the human operator

- In the military, a wide range from a soldier's assistant to swarms of small, smart, autonomous, land-based or flying machines reconnoitering a battle zone or doing battle themselves

In short, an intelligent-controlled machine is a machine that uses sensors to acquire information needed for quick, safe response when the unexpected occurs, with the intelligence to make quick determination of safe responses to changes or unexpected events. Comprehension, reasoning, and learning are the keys to intelligence. The subsequent sections of this chapter address the methodologies that are being practiced and developed by researchers in making a machine intelligent.

1.3 Methodologies of Intelligent Control

Since Fu [15] founded the field of intelligent control where he fused concepts of artificial intelligence and automatic control, researchers have worked extensively on enhancing traditional control concepts and approaches with concepts from information technology and artificial intelligence to make machines more intelligent.

The result is a diversity of topics, which include fuzzy control, neural control, genetic algorithms, learning control, knowledge-based (expert) control, hybrid control, sensing technology, sensory data processing and fusion, task planning, automated fault diagnosis and restoration, obstacle-avoidance, and many more. See Chapters 1 and 5 for the fundamentals.

The methods of intelligent control can be classified into principal, recognizable genre; i.e., knowledge-based or expert systems, fuzzy logic, neural networks, genetic algorithms, hybrid, and other emerging new methods. The general concept of each method will be discussed separately but a more comprehensive treatment will be given to the three relatively new and potentially effective algorithm-based methods; i.e., fuzzy logic, neural networks, and genetic algorithms, which come under the topic of soft computing in intelligent control. In general, all the intelligent control methods that are discussed here can be classified into two distinct approaches; namely, the direct approach and indirect (or supervisory) approach. In the direct approach, the intelligent controller is used as a replacement for the conventional controller, as shown in Figure 2(a). In the indirect approach, the intelligent controller is incorporated into the system as an auxiliary (and supervisory) controller complementing the main conventional controller [16]. This is depicted in Figure 2(b). Some background material on soft computing is found in Chapters 1, 5, and 6.

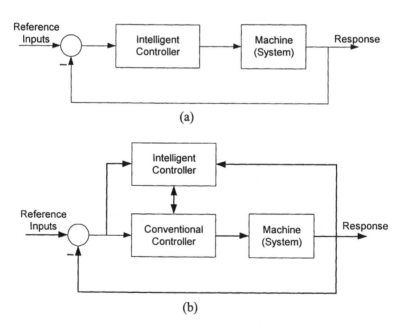

Figure 2: Two general approaches of intelligent control:
(a) direct control, (b) supervisory control.

2 Expert Control

Generally, the focus of automatic control is on the development of algorithms. With the advances in computational technology, elements of logic, reasoning, sequencing, and heuristics can be easily accommodated into the algorithms. In this way, the conventional control algorithms can be extended to expert control in which the heuristic knowledge of a human expert, typically but not necessarily an experienced operator, of the system under control is used to create a knowledge base for a supervisory expert system. An expert control system, also widely known as a knowledge-based control system, has two main components: a knowledge base and an inference engine. The knowledge base contains the known expert knowledge and rules on which the system control is based. The inference engine is a system protocol to navigate through the rules in the knowledge base in conjunction with data in the database, to make the necessary deductions, and to arrive at a satisfactory decision or course of action. This type of control system is capable of perception, reasoning, learning, and making inferences from incomplete information or knowledge of the process.

An expert control system is expected to have the capability to control systems having time-varying, nonlinear characteristics and subjected to a variety of disturbances. With time, the controller is able to gather more information (knowledge) about the process and make the necessary adjustments to enhance its performance automatically. The condition of the process is monitored continuously to detect possible problems before they occur. The expert control system will either take the corrective action or raise an alarm for the human operator. This is done with an array of sensors and actuators. When the user acquires new information about the system, this can easily be used to update the knowledge base to improve control performance. In short, an expert controller is equipped with many algorithms, including control, identification, measurement, monitoring, and design, to effectively monitor and steer the system under control as desired by the user.

Figure 3 shows a typical expert control system structure. It is composed of a basic feedback loop containing a crisp controller. The controller block itself could comprise optimal control, state feedback, state observer, or simple PID controller. In addition, there is an identification block in the outer loop, which can consist of several alternative algorithms. The outermost block is the knowledge-based system or so-called expert system in which reside the supervision, controller design, coordination, and fault detection algorithms. The expert system decides, or rather computes, which control and identification scheme to use and when to switch between control schemes from the information gathered on-line and the a priori knowledge from the human experts. It can also concurrently carry out diagnostic tasks to detect potential faults that could happen and then deduce means of counter action. A rather complete textbook treatment and references of expert control system are given in [17].

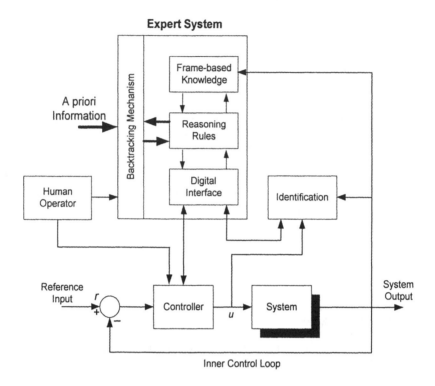

Figure 3: Typical structure of an expert control system.

2.1 Design Principles and Requirements for Expert Control of Machines

The expert control system must have a high *reliability* when it is applied as an auxiliary controller supplementing a conventional feedback controller. This is because the addition of the expert controller will significantly increase the complexity of the control system in terms of software and especially hardware (sensors and actuators). Conventional control approaches are generally not able to deal with problems such as uncertainties, incompleteness, and imprecision. These have to be handled by the expert controller requiring it to be able to cope with different levels of decision making. In knowledge-based control systems, *decision making* is the primary required ability. The expert system must also have *versatility* in its application. i.e., ease of development, diversity, hybrid knowledge representation and global database flexibility, and possession of a multiple reasoning mechanism and an open architecture. The control strategy, data management, expression of expertise, pattern matching, and procedural attachment of the expert schemes must have *flexibility* in principle. In designing an expert system, human domain experts and knowledge engineers are required. The human domain experts provide their necessary expertise and knowledge leading to the solution of the problem at hand while the knowledge engineer converts this information into a structured rule base and programs these rules into the system to provide *human-like capabilities* for the controller. See Chapter 1 for further details of an expert system.

We now discuss the design principles for expert controllers. According to Cai [17], the principle of multiplicity of model description can be used in an expert controller. This principle adopts a multifarious description form of models as opposed to conventional control methods where only one unique mathematical model of the system under control is used. The multiple models can be derived from various methods such as analytical, discrete-event based, fuzzy, rule-based, or model-based. A good example of how model switching is implemented can be found in [12].

The presence of on-line processing dexterity in an intelligent controller is also an important feature. Information processing is capable of dividing and constructing information in useful forms, retaining current important information, and neglecting previous insignificant information. Most industrial processes are stochastic and uncertain in nature with random disturbances. Thus, an expert controller must be flexible in adapting to time-varying changes in the process. In order to adopt the strategy of divide and conquer, the expert control mechanism is structured with different levels of intelligence. Finally, an expert control system, in principle, should have real-time reasoning and decision-making capabilities [18].

3 Fuzzy Control of Machines

The concept of fuzzy logic was first introduced by Zadeh [19] in his effort to overcome shortcomings in those fields where conventional mathematical techniques are of limited effectiveness. From then on, the history of fuzzy logic followed the pattern of many recent key technologies. It was invented in the US, engineered to perfection in Europe, and mass-marketed in Japan. Currently, many researchers all over the world are focusing their efforts on fuzzy logic as the means of realizing intelligent machines which can more easily relate to the linguistic characteristics of humans [20].

3.1 Fuzzy Logic

The concept of linguistic variables [21] plays a central role in the applications of fuzzy logic. The possible values of a linguistic variable are linguistic terms, mostly just referred to as *terms*. These terms are linguistic interpretations of technical variables. For example, the technical variable *distance*, which is measured in meters, can have the linguistic interpretations: very far, far, medium, close, or very close. The technical variable described by a linguistic variable is called the *base variable* in fuzzy logic design. Each linguistic value is elucidated as a label of a fuzzy set in its universe of discourse, and each set is defined by a membership function that maps one or more variables to a degree of membership, usually specified in the range between 0 and 1, in a fuzzy set.

A membership function of a fuzzy set is a possibility function, where a membership function value of zero implies that the corresponding element definitely does not belong to the fuzzy set. When the element is absolutely a member of the fuzzy set, it will have a membership function value of one. An intermediate membership function value between 0 and 1 implies that the corresponding element falls partially inside the fuzzy boundary of the set. This can be seen more clearly from Figure 4. The membership function can be of any shape but, in current practice, it usually assumes a trapezoidal or triangular shape. The number of linguistic variables used is usually in the range between three and seven.

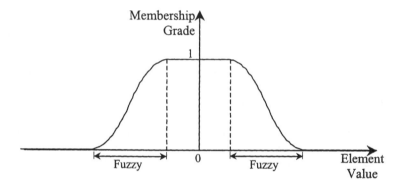

Figure 4: Membership function of a fuzzy set.

The most basic logical operations are NOT (negation), AND (conjunction, $\wedge$) and OR (disjunction, $\vee$). In Boolean logic, NOT X is true if and only if X is not true; X AND Y is true if and only if both X and Y are true; X OR Y is true if and only if at least one of X or Y is true. However, somewhat different means of evaluating results of these operations are used when dealing with fuzzy sets. There is actually an extensive choice for computing fuzzy logic operations but we will present only the original rules proposed by Zadeh. Readers can refer to [22] for other possible fuzzy operations. In Zadeh's original rules, the negation of membership is found by subtracting it from 1. Fuzzy conjunction is found by taking the minimum value while fuzzy disjunction uses the maximum. Specifically,

$$\mu_{\bar{A}}(x) = 1 - \mu_A(x) \tag{1}$$

$$\mu_{A \wedge B}(x) = min[\mu_A(x), \mu_B(x)] \tag{2}$$

$$\mu_{A \vee B}(x) = max[\mu_A(x), \mu_B(x)] \tag{3}$$

The logical operations of negation, conjunction, and disjunction are the foundations upon which much of the fuzzy rule-based processing rests, which are primarily based on inference. Conditional statements, if-then rules, are the key to making

fuzzy logic useful. These statements, when linked through the use of fuzzy operators, can produce quite complicated conditions. A single if-then rule is generally of
the form,

$$\text{If } x \text{ is } A \text{ then } y \text{ is } B \qquad (4)$$

where A and B are linguistic values of variables x and y, respectively. It has become a standard interpretation that Equation (4) is interpreted as a fuzzy constraint
on the variables x and y; i.e., it is equivalent to (AxB), where (AxB) is the Cartesian
product of A and B, which is defined by

$$\mu_{AxB}(u,v) = \mu_A(u) \wedge \mu_B(v), \ u \in U, v \in V \qquad (5)$$

where μ_A and μ_B are the membership functions of A and B, respectively; and U and
V are the universes of discourse of X and Y, respectively. When the dependence of
x on y is characterized by a collection of n rules of the form (4), we have,

$$\text{If } x \text{ is } A_i \text{ then } y \text{ is } B_i, \quad i=1,..,n \qquad (6)$$

where it is interpreted as $(A_1xB_1)+(A_2+B_2)+...+(A_nxB_n)$. Here "+" denotes the OR
operation.

Finally, when fuzziness is not required, for example in the final control action
where only crisp values are useful, the defuzzification process of converting
fuzzy values into crisp values is carried out. Defuzzification is not a straightforward task and there exist quite a few methods, each having its own advantages
and disadvantages for different applications. Interested readers are recommended to refer to [23].

3.2 Fuzzy Control

Figure 5 shows the basic components of a typical fuzzy control system. First, the
crisp input(s) is fuzzified. The inference engine (inference logic) takes these input
and, making use of the knowledge- or rule-base, arrives at the decisions (output).
The fuzzy output produced by the inference engine is then defuzzified in the final
step to produce a nonfuzzy (crisp) control output, which is used to actuate the external plant-under-control.

3.2.1 Design Principles of Fuzzy Control

The first step in designing a fuzzy controller is the selection of a reasonable structure; i.e., determining which of the system parameters are to be used as the input
and output variables. For example, the set-point error and its change can be used as
inputs while the change in actuation signal can serve as the fuzzy output.

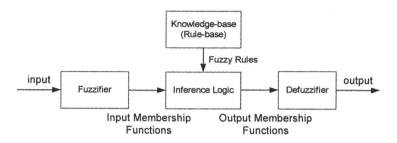

Figure 5: A simple fuzzy controller.

The next step is to select and extract fuzzy control rules. The vocabularies of the input and output variables of the controller are determined. The more vocabularies selected the more flexible the formulation of rules, with the resulting rules being more precise. This is followed by the definition of fuzzy sets, which represent each available fuzzy vocabulary, meaning the shape and span of membership functions. The fuzzy variable normalization range and quantization levels are also determined during this step. After deriving the fuzzy sets, the strategies for fuzzification and defuzzification are sorted out. Finally, the universe of discourse of the quantized value for all input and output variables is decided. This defines the range of the actual voltage or current of the A/D and D/A converters in the fuzzy controller.

3.2.2 Different Approaches of Fuzzy Control

In addition to the basic fuzzy control method presented above, other fuzzy control approaches have been developed. Two distinct approaches, namely, *fuzzy adaptive control* (also called *fuzzy learning control*) and *fuzzy supervisory control*, have proven their superiority. They will be discussed briefly here.

There are three common adaptive techniques that have been introduced to fuzzy control with the objective of optimizing fuzzy rules and their membership functions. These are the *self-organizing fuzzy logic control* (SOFLC), *fuzzy direct adaptive control*, and *fuzzy indirect adaptive control* [4].

Procyk and Mamdani [24] originated the self-organizing fuzzy logic control as an extension to the static fuzzy controller. SOFLC has the advantage of having the ability to adapt to real-time plant model variations besides being robust in dealing with complex, highly nonlinear systems. The SOFLC is structured in such a way that its control policy changes with the instantaneous performance measures. The main feature of this method is that while control actions are generated, the system's rule-base is also continuously altered on-line using a predetermined performance specification. The main advantage of SOFLC is that it does not require the derivation of the fuzzy rule-base during the design stage. The rules are generated through the process of on-line adaptation based on the optimization of a prespecified performance criterion.

SOFLC does have some drawbacks. There is a limitation in having to rely on the specification of an explicit inverse model of the system under control. Its performance criterion is a compromise between rise-time and overshoot requirements, which limits flexibility. Recently, Layne and Passino [25] introduced the Fuzzy Model Reference Learning Control method to overcome the constraints faced by SOFLC through the use of a reference model to quantify any desired closed-loop system behavior.

The direct approach of fuzzy adaptive control proposed by Wang [26] uses some adaptive laws to change the parameters of the membership functions characterizing the linguistic terms in the fuzzy if-then rules with the objective of guiding the system to track a reference trajectory. Fuzzy sets whose membership functions cover the state space are first defined, followed by the construction of an initial adaptive fuzzy controller with parameters that are free to change. Wang adopted the Lyapunov synthesis approach in developing the adaptive law to adjust the parameters of the fuzzy sets, i.e., those represented by membership functions. This direct adaptive approach proved to be globally stable in the sense that all signals are bounded and the tracking error converges to zero asymptotically under some constraints.

The fuzzy indirect adaptive control approach (also referred to as indirect self-organizing fuzzy control) is different from the direct approach in the sense that it performs on-line model or parameter identification and then uses this model to synthesis a fuzzy feedback controller based on some performance criteria. Readers are recommended to refer to [27] for further understanding of this technique.

Moudgal, Passino, and Yurkovich [28] achieved promising results when they investigated the use of a two-level hierarchical rule-based controller, otherwise called *fuzzy supervisory control* (Figure 6). It comprises a simple higher-level "expert controller" which deduces expert knowledge on how to supervise lower-level fuzzy controllers. The higher-level supervisor monitors and adjusts the low-level direct fuzzy controllers. Based on the instantaneous set-point errors, the expert controller decides which rule-base to use and adjusts the universe of discourse of each fuzzy input and output. The control scheme was tested on a flexible-link robot giving promising results.

3.3 Fuzzy Control in the Control of Machines

To date, there have been numerous successful implementations of fuzzy control on machines to realize some degree of intelligence. Here, we discuss only a few specific examples of intelligent fuzzy control of "mechatronics" machines just to provide the readers a feel for the potential of fuzzy control.

Lopez, Gutierrez, and Rosa [29] implemented real-time direct and self-organizing fuzzy control on the microprocessor-based servomotor position control of a machine tool. Today's CNC machines do not perform well under conditions of high

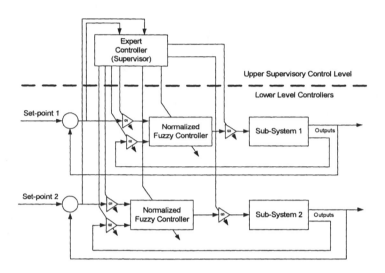

Figure 6: General fuzzy supervisory control system.

speed milling and drilling, and high accuracy workpiece requirements with high throughputs. The aim is to achieve higher production rates and better surface finishes by deriving a better control algorithm. To reduce the computational demands of the fuzzy inference process, metarules are used. This method selects only the necessary rules for inference computation according to the value of the crisp inputs into the fuzzy controller, leaving out rules that have zero-grade membership functions.

Yoshida [30] employed fuzzy control to improve the seek time of magnetic hard disc drives. Fuzzy logic is employed to complement the open-loop, bang-bang seek controller in correcting changes in actuator coil resistance due to temperature changes and actuator force unevenness at different positions. He was able to achieve an improvement of 20 to 30% in seek time with fuzzy logic control as compared to conventional control methods. In addition, correction for coil resistance due to temperature changes improved distance deviation greatly and was found to be effective even when the environment temperature was gradually increased.

Fuzzy control has been used quite extensively in the field of robotics control. Ruspini, Saffiotti, and Konolige [31] applied fuzzy control in the design of highly responsive controllers for autonomous mobile agents. This approach of applying fuzzy logic to mobile robot navigation control with uncertainties in the robot environment extends the concept of behavior into the notion of fuzzy behavior. This involves real-time processing of uncertain, incomplete, and approximate information. A mobile test robot was used by Ruspini and others to test their fuzzy motion control scheme. The robot contained two independently driven wheels for movement while a ring of 12 sonars, wheel encoders, and a video camera were used for sensor feedback. The implemented controllers were capable of implementing motion and perception behaviors, seeking to attain multiple, possibly conflicting, objectives. Similar fuzzy control approaches were also applied by Watanabe [32,33] to autonomous mobile robots.

Another application of fuzzy control in the robotic field is the determination of force and position control gains of a biped robot using fuzzy logic [34]. Kovacic et al. [35] used fuzzy control in joint servo control of a five-axis electrically driven articulated robot arm. They showed that the proposed nonlinear fuzzy controller would provide good trajectory tracking even in the presence of external disturbance. Doersam and Hammerschmidt [36] applied an adaptive fuzzy controller, which allowed automatic controller tuning during system operation, to a three-fingered robot gripper. The gripper was able to perform fine manipulations.

4 Neural Control of Machines

Neural networks are introduced and discussed in Chapters 1, 5, and 6. In this section, we examine in some detail one approach to the use of artificial intelligence techniques for the control of machines: the use of artificial neural networks.

4.1 Artificial Neural Networks

Artificial neural networks are motivated by models of the biological neurons and mimic the most elementary functions of the biological neural networks. They had their beginnings in the 1940s when the model of the elementary computational neuron was first formulated [37]. The *Hebbian learning rule*, a learning scheme for updating the connection weights between neurons, was introduced in 1949 [38] and made significant contributions to the development of neural network theory. In 1958, Frank Rosenblatt introduced the *perceptron* [39], which can modify its interconnections under supervised training to function as an associative memory and thus be used for classifying certain patterns. In 1962, Rosenblatt provided the *perceptron training algorithm*, along with a proof that a perceptron can be trained to learn anything that it can represent [40].

The 1960s saw the introduction of the ADALINE (ADAptive LINEar combiner) and the MADALINE (Many ADALINEs) and a new powerful learning rule, the *Widrow-Hoff* learning rule [41]. These were used in pattern recognition and classification, in weather prediction, and for adaptive control.

Despite the early successes, enthusiasm, and promises, the learning schemes for single-layer perceptrons available at that time were too weak and it was soon found that these networks failed to solve seemingly simple problems superficially similar to those they had been successful in solving. In 1969, Marvin Minsky and Seymour Papert published the book *Perceptrons* [42] in which they proved that the single-layer networks, which were in use then, were theoretically incapable of solving many problems, including the simple Exclusive-OR function. Artificial neural network research then lapsed into a period of stagnation for nearly two decades.

The introduction of the error backpropagation training algorithm for multilayer networks in 1986 by Rumelhart, Hinton, and Williams [43] overcame the limitations of the earlier single-layered perceptrons and sparked a renewed interest in artificial neural networks. This method had earlier been described by Parker [44] and Werbos [45]. Since then, there has been an explosion of research in this field and, today, multilayered neural networks have found successful applications in a wide variety of fields, from medical and process diagnosis to signal identification and process control. They have achieved successes in many applications where conventional approaches have failed.

4.2 Multilayered Neural Network

Figure 7 shows the structure of a single neuron, the fundamental building block for multilayer neural networks. A set of inputs, x, is applied through connecting weights, w, to a summing junction. This summation of products, s, is used as the input to an activation function, f, producing the output y. The equations describing the neuron are

$$s = w_1 x_1 + w_2 x_2 + \cdots + w_n x_n = \sum_{i=1}^{n} w_i x_i$$

or, in vector notation

$$s = w^T x \tag{7}$$

where w is the weight vector and x the input vector.

The output y is given by

$$y = f(s) = f(w^T x) \tag{8}$$

where the activation function, $f(\bullet)$, is typically a continuous *sigmoid* function.

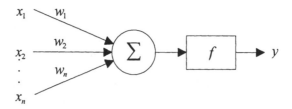

Figure 7: Structure of a neuron.

Multilayer *feedforward* neural networks, sometimes called multilayered perceptrons (MLP), are formed from interconnections of many basic neurons and are
typically of the structure shown in Figure 8. As shown in the figure, in addition to
the necessary input layer and output layer, there are also one or more *hidden layers*. These are called *feedforward* or *nonrecurrent* networks because there are no
feedback connections, that is, connections from the outputs of a layer back to the
inputs of a previous layer. As such, the outputs at any instant are solely determined
by the values of the current inputs and the connecting weights, and not based on
any previous inputs. These networks "remember" what they have been trained to
do through adjustments in the values of their interconnecting weights.

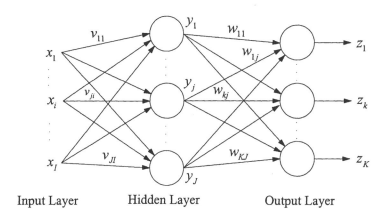

Figure 8: A multilayer feedforward neural network.

For the fully connected network shown in Figure 8, the relevant equations describing the operation are

$$y = \Gamma(vx) \tag{9}$$

$$z = \Gamma(wy) \tag{10}$$

where x is the input vector, y and z are the output vectors of the hidden and the
output layers, respectively, v and w the weight matrices, and $\Gamma[\bullet]$ the diagonal matrices of activation functions.

4.2.1 Network Training

Other than their massively parallel structures, which can be used to great advantage
in achieving greater speeds of processing, a major feature of neural networks is
that they can be trained to map complex functions without the need to have a priori

knowledge about the functions themselves. In other words, a neural network can *learn* to map a function by just having input-output data presented to it. Memory of the network resides in the values of the interconnecting weights, which are adjusted during the training process.

The objective of training the network is thus to adjust the connection weights so that the transfer characteristics of the network between input and output are close to the desired ones. Training is accomplished by presenting the network with a number of training pairs of data, each pair comprising an input vector and the corresponding *desired* output vector. The number of training cycles required to properly train a neural network can range from tens to tens and hundreds of thousands. Sometimes, if improper initial weights or training parameters are used, the network may become unstable during training, that is, values of weights and neuron outputs may increase without bound. For further details on neural networks and their training, readers can refer to [46,47].

The efficiency of training depends on many factors including

- the complexity of the mapping function desired
- the number of nodes
- the initial values of the weights
- the training strategy
- the desired accuracy
- the values of training parameters used

The preferred approach in training a multilayer feedforward neural network is the *error backpropagation* approach or variants of it. In this approach, all the connecting weights are first initialized to small random values. An input data vector is then presented to the network and the network's output vector is computed in a *forward* pass. Then by comparing this output vector with the desired output vector, an error vector at the output layer is determined. This error vector is backpropagated, through the interconnecting weights, so as to determine the error vectors at the outputs of each of the hidden layers. Based on the error vectors so determined, the necessary weight adjustments are made so as to reduce the network errors at the output.

4.3 Neural Networks in Control Applications

The ability of a neural network to map complex functions, through training using input-output data, can be used to advantage in the control of machines. Many successful control schemes are model-based. The basic principle of model-based control techniques is the use of a priori knowledge of the dynamic model of the plant-under-control, in this case a machine or a robot manipulator, to design a suitable controller. Typically, the highly nonlinear and coupled dynamics of the plant are first linearized and decoupled. The resulting linear system can then be controlled using well-developed linear control schemes. Neural network adaptation of this technique generally involves using a neural network trained to map accurately the inverse dynamics of the plant [48,49].

Model-based control techniques can give very satisfactory results and accurate control provided that an accurate dynamic model of the plant is known a priori. Unfortunately, in most applications, it is extremely difficult, if not impossible, to have an accurate dynamic model of the plant, including its parameters. Moreover, plant dynamics can also change over time or during operation, as in the case of a robot manipulator picking up its payload. In such cases, control performance deteriorates [50,51].

With the use of neural networks, the disadvantage of not having an accurate dynamic model of the plant is eliminated. Since the neural network can be trained using *actual* plant input-output data, when properly trained, it can accurately represent the dynamic model of the plant. Furthermore, when used with on-line retraining (again using actual plant input-output data) during operation, the neural network can adapt to plant parameter changes and disturbances during operation and can maintain good control performance continuously.

The following sections describe in detail some approaches for the use of neural networks in control applications together with some actual experimental results.

4.4 Neuro-Computed-Torque Control (NCTC)

The dynamics of any complex mechanical system, including machines and robots, can be described by the following equation:

$$M(q)\ddot{q} + H(q,\dot{q}) = T \qquad (11)$$

with

$$H(q,\dot{q}) = C(q,\dot{q})\dot{q} + F(\dot{q}) + G(q) + d \qquad (12)$$

where q is the $n \times 1$ vector of joint positions, T is the $n \times 1$ vector of applied joint forces/torques, $M(q)$ is the $n \times n$ symmetric positive-definite manipulator inertia matrix, $C(q,\dot{q})\dot{q}$ is the $n \times 1$ vector of centripetal and Coriolis forces/torques, $G(q)$ is the $n \times 1$ vector of gravitational forces/torques, $F(\dot{q})$ is the $n \times 1$ vector representing forces/torques due to friction acting at the manipulator joints, and d is the $n \times 1$ vector of unknown signals due to unmodeled dynamics and external disturbances.

The computed-torque control (CTC) approach involves incorporating the dynamic model into the controller to transform the highly nonlinear dynamics of Equation (11) into equivalent linear systems. Linear control theory can then be applied to synthesize controllers to specify the desired closed-loop response. Figure 9 is a schematic diagram of the computed-torque control system with proportional-derivative (PD) feedback.

As shown in Figure 9, the plant is actuated with the following joint torque vector:

$$T = \hat{M}(q)u + \hat{H}(q,\dot{q}) \tag{13}$$

with

$$u = \ddot{q}_d + K_v(\dot{q}_d - \dot{q}) + K_p(q_d - q) \tag{14}$$

where q_d and q are the desired (reference) trajectory and the output of the plant, respectively, and K_v and K_p are the derivative and the proportional gains (matrices), respectively. In Equation (13), the hats "^" represent the estimates of the matrices $M(q)$ and $H(q,\dot{q})$ of the actual plant dynamics given in Equation (11). Also, D in Figure 9 represents external disturbances.

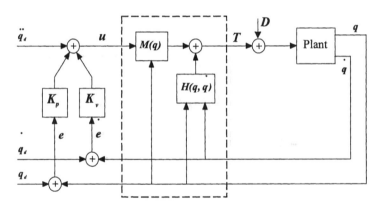

Figure 9: Computed-torque control.

When the robot dynamic model is perfectly known and in the absence of disturbances, equating Equations (11) and (13) and using Equation (14) results in the following error equation:

$$\ddot{e} + K_v\dot{e} + K_p e = 0 \tag{15}$$

where $e = q_d - q$. Equation (15) indicates that, by specifying appropriate values of feedback gains K_v and K_p, the tracking error e, if not already zero, will go to zero asymptotically, and perfect trajectory tracking is possible.

As mentioned in the preceding paragraphs, the performance of the model-based CTC approach depends, to a large extent, upon having an accurate knowledge of the dynamic model of the plant; in other words, how closely the controller as represented by Equation (13) is to the actual plant represented by Equation (11). Mismatch between these can significantly degrade control performance.

In neuro-computed-torque control (NCTC), a neural network is used to replace the portion of the controller within the dashed box shown in Figure 9, generating the control torque as given by Equation (13). The resulting neuro-computed-torque control system is illustrated in Figure 10.

In this control scheme, the requirement for the neural network controller is that it be trained to accurately map the actual plant as given by Equation (11). During the control operation it receives as inputs, the variables u, q and $\dot{q}$, and produces the output T.

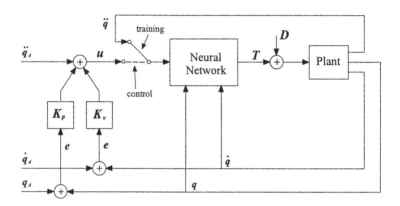

Figure 10: Neuro-computed-torque control

To train the neural network controller according to Equation (11), actual plant input-output data is used to form training sets. A suitable excitation force/torque, T, is used as input to the plant and the corresponding outputs, q, $\dot{q}$, and $\ddot{q}$, are determined through measurements or computation. A training set consists of q, $\dot{q}$, and $\ddot{q}$ as inputs and T as the desired output.

To properly train the neural network over its entire range of operation, a large number of training sets is usually required. The choice of T that is used to excite the plant during training set generation is very important. T needs to be a rich signal which can excite the plant so that the training set generated spans the entire range of operation, in terms of the range of q, $\dot{q}$, and $\ddot{q}$ [52]. A swept sinusoidal signal with a certain proportion of white noise has been found to be a good excitation signal [53,54].

In the NCTC scheme, on-line retraining of the neural network during actual control operation can also be incorporated. This is shown schematically in Figure 10 where a switch is shown switching one of the inputs to the neural network between u (for control) and $\ddot{q}$ (for training). The system then switches alternately between a control phase and a training phase in each sampling period. During the control phase, the aforementioned input to the neural network is switched to u and the neural network is operated according to Equation (13) to compute the required control torque. For the training phase, this same input is switched to accept the actual plant output $\ddot{q}$, which, together with the other plant outputs q and $\dot{q}$, form the input vector of training set. The desired output of the training set is the input torque to the plant, T, at that instance. The advantage of having on-line retraining is that the neural network controller will be continuously retrained with actual plant input-output data and can adapt effectively to variations in the parameters and the model during operation.

4.4.1 Example: Control of a Two-Link Arm

Figure 11 shows a schematic diagram of a two-link robotic manipulator comprising two light links of length l_1 and l_2, each with a distal concentrated mass of m_1 and m_2, respectively.

The dynamic equations for this robot can be written as

$$T_1 = [(m_1 + m_2)l_1^2 + m_2 l_2^2 + 2m_2 l_1 l_2 \cos(q_2)]\ddot{q}_1 + [m_2 l_2^2 + m_2 l_1 l_2 \cos(q_2)]\ddot{q}_2$$
$$- \dot{q}_2 m_2 l_1 l_2 \sin(q_2)\dot{q}_1 - (\dot{q}_1 + \dot{q}_2)m_2 l_1 l_2 \sin(q_2)\dot{q}_2 + (m_1 + m_2)gl_1 \cos(q_1) \qquad (16)$$
$$+ m_2 gl_2 \cos(q_1 + q_2) + f_{v1}\dot{q}_1 + f_{c1} \, sgn(\dot{q}_1)$$

$$T_2 = [m_2 l_2^2 + m_2 l_1 l_2 \cos(q_2)]\ddot{q}_1 + m_2 l_2^2 \ddot{q}_2 + \dot{q}_1^2 m_2 l_1 l_2 \sin(q_2)$$
$$+ m_2 gl_2 \cos(q_1 + q_2) + f_{v2}\dot{q}_2 + f_{c2} \, sgn(\dot{q}_2) \qquad (17)$$

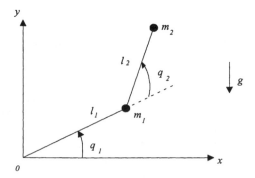

Figure 11: A two-link robot.

where T_1 and T_2 are the joint torques; q_1 and q_2 the joint rotations; f_v and f_c the coefficients of viscous and Coulomb friction, respectively; and g the acceleration due to gravity. It is noted that Equations (16) and (17) are in the form of Equation (11).

The control performance of the conventional computed-torque control (CTC) scheme and the neuro-computed-torque control (NCTC) scheme were compared using computer simulations. In both cases, the links were required to follow an input trajectory in the form of a quintic polynomial [55], moving a total distance of $\frac{\pi}{2}$ rad in 4 s as shown in Figure 12.

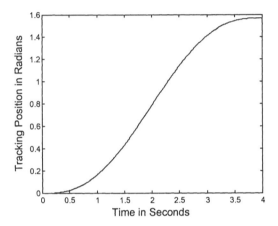

Figure 12: Quintic polynomial input trajectory.

In the NCTC scheme, the neural network controller was pretrained using the "known" plant dynamic model given by Equations (16) and (17). Training sets were generated by choosing random combinations for the variables q_1, $\dot{q}_1$, $\ddot{q}_1$, q_2, $\dot{q}_2$, and $\ddot{q}_2$ within their range of expected operation and using these equations to compute the "desired" values of torques.

In the case of a perfect knowledge of plant dynamics, the CTC scheme was able to achieve "perfect" control with tracking errors in the range of 10^{-4} rad. arising from errors introduced by sampling at 1 ms [56]. The NCTC scheme also did very well giving tracking errors within 10^{-3} rad. The poorer performance of the NCTC scheme as compared with that of the CTC scheme was due to the fact that there were residual mapping errors, because training was stopped when the errors in mapping of the control torques were within 5% of its working range.

The superior performance and adaptability of NCTC over conventional CTC becomes evident in the presence of model uncertainty and external disturbance.

Figures 13 and 14 show the tracking error for the two robot links following the same quintic polynomial trajectory when there is a 10% variation in the masses m_1 and m_2.

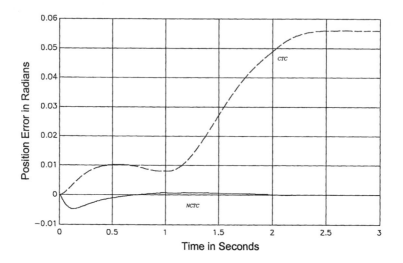

Figure 13: Tracking error for Link 1 when following a quintic polynomial trajectory (Solid line for NCTC and dashed line for CTC).

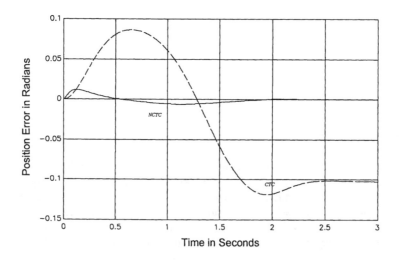

Figure 14: Tracking error for Link2 when following a quintic polynomial trajectory (Solid line for NCTC and dashed line for CTC).

In this case, the controllers of CTC and NCTC both were designed/trained based on an assumed dynamic model for which the values of the two masses were off by 10% of their actual values. It can be seen that while the tracking error performance of the CTC controller deteriorates because of dynamic model mismatch, the NCTC (with on-line retraining) was able to adapt itself quickly and still maintain excellent control performance. Once the NCTC has been retrained, it will adjust its connection weights to properly match actual plant dynamics and will continue to maintain performance at a level comparable to what is possible when trained using a perfect model of the plant. In other words, its tracking error will reduce to within 10^{-3} rad.

In a similar way, while external disturbances will cause deterioration in the control performance of the CTC controller, the NCTC controller will adapt quickly to its changing environment and maintain good performance.

4.5 Neuro-Internal Model Control (NIMC)

Internal model control (IMC) has long been used, mainly in the process industry [57]. Recently, it has also been shown to be suitable for robot manipulator control. As with computed-torque control, it is model-based and can give excellent performance when the dynamic model of the plant is accurately known. In the presence of large modeling uncertainties and external disturbances, its performance too can degrade significantly. When a neural network is incorporated into the control scheme to learn the plant model with on-line retraining, significant improvement in control performance can also be achieved [58].

The structure of a conventional IMC system is shown in Figure 15, where q_d is the reference trajectory, q the plant output, u the controller output, and D is the external disturbance. In an IMC system, the model, G_m, is made to be the same as that of the plant, G_p, and the controller, G_c, is designed to be the inverse of the model, or

$$G_m = \hat{G}$$
$$G_c = G_m^{-1}$$

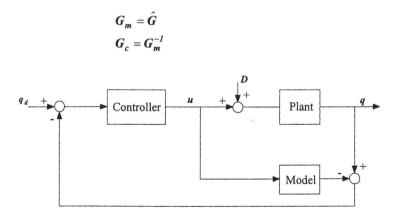

Figure 15: Internal model control system.

A property of IMC is that when the model is an accurate representation of the plant, that is $\tilde{G} = G$, the stability of both the controller and the plant is sufficient for the stability of the overall system. Furthermore, if $G_c = G_m^{-1}$ is realizable, then perfect reference tracking control ($q = q_d$) can be achieved for all $t > 0$, despite any disturbance D. In the case of an open-loop unstable plant, prestabilization of the plant is necessary before IMC can be used.

The ability of neural networks to be trained to map the inverse dynamics of a plant can be used to advantage in an IMC system. Li et al. [58] used a feedforward neural network, trained as the inverse of the plant, to precompensate and linearize a robot before applying IMC. Figure 16 shows the neural network precompensated plant. With the robot having the dynamics as given in Equation (11) and the neural network trained to give the inverse as given by Equation (13), we can write

$$\ddot{q} = u'$$ (18)

and the precompensated plant together with the feedback proportional-derivative control then becomes the linear system

$$q = (Is^2 + K_v s + K_p)^{-1} u'$$ (19)

Equation (19) is then used for the internal model in the IMC system of Figure 15.

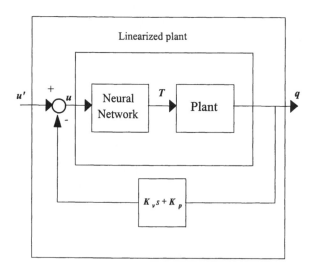

Figure 16: Neural network precompensated plant.

For perfect trajectory tracking, the IMC design rule would provide the controller as

$$G_c = G_m^{-1} = Is^2 + K_v s + K_p \tag{20}$$

To be physically realizable, a prefilter is added and the modified controller [59] is of the form

$$G_m = \frac{1}{(\tau_f s + 1)^N} [Is^2 + K_v s + K_p] \tag{21}$$

where τ_f is the filter time constant and N, its order, is selected to be $N \geq 2$ in this case.

Both IMC and NIMC schemes were implemented on the same two-link arm as described in the previous section with the links required to follow the same quintic polynomial trajectory. With perfect modeling, both schemes showed excellent trajectory tracking performance. Tracking errors were on the order of 10^{-4}, due to errors introduced by sampling at 1 ms.

System uncertainties were then introduced in the form of mass parameters (10% of actual values), disturbance torques (20% of maximum values of torques), viscous friction (0.4), and payload (100% of Link1 mass). Under these uncertain circumstances, the trajectory tracking performance of the NIMC scheme was considerably better than that for the conventional IMC scheme. The results are shown in figures 17 and 18 where it can be seen that the tracking errors for NIMC are about an order of magnitude smaller than that for the IMC scheme.

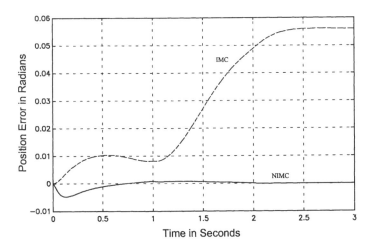

Figure 17: Link1 tracking error for NIMC and IMC with system uncertainties.

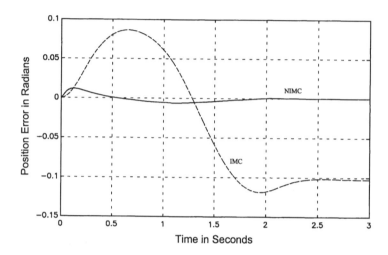

Figure 18: Link2 tracking errors for NIMC and IMC with system uncertainties.

5 Genetic Algorithms Control

Rechenberg first introduced the idea of evolutionary approaches in the 1960s in his work "evolution strategies" [60]. Following this, Holland was reportedly the first to develop this idea further to form the underlying basic principles of genetic algorithms in 1962, and later officially published his work in 1973 [61]. Darwin's "survival of the fittest" strategy basically states that species with good fitness characteristics with respect to their environments are able to survive and evolve over many generations while those with the poor fitness characteristics are unable to survive and eventually become extinct due to natural selection. Inspired by Darwin's principle of genetics and natural selection, genetic algorithms (GAs) are exploratory search and optimization procedures that were based on the principle of natural (biological) evolution and population genetics. Essentially, GA performs a parallel, stochastic, but directed search to evolve the fittest population (see Chapters 1, 5, and 6).

GA is different from traditional optimization techniques in several aspects. As randomized algorithms, genetic algorithms use probabilistic rules to make choices in their operations. The operations optimize the trade-off between exploring new points in the search space and exploiting the information already discovered. GA starts with virtually little or no knowledge of the correct solution, depending entirely on responses from interaction with the environment and evolution operators to arrive at good solutions. The search space is sampled in implicit parallelism, meaning that its effect is equivalent to an extensive, concurrent search of hyperplanes of the given space without directly testing all hyperplanes. This renders GA optimization less susceptible to getting trapped in false "local" optimal solutions as may occur in gradient descent methods. Furthermore GAs can be readily applied to the problem of cost function with discontinuity due to their non-gradient-function-based optimization. Instead of working with the actual parameters that need to be optimized, GA uses a coded genotype representation of the parameters. The binary coding method is usually adopted.

5.1 Simple Genetic Algorithms

As GA is biologically inspired, its search and optimization processes imitates natural evolution, and hence includes biomimetic or genetic operations such as reproduction, crossover, and mutation. Simple GA procedures which operate in cycles called generations are generally composed of coded genotype strings, statistically defined control parameters, a fitness function, genetic operations (reproduction, crossover, and mutation), and mechanisms for selection and encoding of the solutions as genotype strings. The basic flowchart of a genetic algorithm is shown in Figure 19.

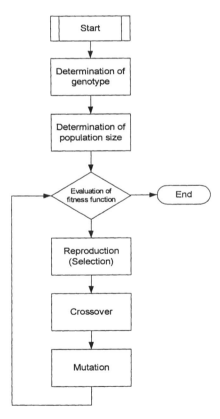

Figure 19: A flowchart for the basic genetic algorithm process.

A population of genotype strings called *chromosomes* is initially generated randomly at the start of the genetic optimization process. At each generation, a new population string is generated based on the previous generation's fitness. Each string in a population is an encoding of the candidate solution. Section 5.1.1 covers some basic proven encoding methods. The existing population is maintained by a selection mechanism. It then goes through three genetic operations; namely, reproduction, crossover, and mutation. Sections 5.1.2, 5.1.3, and 5.1.4 discuss these three common genetic operations.

5.1.1 Encoding Genotype Strings

There are a few choices of genotype encoding methods, which are problem dependent. Binary encoding is commonly used, mainly because the early works of GA used binary encoding. Each chromosome, which represents a probable solution, is a string of zeros and ones, so-called bits (e.g., {1010010101110010101}). Binary encoding gives many possible chromosomes even with a small number of alleles. For cases where binary encoding is not natural, some corrections are required after crossover and/or mutation. When we are required to solve task-ordering problems, permutation encoding is preferred. Every chromosome is represented by a string of numbers in a sequence (e.g., {293741856}). When dealing with special problems where some complicated value such as real numbers is used, value encoding can be a suitable choice. Hence, every chromosome is a string of some meaningful values (e.g., {2.7632, 2.2068, 7.4329, 5.123} or {*back*, *front*, *right*, *left*} or {AFEBCEFDBCFEBAFDCEBA}). An example of such a special problem is finding the weights for a neural network, in which case the real values in the chromosomes represent the weights.

5.1.2 Reproduction

The process of reproduction is governed by the survival of the fittest test. In this process, a new generation of population is formed by randomly selecting strings from an existing population based on fitness. As a result, individuals (parents) with higher fitness values are copied to produce a new population of individuals (offspring) in the subsequent generation, while the less fit individuals are assigned lower probabilities of contributing to subsequent generations.

5.1.3 Crossover

After reproduction, a crossover operation is executed to create new individuals (offspring) with a pair of parent chromosomes. This process, analogous to nature's sexual reproduction, its genetic sexual reproduction, takes two chromosomes and swaps part of its genetic information to produce new chromosomes. The simplest way is to randomly choose some crossover point and bits before this point is copied from the first parent, and then everything after that crossover point is copied from the second parent. For example, the crossover between Parent 1 with binary strings {001101 | 100111010} and Parent 2 with strings {110010 | 010101011} will produce two offspring having chromosomes {001101 | 010101011} and {110010 | 100111010}.

5.1.4 Mutation

Mutation is the last genetic operation in a generation before the performance of each individual of the population is evaluated. It is a localized or bitwise operation, which is applied with a very low probability, to alter the value of a random position in a gene string. Thus, mutation acts as an insurance against total loss of any gene in the population by its ability to introduce a gene which may not initially have existed or which was lost through application of reproduction and/or crossover. It also acts to prevent the falling of all solutions in population into local minima. For binary encoding, this operator simply alters a bit at an arbitrarily chosen site from 0 to 1 or 1 to 0. For example, if a chromosome is represented as {1111111111} and mutation occurs at position 8, the new mutated chromosome becomes {1111111011}.

5.3 Genetic Algorithms for Intelligent Control

The main reason that GA attracted many researchers is its capability to obtain near-optimal solutions to different types of optimization problems without the need to have prior explicit knowledge of the task domain, by simply manipulating bit-strings. However, the development of GA techniques in the control of intelligent machines has been relatively slow compared with fuzzy logic and neural networks. This may be due to the fact that GA is an optimization engine and hence does not appear to be a promising on-line controller on its own. It can only be used to complement other conventional and/or intelligent control methods. In addition, GA processing is very computationally demanding giving rise to difficulties in real-time on-line control, especially of high bandwidth systems such as servomechanisms. Because of this, they are often applied off line to problems such as collision avoidance, path planning, pattern recognition, and other higher level learning and decision-making processes.

Chen and Zalzala [62] applied GA for motion path planning of mobile robots incorporating distance-safety criteria. In motion path planning of a mobile robot, there often exists a large, sometimes seemingly infinite, number of paths between the initial and the target position. In path planning it is usually not necessary to determine the best solution but a good one according to certain constraints or requirements. For this, GA techniques have been shown to perform better than traditional search methods because they combine local and global search methods to avoid being trapped at a local minimum. Thus, computational efficiency, reliability and speed can be greatly increased. Dangprasert and Avatchanakorn [63] proposed a new intelligent GA controller based on the concept of self-tuning regulators. The proposed controller is said to be able to do on-line parameter identification and control law calculation without a priori knowledge of the system or training data to train the system.

6 Hybrid Intelligent Control

The recent years have seen the research activities on intelligent control of machines. Focus has been on the investigation of various fusion possibilities of expert systems, fuzzy logic, neural networks, and genetic algorithms to combine their different strengths while overcoming the weaknesses of individual methods. Although the hybrid intelligent control technique can be developed in a variety of ways, it can generally be classified into two approaches; namely, the function-replacing approach and the intercommunicating approach. In the function-replacing approach, a technique is embedded into another, while the two techniques maintain their functional forms but share data through different degrees of coupling in the intercommunicating approach.

In this section, we introduce the basic concepts of the methods of integrating fuzzy logic, neural networks, and genetic algorithms, and provide some application examples. Interested readers can probe further by referring to the references cited [64-66]. Related topics and applications are presented in Chapter 6.

6.1 Fuzzy-Neural Control

Among the three possible combinations of fuzzy logic, neural networks, and genetic algorithms, the integration of fuzzy logic and neural networks, the so-called fuzzy-neural systems is the most common form. Fuzzy logic has the ability to express control rules in linguistic fuzzy descriptions, but it suffers from the disadvantage that it has no learning ability in its conventional form. On the other hand, neural networks have the capability of generalization and can infer solutions, with quite subtle relationships, from the data presented to them, in the absence of a priori knowledge of the system under control. However, the learned knowledge contained in the neural network is often difficult to be extracted and interpreted. Thus, fusion of these two distinctive approaches has the advantage of capturing and further enhancing the capabilities of both fuzzy logic and neural networks [67].

There are many possible combinations of fuzzy logic and neural network processes and many have been tried. Khalid et al. [68] proposed an adaptive fuzzy-neural control scheme by integrating two neural network models with a basic fuzzy logic controller. The first neural network is trained as a plant emulator using the backpropagation algorithm, with the second used as a compensator to improve the performance of a basic fuzzy controller on-line. The authors claimed that the proposed scheme is able to ease the fine tuning of scale factors and the formulation of correct rules in the basic fuzzy logic controller.

A common trend in fuzzy-neural integration is to use neural networks to tune the fuzzy membership functions and to generate fuzzy control rules autonomously using self-learning methods. One such techniques is found in Kim et al. [69] where they make use of a Fuzzy-Neural Controller (FNC) and a Model Neural Network

(MNN) in their adaptive neural-fuzzy control scheme. In the FNC, the antecedents and consequents of the fuzzy rules are constructed by a multilayer neural network using a clustering method. The FNC is trained to refine the fuzzy rules for the adaptive inference control action by the error backpropagation learning algorithm. On the other hand, the MNN is constructed to identify an unknown system and provide the FNC with the training data. The whole process is done repetitively on-line. This proposed scheme brings out the advantages of fuzzy logic and neural networks, in addition to being easily applied to both nonlinear and linear systems.

A novel learning approach, self-organizing and self-adjusting fuzzy modeling (SOSAFM) has been developed by Kuo et al. [70]. Basically, it consists of two stages, the self-organizing stage (SOS) and the self-adjusting stage (SAS). In the first stage, the input data is divided into several groups by applying Kohonen's feature maps. Methods of statistics are used to determine the center and width of the membership function for each group. The linear regression method is used for the consequents. Thereafter, the initial parameters of the fuzzy system can be decided. Subsequently, the error backpropagation learning method is used to fine-tune the parameters.

Lin and Lee [71] proposed a general neural-network model, hereafter called the connectionist model, for fuzzy logic control and decision or diagnosis systems. In this approach of realizing fuzzy-neural control, the connectionist model can be contrasted with the basic direct fuzzy logic control and decision system in their network structure and learning ability. Such a fuzzy control and decision network can be created from training examples by machine learning techniques, while the connectionist structure can be trained to construct fuzzy logic rules and find optimal input-output membership functions. Also, they have shown that their scheme is able to speed up learning as compared with traditional backpropagation learning algorithms.

Berenji and Khedkar [72] proposed a new way of designing and tuning fuzzy logic controllers based on reinforcements from a dynamic system, which enabled the modeling of the expert knowledge using approximate linguistic terms followed by refinement through the process of learning from experience. Their network architecture, referred to as a generalized approximate reasoning-based intelligent control (GARIC), consists of two feedforward networks one of which, the action selection network, is a fuzzy controller and the other, the action-state evaluation network, a system behavior predictor.

6.2 Genetic-Fuzzy Control

There are a number of parameters in a fuzzy control system that require design specifications. These include the fuzzy sets used for input and output variables, the membership functions that define the fuzzy sets, the structure and entries in the fuzzy associative memory, and, in some cases, the weights of each fuzzy rule. All these parameters are suitable candidates for adaptation with an optimization algorithm. Genetic algorithms have been proposed as a promising approach in enabling automatic generation of optimal parameters for the fuzzy controller.

Various learning methods to provide fuzzy reasoning with learning functions have been investigated but most of these suffer from prerequisite problems. Genetic algorithm is found to be a useful tool in deriving fuzzy inference rules so as to optimize the learning and generalization capabilities of fuzzy reasoning [73]. An information criterion is optimized by using a genetic algorithm to determine the number of inference rules and the shapes of the membership functions in the antecedent parts.

An automatic fuzzy system design method using a genetic algorithm has been proposed by Lee and Takagi [74]. This method determines the membership functions, the number of fuzzy rules, and the rule-consequent parameters concurrently to obtain a complete optimal fuzzy system. A penalty strategy that favors systems with fewer rules is also incorporated.

Song et al. [75] proposed an approach for enhancing the genetic operators' (crossover and mutation) performance with fuzzy logic. Two fuzzy controllers have been designed to adaptively adjust the crossover probability and mutation rate during the optimization process, hence improving the convergence rate of the genetic algorithm based on some heuristics.

6.3 Genetic-Neural Networks Control

The hybrid linkage of genetic algorithms and neural networks, both with self-learning ability, is perhaps the most recently exploited in the hybrid intelligent control field and still very much in its infancy. Neural networks use inductive learning and in general require examples, while genetic algorithms use deductive learning and require an objective evaluation function. A synergism between these two techniques has the potential of enhancing the performance of each in what may be referred to as evolutionary neural networks.

Genetic algorithms can be used to improve the data presented to a neural network. As an example, Brill, Brown, and Martin [76] used a genetic algorithm for feature selection in the context of neural network classifiers; specifically, counterback-propagation networks – Kohonen networks. They were able to increase the computational speed of the classifiers by configuring the genetic algorithm to use an approximate evaluation. In addition, their so-called training set sampling method, in which only a portion of the training set is used on any given evaluation, also showed significant computational savings.

Hung and Adeli [77] integrated genetic algorithms and error backpropagation as an alternative learning technique in place of the latter's gradient descent method that has the possibility of getting trapped in a local minimum. This parallel hybrid neural network learning algorithm exhibits a superior convergence property where the genetic algorithm allows rapid location of the region of optimal performance, followed by the normal backpropagation technique to find the optimal solution.

6.4 Genetic-Neural-Fuzzy Control

Few approaches on synergetic combinations of genetic algorithms, neural networks, and fuzzy logic have been proposed for intelligent control systems. Among the available few, most are still in their algorithm development stage. The trend is usually focused on using genetic algorithms to complement the existing fuzzy-neural control techniques. For example, Mester [78] proposed a genetic-neural-fuzzy controller design of a rigid-link flexible-joint robot manipulator. The control algorithm used fuzzy logic with neural membership functions and a rule-base without needing the knowledge of the mathematical model or the parameter values of the robot. The genetic algorithms were applied for optimization of the fuzzy rule set. The proposed controller was capable of compensating the elastic oscillations of the joints. The obtained membership functions and fuzzy rules were implemented with backpropagation-feedforward neural networks. The membership functions were modified through a learning process for fine tuning. Linkens and Nyongesa [4] proposed a generalized framework for integrating the three intelligent techniques in a real-time learning and control system structure.

6.5 Application of Hybrid Intelligent Control in Machines

The synergistic utilization of fuzzy logic, neural networks, and genetic algorithms to form hybrid intelligent controllers is increasingly applicable in many control technologies. The most explored branch of hybrid methods is the fusion of fuzzy logic and neural networks, often resulting in an entity of its own termed neuro-fuzzy systems.

Stylios and Sotomi [79] have successfully implemented a neuro-fuzzy control model for the next generation of the so-called "intelligent sewing machines." The model incorporates discrimination of fabric characteristics to be stitched by automatic determination of their properties. The fabric–machine interactions at different speeds have been computed in the form of linguistic rules of a fuzzy model and implemented in a neural network to allow for optimization of fuzzy membership functions and, subsequently, self-learning.

In the field of developing intelligent machines, the application of hybrid control in robotics is perhaps the most explored area. Tascillo et al. [80] have developed a neuro-fuzzy hand-grasp of a wheelchair robotic arm with two three-joint fingers and a two-joint thumb. In order to help avoid an extensive search for an optimal grasp each time an object is lifted, the robot is fitted with pressure and force sensors for feedback and a learning mechanism.

Fatikow and Wohlke [81] have used a neuro-fuzzy control approach for intelligent multifinger microrobots in industrial or medical applications. Their concept for the control system architecture is based on a combination of a neural network approach for the adaptation of process parameters and a fuzzy logic approach for the correction of parameter values given to a conventional controller. A planning component deals with the determination of initial manipulator parameters. Together with a sensor fusion procedure and a supervising and reasoning sub-system, this allows reliable operation of a microrobot. The possible applications include robots that can be operated autonomously in changing environments such as flexible inspection and maintenance robots, modular manufacturing robots, and surgery robots.

An intelligent control architecture for a robotic grasping system capable of acquiring an object into a fully enveloping power grasp was developed by Hanes et al. [82]. Control of the internal forces of the grasp is provided, along with trajectory control of object position, as the object is picked up. Fuzzy control techniques are used for control of internal forces in the power grasp, and an artificial neural network provides a means for in-process estimation of nonlinear friction. They also showed that inclusion of the artificial neural network improves the tracking accuracy of the object position.

Besides the domination of neuro-fuzzy methods in the race to achieve hybrid intelligent control, the integration of genetic algorithm and fuzzy logic is gaining popularity. Kelemen et al. [83] reported a genetics-based machine learning (GBML) method for learning and enhancing the control of a microrobot with stepping motor drives. They tried to combine several advantages of fuzzy logic and genetics-based machine learning using slightly modified classifier systems. The PID gains of a conventional controller were tuned on-line in order to minimize the effect of the nonlinear disturbances. The tuning is based on a predictive estimation method of the controller's gain, performed by a genetic algorithm-driven fuzzy classifier system, which has to evolve an adequate rule set to tune the controller gains properly.

In some manufacturing workcells, all the robots cannot communicate globally, but some robots can communicate locally and coordinate to avoid competition for public resources. Thus, it is difficult for each robot to plan its motion effectively while considering other robots. Shibata and Fukuda [84] have proposed a genetic-fuzzy method to enable each robot to plan its motion while considering the known environment and using empirical knowledge. The genetic algorithm is applied to optimize the planning of the motion. Through iterations, each robot acquires knowledge of its unknown environment expressed by fuzzy logic, and the system behaves efficiently as an evolutionary process.

For the remaining two intelligent hybrid approaches, i.e., the genetic-neural and genetic-neural-fuzzy integration, we have yet to find any application that realizes intelligence in machines. Most are still in their simulation or early development stage. It is conceivable, however, that important developments in these areas will be known in the near future.

7 Current Limitations of Intelligent Machines

A number of intelligent control techniques have been developed and implemented, which serve as promising tools towards the realization of intelligent machines. However, there are those who feel that their limitations could cripple or discourage further developments. We will now present some of the barriers that may hinder further developments.

It is important to perform nonlinear analysis on systems or machines to prove that the machine under control is highly reliable because it may be operating in a critical environment. Current nonlinear analysis techniques provide methods to help the designer avoid instabilities and limit cycles. One of the main criticisms that dampen the greater acceptance of intelligent control techniques is that most of the methods used are lacking in practical analysis of stability and robustness. Many proposals for implementing intelligent control in commercial machines have been rejected due to insufficient solid analysis or empirical data for stability and robustness of the systems. Until there is an established method for analyzing stability and robustness and until the intelligent system's behavior can be verified by simulation, modeling, nonlinear analysis, and experiments, as is being done for conventional control techniques, the use of intelligent control schemes in controlling the inner stability loop of machines will not be readily accepted, especially where human safety is of concern [85-88].

In designing a fuzzy control system, it is often time consuming and difficult to translate the expert knowledge into the requisite rule form. There is also a lack of a formal framework or design guidelines for the selection of the relevant controller parameters, such as the type of membership functions, inference methods and tuning criteria in fuzzy control, and the number of layers or nodes and mesh density in neural network control. The realization of intelligent control in multivariable processes might be crippled due to problems with high dimensionality. For example, the number of rules in a fuzzy control system increases rapidly for multiple input systems [4]. This has created considerable skepticism about what can or cannot be achieved by heuristic methodologies of intelligent control.

The Workshop on "Research Needs in Robotics and Intelligent Machines for Emerging Industrial and Service Applications" [14], sponsored by the NSF, the DOE, the IEEE US Activities Board, and the Robotics Industries Association, suggested as institutional barriers to intelligent machines the lack of a coherent national enterprise for research, development, application, and commercialization; a lack of a coherent communication strategy leading to a disconnect between research and commercial needs; and poor dissemination of R&D results from researchers to end users. It also listed, as technology barriers to the development of intelligent machines, the lack of modular and reliable hardware components such as sensors and actuators, a common modular programming language which allows easy integration to hardware, smart advanced sensors for contact force and tactile sensing, 3-D imaging, and high dexterity tools for handling a wide variety of objects.

8 Perspective of the Future

It is clear that conventional control techniques will continue to play a large role in the development of automated machines. However, there will be many opportunities in the open and exciting field of intelligent control to create intelligent autonomous machines that have a competitive advantage. There is still much that is left unexplored. A broad perspective is needed and it is up to our ingenuity to come up with creative solutions – "an intelligent control system is not simply a set-point regulator with an 'intelligent' state feedback law"[87].

Because conventional control techniques are long established, the intelligent control researchers face a formidable task convincing industry to try new techniques. In order to facilitate the control community's acceptance of the relatively new intelligent control techniques, researchers will need to focus on using them as complementary or auxiliary tools, rather than as a complete replacement of conventional controllers [88]. Perhaps intelligent methods are more suitable to handle higher-level, task-orientated, supervisory control that is not achievable by analytical control methods.

It has been indicated in the previous section that one of the weaknesses of intelligent control techniques is the lack of solid theoretical analysis. Since the developments of expert systems, fuzzy logic, neural networks and genetic algorithms typically focus on algorithms, questions regarding stability often arise. Consequently, a great deal of work still needs to be done to address this issue.

Considerable attention has been devoted to the development of intelligent machines in the categories of expert systems, adaptation and learning using fuzzy logic and neural networks, and the fusion of fuzzy and neural networks. It is expected that in the near future, more effort will be focused on the fusion of various intelligent techniques to emulate the processes of reasoning and learning of human behavior. An abstract coverage of intelligent control issues for future investigation has been given by Cai [89].

9 Summary

In this chapter, some approaches in the application of intelligent control techniques for the control of robots and machines were enumerated. First, the essential concepts of intelligence and intelligent machines were addressed. These included a brief background of how the limitations of conventional control techniques have led to the current generation of intelligent machines and some definitions on the fundamental capabilities of intelligent machines. The four common methodologies of intelligent control, namely, expert system, fuzzy logic, neural networks, and genetic algorithms, were presented. The technique of expert systems was given a basic treatment, in which its basic structure and design principles were discussed. Next, the concept of fuzzy logic, followed by the design principles and different approaches of fuzzy control were described. Some fuzzy control application examples were also examined. Then, the method of neural networks for control was introduced in greater detail, covering the fundamentals of artificial neural networks and some detailed application examples. Subsequently, discussion was focused upon the underlying operation of genetic algorithms. As another intelligent control technique, the hybrid intelligent control method was described. A hybrid intelligent controller is formed using possible integration of fuzzy logic, neural networks, and genetic algorithms to combine their different strengths while overcoming the weaknesses of individual methods. The chapter ended with some thoughts on the current limitations faced by the developers of intelligent machines and the future perspective of intelligent control of machines.

References

[1] Porter, B., "Issues in the Design of Intelligent Control Systems," *IEEE Control Systems Magazine*, Vol. 9, pp. 97-99, 1989.

[2] Åström, K. J. and McAvoy, T. J., "Intelligent Control: An Overview and Evolution," *Handbook on Intelligent Control: Neural, Fuzzy and Adaptive Approaches*, Edited by White, D. A. and Sofge, D. A., Van Nostrand Reinhold, New York, pp. 3-34, 1992.

[3] Sinha, N. K., "Intelligent Control of Robots: Status and Future Perspectives," *Proc. 5th IEEE International Workshop on Advanced Motion Control*, Coimbra, Portugal, pp. 356-363, 1998.

[4] Linkens, D. A. and Nyongesa, H. O., "Learning Systems in Intelligent Control: An Appraisal of Fuzzy, Neural and Genetic Algorithm Control Applications," *IEE Proceedings on Control Theory and Applications*, IEE, London, Vol. 143, No. 4, pp. 367-386, 1996.

[5] Forrest, S. J., Milne, J. S., and Taylor, N. G., "Integrating Intelligence into a Mechatronic System," *Proc. IEEE International Symposium on Intelligent Control*, Glasgow, pp. 132-135, 1992.

[6] Fukuda, T. and Arakawa, T., "Intelligent Systems: Robotic versus Mechatronics," *Annual Reviews in Control*, Vol. 22, Elsevier Science, Amsterdam, the Netherlands, pp. 13-22, 1998.

[7] Gupta, M. M. and Sinha, N. K., *Intelligent Control Systems: Theory and Applications*, IEEE Press, Piscataway, NJ, 1996.

[8] King, R. H., "A Survey of Intelligent Control of Mining Equipment and Systems," *International Journal of Intelligent Control and Systems*, Vol. 1, No. 1, pp. 101-117, 1996.

[9] McInroy, J. E. and Saridis, G. N., "Reliable Control and Sensor Fusion in Intelligent Machines," *Proc. IEEE International Conference on Robotics and Automation*, Sacramento, CA, Vol. 1, pp. 487-492, 1991.

[10] Narendra, K., "Intelligent Control," *IEEE Control Systems Magazine*, Vol. 11, pp. 39-40, 1991.

[11] Ollero, A. and Camacho, E. F., "Intelligent Components and Instruments for Control Applications," *International Federation of Automatic Control*, Pegamon Press, Oxford, 1993.

[12] Ravindranathan, M. and Leitch, R., "Model Switching in Intelligent Control Systems," *Artificial Intelligence in Engineering*, Vol. 13, pp. 175-187, 1999.

[13] Rzevski, G., "A Framework for Designing Intelligent Manufacturing Systems," *Computers in Industry*, Vol. 34, Elsevier Science, Amsterdam, the Netherlands, pp. 211-219, 1997.

[14] Robotics and Intelligent Machines Cooperative Council, "The Future and Intelligent Machines: Charting the Path," Proc. Workshop on Research Needs in Robotics and Intelligent Machines for Emerging Industrial and Service Applications, *IEEE Robotics and Automation Magazine*, Vol. 4, pp. 12-16, 1997.

[15] Fu, K. S., "Learning Control Systems and Intelligent Control Systems: An Intersection of Artificial Intelligence and Automatic Control," *IEEE Transactions on Automatic Control*, Vol. 16, pp. 70-72, 1971.

[16] Tzafestas, S. G., *Methods and Applications of Intelligent Control*, Kluwer Academic Publishers, Dordrecht, the Netherlands, 1997.

[17] Cai, Z. X., *Intelligent Control: Principles, Techniques and Applications*, World Scientific, Singapore, 1997.

[18] Moronuki, N. and Lee, K. H., "Design Principles of Intelligent Machines – Design Evaluation from Information Aspect," *Proc. IEEE International Conference on Systems, Man and Cybernetics*, Vancouver, BC, Vol. 2, pp. 1819-1824, 1995.

[19] Zadeh, L. A., "Fuzzy Sets," *Information and Control*, Vol. 8, pp. 338-353, 1965.

[20] Driankov, D., Hellendoorn, H., and Reinfrank, M., *An Introduction to Fuzzy Control*, Springer, Berlin, 1996

[21] Zadeh, L. A., "The Concept of a Linguistic Variable and Its Applications to Approximate Reasoning," *Information Sciences*, Vol. 8, pp. 199-249, 1975.

[22] Klir, G. J. and Folger, T. A., *Fuzzy Sets, Uncertainty and Information*, Prentice Hall Publishing, Englewood Cliffs, NJ, 1988.

[23] de Silva, C. W., *Intelligent Control: Fuzzy Logic Applications*, CRC Press, Boca Raton, FL, 1995.

[24] Procyk, T. J. and Mamdani, E. H., "A Linguistic Self-Organizing Process Controller," *Automatica*, Vol. 15, pp. 15-30, 1977.

[25] Layne, J. R. and Passino, K. M., "Fuzzy Model Reference Learning Control," *Advances in Fuzzy Control*, Edited by Drainkov, D. and Palm, R., Physica-Verlag, NewYork, pp. 263-282, 1998.

[26] Wang, L. X., "Stable Adaptive Fuzzy Control of Non-Linear Systems," *IEEE Transactions on Fuzzy System*, Vol. 1, No. 2, pp. 146-155, 1993.

[27] Harris, C. J., Moore, C. G., and Brown, M., *Intelligent Control: Aspects of Fuzzy Logic and Neural Nets*, World Scientific Publishing, Singapore, 1993.

[28] Moudgal V. G., Passino, K. M., and Yurkovich, S., "Rule-Based Control for a Flexible-Link Robot," *IEEE Transactions on Control Systems Technology*, Vol. 2, No. 4, pp. 392-405, 1994.

[29] Lopez, J. R. A., Gutierrez, E. A., and Rosa, L. C., "A Fuzzy Logic Based Approach to Machine Tool Control Optimization," *Fuzzy Control Systems*, Edited by Kandel, A. and Langholz, G., CRC Press, Boca Raton, FL, pp. 523-540, 1994.

[30] Yoshida, S., "A Fuzzy Controller for a Rigid Disk Drive," *Fuzzy Control Systems*, Edited by Kandel, A. and Langholz, G., CRC Press, Boca Raton, FL, pp. 580-599, 1994.

[31] Ruspini, E. H., Saffiotti, A., and Konolige, K., "Progress in Research on Autonomous Vehicle Motion Planning," *Industrial Applications of Fuzzy Logic and Intelligent Systems*, Edited by Yen, J., Langari, R., and Zadeh, L. A., IEEE Press, Piscataway, NJ, pp. 156-174, 1995.

[32] Watanabe, K., "Intelligent Control for Robotic and Mechatronic Systems – A Review," *Proc. IEEE International Conference on Systems, Man and Cybernetics*, Beijing, Vol. 1, pp. 322-327, 1996.

[33] Pin, F. G. and Watanabe, H., "Autonomous Navigation of a Mobile Robot Using the Behaviorist Theory and VLSI Fuzzy Inference Chips," *Industrial Applications of Fuzzy Logic and Intelligent Systems*, Edited by Yen, J., Langari, R., and Zadeh, L. A., IEEE Press, Piscataway, NJ, pp. 156-174, 1995.

[34] Shih, C. L., Gruver, W. A., and Zhu, Y., "Fuzzy Logic Force Control for a Biped Robot," *Proc. IEEE Int. Symp. Intelligent Control*, Arlington, VA, pp. 269-274, 1991.

[35] Kovacic, Z., Bogdan, S., and Laci, V., "Fuzzy Servo Control of an Articulated Robot Arm," *Proc. IEEE/RSJ/GI Int. Conf. Intelligent Robots and Systems*, Munich, Vol. 1, pp. 641-648, 1994.

[36] Doersam, T. and Hammerschmidt, O., "An Adaptive Fuzzy Control for a Three Fingered Robot Gripper," *Proc. Third Australian and New Zealand Conference on Intelligent Information Systems*, Perth, Australia, pp. 158-163, 1995.

[37] McCulloch, W. S. and Pitts, W. H., "A Logical Calculus of the Ideas Imminent in Nervous Activity," *Bull. Math. Biophy.*, Vol. 5, pp. 115-133, 1943.

[38] Hebb, D. O., *The Organization of Behavior: A Neuropsychological Theory*, Wiley, New York, 1949.

[39] Rosenblatt, F., "The Perceptron: A Probabilistic Model for Information Storage and Organization in the Brain," *Phych. Rev.*, Vol. 65, pp. 386-408, 1958.

[40] Rosenblatt, F., *Principles of Neurodynamics: Perceptrons and the Theory of Brain Mechanisms*, Spartan Books, Washington, D.C., 1962.

[41] Widrow, B. and Hoff, M. E. Jr., "Adaptive Switching Circuits," *IRE WESCON Convention Record, Part 4, Institute of Radio Engineers*, New York, pp. 96-104, 1960.

[42] Minsky, M. L. and Palpert, S., *Peceptrons*, MIT Press, Cambridge, MA, 1969.

[43] Rumelhart, D. E., Hinton, G. E., and Williams, R. J., "Learning Internal Representations by Error Propagation," *Parallel Distributed Processing*, Vol. 1, MIT Press, Cambridge, MA, pp. 318-362, 1986.

[44] Parker, D. B., "Learning Logic," *Invention Report S81-64, File 1. Office of Technology Licensing*, Stanford University, Stanford, CA, 1982.

[45] Werbos, P. J., *Beyond Regression: New Tools for Prediction and Analysis in the Behavioral Sciences*, Ph.D. Thesis, Harvard University, Cambridge, MA, 1974.

[46] Haykins., S., *Neural Networks: A Comprehensive Foundation*, Macmillian Publishing Co., New York, 1994.

[47] Zurada, J. M., *Introduction to Artificial Neural Systems*, West Publishing Co., St. Paul, MN, 1992.

[48] Poo, A. N., Ang, M. H. Jr, Teo, C. L., and Li, Q., "Performance of a Neuro-Model-Based Robot Controller: Adaptability and Noise Rejection," *Intelligent System Engineering*, Vol. 1, pp. 50-62, 1992.

[49] Li, Q. A., Poo, A. N., and Teo, C. L., "Parameter Variation Compensation of a Robotic Manipulator Using a Neural Network Structure," *Proc. International Conference on Machine Dynamics and Engineering Applications*, Zhenjiang, PRC, pp. 413-419, 1992.

[50] Yuan, M., Hong, G. S., and Poo, A. N., "Neural Adaptive Controller: Application to Robotic Manipulator," *Proc. International Conference on Automation, Robotics and Computer Vision*, Singapore, pp. 1734-1737, 1994.

[51] Yuan, M., Poo, A. N., and Hong, G. S., "Direct Neural Control System: A Non-Linear Extension of Adaptive Control," *IEE Proceedings, Part D, Control Theory and Application*, Vol. 142, pp. 661-667, 1995.

[52] Chan, K., *A Study of Neural Network Model-Based Controller*, B.Eng. Thesis, Department of Mechanical and Production Engineering, The National University of Singapore, Singapore, 1996.

[53] Xi, W. Y., *Neural Network Inverse Control*, M.Eng Thesis, Department of Mechanical and Production Engineering, The National University of Singapore, Singapore, 1998.

[54] Boo, K. H., *A Study of the Feedforward Neural Network as a Controller*, B.Eng. Thesis, Department of Mechanical and Production Engineering, The National University of Singapore, Singapore, 1997.

[55] Craig, J. J., *Introduction to Robotics: Mechanics and Control*, Addison-Wesley Publishing Co., Reading, MA, 1986.

[56] Ang, M. H. Jr, Poo, A. N., Teo, C. L., and Li, Q., "Compensation of Trajectory Tracking Errors Introduced by Sampling in Computer Control Implementations of Model-Based Robot Control," *Proc. International Conference on Industrial Electronics, Control and Instrumentation*, Maui, HI, pp. 1651-1653, 1993.

[57] Morari, M. and Zafiriou, E., *Robust Process Control*, Prentice-Hall, Englewood Cliffs, NJ, 1989.

[58] Li, Q. A., Poo, A. N., Lim, C. M., and Ang, M. H. Jr, "Neuro-Based Adaptive Internal Model Control for Robot Manipulators," *Proc. IEEE International Conference on Neural Networks (ICNN'95)*, Perth, Australia, pp. 2353-2359, 1995.

[59] Fisher, D. G., "Process Control: An Overview and Personal Perspective," *The Canadian Journal Chemical Engineering*, Vol. 69, pp. 5-26, 1991.

[60] Obitko, M., *Genetic Algorithms*, http://www.datakit.cz/ga/main.html, 1998.

[61] Holland, J. H., "Genetic Algorithms and the Optimal Allocation of Trials," *SIAM Journal of Computing*, Vol. 2, No. 2, pp. 89-104, 1973.

[62] Chen, M. and Zalzala, A. M. S., "Safety Considerations in the Optimization of Paths for Mobile Robots Using Genetic Algorithms," *Proc. First International Conference in Genetic Algorithms in Engineering Systems: Innovations and Applications*, IEE, University of Sheffield, Sheffield, UK, pp. 299-306, 1995.

[63] Dangprasert, P. and Avatchanakorn, V., "Genetic Algorithms Based on an Intelligent Controller," *Expert Systems with Applications*, Vol. 10, No. 3, pp. 465-470, 1996.

[64] He, L., Wang, K. J., Jin, H. Z., Li, G. B., and Gao, X. Z., "The Combination and Prospects of Neural Networks, Fuzzy Logic and Genetic Algorithms," *Proc. IEEE Midnight-Sun Workshop on Soft Computing Methods in Industrial Applications*, Kuusamo, Finland, pp. 52-56, 1999.

[65] Saridis, G. N., "On the Theory of Intelligent Machines: A Comprehensive Analysis," *International Journal of Intelligent Control and Systems*, Vol. 1, No. 1, pp. 3-14, 1996.

[66] Song, Y. H., Johns, A., and Aggarwal, R., *Computational Intelligence Applications to Power Systems*, Science Press, New York, 1996.

[67] Tsoukalas, L. H. and Uhrig, R. E., *Fuzzy and Neural Approaches in Engineering*, John Wiley and Sons, New York, 1997.

[68] Khalid, M., Omatu, S., and Yusof, R., "Adaptive Fuzzy-Neuro Control with Application to a Water Bath Process," *Proc. IEEE International Conference on Control Applications*, Glasgow, pp. 173-178, 1994.

[69] Kim, S. H., Kim, Y. H., Sim, K. S., and Jeon, H. T., "On Developing an Adaptive Neural-Fuzzy Control System," *Proc. IEEE/RSJ International Conference on Intelligent Robots and Systems*, Yokohama, Japan, pp. 950-957, 1993.

[70] Kuo, R. J., Cohen, P. H., and Kumara, S. R. T., "Neural Network Driven Fuzzy Inference System," *Proc. IEEE International Conference on Neural Networks*, Orlando, FL, Vol. 3, pp. 1532-1536, 1994.

[71] Lin, C. T. and Lee, G. C. S., "Neural-Network-Based Fuzzy Logic Control and Decision System," *IEEE Transactions on Computers*, Vol. 40, No. 12, pp. 1320-1336, 1991.

[72] Berenji, H. R. and Khedkar, P., "Learning and Tuning Fuzzy Logic Controllers through Reinforcements," *IEEE Transactions on Neural Networks*, Vol. 3, No. 5, pp. 724-740, 1992.

[73] Nomura, H., Hayashi, I., and Wakami, N., "A Self-Tuning Method of Fuzzy Reasoning by Genetic Algorithm," *Fuzzy Control Systems*, Edited by Kandel, A. and Langholz, G., CRC Press, Boca Raton, FL, pp. 337-354, 1994.

[74] Lee, M. and Takagi, H., "Integrating Design Stages of Fuzzy Systems Using Genetic Algorithms," *Proc. Second IEEE International Conference on Fuzzy Systems*, San Francisco, CA, Vol. 1, pp. 612-617, 1993.

[75] Song, Y. H., Wang, G. S., Johns, A. T., and Wang, P. Y., "Improved Genetic Algorithms with Fuzzy Logic Controlled Crossover and Mutation," *Proc. UKACC International Conference on Control*, University of Exeter, Exeter, UK, Vol. 1, No. 427, pp. 140-144, 1996.

[76] Brill, F. Z., Brown, D. E., and Martin, W. N., "Fast Genetic Selection of Features for Neural Network Classifier," *IEEE Transaction on Neural Networks*, Vol. 3, No. 2, pp. 324-328, 1992.

[77] Hung, S. L. and Adeli, H., "A Parallel Genetic/Neural Network Learning Algorothm for MIMD Shared Memory Machines," *IEEE Transactions on Neural Networks*, Vol. 5, No. 6, pp. 900-909, 1994.

[78] Mester, G., "Neuro-Fuzzy-Genetic Controller Deign for Robot Manipulators," *Proc. IEEE IECON 21st International Conference on Industrial Electronics, Control and Instrumentation*, Orlando, FL, Vol. 1, pp.97-92, 1995.

[79] Stylios, G. and Sotomi, O. J., "A Neuro-Fuzzy Control System for Intelligent Sewing Machines," *Proc. 2nd International Conference on Intelligent Systems Engineering*, Hamburg, pp. 241-246, 1994.

[80] Tascillo, A., Skormin, V., Crisman, J., and Bourbakis, N., "Intelligent Control of a Robotic Hand with Neural Nets and Fuzzy Sets," *Proc. IEEE International Symposium on Intelligent Control*, Chicago, pp. 232-237, 1993.

[81] Fatikov, S. and Wohlke, G., "A Neuro-Fuzzy Approach for Intelligent Microrobots," *Proc. International Conference on Systems, Man and Cybernetics*, Le Touquet, France, Vol. 4, pp. 441-446, 1993.

[82] Hanes, M. D., Ahalt, S. C., and Orin, D. E., "Intelligent Control of Object Acquisition for Power Grasp," *Proc. IEEE International Symposium on Intelligent Control*, Columbus, OH, pp. 303-308, 1994.

[83] Kelemen, A., Imecs, M., Rusu, C., and Kis, Z., "Run-Time Autotuning of a Robot Controller Using a Genetics Based Machine Learning Control Scheme," *Proc. First International Conference on Genetic Algorithms in Engineering Systems: Innovations and Applications*, University of Sheffield, England, pp. 307-312, 1995.

[84] Shibata, T. and Fukuda, T., "Coordinative Behavior by Genetic Algorithm and Fuzzy in Evolutionary Multi-Agent System," *Proc. IEEE International Conference on Robotics and Automation*, Atlanta, GA, Vol. 1, pp. 760-765, 1993.

[85] Passino, K. M., "Intelligent Control for Autonomous Systems," *IEEE Spectrum*, Vol. 32, pp. 55-62, 1995.

[86] Chiu, S., Cheng, J. J., Sitter, C., and Fooks, E., "Perspectives on the Industrial Application of Intelligent Control," *Proc. 34th IEEE Conference on Decision and Control*, New Orleans, LA, Vol. 1, pp. 757-761, 1995.

[87] Chiu, S., "Developing Commercial Applications of Intelligent Control," *IEEE Control Systems Magazine*, Vol. 17, pp. 94-97, 1997.

[88] Passino, K. M., "Bridging the Gap between Conventional and Intelligent Control," *IEEE Control Systems Magazine*, Vol. 13, pp. 12-18, 1993.

[89] Cai, Z. X., "Prospect for Development of Intelligent Control," *Proc. IEEE International Conference on Intelligent Processing Systems*, Beijing, Vol. 1, pp. 625-629, 1997.

9 | INTELLIGENT MACHINE TO MODIFY OR ADAPT HUMAN BEHAVIOR

D. W. Repperger
Air Force Research Laboratory
Wright-Patterson Air Force Base
Dayton, Ohio 45433-7902

In this chapter, a definition of an intelligent machine is presented which is predicated on how an inanimate device may modify human behavior. The efficacy or intelligence of the machine is then quantified (objectively) based on how it enhances the performance of the overall human–machine interaction. After an adaptation of human behavior is observed, a number of new issues arise, e.g. has this adaptation been for the better, is the machine that produced this effect now still intelligent, and what is the next and final step in this process? A simple example involving a human-interface device is presented to illustrate how an intelligent machine is developed. In a post hoc sense, the resulting modification of the overall interaction is then examined to evaluate the utility of the device in question.

1 Introduction

Intelligence is usually considered as a human attribute. Can other animals be viewed as intelligent? Certainly many aspects of animal behavior can be viewed within the context of being intelligent as observed in the responses made by porpoises, chimpanzees, etc. [1,2]. Animal biologists commonly refer to certain animals or species as having "high intelligence" when comparing across animals in terms of how well they perform tasks, as well as the degree of complexity of the chore involved. If animals, other than humans, can be considered intelligent in their behavior, then one may be able to extrapolate or generalize this concept to machines or to other inanimate creations of man. A device is considered herein which may appear to be producing intelligent behavior when utilized by humans. A definition of what may be contemplated as *machine intelligence* is given in a somewhat objective manner. If the overall interaction (human and intelligent machine) is much improved, within a framework that appears as intelligent, after the interaction with the machine, as contrasted with the performance in the absence of the machine, then the inanimate object has added with the efficacy of the human–

0-8493-0330-3/00/$0.00+$.50

machine combination to improve its capability in some sense. To add credence to these concepts, a recently developed human-interface device (involving pilots flying simulators) is examined which is known to modify human behavior. Understanding why and how the behavior modification comes about is essential in comprehending the ability of a machine to induce an adaptation in human behavior. First, a definition of an intelligent machine is introduced.

2 Definition of an Intelligent Machine

For initial purposes, a machine is considered intelligent if, when interacting with a human, the person increases his/her knowledge base, or if the overall human–machine performance is enhanced as manifested by an adaptation of behavior. This change must appear to provide a higher intelligence level of operation (as measured by improved performance, better decision-making capability, or greater throughput capability on complex tasks). Such a definition, however, has both temporal and other attributes which affect the machine's ability to appear intelligent. To provide credence to this point, the first example considered involves a machine which initially appears to have intelligence. Some background material is found in Chapters 1 and 2.

2.1 Example 1 – Intelligent Machine 1?

Suppose the clock were turned back to 1981, and we are presented with an intelligent machine. The object of interest is classified, at this time, as a 286 personal computer with a disk operating system called DOS 2.1 with a 10 Megabyte hard drive. To ably assist us, we are given software involving a word processor which is called Word Star 2.3. In this era, such a mechanism was extremely unfamiliar to the general user, but within a year or so of operation, this device radically changed how we performed mundane tasks, how data were analyzed, but how we composed manuscripts, etc. As we enter the year 2000, such a device now appears to be laughingly useless, yet 19 years earlier, it appeared as a revolutionary development in the workplace. Such a contrivance laid the foundation for much advanced technology to come. In the year 2000, this 286 computer may not be viewed as "intelligent." Therefore, the utility of an intelligent machine seems to be predicated on its ability to provide learning to the user and results in adapting his/her behavior. Accordingly, with the addition of an intelligent machine, the overall human–machine system would be more productive in some sense or operate at a higher intellectual level. Hence, the machine has added "value" in the sense the human–machine system now operates at a more elevated level. Thus machine intelligence is dependent not only on the time frame in which it appears, but also on its apparent utility to the human. The 286 computer may not be viewed as intelligent by today's standards if we do not learn from it or if it fails to provide us with information we normally would not get otherwise. Example 2 demonstrates how the temporal aspects of the device in question may suddenly change under untoward circumstances.

2.2 Example 2 – Machine 1 Now Becomes Intelligent

From the definition given previously, the 286 computing machine appears to have little utility in the year 2000. However, suppose a catastrophe of major proportions suddenly occurs without warning. All present day computer systems were instantly disabled and we are left (in the year 2000) with only one working computer (the 286 machine). With the loss of all alternative prior technology, the human would then have to relearn this primitive system, this last working computer left in operation. Such a mechanism would now provide some level of intelligence to the user since it would still modify his/her lifestyle, increase his/her ability to perform tasks, and let the human operate at a higher intelligence level. Thus, the intelligence of the machine (its utility to improve human life in some sense) has increased when the competing technologies have been modified. Hence, environmental factors and rival technologies influence the utility and efficacy of an existing machine to appear intelligent. This motivates the list given in the next section on a possible taxonomy (rules) involving machine intelligence.

2.3 A Possible Taxonomy (Rules) for Machine Intelligence

1. Measures of intelligence for machines must have analogies to related metrics involving humans/animals.

2. When a human interacts with an intelligent machine, the overall synergy, in some sense, must improve the ability of the human–machine system to perform a given task (or have improved decision-making capability). The basis of comparison is the human performing the same task without the use of the intelligent machine.

3. Machine intelligence may be task specific. Thus, a machine which is intelligent for one task may not be intelligent for another task.

4. Machine intelligence may consist of relative measures, not absolute measures. This is a result of the prior discussion of the 286 computer which may be viewed as intelligent or not depending on its relative utility and other circumstances. The relative measure may be associated in a time sense, in a complexity sense, or in an improved decision-making capability. Also, given two machines, it is desired to be able to say that machine 1 is more intelligent than machine 2 for a given task. Some quantitative (objective) measures should concretely discern the degree of difference in machine intelligence between two systems.

5. The units of machine intelligence may be related to throughput measures such as capacity (bits/sec) which is used in information theory to characterize the attribute of an information channel to transmit data. For example, a high capacity channel or system can process information more quickly and is sometimes regarded as a trait generally associated with intelligence. Improved intelligence may be akin to improved decision-making ability.

3 Human–Machine Device to Adapt Behavior

To develop these arguments further, a specific example involving a human inter-face system (pilot–aircraft simulator) is now presented to show an assemblage which modifies human behavior and appears to add to overall increased intelligence of the human–machine system. To show the efficacy of a machine to modify and adapt human behavior (for the better), a three-step procedure will be employed. The first step is to create a scenario in which the human dealing with a given system (aircraft or simulator) is not performing well. The second step would be to introduce an assistive device (intelligent machine) which then improves the interaction to the point where the combined human–machine system performs much better as a team as contrasted with the case of the assistive device's being absent. The last step is to examine the ramifications of the design thus considered. That is, what type of interaction is likely to occur next? Is the consequence of this interaction for the better? The first step is to introduce a problematic human situa-tion where there is a documented case of undesired performance with no assistive device (intelligent machine) in the process.

3.1 Step 1 – Creating an Undesired Human Performance Interaction

Figure 1 illustrates a block diagram of a human–machine interaction which is commonly studied in applications involving pilots' flying aircraft or simulators. In this diagram, the pilot–aircraft combination is modeled via the inner block con-taining the transfer function $H(s)$ which is a linearization, using describing func-tion techniques, of a human–aircraft interaction. This type of system description represents a target tracking task. The desired target to be tracked is symbolized by $f_t(t)$ and may portray a landing path profile, tracking another aircraft, or following some given motion profile known in Cartesian space. The output of the human–machine system (pursuer aircraft pose vector) is denoted as $f_p(t)$ and the tracking error signal $e(t)$ satisfies:

$$e(t) = f_t(t) - f_p(t) \tag{1}$$

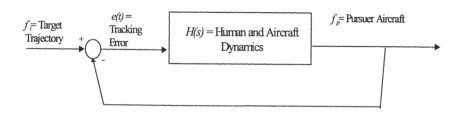

Figure 1: The original human task — target tracking.

Thus, good performance is quantified, in some sense, by small values of the tracking error $e(t)$ since the pursuer aircraft (under our control) then follows the desired tracking trajectory (or aircraft) $f_t(t)$. In the sequel, different (small, in some sense) measures of $e(t)$ will be related to good performance in this scenario involving target tracking.

Figure 2 now extrapolates this problem into a more detailed analysis to include an enhanced description of the human–machine task that will be considered in this study. In Figure 2, it is seen that the solid blocks are an extension of Figure 1. The essential elements include the human operator, a control stick, and the aircraft dynamics. To create the first step of synthesizing a human–machine interaction where performance is substandard in Figure 2, a pure time delay τ is inserted between the stick's output and its influence on the aircraft's dynamics. A second way to make the task more challenging to the pilot is by inserting roll and pitch air turbulence which has been included in Figure 2 to affect the variable f_p (the pursuer's pose vector). Also in Figure 2, the dotted blocks describe the intelligent machine or assistive device that will be included later to work with the human to mitigate the two undesired system properties (time delay τ and air turbulence). The first step is to demonstrate that an untoward pilot–aircraft interaction situation has been created which is problematic and requires the addition of an assistive device (dotted blocks in Figure 2) to help improve the situation. The historical perspective of this problem will help explain the rationale for this design.

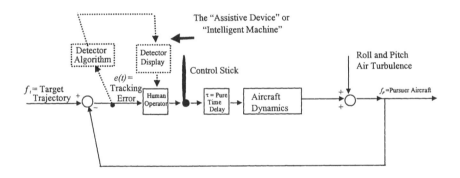

Figure 2: A more detailed version of the pilot's task.

3.2 Historical Perspectives of the Untoward Human-Machine Interaction

Human–machine interactions may exhibit certain loss of control which is manifested by characteristics of the tracking error. At the brink of instability, an interaction termed a *pilot-induced oscillation* (PIO) can occur typified by oscillatory behavior of an aircraft which can lead to a crash [3]. The PIO problem has been known since the early days of the Wright Brothers and their first flyer [4], and there are several theories to help explain this phenomenon. A far more serious instability that occurs in human–machine interactions can be characterized as a complete loss of control. Methodologies exist to delineate controllable and stable behavior and to distinguish it from unstable behavior [4,5] typical of what leads to the crash of an aircraft. With a credible (prior) warning, the display or controller of the human–machine system could be updated to possibly reduce the chance of a crash, or some more drastic procedures could be instituted. For example in troubled situations, control could be taken away from the pilot and the process could be completely automated. Thus, the intelligent machine considered here would be the detector device (dotted blocks in Figure 2) the theoretical issues of which are presented in Appendix A. The goal of the detector would be to alert the pilot to a potential loss of control and consequently lead to an adaptation of his/her behavior.

3.3 An Experimental Scenario to Study the Human–Machine System at Instability

At the Air Force Research Laboratory, Wright-Patterson Air Force Base, Dayton, Ohio, studies are on-going to develop assistive systems (adaptive joystick controllers or displays) that may accommodate when particular situations arise. The potential loss of control or PIO is a critically important situation to study. If a detector can predict this untoward event a priori, then perhaps the display or controller may be adjusted to help prevent a crash or other undesirable event. At least such a system may increase the alertness level of the pilot and induce a productive change in his/her behavior. To replicate a situation likely to cause a loss of control, four experimental variables were manipulated in a laboratory experiment.

1. A time delay τ was introduced between the stick's output and the effect (input) it produces on the aircraft dynamics under control of the operator (f_p) in Figure 2. In conjunction with this delay, a difficult task condition, the construction of a combined high (roll and pitch) noise turbulence as displayed in Figure 2, was included. These high turbulence conditions are known to help trigger a PIO in the presence of a large time delay in the pilot–vehicle loop.

2. A force-reflecting joystick versus a non-force-reflecting joystick was employed. Certain paradigms of this type are known to enhance tracking performance (see [6-8]).

3. A 3-D audio system was included to investigate audio enhancements.

4. The detector condition (intelligent machine denoted by the dotted blocks in Figure 2) was either on or off. Thus, the closed-loop system would presumably operate at a lower or possibly higher level of intelligence.

Seven subjects ran a total of eight data days with 16 trials per day of the experimental conditions presented in random order. Both objective and subjective data were collected. The subjective data included Cooper–Harper ratings of the task and a PIO questionnaire [9]. This provided a verbal indication of the potential for the closed-loop system to oscillate or be on the verge of loss of control. It was necessary to collect the subjective data to provide concurrence with the objective data to help make a determination of an actual loss of control or oscillatory behavior. Training of subjects was accomplished by gradually increasing the time delay and intensity of the noise turbulence variables until oscillation and/or loss of tracking control was evident. The 16 daily trials consisted of low and high values of the four experimental variables presented in randomized order. It is necessary to discuss why this situation will lead to a difficult human–machine interaction that may require an assistive device (intelligent machine) to improve this interaction.

3.4 The Rationale for Why the Human–Machine System Must Become Unstable

Figure 3 is an abstraction of some of the key experimental design variables under study to portray a brief description of their role in inducing a loss of control or a pilot induced oscillation. In Figure 3, the starting point is *a* where the stressor variables ($\tau = 0$, and the roll and pitch noise variance) are zero. Starting at point *a* and going upward to point *b*, the time delay which was $\tau = 0$ at point *a*, increases to $\tau = 600$ ms near point *b* which is generally the point where a loss of control of the closed-loop system occurs. A critical boundary of the trapezoid is indicated near point *b* showing that, inside the trapezoid, acceptable tracking occurs and, outside the trapezoid, loss of control transpires after crossing the critical boundary. To see the effect of the turbulence, starting at point *a* and going to point *c* would result in a roll PIO for a sufficiently high variance of the roll turbulence (assuming this noise source is to be zero mean). The critical boundary is thus reached to the right of point *c*. For pitch turbulence, starting at point *a*, and traversing to point *d*, for a sufficiently large value of pitch noise variance, the corresponding pitch PIO occurs. Again the critical boundary is reached for a sufficiently large pitch noise variance.

For the experiment described in this chapter, the actual paths were along the direction of points *a* to *e* or *a* to *f* in which both time delay and turbulence occurred simultaneously. Thus for a sufficiently large value of time delay and variance of the turbulence stressor, the critical boundary would be reached. In the described experiment, both the delay and variance of the turbulence were increased to produce either a loss of control or an oscillatory behavior as indicated in the closed-loop error data displayed in Figure 4. Thus, each subject has his/her own critical boundary which was determined empirically. Appendix B demonstrates that the experimental variables showed their efficacy in the role of producing a compromise of the tracking performance and the critical boundary was reached. The goal of this chapter, however, is to introduce the intelligent machine which would help improve upon this undesirable situation.

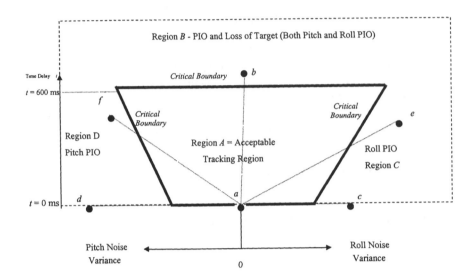

Figure 3: An abstraction of the experimental design variables.

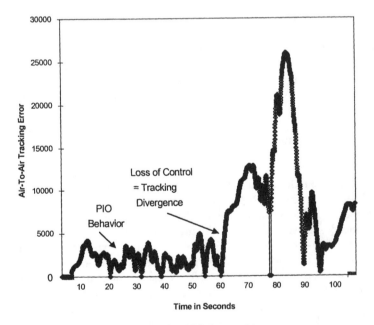

Figure 4: Closed-loop tracking error.

3.4.1 Step 2 – The Introduction of a Machine to Improve the Human–Machine Interaction

With reference to Figure 2, the goal was to now insert a detector algorithm and provide a detector display to the pilot to help him/her gain more information on the tracking task especially when the stressor variables would create a situation in which loss of control or a pilot induced oscillation were imminent. Thus, the two conditions: detector-on versus detector-off would constitute the "intelligent machine" being on or off in this case. Data will be compared across the two conditions: detector-on versus detector-off to evaluate the efficacy of the assistive device to improve the human–machine interaction. It will now be demonstrated that the assistive device improved the efficacy of the overall closed-loop system.

4 Demonstrating the Efficacy of the Overall Human–Machine System

To show that the overall human–machine system has benefited from the interaction with the intelligent machine, the presumption will be that improved intelligence is consistent with improved decision-making capability. To explain this performance metric, simple concepts are borrowed from signal detection theory [10]. Figure 5 illustrates the density functions of a simple decision rule based on two alternatives of choice. We denote e_k as the event of interest and $P(h_i|e_k)$ as the a posteriori probability that hypothesis h_i is true given that the event e_k has occurred. The a priori probability of the state occurring prior to its observation is given by $P(h_i)$. Two possible hypotheses h_0 and h_1 will be considered. The actual responses by the decision maker to these hypotheses will be denoted by H_0 and H_1, respectively. For any number of hypotheses h_k containing h_i and h_k with an event e_k occurring, another variable of interest is specified by:

$$L_{ij}(e_k) = p(e_k|h_i)/p(e_k|h_j) \qquad (2)$$

where $L_{ij}(e_k)$ is the likelihood ratio of event e_k for hypothesis i relative to hypothesis j. Table 1 illustrates a response matrix which describes the conditional probabilities and the four possible events that might occur (Hit, Miss, False Alarm, and Correct Rejection) in making decisions for two alternatives of choice.

Table 1: Response matrix of the ROC

Response	Truth = h_1	Truth = h_0
H_1	$p(H_1|h_1)$ = Hit, Cost = V_1	$p(H_1|h_0)$ = Miss, Cost = V_2
H_0	$p(H_0|h_1)$ = False Alarm, Cost = V_3	$p(H_0|h_0)$ = Correct Rejection, Cost = V_4

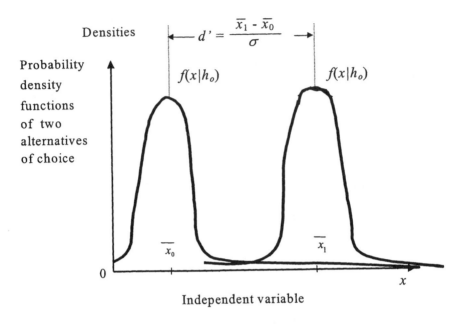

Densities

$$d' = \frac{\overline{x}_1 - \overline{x}_0}{\sigma}$$

Probability
density
functions
of two
alternatives
of choice

$f(x|h_o)$ $f(x|h_o)$

x_0 x_1

0

x

Independent variable

Figure 5: Densities of two alternatives of choice.

Figure 6 illustrates the relative operating characteristic (ROC) curve for the human operator. Appendix C describes the derivation of such a diagram. To briefly describe its utility, in Figure 6 the line AC describes random guessing and corresponds to the case $d' = 0$ in Figure 5 when the two density functions are directly on top of one another. When $d' > 0$ then the human operator is a better decision maker as the point B is a more efficient operating point as compared with point D. As $d' \to \infty$, then the ROC curve approaches an optimal decision maker (line AEC in Figure 6) and can be shown to maximize the following cost function:

$$\max \; J_1 = p(H_1|h_1) - p(H_1|h_o) = \text{Hits} - \text{False Alarms} \tag{3}$$

subject to the following constraints:

$$p(H_0|h_o) + p(H_1|h_o) = 1 \tag{4}$$
$$p(H_0|h_1) + p(H_1|h_1) = 1 \tag{5}$$

It can be shown [10] that the slope of the ROC curve at point A in Figure 6 (maximum slope) is precisely the likelihood function as described in Equation (2).

What is of use for this study is the following lemma that we state without proof but which is easily corroborated from inspection of Figure 6 and is well known from signal detection theory.

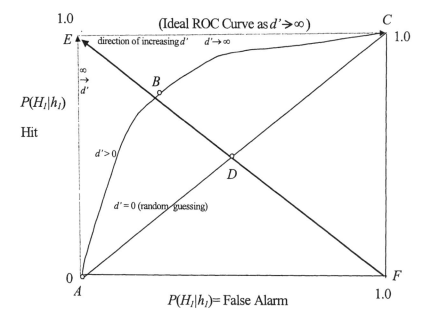

Figure 6: ROC (relative operating curve for the human operator).

Lemma (1): Maximizing J_1 of Equation (3) is equivalent to maximizing the area under the ROC curve of Figure 6. This is easily shown since the figure to the right of the ROC curve is a convex region and the slope of the line ABC is a monotonically decreasing function in moving to the right of point A.

4.1 Criteria for an Intelligent Machine

In this section, the main criteria for an intelligent machine are summarized, in the context of the present chapter.

1. If the intelligent machine interacting with the human operator results in a larger area under the ROC curve as compared with the case of not being used, then the overall human–machine interaction has been improved. Higher intelligence is demonstrated, which is reflected by an improved decision-making capability.

2. In comparing the use of two intelligent machines, if machine$_1$ produces a larger area under the closed-loop (human in the loop) ROC curve than machine$_2$ for a given task, then machine$_1$ is defined as having a higher intelligence than machine$_2$. Thus the method to objectively compare machines is via the relative area to the right of the ROC curve (which maximizes J_1 of Equation (3)).

Finally to extrapolate these results to the experiment thus described, we now relate these results to the detector system (intelligent machine).

5 Results of the Validation of the Intelligent Machine with Empirical Data

From the explanation of Appendix C, comparisons are made of the area to the right of the ROC curve in Figure 13 (see Appendix C) with or without the detector's being active. Table 2 is a shortened version of data from [11] which shows the human–machine system is more improved with the detector active versus having the detector turned off. Also note, the data were calculated for different parameters within the detector that may have affected its efficacy (α = bandwidth in radians/second, N_x = window samples).

Table 2: Normalized area on Figure 13 (averaged across subjects)

Detector Parameters	Closed-Loop Detector on	Detector off
α =1, N_x= 80 samples	.95	.858
α =5, N_x=80 samples	.96	.867
α =10, N_x= 80 samples	.93	.805

Thus the presence of the detector in the loop improved the human–machine decision-making process. The conclusion is that the intelligence of the closed-loop system has been refined with the addition of the assistive device, the detector.

5.1.1 Step 3 – Predicting the Next Step in the Evolution of the Human–Machine System

The final step in this process would then be to observe if the Figure 13 plot could have been improved upon or if the maximum area for a particular machine had been obtained. In actuality, this may always be difficult to demonstrate but a paradigm has been put in place to compare relative machines or to compare the case of being with or without a given intelligent machine.

6 Summary

This chapter presented a study that has been conducted on an assistive device which improves the decision-making capability of a pilot in a closed-loop system. An objective metric (area to the right of the ROC curve in Figure 13) allows a comparison of the efficacy of a system to improve the overall intelligence of the human–machine system. Machine intelligence is assumed to provide the human improved decision-making ability. Analogies from studies involving signal detection theory were used to illustrate the procedure.

References

[1]   Hunt, E., "The Role of Intelligence in Modern Society," *American Scientist,* pp. 356-368, July-August, 1995.

[2]   Albus, J. S., "Outline for a Theory of Intelligence," *IEEE Transactions on Systems, Man, and Cybernetics,* Vol. 21, No. 3, pp. 473-509, May/June, 1991.

[3]   Dorheim, M. A., "Report Pinpoints Factors Leading to YF-22 Crash," *Aviation Week and Space Technology,* pp. 53-54, Nov. 9, 1992.

[4]   Stengel, R. F., "Toward Intelligent Flight Control," *IEEE Transactions on Systems, Man, and Cybernetics,* Vol. 23, No. 6, pp. 1699-1717, Nov/Dec 1993.

[5]   Repperger, D. W., Ward, S. L., Hartzell, E. J., Glass, B. C., and Summers, W. C., "An Algorithm to Ascertain Critical Regions of Human Tracking Ability," *IEEE Transactions on Systems, Man, and Cybernetics,* Vol. SMC-9, No. 4, pp. 183-196, April 1979.

[6]   Repperger, D. W. "Active Force Reflection Devices in Teleoperation," *IEEE Control Systems Magazine,* pp. 52-56, January 1991.

[7]   Repperger, D. W., Phillips, C. A., and Chelette, T. L., "A Study on Spatially Induced 'Virtual Force' with an Information Theoretic Investigation of Human Performance," *IEEE Transactions on Systems, Man, and Cybernetics,* Vol. 25, No. 10, pp. 1392-1404, October, 1995.

[8]   Repperger, D. W. Haas, M. W. Brickman, B. J, Hettinger, L. J, Lu, L., and Roe, M. M., "Design of A Haptic Stick Interface as a Pilot's Assistant in a High Turbulence Task Environment," *Perceptual and Motor Skills,* Vol. 85, pp. 1139-1154, 1997.

[9]   Bjorkman, E. A., *Flight Test Evaluation of Techniques To Predict Longitudinal Pilot Induced Oscillations,* MS Thesis, Air Force Institute of Technology, Wright-Patterson Air Force Base, Dayton, OH, AFIT/GAE/AA/86J-1, 1986.

[10] Sheridan, T. B., *Telerobotics, Automation, and Human Supervisory Control,* MIT Press, Cambridge, MA, 1992.

[11] Repperger, D. W., Haas, M. W., Schley, P. C. and Koivo, A. J., "Failure Detection Methods to Predict Loss of Control Involving Human-Interface Devices, Part I: Theory and Part II: Empirical Validation," *Proceedings of the 1998 American Control Conference,* pp. 444-446, pp. 2862-2866, June 1998.

Appendix A – Development of a Detector System – Theoretical Issues

The theoretical arguments that provide a basis for the detector system can be gleaned from studies involving a phase plane analysis of the closed-loop tracking error. Phase plane methods provide an ideal venue for studying characteristics of human–machine interactions because patterns of responses can be studied in such a pictorial framework when the underlying dynamics may not be completely known or understood.

A.1 Phase Plane Analysis and the Closed-Loop Tracking Error

The first step in developing a detector system is to understand how to estimate derivatives of the closed-loop tracking error signal $e(t)$. The underlying presumption is that the signal $e(t)$ (derived from measurements of $f_t(t)$ and $f_p(t)$) is gleaned from sources such as radar, global positioning systems (GPS), other aircraft, way-point display symbology, or inertial guidance systems.

A.2 Estimating Higher Derivatives of $e(t)$

To develop an estimator of the higher derivatives of this signal, let $\hat{e}$ express a low-pass filtered estimate of $e(t) = f_t - f_p$ with $\hat{E}$ and E denoting their respective Laplace-transformed quantities. A transfer function is formed via:

$$\frac{\hat{E}}{E} = \frac{1}{\left(1 + s/\alpha\right)^3} \tag{6}$$

where α is the low-pass filter breakpoint. State variables are selected ($x_1 = \hat{e}$, $x_2 = \dot{\hat{e}}$, $x_3 = \ddot{\hat{e}}$) and a state vector $x = [x_1, x_2, x_3]^T$ is integrated forward using a first-order Euler approximation:

$$x_{t+\Delta t} \approx x_t + \dot{x}_t \Delta t \tag{7}$$

with initial conditions based on similar approximations in the error data. Figure 7 illustrates the block diagram form of the low-pass filter method to estimate the higher derivatives which can be easily implemented in either software or hardware. The output of Figure 7 feeds directly into Figure 8, the detector algorithm.

A.3 The Detector and the Prediction of Error Divergence – Defining the Paradigm

Figure 8 illustrates how the detector system works in principle. The output of Figure 7 is used to estimate the first three derivatives of the error signal utilizing the low-pass filter framework. The methodology of the detector system is described in the right block in Figure 8 and now described in detail.

A.3.1 The Detector Block

Since the variables ($\hat{e}, \dot{\hat{e}}, \ddot{\hat{e}}$) and also ($\dddot{\hat{e}}$) are known or estimated, the rationale for predicting error divergence can now be developed. Figure 9(a)-(c) demonstrates the three phase planes ($\dot{\hat{e}}$ vs. $\hat{e}$), ($\ddot{\hat{e}}$ vs. $\dot{\hat{e}}$) and ($\dddot{\hat{e}}$ vs. $\ddot{\hat{e}}$) if the human–machine

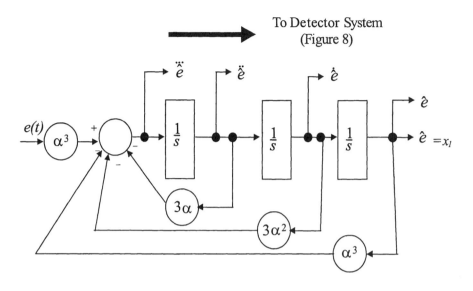

Figure 7: Low-pass filter to estimate higher derivatives.

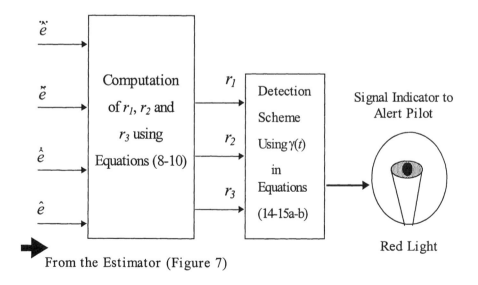

Figure 8: System description of detector system.

system were at a perfect oscillation. In a perfect oscillation, 50% of the time is spent in quadrants I and III of the phase plane. It will be shown in the sequel that this type of pattern of tracking behavior is extremely destructive. We state certain lemmas but due to space restrictions, only briefly sketch out the proofs. Some definitions are introduced to better explain the lemmas.

Definitions: Let

$$r_1 = n_1/n \tag{8}$$

$$r_2 = n_2/n \tag{9}$$

$$r_3 = n_3/n \tag{10}$$

and

$$\gamma(t) = r_1 + r_2 + r_3 \tag{11}$$

where n is the total number of data samples under consideration (one cycle in the phase plane) and n_1 of these data samples fall in quadrants I and III of Figure 9(a), n_2 fall in quadrants I and III of Figure 9(b), and n_3 fall in quadrants I and III of Figure 9(c). Lemma 2 addresses the approximate value of these r_i quantities when the human–machine system is in or at a near PIO mode of operation.

Lemma 2:

If $e(t)$ is dominated by a single sinusoid, the following relationship is approximately true for a complete cycle of the sinusoid $e(t) = A \sin (\omega t)$: $r_1 \approx .5$, $r_2 \approx .5$, $r_3 \approx .5$, and $\gamma(t) = 1.5$.

Remark:

Lemma 2 is obvious for a complete cycle of the sinusoid. This would be typical of a PIO situation. The next lemma addresses when a trajectory will show a tendency to diverge in a phase plane.

Lemma 3:

Trajectories that enter and remain in quadrants I and III of Figure 9(a), (b), or (c) lead to divergence in the sense that $\| \hat{e}_{t+\Delta t} \| > \| \hat{e}_t \|$. (A Euclidean norm is assumed.)

Proof of Lemma 3:

Using a first order Taylor's series expansion of $\hat{e}_{t+\Delta t}$ yields the Euler approximation:

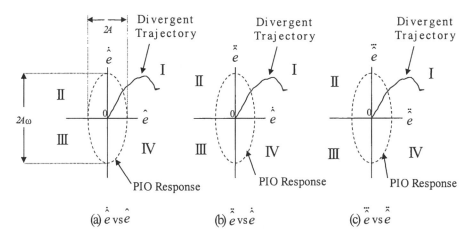

Figure 9: Phase planes of estimated scalar error.

$$\hat{e}_{t+\Delta t} \approx \hat{e}_t + \Delta t \; \dot{\hat{e}}_t \tag{12}$$

Thus, from inspection of Equation (12) and Figure 9(a), if $\hat{e}_t$ and $\dot{\hat{e}}_t$ both have the same sign, the magnitude of $\hat{e}_{t+\Delta t}$ can only increase. By differentiating Equation (12), the obtained results then extrapolate to Figures 9(b) and 9(c) using the same arguments. An alternative way to show this result is to use a second-order Taylor's series expansion which would be of the form:

$$\hat{e}_{t+\Delta t} \approx \hat{e}_t + \Delta t \; \dot{\hat{e}}_t + (1/2)\,(\Delta t)^2 \; \ddot{\hat{e}}_t \tag{13}$$

From observation of Equation (13), one can see that if the three variables ($\hat{e}, \dot{\hat{e}}, \ddot{\hat{e}}$) have the same sign, this produces a definitive increase in the magnitude of $\hat{e}_{t+\Delta t}$.

Lemma 4 addresses the converse argument and combines this measure of tracking divergence into the one variable $\gamma(t)$.

Lemma 4:

Trajectories that enter and remain in quadrants II and IV of Figure 9(a), (b), or (c) lead to convergence in the sense that $\| \hat{e}_{t+\Delta t} \| < \| \hat{e}_t \|$. A rule for determining convergence or divergence of a trajectory could be specified via:

If $\gamma\,(t) > 2.0$, then the trajectory is diverging.
If $\gamma\,(t) < 1$, then the trajectory is converging.

Proof of Lemma 4:

By examination of Equation (13), if there is no common sign agreement among the three variables ($\hat{e}_t$, $\dot{\hat{e}}_t$, $\ddot{\hat{e}}_t$), then the magnitude of the variable $\hat{e}_{t+\Delta t}$ can only decrease in magnitude. With this concept in mind, a detector system can now be constructed.

A.3.2 The Detection Algorithm

With reference to Figure 8 and 9(a)-(c), the detection algorithm calculates γ(t) via:

$$\gamma(t) \; = \; r_1(t) \; + \; r_2(t) \; + \; r_3(t) \tag{14}$$

Thus, the decision on whether tracking control is to be lost requires concurrence from the majority of the three phase planes as demonstrated in Equation (14). To improve the quality of the detection scheme, tests were made on empirical data, and [11] describes much of this detail. To summarize, two criteria were selected to help detect a loss of control or a possible PIO:

(a) γ (t) must be greater than some threshold value, e.g.:

$$\gamma(t) > 2.0 \text{ for divergence to be precipitated} \tag{15a}$$

(b) The rate of change of γ(t) is required to be positive prior to the loss of control.

$$\dot{\gamma}(t) > 0 \tag{15b}$$

Further discussions and validation of this algorithm are contained in [11].

Appendix B – Implementation of the Detector Device

Figures 7 and 8 illustrate the system operation and implementation of the device that makes estimates of the closed-loop tracking error and its higher derivatives via a method such as a low-pass filter model. Figure 10 illustrates a US Air Force subject involved in the experimental tracking paradigm. When controlling a task of this nature, the characteristics of the closed-loop tracking error capture the essence of whether the overall system is in a mode of operation which can be classified as controllable or noncontrollable. Figure 4 illustrates the tracking error versus time with notations indicating when tracking divergence occurs as well as the possible incidence of PIO behavior. Studying the human–machine system within a PIO context is extremely important because the sensitivity of the interface to all design parameters is significantly enhanced at this point where the human–machine system is at the brink of instability.

Figure 10: Military subject performing critical tracking task.

B.1 Results from the Data

Figure 4 illustrates not only $e(t)$, the actual data from a run, but also $\hat{e}\,(t)$, a low-pass filtered estimate of this variable. If $|e(t)| > 3000$, the target aircraft is off the screen and the subject has failed at the task. Thus the magnitude of $e(t)$ defines failure, as well as the properties of $\gamma(t)$. The data presented here were analyzed across seven subjects who were paid for their participation in this study.

B.2 Statistical Analysis of the Independent Variables

From the subjective data (Cooper–Harper (C–H) ratings and PIO ratings) as well as from objective measures (magnitude of the tracking error, crashes, etc.), it was necessary to demonstrate that the subjects were sufficiently stressed to lose control of the tracking task as a consequence of the independent variables selected in this experiment. A complete analysis of variance (ANOVA) was conducted across subjects in terms of the independent variables that affected their behavior. Table 3 illustrates the effect of each of the independent variables on tracking considered to be in a controllable mode versus runs that indicated tracking behavior which was not controllable. Here F connotes F ratio, τ is the delay variable, and p is the level of statistical significance.

Table 3: Significant effects of the independent variables.

C–H Ratings	$\tau = .179$ s	$\tau = .763$ s	$F=6.88$	$p < .0001$
e_{RMS} error involving Pitch and Roll Noise with Delay	Low delay and turbulence	High delay and turbulence	$F=3.36$	$p=0.006$
e_{RMS} error involving Force On/Off	Force on	Force off	$F=5.64$	$p=.002$

Thus, increasing the stressor variables, including noise turbulence, results in an increase of the C–H ratings as well as the root mean square tracking error (e_{RMS}). The force stick condition being active helped reduce this performance variable (reduced e_{RMS}).

Appendix C – Derivation of the ROC Curve of Figure 6

To understand how the ROC curves can be applied to human interface systems, this Appendix will consist of two parts. Part I will discuss the theoretical aspects of this approach and Part II will describe how to apply this technique to the experiment described herein.

C.1 Part I – Theoretical Issues Regarding the ROC Curve

The relative operating characteristic (ROC) curve provides a compact and versatile representation of the crossplot of hit rate versus false-alarm rate. It will be shown that ROC curves represent the best possible decision performance with the given data because of the optimality of the decision method. First, a paradigm for the construction of a continuous ROC curve is presented.

C.1.1 Construction of a Continuous ROC Curve

Figure 11(a) portrays an expansion of Figure 5 with areas under the respective curves denoted. The independent variable is x, and the variable x_c refers to a value of x for a decision rule cutoff. Figure 11(b) shows the respective cumulative distribution function plots of Figure 11(a) with the ordinate values as indicated for an abscissa value of x_c. The cumulative distribution function is simply a first integral of the plot of Figure 11(a) with respect to the independent variable. Figure 11(c) now portrays the resulting plot of the ROC curve extracted from Figure 11(b). The operating point is indicated which corresponds to the resulting slope of L_c units. To better understand these figures, Lemma 5 is now introduced to illustrate the optimality properties of the decision rule and how it is utilized in the application presented here.

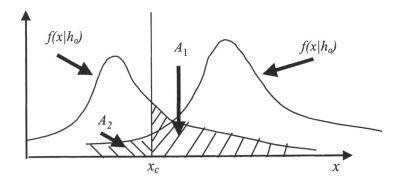

Figure 11(a): Areas under densities for decision rule.

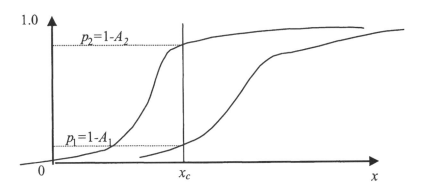

Figure 11(b): Cumulative distribution functions.

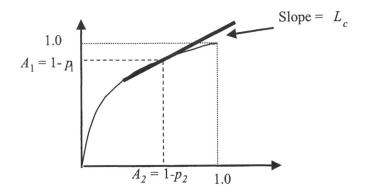

Figure 11(c): Resulting ROC curve.

Lemma 5: The optimal decision rule is to select hypothesis h_1 if and only if:

$$E\{h_1\} \geq E\{h_0\} \tag{16}$$

where $E\{.\}$ is the probabilistic expectation operator. The sense of an optimal decision rule is that no other rule can do better, "on the average."

Proof:

With reference to Table 1, the reward for choosing h_1 is:

$$E\{h_1\} = p(h_1) \, V_1 - p(h_0) \, V_2 \tag{17}$$

Correspondingly, the reward for choosing h_0 is:

$$E\{h_0\} = p(h_0) \, V_4 - p(h_1) \, V_3 \tag{18}$$

Combining Equations (16) and (17)-(18) yields the decision rule to select h_1 if and only if:

$$p(h_1) \, V_1 - V_2 \, p(h_0) \geq p(h_0) \, V_4 - p(h_1) \, V_3 \tag{19}$$

But $p(h_1) + p(h_0) = 1$ implies we wish to select:

$$\frac{p(h_1)}{p(h_0)} \geq \frac{V_4 + V_2}{V_1 + V_3} \tag{20}$$

which is a constant and only depends on the response matrix in Table 1. This is sometimes termed the *ratio of regrets*. To generalize this result, assume the observer (decision maker) obtained measurements during the interval (x in length) and the expression in (20) can be written:

$$\frac{p(h_1 \mid x)}{p(h_0 \mid x)} \geq \frac{V_4 + V_2}{V_1 + V_3} \tag{21}$$

Now applying Bayes' rule:

$$p(h_1 \mid x) = \frac{p(x \mid h_1) \, p(h_1)}{p(x)} \tag{22}$$

and

$$p(h_0 \mid x) = \frac{p(x \mid h_0) \, p(h_0)}{p(x)} \tag{23}$$

which implies:

$$\frac{p(x|\ h_1)\ p(h_1)}{p(x|\ h_0)\ p(h_0)} \geq \frac{V_4 + V_2}{V_1 + V_3} \tag{24}$$

Define a constant K via:

$$K \;\underline{\Delta}\; \frac{p(h_0)}{p(h_1)}\ \frac{V_4 + V_2}{V_1 + V_3} \tag{25}$$

Then Equation (24) can be written:

$$\frac{p(x\mid h_1)}{p(x\mid h_0)} \geq K \tag{26}$$

which implies, pick the hypothesis h_1 if and only if:

$$L(x) \geq K \tag{27}$$

To summarize, the observer collects data and calculates $L(x)$ from an observation and compares $L(x)$ with K. If $L(x) \geq K$, the observer selects the response H_1; otherwise H_0 is chosen. In the long run the observer maximizes his/her average reward.

The following additional attributes can similarly be shown to hold for Figure 6.

1. The slope of the ROC at any point is the likelihood ratio for the cutoff associated with that point (see Figure 11(c)). Thus, the ROC curve can be viewed as a first integral of the liklihood ratio if it can be expressed in closed form.

2. An optimal observer will have a monotonically decreasing slope, going to the right. Hence, point A in Figure 6 has the maximum slope.

3. The ROC is symmetric about the negative diagonal (line FE in Figure 6) if the variances of the underlying distributions (Figure 5) are assumed equal.

4. The ROC is density independent (normality does not need to be assumed).

The final part of this Appendix will show how to apply the experiment described in this chapter within the context of the discussion on intelligent machines.

C.2   Part II – Relating the Experiment to the Intelligent Machine Discussion

The last step in this process is to consider the experiment discussed herein to a similar signal detection problem commonly studied. Generally the choice is made between two alternatives and Figure 12 illustrates such a two-state model. For brevity, the notation $q(s) = p(H_1|h_1)$ and $q(n) = p(H_1|h_0)$ will be suitable for the two-state analysis. The corresponding likelihood ratio is $L = q(s)/q(n)$. The notations s and n refer, in an analogous manner, respectively, to signal and noise. The resulting ROC curve with this model would appear as in Figure 13 and is extremely simple to deal with. In Figure 13, the area to the right of the ROC curve is a measure of the maximization of J_1 of Equation (3), and from the prior discussion provides a closed-loop intelligence metric and means of comparing alternative machines. To generate this ROC curve for the experiment described herein, the following assumptions were made:

1. Subjective data were collected from the pilots responding via their PIO ratings and Cooper–Harper ratings. The presumption was made that if the PIO rating of 3.0 or larger was elicited, then the subject predicted the s response (analogous to signal or potential loss of control). If the PIO rating was under 3.0, then the presumption was that the subject predicted the n response (analogous to noise).

2. The frequency of correction decisions made by the detector could then be compared to the truth condition (made by the human and his/her PIO rating). Thus, the detector's response could be compared to the true situation. Both hits and false alarms could then be calculated.

3. The closed-loop machine would be more intelligent if, when using the detector, the closed-loop system would have a larger area to the right of the ROC curve in Figure 13. Thus, the efficacy of the detector to appear intelligent is to improve the awareness of the operator to better understand his/her true situation. This is a manifestation that the human–machine system is improved by including the machine compared with the case where the machine is absent from the process. The human–machine system is more intelligent (improved decision maker), because it is more aware of the true world situation.

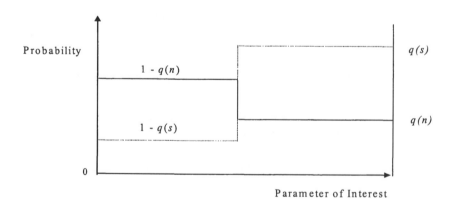

Figure 12: Two-state model — probabilities.

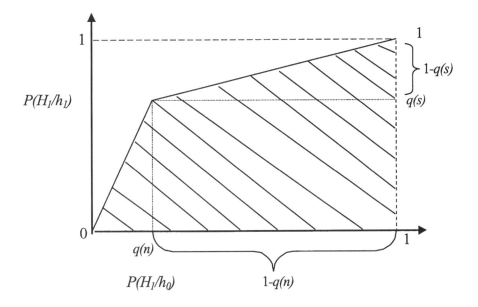

Figure 13: Two state model — ROC curve.

INDEX